BOYS IN THE PITS

Child Labour in Coal Mines

Beginning early in the nineteenth century, thousands of Canadian boys, some as young as eight, laboured underground – driving pit ponies along narrow passageways, manipulating ventilation doors, and helping miners cut and load coal at the coalface to produce the energy that fuelled Canada's industrial revolution. Boys died in the mines in explosions and accidents, but when they organized strikes for better working conditions, they were often expelled from the mines.

Boys in the Pits shows the rapid maturity of the boys and sheds light on their role in resisting exploitation. In what will certainly be a controversial interpretation of child labour, Robert McIntosh recasts wage-earning children as more than victims, showing that they were individuals who responded intelligently and resourcefully to their circumstances.

Boys in the Pits is particularly timely as, despite the United Nations Convention on the Rights of the Child, accepted by the General Assembly in 1989, child labour still occurs throughout the world and continues to generate controversy. McIntosh provides an important new perspective from which to consider these debates, reorienting our approach to child labour, explaining rather than condemning the practice. He examines the role of changing technologies, alternative sources of unskilled labour, new divisions of labour, changes in the family economy, and legislation within the broader social context of the period from 1820 to 1940 – when the place of children was being redefined as home, school, and playground – to explore the changing extent of child labour in the mines.

ROBERT MCINTOSH is employed at the National Archives of Canada.

Boys in the Pits:
Child Labour in Coal Mines

ROBERT McINTOSH

McGill-Queen's University Press

Montreal & Kingston · London · Ithaca

© McGill-Queen's University Press 2000
ISBN 0-7735-2093-7

Legal deposit fourth quarter 2000
Bibliothèque nationale du Québec

Printed in Canada on acid-free paper

This book has been published with the help of a grant
from the Humanities and Social Sciences Federation of
Canada, using funds provided by the Social Sciences
and Humanities Research Council of Canada.

McGill-Queen's University Press acknowledges the
financial support of the Government of Canada
through the Book Publishing Industry Development
Program (BPIDP) for our publishing activities. It also
acknowledges the support of the Canada Council for
the Arts for its publishing program.

Canadian Cataloguing in Publication Data

McIntosh, Robert G. (Robert Gordon), 1960–
    Boys in the pits : child labour in coal mining
    Includes bibliographical references and index.
    ISBN 0-7735-2093-7
    1. Child labor – Canada – History. 2. Coal miners –
    Canada – History. I. Title.
    HD6247.M6152C3 2000   C00-900305-3
    331.3'822334'0971

Typeset in Palatino 10/12
by Caractéra inc., Quebec City

To my parents

Contents

as I admire these boys, I am thankful our children – like all Canadian children today – are spared the experience of growing up in the pit. At the same time, I regret that child labour remains a contemporary injustice in many parts of the world.

Acknowledgments

The Department of History at Carleton University provided the very collegial environment in which this book first took shape. I would like to thank numerous individuals there who read and commented on early versions of this research: Kerry Badgley, Carman Bickerton, Robert Goheen, Jim Kenny, Duncan McDowall, and Stan Mealing. My more recent colleagues at the National Archives of Canada – they are too numerous to mention by name – have continued to support this research. I am grateful to them. Ian McKay, of Queen's University, very kindly opened to me his remarkable collection of material on the Maritime working class. He has also generously commented on an earlier version of this study. I am very indebted to him. I would like to thank also the reviewers for McGill-Queen's University Press and the Aid to Scholarly Publications Program for their very valuable comments. The National Museum of Science and Technology kindly granted permission to republish sections which had previously appeared in a volume in their Transformation series, entitled *Coal Mining in Canada*, co-written with Del Muise. I wish to acknowledge in particular Louise Trottier, curator, Energy and Mining, for her support for my work on the technology of coal mining. In addition, I wish to express my gratitude to the Social Sciences and Humanities Research Council of Canada, which originally funded the research on which this book is based.

I accumulated my greatest debts to Del Muise of Carleton University. Always encouraging, he first introduced me to the history of coal mining. His influence is reflected throughout this book.

Finally, I wish to thank my wife, Rolina van Gaalen. We have raised two children, Anna (now eleven) and Robert (nine), with this book. Our children live lives far removed from those of pit boys. As much

Tables

Abbreviations

BESCO	British Empire Steel Corporation
CCCW	Canadian Council on Child Welfare
CGIT	Canadian Girls in Training
CPR	Canadian Pacific Railway
DOMCO	Dominion Coal Company
DOSCO	Dominion Coal and Steel Company
GMA	General Mining Association
HBC	Hudson's Bay Company
IODE	Imperial Order of the Daughters of the Empire
NCMI	Nova Scotia Museum of Industry
NCWC	National Council of Women of Canada
POH	Protestant Orphans' Home
PWA	Provincial Workman's Association
UMWA	United Mine Workers of America
WCTU	Woman's Christian Temperance Union
WFM	Western Federation of Miners
YMCA	Young Men's Christian Association
YWCA	Young Women's Christian Association

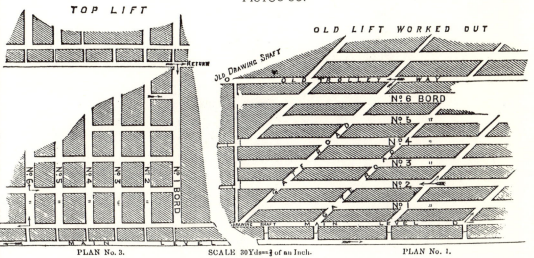

Illustration 1 Bord-and-pillar mining, Pictou County. The "bord and pillar" method was the standard mining technique in Victorian Canada. In the first round of mining, pillars were left standing to support the roof of the mine while adjacent coal was removed, producing a characteristic checkered pattern. In a second round, the pillars themselves were removed by careful cutting with a handpick, leaving the mine ceiling to settle against the floor. (Gilpin, "Coal Mining in Nova Scotia," 358)

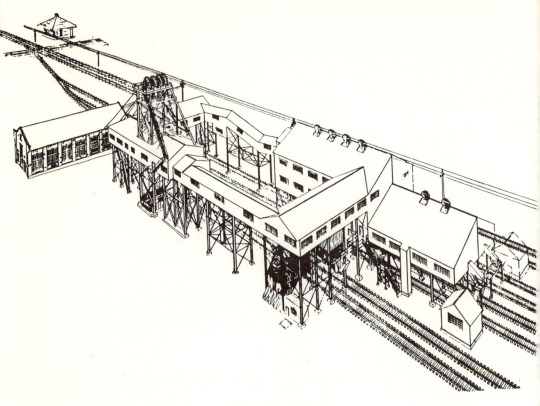

Illustration 2 Bankhead, Sydney Mines, 1912. Coal was raised from the mine into the bankhead, where it was cleaned, sorted by size, and loaded into railcars for transportation to the shipping dock or directly to market. (Dawes, "Coal Raising and Screening," 300)

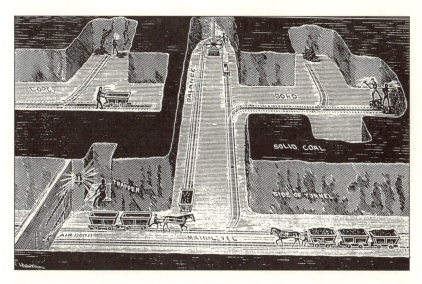

Illustration 3   Back-balance, Joggins. This illustration gives a primitive view of the underground operations of a mine. The "back-balance" consisted of two mine cars, one of which carried ballast, joined by a rope run around a pulley placed at the top of an inclined underground road. By the use of a lever the empty car was brought to any point along the inclined road. When filled with coal, the car was re-attached and lowered by gravity to an underground road. (Morrow, *Springhill Disaster*, 60)

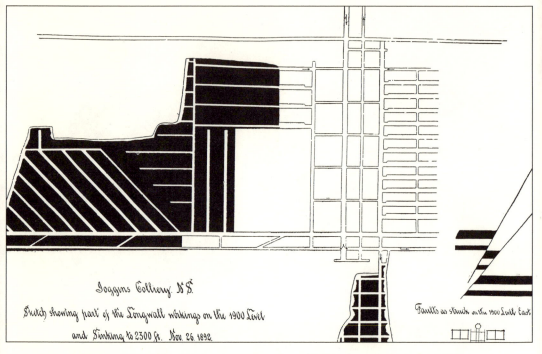

Joggins Colliery. N.S.

Sketch showing part of the Longwall workings on the 1900 Level
and Sinking to 2300 ft. Nov. 26. 1892.

Faults as struck on the 1900 Level East

Illustration 4   Longwall mining, Joggings. With longwall mining employed
increasingly in the twentieth century, all coal was removed in a single operation. In "retreating longwall" mining, two parallel roads were driven from
the level to the edge of the seam. The coal was then mined along a continuous
face back to the level, the roof being allowed to settle behind the face
workings. In "advancing longwall" the coal was worked from the level to
the edge of the seam, with travelling roads built and maintained in the refuse
left after the collapse of the roof. (Baird, "Joggings Mine," 60)

Illustration 5   Springhill disaster, 1891, mine surface. News of an explosion in a mine always drew an anxious crowd to the mine surface. At Springhill, the crowd witnessed the removal of 125 corpses from the stricken colliery, the youngest a twelve-year-old boy. (Morrow, *Springhill Disaster*, 35)

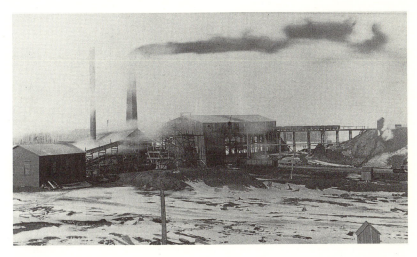

Illustration 6   Surface buildings, east side of No. 3 Slope, Springhill, 1897. The mine was marked by the prominent bankhead at the top of the pit that housed its hoisting, dumping, and screening equipment. In close vicinity were pump and winding-engine houses and their large smokestacks, the lamp cabin, the fan house, stables, carpenter's and blacksmith's shops, mine offices, and storehouses. Huge mounds of coal, awaiting shipment out, were adjacent to the bankhead, as were the substantial mounds of waste removed from the coal at the picking table. (NA, PA 147625)

Illustration 7 Coal picking, Drummond Colliery, Pictou County, Nova Scotia. In the bankhead, men and boys laboured at the picking belt, removing rock and other waste material from the coal. (NA, PA 53603)

Illustration 8   Pit pony, New Aberdeen, Cape Breton, 1946. Pit ponies were employed to haul coal out of the mine and equipment and supplies into the mine. While gradually displaced by mechanized means of haulage, the last ponies were not removed from Cape Breton mines until about 1960. (NA, PA 116676)

Illustration 9   Pit boy, Cape Breton, 1909. "The boys seem happy enough, and were bright little fellows from 11 to 15 years of age." (NA, C-030944)

Illustration 10 Fourteen-year-old pit boy, 1912. "Sitting so long alone in the darkness they become thoughtful, sober, sometimes melancholy. They go silently to their homes when they leave the mine; they do not stop to play tricks or joke with their fellows; they do not run, nor sing, nor whistle. Darkness and silence are always depressing, and so much of it in these young lives cannot help but sadden without sweetening them." (NA, C-030945)

Illustration 11   Boy miners at the Six Foot Mine, Thorburn, 1900. Pit boys, in the opinion of mine officials, were "a very troublesome element to manage." (NSMI, N-22914)

Illustration 12   Early GMA housing, Stellarton – "Miners' Row." Many coal companies built housing as a strategy to attract and retain a workforce. These dwellings were constructed in Pictou County in the mid-nineteenth century. (NSMI, N-22914)

Illustration 13 Miners on riding rake, Acadia No. 3 Mine, Thorburn, c. 1910. As mines extended deeper underground, coal companies used riding rakes to bring workers into and out of the mine. (NSMI, N-19693)

Illustration 14   Extension coal mines, Vancouver Island. Mules, alleged to be less temperamental, more sensible, less likely to bolt than ponies, were the beast of choice on Vancouver Island. (PABC, E-01185)

Illustration 15   Vancouver Coal Company wharves, Nanaimo. Coal's low value relative to its weight made shipping a preferred means of transport to market. Enormous
wharves were constructed to speed the loading of ships. (PABC, A-06509)

BOYS IN THE PITS

increasingly exposed to dangerous machinery – unprotected gearing, belts, fly-wheels, saws – and noxious materials. Traditional safe-guards for labouring children such as legal apprenticeships either fell into disuse or, as in the case of the tobacco and cigar-making trades, were corrupted so as to minimize the child's acquisition of a valued skill and maximize corporate profits from ill-paid youngsters. "The apprentice system is almost a thing of the past," reported the federal Royal Commission on the Relations between Capital and Labour in 1889. "The introduction of machinery and the division of labor have nearly put an end to it."[19]

New, unsettling, and above all public contexts of children's labour helped to undermine the widely held opinion that the child's early initiation to work was both natural and necessary within the labouring classes. They also prompted the rethinking of traditional attitudes that had shown far more concern over idle than over working children.[20] In contrast to the relative seclusion of the household, where they had traditionally laboured, children entered the massive factories, or descended into large mines, or thronged city centres peddling goods and services, visibly in large numbers. When witnessed in the light of post-Enlightenment ideas about childhood in Victorian Canada, child labour was first defined as a social problem.[21] In 1861 John A. Macdonald could celebrate the advent in Canada of the factory as a place of employment for children. No prime minister from the time of Wilfrid Laurier would be likely to do so.[22]

In the late nineteenth and early twentieth centuries, a new model of appropriate childhood was constructed, underpinned by an emerging view of children as dependent, weak, vulnerable, and incompetent. Defined in legislation on the basis of chronological age, childhood was also marked by a growing range of special organizations and segregated institutions. Shifting views of what was an appropriate childhood produced growing tension over this period: were labouring children capable contributors both to industry and to strained and vulnerable working-class budgets; or innocent victims of grasping employers and parents?

Much of childhood, as Neil Sutherland has observed, is "a matter of human decision rather than biological necessity."[23] Today, the young boy labouring in a mine ten or twelve hours daily is considered to be victimized. Contemporaries viewed him differently. As a Nova Scotian miner explained in 1891, "there are no children working in the mine. They may be children when they go in at ten or twelve years of age, but a fortnight or so thoroughly works that out of them. They then become very old fashioned boys. They get inured to all sorts of danger and hardship; they have, in a word, to think for themselves, as regards their work. As a matter of necessity, and as a matter of course, they soon presume to think for themselves on all matters."[24]

This study examines child labour from the perspective of a single industry, coal mining. Coal was the basic fuel of the industrial transformation of the nineteenth century. From the 1850s onward, it was used increasingly in both railway and stationary steam engines, to propel ocean shipping, and to heat homes and other buildings. Coal's importance to nineteenth-century industrial society can scarcely be overestimated – a significance akin to petroleum's role today. It was "the mainspring of our civilization," in the opinion of one Victorian, "the highest material boon that can be craved by community or nation."[25] Annual coal consumption increased from perhaps three-quarters of a million tons at Confederation to three and a half million tons in 1886. By 1902 it had risen to over ten million tons; it reached 31.5 million tons in 1913.[26] As demand for coal grew, so did the coal industry. Canadian coal production increased from less than ten thousand tons in 1800 to nearly six million tons a century later. By 1920 nearly 17 million tons of coal were raised at Canadian mines. Coal production remained at this approximate level until the Second World War.[27]

The mines workforce grew apace. In 1820 perhaps a few dozen people laboured in shallow Nova Scotian mines. At Confederation, nearly 4,000 were employed in coal mines on Vancouver Island and in Nova Scotia. By 1900 nearly 10,000 men and boys worked at collieries in five Canadian provinces.[28] The numbers employed in coal mining in Canada grew very rapidly over the following decade. In 1911, 12,500 mine workers were employed in Nova Scotia alone, a further 6,700 in Alberta and nearly 6,900 in British Columbia.[29] Employment figures in coal mining stagnated at approximately this level until the Second World War. In 1939, 26,472 remained employed mining coal in Canada. Nova Scotia continued to account for half; nearly 8,000 were employed in Alberta and a further 3,000 in British Columbia. The balance were employed at smaller mines in Saskatchewan and New Brunswick.[30]

Coal mining provided the basis of a number of regional economies. Coal was mined on a small scale on Cape Breton Island from the seventeenth century. The first large-scale mines in British North America, dependent on cheap seaborne transportation, were developed in the 1820s at the Albion Mines, in Pictou County, and at Sydney Mines, on Cape Breton Island. The end of the General Mining Association (GMA) monopoly of mining in Nova Scotia in 1858 led to a proliferation of new mines in the province, notably on Cape

Table 1.1
Canadian Coal Production by Province (millions of short tons)

	Canada	NS	NB	Sask	Alta	BC
1870	0.75	0.72	–	–	–	0.034
1880	1.48	1.16	–	–	–	0.305
1890	3.08	2.22	0.007	–	0.129	0.767
1900	5.78	3.69	0.01	0.041	0.311	1.78
1910	12.91	6.52	0.055	0.181	3.04	3.52
1920	16.95	6.5	0.172	0.335	6.91	3.02
1930	14.88	6.25	0.209	0.579	5.76	2.12
1940	17.57	7.85	0.547	1.1	6.21	1.87

* Indicates little or no coal production.

Note: Figures may not add up due to rounding.

Source: Canada [Carroll], *Royal Commission on Coal*, 61–71.

Breton Island. The Hudson's Bay Company initiated commercial mining on Vancouver Island in 1849, where large collieries were operating by the 1870s. Railway construction led to the development of important coalfields in Nova Scotia's Cumberland County, at Springhill and Joggins, as well as in Inverness County, Nova Scotia; and encouraged the expansion of long-worked smaller mines in central New Brunswick.[31] Following transcontinental railroad construction towards the end of the century, commercial mines were opened in the interior of British Columbia, Alberta, and Saskatchewan.[32]

The heart of Canada's late-nineteenth-century coal industry remained in Nova Scotia, despite increasing activity on the Pacific coast. At Confederation, British Columbia's output amounted to just 30,000 tons; in Nova Scotia 532,000 tons were lifted and sold, well over half from Cape Breton.[33] By 1890 the gap had narrowed somewhat: British Columbia produced 767,000 tons of coal, Nova Scotia about three times as much. Only at the beginning of the twentieth century did the coal industry begin to shift west, although Nova Scotia continued to account for over half of Canada's coal production as late as 1910 and remained the largest coal-producing province in most years until after the Second World War (see Table 1.1).

Boys were brought into the mine by their fathers, experienced miners who had been recruited in the United Kingdom to develop the Canadian industry. Growth in colliery size was accompanied by ever greater calls for child labour. At the earliest mines the presence of just a handful of boys is recorded.[34] But their numbers increased considerably. Perhaps 450 boys laboured in British North American coal mines in 1866; in 1890 nearly 1,000 worked in Canadian mines. At large Victorian collieries such as the Albion Mines or Sydney

Mines, at times up to one-quarter of the underground workforce was under eighteen years of age. The employment of boys at Canadian coal mines reached its peak during the first decade of the twentieth century, when over 1,200 boys laboured at any given time, although as a proportion of the mine labour force their numbers had peaked several decades earlier.[35]

The colliery was a particularly inhospitable workplace. The routine of work compelled the boys to rise early, make their way wearily to the pithead, and be plunged hundreds of feet underground. In utter darkness, relieved only slightly by the uncertain light of their lamps, day after day, for up to twelve hours or longer, boys manipulated ventilation doors, led horses along lengthy and treacherous underground roads, or lifted tons of coal daily, filling wagon after wagon with freshly mined coal as the first step in its removal from the mine. For boys, work in a coal mine was hard – in the eyes of early historians of the industrial revolution, a fitting symbol of the "bleak age."[36]

The hardships boys faced in the mine were exacerbated by the tender age at which they first entered it. While the evidence is patchy, it appears that by the end of the nineteenth century most pit boys were aged between thirteen and sixteen.[37] Some boys began to labour in Canadian mines at the age of eight or nine. Into the 1880s, boys were quitting school at thirteen in Springhill, Nova Scotia, to work in local collieries; on Cape Breton, boys were entering the mines at even younger ages at that time.[38] As late as 1920, boys as young as thirteen continued to labour in New Brunswick's coal mines.[39] After the First World War, boys typically started to work in Canadian mines, at the earliest, at fourteen or fifteen years of age.[40] Toots MacNeil, who started to work in a Cape Breton mine in 1924 at the age of twelve, was an exception.[41] By about the age of eighteen, the pit boy was expected to have taken on adult work, generally as a coal miner.[42]

This is a history of boys in coal mines in Canada. Although boys laboured in every province in which coal was mined, Nova Scotia is examined most closely in this study. By far the dominant coal-producing province throughout this period, Nova Scotia was where most boys laboured and where, in fact, boys constituted a considerable portion (roughly one-sixth) of the mine workforce until late in the nineteenth century. Frequent comparisons are drawn with Vancouver Island, also a site of early mining, where boys continued to work until well into the twentieth century, although British immigrant miners encountered frustrations in their efforts to bring their boys into the mines there. In coalfields developed later (in New Brunswick, in the interior of British Columbia, in Alberta, and in

Saskatchewan), far fewer boys were employed, and these districts receive relatively little attention.

Boys' subsequent exclusion from colliery work is also examined. The degradation of the miner's traditional skills, changing technologies, alternative sources of unskilled labour, new divisions of labour, and changes in the family economy all had their part to play within the broader social context where children's place was being redefined as (and limited to) the home, school, and playground. The mine was the object of the first legislated efforts to restrict children's labour in Canada, and the impact of such legislation should not be underestimated, particularly on Vancouver Island. By the 1930s, boys were rarely employed at Canadian collieries.

Pit boys did not document their experience. Even the handful of miners who wrote autobiographies as adults had little to say about their childhood experience in the mine.[43] Nor did others pay particular attention to pit boys. Nonetheless, they laboured in an industry perhaps unparalleled for the quantity of documentation it generated. Industrial publications described the physical environment in which boys laboured. The social context of the mine was outlined in union publications and records. Glimpses of the boys were also caught in the popular press, in travellers' accounts of their visits to mines, and in the publications of students of the industry such as Edwin Gilpin, R.H. Brown, C.O. Macdonald, and Robert Drummond. Boys also crossed the path of government. The coal industry was the subject of a considerable range of royal commissions and of more modest inquiries; provincial Departments of Mines published annual reports from 1866 in Nova Scotia, 1877 in British Columbia, and 1905 in Alberta and Saskatchewan.[44] After 1900 the federal Department of Labour collected information on work in the industry. From these records, the history of boys in the mines can be reconstructed.

Any study of child labour sits at the intersection of working-class history, the history of childhood, and the history of the family. The child as worker has preoccupied historians in none of these fields. More than two decades after "labour" history became "working-class" history, most of the historical experience of labouring children remains unexplored.[45] The literature continues to be dominated by the skilled worker, his workplace, his industrial conflicts, his trade unions, his culture – and, most recently, constructions of his gender identity. Working women are only beginning to find a place. Children remain neglected.[46] The literature on coal mining reflects this general inattention to labouring children. Despite the research interest shown in recent years in Canadian coalfields, mine workers have been depicted with rare exceptions as adult.[47]

Historical writing on childhood has also failed to recognize the extent to which the working-class experience of childhood has been shaped by work. Rather, it favours descriptions of how public institutions have been developed in response to (the special problem of) children. In these studies, children have become historical objects for whom adults devise appropriate strategies. A number of distinct streams within this literature can be identified, focusing on child welfare, education, health, and juvenile delinquency.[48] Family history has usefully examined child labour as a survival strategy within the family economy, but it has left undeveloped the industrial context of this labour and children's experience of and response to labour. Boys and girls are depicted as family economic resources, not historical agents.[49]

Internationally, the labouring child has received more attention. But even here only a partial picture of child labour has been offered. Children have no history of their own: their "history" is the account of action undertaken by others to improve their condition.[50] Implicitly, children are impotent; their welfare is the object of others' efforts. They are mere victims of history. "Man's inhumanity to man has, over the centuries," runs the familiar refrain, "been surpassed only by his inhumanity to women and children."[51] In the United Kingdom, where the process of industrialization has spawned a vast literature, the image of the child of the industrial revolution as a victim persists tenaciously – despite a handful of recent efforts to underscore the agency of urban adolescent males.[52] Originating in a series of early-nineteenth-century commissions of inquiry, the conventional portrait of the child of the industrial revolution has been developed by historians as diverse in views as Marx and Engels, the Hammonds, Clapham and Trevelyan, Briggs and Thompson.[53] They all offer litanies of the degradation of the labouring child.[54] Clapham laments their "ignorance, overwork, degrading conditions."[55] Trevelyan and Briggs outline the brutal conditions legislative action sought to remedy.[56] E.P. Thompson, in closing his section in *The Making of the English Working Class* on the child worker, argues that "the exploitation of little children, on this scale and with this intensity, was one of the most shameful events in our history."[57] The history of child labour is reduced to a chronicle of blighted childhood.

This book reassesses this orthodoxy. In the first part, it examines how changing attitudes and practices regarding childhood, class relations at the colliery, mining technology, the state, the working-class family, and the mining community shaped the world pit boys encountered. These circumstances drew boys into the mine, defined their place there, and eventually expelled them from the colliery. Yet an analysis confined to them simply objectifies the boy. In the second part, the pit boys' limited but clear margin of manœuvre is reflected in the single chapter examining their response to the mine.

Chapter 2 outlines the context in which child labour came to be defined as illegitimate. A broad reform coalition, emphasizing the dependence of children, their immaturity, their need for protection, sought to reshape childhood over the nineteenth century. These efforts were expressed concretely in a range of legislation, institutions, associations, and conventions which, increasingly, defined and segregated children. Adults were to work. Children were not to work. The pit boy laboured in an ever more hostile social environment.

Chapter 3 explores class relations at the time, the struggle over the allied questions of who was qualified to work at the colliery and who was qualified to cut coal and promoted to the work of a miner. It describes the development of distinct markets for child workers in nineteenth-century Canadian coalfields. British immigrant miners encountered few obstacles in Nova Scotia to their customary early initiation of boys to mine labour. In contrast, they were far less successful on Vancouver Island in their efforts to employ their boys. Employers' ready access to Asian labourers, linked with provincial legislation in 1877 restricting child mine labour, produced relatively low levels of child labour on the Pacific coast. And in the mines of the western interior, developed at the end of the nineteenth century, immature local coal communities offered a limited local supply of boys. Their workforces were based on transient adult males, and only a handful of boys ever laboured in these mines.

The impact of technical changes on child labour is discussed in Chapter 4. Techniques of mining changed extensively, if unevenly, over the nineteenth century as rapidly growing markets for coal stimulated vastly increased production. A series of innovations in the methods used to mine coal, associated with the introduction of steam power, transformed mine work at the largest collieries, lessening the need for sheer brute strength among mine labourers. These changing technologies greatly increased the range of mine jobs boys were competent to fill. But as early as the 1880s, with the mechanization of underground haulage, this trend was reversed and subsequent technical innovations discouraged the employment of boys in mines. At the same time, these new techniques of mining, in jeopardizing the collier's traditional skills, encouraged miners to steer their sons away from what they viewed as a declining craft.

Over the nineteenth century, the state assumed growing prominence in the articulation of the rules governing participation in the mine workforce. Chapter 5 focuses on the ways in which the state defined sex- and age-based eligibility for specific employment and at whose initiative it acted. Legislation directly affecting pit boys took two forms. First, school legislation, particularly compulsory attendance laws, began to shape child labour markets. Subsequently, Mines Acts, wherein children's right to work in the mines was restricted by minimum-age requirements and by limitations on the length of their working day and week, had a major impact on boys' access to the mines, particularly in British Columbia. The trade unions played a key role. Relatively weak elsewhere in Canada until after the turn of the twentieth century, in Nova Scotia they clearly spearheaded efforts to remove boys from the mine, encouraging school attendance and sponsoring the legislative amendments to the Mines Acts that defined the reconstructed childhood.

Class relations at the mine, the nature of the adult mining workforce, mining technology, and legislation help to account for the much higher levels of child labour in Nova Scotian mines than elsewhere in Canada. Chapter 6 considers the mining family economy in Nova Scotia, the gender-based division of labour in coal communities, and the continuing significance of non-wage forms of family income. It then assesses the place of boys' wage earnings in the efforts of mining families to earn a living. The argument is developed in part by statistical data from the manuscript census for Sydney Mines, Nova Scotia, for 1871 through 1901. While boys' wage earnings were only necessary to family subsistence in rare instances, they retained a crucial role in giving mining families a cherished margin of security until higher turn-of-the-century adult wages, improved insurance programs, pensions, and other benefits helped to attenuate traditional financial concerns.

Chapter 7 examines mining communities. In the nineteenth century, boys raised in these communities were expected to enter the mine – they followed the trade of their father and older brothers. Dependent on the employment offered by the mine, mining towns and villages had typically only few thousand inhabitants, on occasion just a few hundred. Nonetheless, they were marked by sharp social divides. Class differences led to struggles over power within the community; relations between men and women were marked by inequities and silences; cultural conflict was underscored by the scorn that the liberal trade union leadership poured on miners' "rough" behaviour. But an emerging consensus around child labour in the pits transcended these differences. New views of an appropriate childhood slowly percolated into coal towns and villages. Agents of the reconstructed childhood had a growing place in the community: the juvenile temperance groups, the Woman's Christian Temperance Union, the Boys' Brigade, the YMCA, the Boy Scouts, and Children's

Aid Societies. Miners' unions warmly endorsed new definitions of childhood. Over the late nineteenth and early twentieth centuries, the mining community began to shift its views regarding the employment of boys in the pits.

Chapter 8, which examines boys' response to their experience in the coalfields, looks at the relationships that boys entered into within the mine and the unique identity they acquired through these relationships. This enabled them, in small but meaningful ways, to exercise limited power. If the world they encountered was harsh, they nonetheless rebelled against its most oppressive aspects. While tensions existed between boys and older mine workers, their most vigorous challenges were to mine management. As vulnerable, as victimized by circumstances as these children appear to have been, they were an independent and recognized force in the mines where they laboured.

Chapter 9 briefly considers the pit boys' ultimate exclusion from Canadian coal mines in the context of the decline of the traditional (underground) mining industry between the world wars. Concluding with an evaluation of the labour performed by the boys in the pits, it argues that our contemporary view of child labour owes as much to the modern definition of childhood, which interprets child labour as offensive, as it does to the actual experience of labouring children. But today's judgment has nineteenth-century antecedents: the growing tension that began in the late nineteenth century between new definitions of childhood and the boys' experience of the pits was only resolved many decades later, when boys were finally excluded from the mines.

Pit boys were born into circumstances over which they had no control: their world was framed by class relations and industrial technology, the state's laws, family constraints, and community expectations. But the boys responded maturely and intelligently to these restrictive circumstances, demonstrating a clear, if limited, ability to resist others' efforts to take advantage of them. The history of pit boys is more than a record of their victimization. They participated in their own making.

CHAPTER TWO

The Making of Modern Childhood

"What I have claimed for, and struggled to give to my own children ...
I want to see other people's children enjoy."
C.W. Vernon, "Child Labour in the Country"

The activity of most children in Canada today is divided between school and play. Typically, boys and girls reside in an urban community. They are raised in a nuclear family of on average under two children, although much of their day is spent outside their parents' supervision. While they may assist in household chores or take part-time jobs as adolescents to earn some spending money for themselves, expert advice and popular belief emphasize the crucial role of play in children's development into healthy adults. Gender roles – how boys are to behave as boys, and girls as girls – are learned early within the family and are reinforced at school and in play.[1]

In contrast, until well into the twentieth century, children worked from an early age, contributing their labour under their parents' direction in support of the household.[2] Most lived in rural districts, within a large nuclear family.[3] If children went to school, attendance was irregular, subject to the demands of the family economy.[4] Play-time was stolen from work and school time. Folk wisdom directed that boys and girls be trained to be submissive and obedient.[5] Children learned gender roles early by observing and imitating adults at work and play.[6]

Although work retained a large place in the life of the overwhelming majority of children, childhood changed radically over the nineteenth century in the wake of the Enlightenment. A heightened awareness of childhood as a distinct and special stage in life developed.[7] Far greater concern was shown for the inner, emotional life of children.[8] New attitudes towards childhood were also marked by an increasing emotional investment in children.[9] Children were "sacralized" as an "emotional and affective asset" within the family, rather than valued for their economic contributions.[10] At the same time, childhood became sentimentalized: children were portrayed so as to

evoke an emotional response.[11] Greater sensitivity to children translated into increasing sensitivity to the gradation of age.[12] Even their
dress became distinct.[13]

The defining characteristic of the reconstructed childhood was the
emotional and psychological dependence of the child.[14] From this
assumption others were derived: labelled weak and innocent, children
were thus also vulnerable. Defined as fundamentally immature, they
were defined as corruptible. Stigmatized as incompetent, they were
considered unfit to assume adult responsibilities. These disabilities
required responses. New views of childhood, Neil Sutherland
observed, reflected the "strongly developing belief in the influence of
environment on children." The child, a "partially formed and potential
adult," was defined as "basically plastic raw material."[15] The articulation of appropriate responses produced the reconstructed childhood.

Children were segregated so that they could be protected from the
coarse and vicious examples found in adult society. The preferred
environment for the child was to be the nurturing family. But for
delinquent children, or for those who had lost their natural family,
special institutions were created by the middle of the nineteenth century, and before its close, systems of juvenile justice and child welfare
had emerged. Children's responsibility under the law was attenuated,
and stronger efforts were made to rehabilitate rather than punish
wayward children. These efforts were accompanied by a vast range
of institutions developed for all children, most notably the common
school. Even children's leisure activities were organized independently from adults'. Most significantly, the traditional preoccupation
with finding gainful employment for children was eclipsed by systematic efforts to defer boys' and girls' entry into the world of work,
at least until the relatively mature age of twelve, fourteen or older.[16]

Crucially, the transformed childhood was universal. The powers of
the state were used to ensure that all children *had* a childhood.
Members of the Montreal Society for the Protection of Women and
Children, in advocating criminal law amendments for the protection
of young girls in 1889, made explicit that their aim was "so that the
poor and friendless will be as well protected as the rich and powerful."[17] "What I have claimed for, and struggled to give to my own
children," an Anglican clergyman affirmed in 1923, "I want to see
other people's children enjoy."[18] The principal instrument employed
to shape childhood was the common school. Public school systems
were designed to educate the offspring of the urban middle classes
as well as of immigrant and labouring classes. The National Council
of Women of Canada (NCWC), in advocating in 1912 that all children
between the ages of five and fourteen be "devoted entirely to getting

a general education," echoed the statements of two generations of
school promoters.[19]

A central aspect of the reconstruction of childhood over the nineteenth century was its progressive prolongation.[20] The child was
considered dependent, in need of special treatment, to an ever greater
age. This was expressed most clearly in legislation. Under a variety
of pressures, governments steadily extended the age of legal minority. The first provisions for compulsory school attendance in the
nineteenth century applied to children under the age of twelve or
fourteen; by early in the twentieth century, education was compulsory in most provinces until the age of fourteen or sixteen. Fears
regarding the white slave trade were widespread in the late nineteenth century.[21] From Confederation, federal law defined "carnal
knowledge" of girls under ten years of age as a felony (from 1906,
as an indictable offence).[22] This age was raised to fourteen in 1890,
and to sixteen in 1920.[23] When Parliament passed legislation enabling
the provinces to establish juvenile courts in 1892, provision was made
for the separate trial of children to the age of sixteen; in 1921 the
threshold was raised to eighteen.[24] Likewise, the minimum age for
legal participation in the wage labour force was progressively raised.
In the coalfields of Nova Scotia, the minimum age for underground
employment was set at ten in 1873 and raised to twelve in 1891. It
was extended to sixteen in 1923, to seventeen in 1947, and to eighteen
in 1954.[25] Ontario passed the first Factory Act in Canada in 1884,
which set the minimum age of employment in factories at twelve for
boys. This legislation was amended in 1895 to raise this age to
fourteen.[26] Quebec, slow to legislate compulsory school attendance,
necessarily relied more heavily on its Factory Act to restrict child
employment. First establishing a minimum age for boys at twelve in
1885, this was raised progressively to thirteen in 1903, fourteen in
1907, and, unless the child was able to read and write fluently, sixteen
in 1910.[27] Similarly, children's protection legislation in Quebec, as first
drafted in 1884 and amended in 1912, addressed those under fourteen
years of age. As revised in 1950, this legislation applied to those
under eighteen years of age.[28] Legal status as a minor – childhood –
has become an ever more inclusive category.

THE REFORMERS OF CHILDHOOD

The original model for the reformed childhood was urban, emerging
within relatively affluent and well-educated milieux – what contemporaries labelled the "respectable" or "middle" classes.[29] But the
transformation of childhood can not be reduced to the efforts of

urban bourgeois to use the state to reshape the rural and working-class experience of childhood to their specifications. Reformers from a wide range of backgrounds contributed for a variety of motives, by no means uniformly altruistic, to the reconstructed childhood.[30] Acknowledging considerable overlap among his categories, Neil Sutherland identified three "clusters" of social reformers who provided the impetus to the reconstructed childhood: Christians with a "social passion" who aimed to construct a Protestant society; members of the urban middle class "who saw a reconstructed childhood as part of their effort to make the new environment a place of order and prosperity for themselves and their offspring"; and finally, members of the new professions such as social work who sought to extend their authority and influence.[31] This broad reform movement, Sutherland emphasized, had by the turn of the twentieth century "draw[n] the plans for and rough[ed] in many of the dimensions of a transformed childhood."[32]

The English-speaking British North American colonies were marked by tremendous religious diversity based on ethnic background and denominational affiliation.[33] Crossing sectarian boundaries within nineteenth-century Protestantism was the evangelical impulse. "The distinguishing feature of the evangelical faith," David Marshall explains, "was its emphasis on becoming aware of God in the depths of the heart. Evangelicals were convinced that God was constantly rewarding, admonishing, and punishing individuals."[34] Notwithstanding their preoccupation with the individual's personal relationship with God, Marshall stresses evangelicals' social activism. "Within evangelicalism there was no clear-cut dichotomy between one's personal relation with God and commitment to building a social order based on Christian principles; they were integrally related."[35] Reform movements advocating the abolition of slavery, prison reform, temperance, and assistance to the poor were commonly led by evangelicals.[36] And, as Alison Prentice observed, "[t]he evangelical belief that, despite the persistence of sin in the world all people were capable of being saved, was fundamental to the crusade for educational reform."[37]

Concern grew among Christian communities early in the nineteenth century over the conditions in which children were raised. For the vast majority of children, their first encounter with Christian reform was in the Sunday School.[38] But the evangelical impulse also led to "philanthropic abduction," intervention to remove children from family environments considered unsuitable. This work, premised on the "individual rather than communal nature of corruption," focused on the rescue of individual souls rather than the reform of society.[39] Often called "child-saving," these efforts extended beyond a concern with orphans to encompass a range of children who were deemed to be inadequately provided for, notably, boys and girls from poor families.[40]

Efforts to "rescue" children reached their largest scale in the programs to bring juvenile emigrants from the United Kingdom to Canada.[41] These extended back at least to 1835, when the Children's Friend Society was founded in Toronto.[42] Maria Susan Rye brought her first group of children to Canada in 1869; Annie MacPherson brought hers the following year. Churches sponsored their own juvenile emigration programs, such as the Church of England's Waifs and Strays Society. Most active of all was Thomas John Barnardo, who sent 24,000 children to Canada between 1882 and the start of the First World War.[43] Between 1868 and 1925, these organizations brought 80,000 British children to Canada.[44] From the perspective of child-savers, the benefits of emigration were patent. At a relatively modest cost, children were removed from environments considered harmful – the poor families of urban Britain – and placed in those considered healthy – rural Canadian families. The results, in the testimony of the children themselves, fell far short of the child-savers' expectations.[45]

Evangelicals were also ultimately disappointed in their campaign against drink, another principal thrust of their reform activity. Alcohol was widely blamed for the perceived breakdown in family life – as a basic threat to society.[46] Among the first Victorian organizations to deal actively with children were those enlisting them in the campaign against drink. British children's temperance groups, most notably the Band of Hope, were present in Canada within a generation after their formation in the United Kingdom, organized by adult male temperance societies like the Sons of Temperance or the International Order of Good Templars.[47] The Woman's Christian Temperance Union (WCTU), whose first locals were formed in Canada in 1874, the year the union was founded in the United States, subsequently organized Bands of Hope. The WCTU was the most consequential of the evangelical temperance organizations, and the most involved with children. Boys and girls were seen as impressionable – uniquely susceptible to temperance appeals. At the same time, they were seen as persuasive advocates of the cause with adults. The WCTU showed a particular sensitivity to age. Children under seven years of age were organized in playgroups as "Little White Ribboners." Bands of Hope and their successor, Loyal Temperance Legions, organized boys and girls from seven to approximately fifteen years of age. These groups administered the "triple pledge" to children to forswear intoxicating liquors, tobacco, and bad language. Older girls were encouraged to join the Young Woman's Christian Temperance Union, and were given primary responsibility for organizing the activities of the Bands of Hope and other educational work with children, commonly in association with Sunday Schools. The WCTU also attempted, with mixed success, to have temperance literature placed on the public school curriculum.[48]

Growing evangelical concern over declining religious practice, particularly among young boys, produced a variety of responses.[49] John Webster Grant has argued that it is "difficult to exaggerate the importance" of the Young Men's Christian Association (YMCA), whose first Canadian branch was established in Montreal in 1851. Focusing first on the evangelization of poor youth, the YMCA emphasized recreational needs, viewing "sin as a spare time activity." By the end of the century, its attention encompassed all boys and it was hiring salaried workers.[50] Seeking to construct "a quarantined world of boyish recreation and attenuated moral and religious questioning," the YMCA developed an age-based program of training, including a progressive curriculum, manuals, and tests.[51]

The Young Women's Christian Association (YWCA) was organized a generation later than the YMCA and took as its focus of concern the growing number of young women entering the wage labour force. Its locals often worked closely in tandem with the Protestant churches. The Saint John local, founded in 1870, established a mission school to educate young working women. Toronto's, established in 1873, offered cheap, "respectable" accommodation to young women often from rural areas, new to the city. In 1874 the Halifax YWCA established a home for delinquent girls. The national YWCA union was established in 1893.[52] The Canadian Girls in Training (CGIT) curriculum was developed in 1917 by the YWCA to provide a Protestant education for girls aged twelve to seventeen. In contrast to the equivalent programs for boys (the Trail Rangers and the Tuxis Boys), the CGIT enjoyed popularity. By the end of its first decade, 75,000 girls had participated in Canadian Girls in Training.[53]

Churches too confronted the problem of maintaining the interest of the young, particularly boys, in organized religion. Recognizing the limited attractions of Sunday Schools, Protestant churches turned to the new instrument of boys' groups. The Boys' Brigade was founded in 1883 by William Smith in Glasgow. Offering the enticement of military-style drill and marches through city streets, it expanded rapidly.[54] Boys' Brigades were in Canada within a few years.[55] For older children, late nineteenth century churches sponsored many leisure activities including literary and debating clubs and organized sports and games.[56] By the 1890s, denominational organizations for the young had been formed: Epworth Leagues among Methodists, the Presbyterian Westminster Guilds, the Baptist Young People's Unions, and the King's Daughters and Sons among Anglicans.[57] Catholics also had a variety of confraternities for children and youths. Within Irish parishes, literary and debating societies were commonly sponsored.[58]

Late in the nineteenth century, liberal evangelicals spearheaded the emergent social gospel movement. Placing far less emphasis on the Christian basis of reform, focusing on social ills, and rejecting an individual basis for such ills, their motives were marked far more by secular and humanitarian concerns. This movement can be linked with the second cluster of reformers of childhood that Sutherland identified within the Anglo-Saxon urban business and professional groups emergent over the second half of the nineteenth century.[59]

Women's organizations, very prominent within middle-class reform, reflected the rise of social service as a feminine ideal.[60] They were responsible for many of the earliest orphans' homes and kindred facilities such as infants' homes. Although special homes for the shelter and care of dependent children had appeared in Canadian urban centres from an early date, they were exceptional. In Halifax, for example, an orphans' home had operated between 1752 and 1787.[61] Only from the middle third of the nineteenth century were distinct institutions for dependent children commonly established. Among Protestant communities, Ladies' Aid Societies generally took the lead in establishing Protestant Orphans' Homes (POHs); among Catholics, various religious orders cared for orphans as one of their many welfare functions.[62] The name "orphan home" is misleading insofar as most housed more non-orphans than orphans. Children were commonly temporarily consigned to an institution by a single parent unable to manage, or by a family undergoing a short-term crisis.[63]

The POHs constituted the first systematic attempt to create specialized institutions for children. Efforts were made to establish a family-like environment, probably far more successfully at the homes with two dozen children than at those with two hundred. At the same time, the coercive aspects of these institutions are clear. Children were segregated from undesirable influences. Their families were refused contact or saw their visiting privileges limited to a specified hour or two weekly. Children's activities were closely controlled. Schoolrooms were established in the Homes for the purpose of isolating POH children from those attending the neighbourhood school.[64]

Alternatively, women's reform activity took children's health as its primary focus, seeking to make childhood more secure from the threat of disease. Rates of infant and early childhood mortality remained staggeringly high until after the First World War.[65] Ad hoc initiatives were taken in response. Locals of the National Council of Women of Canada (founded in 1893) opened Well-Baby Clinics and milk depots and undertook campaigns for tuberculosis control, improved housing, home nursing, and "Little Mother Classes" in schools, in addition to the NCWC's better-known role as a national forum and lobby focusing on issues relating to women and children.[66] The Imperial Order of the Daughters of the Empire (founded in 1900) also sponsored well-baby clinics and made efforts to improve rural standards of hygiene, as did the Cercles des Fermières (from 1915) and the Fédération des femmes canadiennes-françaises in French-speaking districts. Women's Institutes (from 1903) provided health education and medical services in schools, and campaigned for pure milk and improved sanitation in small municipalities and rural schools.[67] In 1914 the Canadian Red Cross Society initiated a program of health instruction to young children through Junior Red Cross Societies, which had enrolled 75,000 children by 1923.[68]

As the nineteenth century approached its close, women's organizations widened in scope. While the WCTU, for instance, continued to focus on prohibition, it came to advocate a range of other state actions. WCTU locals lobbied for curfews, stiffer compulsory education laws, stronger legislation to address cruelty to children, and more effective anti-procuring legislation.[69] These broadened concerns extended to children's leisure pastimes. Children's use of tobacco was dismissed as harmless until the 1860s, when it began to be redefined as a waste of money, harmful to health, and, because of its narcotic effects, as a path to stronger drugs and alcohol.[70] The sight of boys of eight and nine years of age "puffing away at cigarettes with all the nonchalance of experts at the business" was a source of indignation by 1892.[71] Locals of the NCWC were active in campaigns to ban tobacco sales to children, to limit sales outlets, and to increase licence fees for vendors.[72]

Increasing literacy led to the development of mass markets, the publication of cheap and accessible reading material, and a range of specialized publications for children. "Everybody has a paper, even to the children," reported the *Journal of Education* in 1861.[73] The (British) *Boy's Own Magazine*, founded in 1855, was among the first and the most widely distributed specialized publications for children. The English public school boy was held up as the model child; girls' place was depicted as in the home. Adventure stories, commonly set in the Canadian North-West, were the staple of the *Boy's Own Paper*, published from 1879.[74] By the end of the century, age and gender sensitivity led to increasingly age-specific publications: for young children, adolescents, and young adults.[75] Didactic literature for children was a staple of temperance societies, which also took it upon themselves to monitor literature and censor publications deemed unfit for children.[76] In Canada, the churches were also energetic producers of children's publications. The Presbyterian Church published *East and West* for ten- to fourteen-year-olds, and the *Pathfinder* for children from fifteen to eighteen. The Methodists produced *Playmates*, for six- to nine-year-olds, and *Onward*, directed at children ten to fourteen. All emphasized moral teaching in the form of stories, parables, and accounts of good deeds.[77]

Public and school libraries followed closely after the establishment of free and common schools, with the object as much to monitor reading material as to ensure its availability.[78] "Pernicious" literature was an early concern of the National Council of Women of Canada, whose Committee on Objectionable Printed Matter extended its mandate in 1903 to improper plays and posters, in 1908 to picture cards, and in 1909 to children's newspaper supplements. The contents of local libraries were also scrutinized (French novels were reviewed particularly closely). Keeping pace with changing popular media, the NCWC monitored motion pictures until the Second World War.[79]

The street, traditionally a favourite arena of play, was redefined as early as the 1850s as constituting an environment where children at best loitered and at worst were initiated into criminal activity through temptations such as "drinking saloons and dance-houses ... the ball-alley, [the] gambling room, and places of a still worse character."[80] Concern began to be raised over juvenile gangs.[81] As early as the 1890s, NCWC locals were lobbying for curfew by-laws and truancy acts to "drive children back to the control of parents and schools."[82] "Children left to themselves in the street do not play, but learn most vicious habits," members of the NCWC were told in 1908.[83] The emergence of organizations such as Bands of Hope, Boys' Brigades, Scouts and Guides, or the Junior Red Cross reflects the determined effort to exercise a much stricter supervision over children's leisure and recreation.

The concern to establish suitable environments for play led to calls early in the twentieth century for supervised urban playgrounds.[84] Here too the NCWC took a leading role. In 1900 the Saint John's Local Council of Women established a committee dedicated to convincing parsimonious local officials of the virtues of municipal playgrounds. The following year, the NCWC established the National Committee on Vacation Schools and Supervised Playgrounds. By 1913, thirteen local councils had formed playground committees, with varying levels of success.[85]

In another avenue of activity, a number of organizations sponsored "purity lectures," often in schools. The young child was seen as sexually innocent. To prolong this desired state, the experts advised restraint: late hours, sensational novels and illustrations, even the ballroom, were all considered to hasten the problematic puberty. Adolescents were advised to exercise continence.[86] Considerable attention was directed to this end in the British "Duty and Discipline" series and the American "Self and Sex" series, adopted by the WCTU and the Methodist Church.[87] The Church of England took a further step in 1883, initiating the White Cross Society, "to promote social purity and to assist young men in their resistance to illicit sexual relations."[88] And at a time when the Criminal Code defined the age of female consent at sixteen, the National Council of Women of Canada called for it to be raised to eighteen.[89]

Cruelty to children was a particular focus of concern, and one area where men were as prominent as women. Often growing out of initial efforts to protect animals, anti-cruelty societies shifted the focus of their concern in light of evidence of widespread neglect and abuse of children. The Halifax Society for the Prevention of Cruelty, founded in 1876 by young businessmen, directed its efforts towards neglected and homeless children, notably those found begging in the streets.[90] The Montreal Society for the Protection of Women and Children, organized in 1882 by a group of philanthropically inclined businessmen, waged campaigns for legislated restrictions on child labour and also focused on cruelty to children, street-trading, prostitution, compulsory education, and a juvenile court system. It lobbied politicians and public officials (both for new laws and the firmer enforcement of existing legislation); approached parents whose young children were found out on the streets; and prosecuted offending parents or other adults it deemed exploitative.[91] Toronto's Humane Society was organized in 1887 to combat cruelty to and neglect of both children and animals. An early focus of its efforts was to gain legal authority to address the problems of children victimized by "drunken, cruel and dissolute parents or guardians." Particularly concerned by the street trades, the Humane Society called for licensing and closer police supervision of shoe-shine boys, newsboys, and other street vendors, the banning of young girls from street trades, and an extended use of industrial schools.[92] By the turn of the twentieth century, fears over the health of the empire in the wake of the Boer War sharpened concerns about children. These concerns buttressed support for children's health campaigns that were a response to infant mortality and "feeble-mindedness" at the same time as they bolstered the cadet movement.[93] They also underlay interest in the Boy Scouts movement.[94] In

Quebec, the formation of the Catholic and nationalist Association catholique de la jeunesse canadienne-française reflected fears arising from urbanization and secularization.[95]

The third major cluster of childhood's reformers were the new professionals: mostly educators, but also factory inspectors, recreational and social workers, juvenile court judges, morality squad police officers, and public health officials who emerged with the burgeoning new systems for the regulation and reconstruction of childhood. The rise of child welfare professionals marked the shift from voluntary efforts, often by women, to a male-dominated, state-sponsored era of professionalism, where formal training, accreditation, and recognized expertise were preferred to the moral and evangelical thrusts of voluntary efforts. Associated with this trend was increasing coordination and institutionalization of activity.

By far the most numerous and influential of the new professionals were the educators who emerged with the vast systems of public schools developed over the late nineteenth and early twentieth centuries.[96] Their interest in children's education came to encompass many other aspects of children's lives, including their health, their home life, delinquency, and wage labour.[97] And at the university, the growing interest among psychologists in child development was reflected in the St George's School for Child Study, established in 1925 at the University of Toronto.[98] Patterns of normative child growth were outlined subsequently by widely read developmental psychologists such as S.R. Laycock of the University of Saskatchewan.[99]

Factory inspectors, although never numbering more than a few dozen nation-wide, were outspoken in their advocacy of more stringent protective legislation, even if they were seldom aggressive in sanctioning infractions of legislation by factory owners.[100] Their annual reports to legislators deplored the circumstances in which children laboured, and made regular calls for stricter legislation. "With regard to the questions of employment of children, I can only repeat what I have said in my previous reports," argued the factory inspector for Eastern Ontario, O.A. Rocque, in 1892: "that the school laws compelling children to attend schools should be enforced, and that the minimum age of employment be raised two years. I would also add that no children under sixteen years of age be employed unless they can read and write, and that their time of labor should not exceed say eight hours per day."[101] The first efforts to restrict at law children's employment in shops met with a similar reaction from another factory inspector: "The Shops Act calls for an age limit of ten years. In my opinion, this is far too young for children to go out into the world and fight the battle of life. If we expect to build up a strong nation, both physically and mentally, it cannot be done by sacrificing our children to the greed of commercialism."[102] Factory inspectors' concern helped to keep child labour on the public agenda.

To the groups responsible for the reconstruction of childhood that Sutherland enumerated, a fourth has to be added: trade unionists. Working people across the country shared concerns about both the condition of children and the threat to adult wages presented by child labour. The short-lived Canadian Labour Union of 1873 called for a legislated minimum age of ten for factory employment.[103] From its first session in 1883, the Trades and Labour Congress called for Factory Acts and improved access to public education by the free provision of books. In 1887 it called for the enforcement of provincial laws "compelling children of a certain age to attend school." By the 1890s its platform called for free and compulsory education and the abolition of child labour to fourteen years of age. Union locals, provincial federations, and international unions all reiterated similar concerns.[104] Organized labour was among the most conspicuous advocates of the reconstructed childhood.[105]

In the nineteenth century, child-centred reform was led by isolated and often single-issue groups, with little coordination of effort. While voluntarism, an ethic of unpaid service, had marked the efforts of the Protestant Orphans' Homes, the early Children's Aid Societies, and a range of other welfare organizations working with children in the nineteenth century, professionalism was the watchword of social work in the twentieth century.[106] With professionalization, coordinated reform networks emerged. The Protestant churches played a key role. The Presbyterian Board of Moral and Social Reform was organized in 1908; its secretary, J.G. Shearer, wrote articles on social evangelism for the labour press, advocating closer regulation of child and sweated labour and shorter hours of work. The Methodist Department of Temperance and Social Reform, established in 1902, considered questions including children's playgrounds, homes for juvenile delinquents, legislation regarding child labour, and the promotion of sex education. These two churches formed in 1908 the interdenominational Moral and Social Reform Council of Canada. Renamed the Social Service Council of Canada in 1913, it aimed to integrate social reform activity and act as a springboard for efforts to built a national reform coalition involving the churches, women's groups, organized labour, and rural organizations.[107] The reform coalition reached its peak of strength in 1920s; the Dominion Grange, the YMCA, the WCTU, the NCWC, the Victorian Order of Nurses, the Federation of Women's Institutes, the Canadian Council of Agriculture, the Canadian Prisoner's Welfare Association, the Salvation

Army, and other smaller groups all joined the Social Service Council of Canada between 1921 and 1925.[108]

Under the influence of women's organizations, organized reform focused increasingly on government efforts expended on behalf of women, children, and the family. The reform measures that were advocated concerned child welfare, public health, unemployment insurance, old-age pensions, and the reform of rural life.[109] The British Columbia campaign for mothers' pensions (provided by the province to women without an adult male breadwinner and with dependent children) provides an example of a typical reform coalition. In Vancouver, the Local Council of Women was lobbying as early as 1901; it later gained support from the University Women's Club, the Children's Aid Society, the WCTU, the IODE, the Equal Franchise Association, and local organized labour. (British Columbia was unusual for the modest role played by the clergy in this effort.)[110]

A major thrust of child welfare activity focused on children's health. Early efforts were associated with the domestic science movement. Popular education was seen as essential to reducing infant mortality rates.[111] In Quebec, the "Gouttes de Lait" program, designed to educate mothers in both pre- and post-natal care, in addition to dispensing pure milk, established supervisory infant clinics after 1911. Some clinics also operated programs of home visits.[112] By the First World War, public health had passed into the hands of – generally male – medical professionals and out of those of the Local Councils of Women, which had dominated efforts in the late nineteenth century. The Canadian Public Health Association was formed in 1910. The federal Department of National Health was founded in 1919, and a separate Child Welfare Division was organized the following year under Dr Helen MacMurchy. Although largely limited to an advisory role, its famous Little Blue Books were consulted by tens of thousands of anxious parents. Advice literature for parents proliferated from the turn of the twentieth century.[113]

The child welfare movement was institutionalized nationally in 1921 in the form of the Canadian Council on Child Welfare (CCCW). A quasi-public agency, funded by grants from the federal government and the Canadian Life Insurance Officers' Association, its original aims included the study of child hygiene, employment, education and recreation, and the special care of dependent, delinquent, neglected, and disabled children. It disseminated information on all aspects of child life, developed mother-care kits, and advised on legislation. Many groups, including the National Council of Women of Canada, the Federated Women's Institutes, the Women's Section of the Grain Growers Association, the IODE, the Cercles des

Fermières, and the Fédération des femmes canadiennes-françaises, assisted in the distribution of CCCW literature. Under the direction of Charlotte Whitton, the council stood as a focal point within the child welfare network.[114]

Reform groups increasingly expressed their concern over the labouring child, who became in the 1900s a metaphor for social injustice.[115] The Halifax *Herald* put the question in 1909: "Child Labor: Is There a Problem?" It responded emphatically: there was a problem. Many reasons were outlined: work denied the child the right to be schooled. It compromised home life and children's health. It took away jobs from men. It brought the law into disrepute by underlining that legislation was commonly unobserved and unenforced. Most importantly, labour denied the child the time to play.[116]

On the question of child labour, the various strands of reform united. Evangelical concerns over children's spiritual condition found focus in the emergent social gospel movement's lobby for stronger legislative controls to suppress child labour.[117] W.G. McKinnon, speaking to the YMCA Sociological Club in Halifax on "the exploiting of children for gain," argued, "If we substitute the association of profane men, for a mother's care, can we expect anything but a profane race?"[118] Women's groups, from the National Council of Women of Canada to the Halifax Local Council of Women, fought for tighter legislative controls over child labour.[119] The new professionals continued their efforts to restrict the employment of children. The Canadian Council on Child Welfare's campaign for Canadian adherence to the child labour standards established by the International Labour Organization (ILO) during the 1920s linked federal and provincial Departments of Labour, local and provincial social welfare councils, clergymen, trade unions, provincial federations of labour, councils of women and juvenile court officials. All were agreed that children's labour was to be subordinated to their need for schooling and play.[120]

THE STATE AND CHILDHOOD

Reformers recognized early that their powers of coercion were limited in the absence of participation by the state. They could organize boys' and girls' associations but not compel anyone to join them; produce literature but not guarantee a readership; condemn abusive households but not remove children from them; advocate schooling but not ensure attendance; protest against child labour but not end it. The state was a necessary instrument for the regulation and reformation of childhood.[121]

Yet the Victorian state was very reluctant to take on this role. Ivy Pinchbeck underscored the profound resistance of British legislators to "interposing in the life and organization of the many families who were able to support themselves and their children."[122] In taking this position, they were only responding to their constituents. "[O]ne would almost think that a man's children were supposed to be literally, and not metaphorically, part of himself," observed John Stuart Mill in 1859, "so jealous is opinion of the smallest interference of law with his absolute and exclusive control over them; more jealous than of almost any interference with his own freedom of action."[123] The traditional legal framework in Great Britain, emphasizing paternal authority rather than children's rights, was implanted in the English-speaking British North American colonies. In Lower Canada, the father's right to raise his children as he saw fit – *la puissance paternelle* – was enshrined in the Civil Code.[124] Intense respect for the integrity of the family placed a powerful obstacle in the path of those who wished to provide guarantees in law of the independent rights of the children both inside and outside the household.[125]

Two categories of children first drew the attention of public officials: neglected children, who lacked adequate care, and delinquent children. These two groups were not necessarily clearly differentiated: wayward children were viewed as actual criminals and neglected children as future criminals.[126] At the start of the nineteenth century, public welfare in British North America was a haphazard patchwork, both in colonies that adopted the Poor Law (which compelled local assessment for maintenance of the poor), such as Nova Scotia and New Brunswick, and those colonies like the Canadas, that did not. Both local authorities and private charities, with funds raised by voluntary subscription, provided out-relief.[127] Even so, institutions existed from an early date. Poor law colonies operated poorhouses. All colonies made public grants to privately run welfare institutions, mostly hospitals but also orphanages, almshouses, houses of industry, and other refuges.[128]

Little effort was made to treat children differently from adults. Particularly in the early part of the nineteenth century, necessitous but able-bodied adults were bound out at public expense as labourers. Children without adequate adult care were also bound out at the first opportunity.[129] Binding out was viewed as a more economical means of dealing with the dependent of all ages than institutionalization.[130] The two responses were not necessarily exclusive of each other. The Toronto House of Industry, for instance, had a policy of placing able-bodied children as apprentices.[131] An apprenticeship served the immediate goal of placing a dependent child, while teaching him or her a valued skill.[132]

Until late in the nineteenth century, legislation relating to dependent children remained one of the rare contexts where public authorities would intervene in family life. The coercive aspects of this practice are evident. The price of public support for a poor family might be the binding out of the children, as striking miners at the Albion Mines in Nova Scotia were reminded by a hostile journalist in 1842: "Some of the men have set off for the United States, leaving their wives and children behind them, presuming, no doubt, that they will be provided for from the Poors' fund. But they ought to remember that if the overseers of the Poor undertake the care of their families, they are empowered to bind out their children as apprentices; and it would be no pleasant circumstance for fathers to return and find their little ones so disposed of."[133]

In practice, Poor Law and non-Poor Law colonies operated similarly. The poor, orphaned, criminal, and/or unlucky children who found themselves in the hands of public authorities at this time (and for whom an apprenticeship was not found) were mixed promiscuously with adults in a local public institution that catered to the dependent or wayward of all ages. A committee inquiring into conditions in Halifax's Poor Asylum in 1832 condemned the absence of "comfort and cleanliness" and noted that the seventy-four orphan children in the institution slept with adults "without any regard to fitness of health or morals."[134] William Jaffray observed in 1870 that the Waterloo (Ontario) Poor House was home to sixty-two people of all ages. Eight were children aged between four and twelve. He recommended that the sexes be separated – he had no particular observation to make on the children's presence.[135] In nineteenth-century communities across Canada, the local jail, the most common facility, had a particularly wide clientele.[136]

The law, too, failed to discriminate clearly between young and old. If youthfulness was recognized in British North America as an extenuating circumstance in capital crimes – as a ground for a pardon or alternative punishments such as banishment or penitentiary terms – children over seven years of age had little special status otherwise in the justice system.[137] George Brown discovered during his commission of inquiry into the Kingston Penitentiary in 1849 that boys and girls shared not only the institution with adults, but also its brutal disciplinary regime. Alexis Lafleur, for instance, was first incarcerated in the penitentiary at the age of eleven. He soon found himself placed on bread and water, confined by himself to a dark cell, and lashed regularly. By the time he reached the age of fifteen, he was being whipped with the cat. His offences on various occasions? – disobedience, talking, laughing, and insolence ("sauciness"). Other children were similarly punished: fourteen-year-old Sarah O'Connor had been lashed with a rawhide five times in a recent three-month period; twelve-year-old Elizabeth Breen, seven times in fifteen months; eight-year-old Antoine Beauche, forty-eight times in ten months; and ten-year-old Peter Charbonneau had been "stripped to the shirt, and publically [sic] lashed 57 times in eight and a half months."[138]

Confronted with this situation, Brown and the other commissioners advocated that immediate steps be taken to segregate juvenile offenders from the corrupting influence of adult criminals by their removal from common jails and penitentiaries: "It is distressing to think that no distinction is now made between the child who has strayed for the first time from the path of honesty, or who perhaps has never been taught the meaning of sin, and the hardened offender of mature years. All are consigned together to the unutterable contamination of the common gaol; and by the lessons there learnt, soon become inmates of the Penitentiary." Extolling the merits of "strict discipline, with good education, invigorating relaxation and healthful labor" for children within the context of an institution, the commissioners recommended the establishment of "Houses of Refuge for the reformation of juvenile offenders" for both neglected children and children convicted of crime. When at "a proper age," children would be apprenticed.[139]

At least in part because of the commission's concerns, legislation was passed in 1857 providing greater latitude for summary trials for juveniles of both sexes under sixteen "to avoid the evils of their long imprisonment before trial," and the construction of special reformatories for young people under twenty-one.[140] As a consequence, juvenile prisons were opened at Penetanguishene (Canada West) and Île aux Noix (Canada East) in 1859. These institutions segregated children from more hardened criminals. They were also designed to make a greater attempt at rehabilitation by teaching children trades.[141] Despite these efforts, juvenile reformatories remained harsh environments, especially for the very young.[142] Emphasis was placed on work and discipline. Until 1880, boys were locked in their cells when not eating, working, or at religious services.[143] Controversy arose almost as soon as the reformatories were opened as to whether most acts of petty crime – let alone vagrancy or destitution – warranted incarceration in a juvenile prison.[144]

The problem was compounded with the emergence of publicly funded school systems. Legal provisions for compulsory attendance invented a new category of delinquency labelled truancy. Another institution, the industrial school, was designed to house truants and other minor delinquents in an environment less harsh than the reformatory.[145] As was the case with so many other nineteenth-century welfare institutions, public funds were used to support private initiative. The Protestant Halifax Industrial School was founded in 1863; in 1885 the St Patrick's Industrial School was established in the city for wayward Catholic boys. Whereas both received a civic grant, they were operated under church auspices.[146] In Quebec, legislation was first passed in 1869. Magistrates who deemed children under fourteen to be "orphelins, errants ou incontrôlables" were empowered to place them summarily in a church-operated industrial school. The law's range was extended in 1884 to neglected children and in 1912 to children abused by their parents.[147] In Ontario, the first industrial school was established for boys at Mimico in 1887.[148] Three other industrial schools followed in the province before the turn of the century, including the Alexandra School for Girls in east Toronto, opened in 1891.[149] The New Brunswick Boys Industrial School was opened in Saint John in 1893.[150] By 1910, industrial schools had also been established in British Columbia and Manitoba.[151]

The Ontario Royal Commission on the Prison and Reformatory System (the Langmuir Commission) marks a watershed in Victorian approaches to delinquent children. The commission conducted a broad survey of opinion on the child welfare system and its recommendations in 1891 provided a blueprint for future child welfare activity. The commissioners reiterated a traditional view in linking neglected children and criminality. On account of this tie, they advocated public intervention in the lives of children labelled neglected as a means of curtailing delinquency. They recommended the separate trial and detention of delinquent children; they questioned the merits of institutionalization, even when catering specifically to children, in affirming that the best environment for a child to be raised was the family, if not the child's own, then a foster home. They urged the establishment of industrial schools in every city and large town and the fostering of children attending such schools. To oversee this activity, they recommended the formation of voluntary organizations along the lines of the Children's Aid Societies (CAS) operating in a number of American states.[152] In affirming the family as the principal buttress of the reformed childhood, the commission reflected new thinking about child rescue.[153]

The Children's Protection Acts passed in most provinces before the First World War marked this profound change in orientation towards wayward children, providing not only for distinct institutions for children but for entirely separate legal systems. These acts contained provisions for the detention and trial of juvenile offenders apart from adults. They also provided for liberal and flexible sentencing practices. In Ontario, for instance, magistrates were empowered to send juvenile offenders to industrial schools, rather than prisons, for infractions of provincial law.[154] The 1908 federal Juvenile Delinquents Act was the culmination of efforts to segregate children, so that they were "guarded against association with crime and criminals."[155] The act defined the juvenile offender as anyone apparently under the age of sixteen, irrespective of the severity of the offence.[156] He or she was to be detained pending trial separately from adults, and tried summarily in a special juvenile court, without publicity. The juvenile court, given wide latitude in dealing with young offenders, was empowered to place them in the custody of their own parents, of foster parents, of a probation officer, of an industrial school or a reformatory, or even of a CAS or a provincial Superintendent of Neglected and Dependent Children.[157] Under the Juvenile Offenders Act, the delinquent child was defined "not as a criminal, but as a misdirected and misguided child, and one needing aid, encouragement, help and assistance."[158] Fostering and school attendance, rather than a combination of institutionalization and apprenticeship, was the new preferred option for dependent and delinquent children.

UNIVERSALIZING CHILDHOOD

Systems of child welfare and juvenile justice had an impact on only a minority of children, but state initiatives reached all children through legislated efforts to place them in schools, supplemented by a range of legislation prohibiting them from a wide variety of workplaces and leisure activities. And finally, legislation penetrated the household in the effort to protect children from abusive or otherwise substandard parents. The most striking feature of the Victorian redefinition of childhood was its universality: the life of every boy and girl was at issue.

Central to efforts to reform and prolong childhood was the free and common school, at which attendance was required. Whatever its educational merits, compulsory school attendance was "one of the most effective forms of child labour legislation," as an official of the federal Department of Labour observed in 1930.[159] Its origins were modest, owing to a reluctance to challenge parental authority, cost considerations, concern over government's role, and suspicion or scepticism regarding the aims of school promoters.[160] The system aimed to be universal, but in the absence of compulsion it failed to meet this objective. Referring to "street arabs," an Ontario official observed in 1866 that "for this large class of children, our admirable and costly Common Schools are perfectly useless."[161] The first steps towards compulsory education were tentative and did not necessarily closely follow the establishment of state-sponsored free and common school systems. Initially, only the youngest children were required to attend school, and only for a few months annually. Ontario, which passed the first legislation for compulsory schooling in 1871, called for seven- to twelve-year-olds to attend school at least four months a year. Prince Edward Island, in 1877, was the second to inaugurate province-wide compulsory education (eight- to thirteen-year-olds were to attend for at least twelve weeks each school term). Other provinces, including British Columbia (1873), Nova Scotia (1883), and New Brunswick (1906), addressed the delicate question of compulsory school attendance by adopting the model of the English Act of 1870: they empowered local authorities to legislate compulsory school attendance by means of by-laws.[162] But over time, although progress was uneven and favourable labour markets could lure boys and girls from the classroom until well into the twentieth century, an ever greater proportion of children, for an ever greater portion of their lives, attended school. By the Second World War, provisions were in place in every province whereby children aged from six to sixteen were expected to attend school regularly over a school year up to ten months long. Even in Quebec, where resistance to compulsory schooling had been tenacious, a compulsory education law was passed in 1943.[163]

The first tentative efforts to impose legal restrictions on child labour in Canada were contemporary with compulsory schooling legislation: Mines Acts were passed in Nova Scotia (1873) and in British Columbia (1877), followed by Ontario (1890) and Quebec (1892). Their provisions regarding child labour were broadly similar: a minimum age for employment was set, there were restrictions on the daily and weekly permissible hours of work, and the young were prohibited from performing certain kinds of hazardous tasks and from operating certain kinds of machinery. Educational standards might be required of young mine workers. Invariably, there was a clause prohibiting women and girls from employment in a mine.[164]

Factories employed children far more than mines did in late-nineteenth-century Canada. The first efforts to legislate restrictions on the employment of children in factories were made in Ottawa. Darby Bergin, member of Parliament for Cornwall, where hundreds of boys and girls toiled in large textile mills, introduced bills on the issue into the House of Commons in 1880 and 1881.[165] His efforts led to a federal commission "to enquire into the working of the Mills and Factories of the Dominion, and the labor employed therein." The commission reported in 1882:

The employment of children and young persons in mills and factories is extensive, and largely on the increase, the supply being unequal to the demand, particularly in some localities, which may partially explain why those of such tender years are engaged. As to obtaining with accuracy the ages of the children employed, we found some difficulty, insomuch as the employer has no record thereof, having no interest or obligation in so doing ... We are sorry to report that in very many instances the children, having no education whatever, could not tell their ages; this applies more particularly to those from twelve years downwards – some being found as young as eight or nine years ... It must be born in mind that the children invariably work as many hours as adults, and if not compelled, are requested to work overtime when circumstances so demand, which has not been unusual of late in most lines of manufactures. The appearance and condition of the children in the after part of the day, such as may be witnessed in the months of July and August, was anything but inviting or desirable. They have to be at the mills or factories at 6:30 a.m., necessitating their being up from 5:30 to 6 o'clock for their morning meal, some having to walk a distance of half a mile or more for their work. This undeniably is too heavy a strain on children of tender years, and is utterly condemned by all except those who are being directly benefitted by such labor.[166]

In response, a government bill was introduced in the Senate in 1882, and revised bills in the House of Commons the following two years. None resulted in legislation, as protests from individual manufacturers and the Canadian Manufacturers' Association stalled the bills' progress. Ottawa's efforts in this area ceased altogether in 1886, when a court decision indicated that a factory act was almost certainly outside of federal jurisdiction.[167]

Provinces had already started to legislate in this area. Factory Acts were passed in Ontario (1884), Quebec (1885), Manitoba (1900), and Nova Scotia (1901). These acts were broadly similar to Mines Acts insofar as they aimed to establish minimum ages for work and hours of work, and to regulate working conditions. While they did not seek to exclude girls from employment in factories, they discriminated between boys and girls. In Ontario and Quebec, for instance, the minimum age of factory employment was twelve for boys and fourteen for girls; boys of twelve and thirteen and girls of fourteen to seventeen were normally restricted to ten hours of work a day and sixty hours a week.[168]

Recognizing the extent to which children were employed in retailing, the Shops Acts were another form of protective labour legislation passed on children's behalf. Ontario and Manitoba passed identical acts in 1888: no boy under fourteen or girl under sixteen was to be employed in a shop for more than seventy-four hours a week, or more than fourteen hours on any given day. Before the turn of the century, Nova Scotia had passed a similar law.[169] Ontario also took the lead in restricting children's retailing activities. The Ontario Municipal Act was amended in 1886 allowing local police boards to pass by-laws regulating child street vendors. The Toronto Humane Society was lobbying the Police Commission shortly afterwards to enact such a by-law. Passed in 1890, it banned boys under eight and girls of any age from the street trades. All street vendors under sixteen years of age were to apply for a badge. Vendors had to demonstrate a good record and attend school at least two hours daily. Strongly attacked in the Toronto press (it was an assault on newsboys), the police failed to enforce the law and it soon fell into disuse, although it appears to have eliminated girls permanently from the street trades.[170] Children were also restricted in their common task of scavenging items for sale to junk dealers.[171] Ontario was the first province to amend its Municipal Act to allow local councils to pass by-laws prohibiting junk dealers and second-hand merchants from buying from anyone under eighteen years of age "without written authority from a parent or guardian."[172]

The state also took a role in regulating children's leisure through provincial legislation (notably in clauses of Children's Protection Acts) and municipal by-laws banning unaccompanied children from saloons and other places where alcohol was sold, as well as from dance halls and billiard rooms; and prohibiting children altogether from houses of ill-fame.[173] The WCTU and Children's Aid Societies actively lobbied municipalities to implement the clause in the Ontario Children's Protection Act authorizing them to restrict children from the streets altogether at certain hours – a direct challenge to the "vibrant and colourful street culture" of children identified by John Bullen.[174] Ultimately, forty cities and towns passed a curfew by-law.[175] Later laws prohibited children from smoking.[176] Subsequently, legislation barred children from specified categories of motion pictures.[177]

Children were also subject to yet another variety of special legislation. The Children's Protection Acts that provinces began to pass in the 1880s had as their principal aim to protect children from cruel parents. Nova Scotia passed the first Children's Protection Acts in Canada in 1880 and 1882, largely at the behest of the Halifax Society for the Prevention of Cruelty, to empower magistrates to remove

children from abusive households.[178] Other provinces followed Nova
Scotia's lead. In Ontario, "An Act for the Protection and Reformation
of Neglected Children" (1888), like the earlier Nova Scotian act,
authorized courts to commit abused or neglected children to industrial schools or an equivalent institution.[179] The model for Canadian
provinces was the subsequent Ontario Children's Protection Act,
often called the "Children's Charter," passed in 1893. In part a
response to the recommendations of the Langmuir Commission discussed earlier, its clauses dealing with cruelty to children (defined as
boys under fourteen and girls under sixteen) were taken from a
United Kingdom statute of 1889.[180] Cruelty was defined to encompass
not only neglect and physical cruelty, but also begging in the streets.
Street performances, or peddling goods, fell under this provision of
the act if they occurred at night, and in the case of children under
ten years of age, were prohibited altogether. The legislation carried
provisions for a fine of up to $100, or three months in jail, for adults
found guilty of cruelty to children. The act provided a novel mechanism for the care of children: the new Office of Superintendent of
Dependent and Neglected Children was responsible for a range of
activities, including the inspection of industrial schools, temporary
homes and shelters, and foster homes, and was to assist in the
organization of Children's Aid Societies.[181]

The Ontario model was adopted in other provinces and continues
to serve as the basis for child welfare activity in Canada today.
Children's Protection Acts were passed in Manitoba in 1898, in British
Columbia in 1901, in Alberta in 1909, and on Prince Edward Island
in 1910.[182] Nova Scotia established the office of provincial superintendent of neglected and dependent children in 1912.[183] Quebec stood
as the principal exception. Only in 1930 did the provincial Montpetit
Commission recommend the establishment of a Children's Bureau
and CAS-like organizations in Quebec. While some were subsequently formed, they lacked any authority in law for their actions.[184]
An intense suspicion within the Roman Catholic hierarchy both of
state legislation and any effort to move away from institutionalization (the church operated extensive welfare institutions in the province) led to a distinct Quebec response to child welfare, marked by
a far greater resort to the institutionalization of dependent children,
until the 1970s.[185]

Over the nineteenth century, reformers articulated basic standards
and rights to which all children were entitled. To ensure they were
met, clusters of concerned individuals and organizations, often local
in their focus, with a range of specific goals, sometimes working at

cross-purposes, contributed in their own way to the codification in law of these new notions of childhood.[186] Lawmakers reacted, hesitantly. "Prodded by the need to solve newly emerged, perceived, or discovered practical problems," Neil Sutherland has observed, "Canadians gradually sorted out various groups of children who needed particular kinds of care. As they did so, they set more and more precise and increasingly high standards for various phases of a 'proper' childhood and proposed remedies for those who did not meet them. It was a very *ad hoc* process with few precedents for anyone to follow."[187] The legal framework for the reconstituted childhood was slowly erected.

This growing variety of activity by legislators marked a clear shift in the position of the state with respect to children. Early reluctance to act gave way to a wide range of legislation. Early stress on the demands of industry surrendered to a growing concern for the child. Early concern to tread warily regarding parental prerogatives shifted to a definition of the child as, universally, the "irresponsible ward of the state."[188]

Initial legislation was, if not necessarily effective, certainly prescriptive. It laid out in very general terms what a normal childhood was to look like: that all boys and girls required special care in a family environment, that children within a certain age bracket, for a certain minimum number of days annually, attended school; that boys and girls did not work for wages until they reached a minimum age, after which only certain workplaces were considered suitable for them, and only for a limited number of hours daily and weekly; and finally, that children's legitimate leisure activities were more circumscribed than adults'. More importantly, early legislation laid the groundwork for state action. The importance of this base must not be underestimated. Once the state's initial role in children's lives was recognized, its subsequent steps were relatively unopposed.[189]

CHILDHOOD TRANSFORMED

To well into the nineteenth century, children were trained, disciplined, and worked much like adults. Special institutions for delinquent and dependent children, emerging by the middle of the nineteenth century, marked very early efforts to redefine childhood. While experimentation with a variety of institutional environments continued into the twentieth century, particularly in Quebec, from the 1880s increasing emphasis was placed on the home environment, either in natural families or in a reconstituted (foster) family, for the raising of children. Outside of the home, the emergence of special

organizations, literature, and playgrounds for children, in addition
to the critically important common school, reflected the redefinition
of childhood as a special and distinct period in life requiring segregated environments. Above all, the modern childhood was characterized by the deferred start of working life in favour of a balance
between play and schooling, the paramount features of children's
lives in Canada today. Children's right "to freedom from toil of a
character, calculated to stunt their physique and to prevent their full
maturing of their mental and spiritual powers ... to play so that their
gifts of imagination, of imitation, of comradeship might be developed; and ... to such an all-round education as will best enable them
to become themselves" was generally acknowledged.[190]

The drive to give the new views of childhood the force of law was
an intrusive assault on traditional parental prerogatives. Relative to
a generation or two earlier, the state engaged in unprecedented levels
of scrutiny of the family.[191] The state's laws increasingly circumscribed the power parents exercised, over their children's work and
education, most notably. At the same time, it prescribed penalties for
substandard parents. By the late nineteenth century, most provinces
had assumed the right and responsibility to remove children from
their home in the event of parental mistreatment or neglect.[192] They
had also redefined the law so as to affirm the best interest of the child
in custody decisions – abrogating the father's earlier "virtually absolute" right to custody.[193]

Members of an Ontario legislative committee struck in 1907 to
examine child labour stated their views bluntly. "The state is impoverished when from any cause the material out of which useful citizens could be made is ruthlessly wasted ... The child of to-day is the
man of tomorrow. As the irresponsible ward of the state, he should
be protected against neglect and greed on the one hand, and on the
other, he should be given a fair opportunity to secure at least an
elementary education, to attain physical strength, and to develop
good health, sound brains and a clean life." The child was entitled
to minimum standards of treatment to be enforced by the state.[194]

But state undertakings towards children at the turn of the twentieth century remained limited. They aimed to ensure that children
were not beaten, at least not in a manner to become life-threatening,
attended school, did not work full-time for wages, and abstained
from a defined range of leisure activities. But the state, outside of the
very small numbers of children in public institutions or who were
wards of a Children's Aid Society, did not attempt to ensure that boys
and girls were fed regularly or were adequately dressed and sheltered. Only with the First World War did select categories of children

benefit from state efforts to ensure minimal standards of financial support, when the privately organized Patriotic Fund and federal Separation Allowances were introduced to protect on a vast scale family-income levels in the absence of the soldier breadwinner. At the same time, starting with Manitoba in 1916, provinces began to introduce Mother's Allowances. But only with the family allowance program, introduced in 1944 and designed "[t]o aid in ensuring a minimum of well-being to the children of the nation and to help gain for them a closer approach to equality of opportunity in the battle of life" was the "language of children's rights" extended and universalized to encompass financial aid to all families for all children.[195]

Despite the considerable range of consensus that the legislation respecting children reflected, misgivings extended throughout Canadian society. In light of the hostility or indifference with which so much of this legislation was met, the extent to which it shaped popular practice has to be closely scrutinized. At the core of middle-class objections to the expanding state role were protests against dwindling parental responsibility. A *Saturday Night* journalist spoofed efforts to use legislation to create the new model child:

They should frame a Spanking Act intended to prevent the squalling of babies, the chewing of gum and refusal to take the matutinal bath. Enactments should be provided for the imprisonment of boys who insist on sliding down hill to the detriment of their trousers, and for the making of dreadful examples of girls who let their stocking sag around their ankles. By proper attention to these domestic details the responsibility of parents may be greatly decreased. All they will have to do shall be to provide nourishment and raiment for their offspring, the policeman will do the rest. What a delightful vista is opened for the coming parent when the Kodak[196] theory of parental responsibility is perfected. They will bring the child into the world, the police magistrate will do the rest.

The journalist continued on the topic of compulsory schooling:

[N]eglect in providing parental precept and example is having its effect ... I think the whole business would be laughable if it were not an innovation of that outrageous and fool idea that good boys and good girls and good men and good women are to be made by statute.[197]

Many others raised concerns over public expenditures and the state's expanded role.[198] Employers were resentful of any restriction on their access to labour. As late as 1929, a Manitoba employer expostulated on the subject of a minimum-wage bill for boys: "Take from the boy and his parents the right to freely contract and sell his labour for the highest wage which his individual skill will command and the boy would be reduced to an automaton – a mere creature of the state."[199] The Roman Catholic Church in Quebec resisted state activity in areas of its traditional prerogative.[200]

State activity, despite its universal application, in fact aimed primarily at the rural and working-class experience of childhood, seeking to make it conform to urban middle-class models. While wide support, notably on the part of the trade unions, emerged within the working class for these efforts (the transformed childhood was not imposed unilaterally by one class on another), it is with respect to working-class and farm children that the success of reformers' efforts has to be measured. Efforts to define children's dependence clashed sharply with the working-class family wage economy, whereby boys and girls began to labour for wages at a young age as a key survival strategy.[201] For this reason, working-class parents were among the principal opponents of legislation aimed to restrict children's employment.[202] In the eyes of social reformers, children laboured because of idle, greedy, or unthinking working-class parents. Federal commissioners in 1882 affirmed that children laboured on account of "the cupidity of their parents who have good positions as mechanics"; others laboured because of "the idle habits of the parents, who live on the earnings of the children." Two generations later, such observations persisted. "Some [parents] are concerned with the immediate financial return," ran a typical complaint, "and are willing to sacrifice their children's future for the present enjoyment of added luxuries or comforts."[203] Increasingly, parents of working children were condemned for their alleged exploitation of their children. Yet many families remained heavily dependent on children's wage earnings until well into the twentieth century.[204] Similarly, the labour contributions of children were crucial to the farm family economy.[205]

One of the most bitterly contested aspects of the debate over childhood was its extent. Few disputed the existence of a period of dependence. At issue was when this period ceased. For the most part, the children whom the debate addressed as it emerged in the mid-nineteenth century – and continues today – were those from eight to eighteen years, the specific ages in question increasing over time. Children younger than eight, while certainly helpful in the home, were of limited use in the labour market, although Andrew Doyle, a British official sent to Canada in 1874 to enquire into the condition of British juvenile emigrants, observed that Canadians put their children to work "at a very early age."[206] Those older than eighteen were viewed as mature (for the purpose of wage labour, although those choosing to marry generally did not do so until they were well into their twenties). A British mines inspector was arguing as late as 1870 against protective legislation: "To keep young persons from work till they are 12 years of age will, I fear, create the objection to labour which through their life they will be unable to overcome."[207] Even as active a crusader for children's protection as J.J. Kelso wrote in 1894 that girls should be self-supporting at twelve years of age, and boys at fourteen.[208]

The failure to universalize the reconstructed childhood is as patent now as it was in Kelso's day. The development of secondary education in the twentieth century underlines the class-based bifurcation that still marks childhood. Within poorer families, economic pressures have contributed to much lower school-leaving ages than among more affluent Canadians.[209] But class apart, gender, ethnicity, community – not to mention the parents one happens to be given – all continue to shape an individual's experience of childhood. Yet the partial successes of the deliberate efforts of reformers must be acknowledged. Canadian childhood changed by virtue of their activity. And this change touched all Canadian children.[210]

It is in the context of the reformed childhood that child mine labour is examined here. Boys had entered British North American coal mines before any concern was expressed on the question of child labour. As a proportion of the workforce, boys' presence in the mines was greatest when the first efforts were being made to introduce common school systems. Boys worked in Canadian mines in largest numbers immediately prior to the First World War, as the campaign against child labour emerged in strength.

In the light of modern prescriptions for childhood, the pit boy became ever more offensive. The clamour, filth, dangers, and responsibilities associated with work in the mine were not seen to constitute an appropriate environment for children. Outside of the mine, pit boys' fondness for tobacco, use of alcohol, penchant for loitering on the streets, and other "disreputable" leisure activities scarcely resembled the prescribed conduct of the reconstructed child. Their self-confident behaviour and colourful language were discordant in an era when, increasingly, mature thought and action by children were labelled precocious and actively discouraged. In an age of reform, marked by metaphors calling for the application of "light, soap, and water" to social problems, the pit boy laboured deep underground, in the dark. And he was dirty.

CHAPTER THREE

Miners, Mine Operators, and Child Labour

"[O]ur boys have very little chance to be employed in the mines ...
[they] grow up to near manhood without an opportunity to earn
any part of their living such as they might have were there no Chinese,
and such as boys have in other parts of the world."
Vancouver Island trade unionist, 1885

Boys were first brought into the coal pits by their father or an older relative, immigrant miners recruited in Great Britain for the large commercial mines introduced in Nova Scotia during the 1820s and on Vancouver Island in the 1850s. These experienced miners demanded the traditional prerogative of craftsmen, the right to control entry into their trade by means of rules of apprenticeship. They would hire mine labourers, generally young kin; educate them in mine work; pay, supervise, and discipline them; and determine their readiness to cut coal as qualified miners. For miners, this family-based organization of labour was at the base of their traditional authority in the workplace.

Employers welcomed boys' presence in the mines both as an inexpensive source of necessary labour, and as a means of reproducing the skilled mine labour force. But they did not want boys to be used to buttress miners' authority in the mine, with all its consequences for uncontrollable production costs. More importantly, employers intent on cutting their costs by introducing new mining techniques and new machinery could not leave control over the work process to miners. When mine operators had greater access to labour, miners' control over their conditions of work was challenged. Large numbers of inexperienced workers were hired to labour in the proliferating number of coal mines developed from the mid-nineteenth century.

The miners' response was to organize unions to win recognition at the pit and in law for the qualifications they felt boys' lengthy experience in the mine bestowed. Although miners were unsuccessful in their efforts to win legal recognition of boys' informal apprenticeship, provincial governments passed at their behest numerous pieces of legislation that, in the name of mine safety, restricted access to the mine. The most important legislation, although never as effective as miners wished, required the certification of miners and mine officials. The struggle between workers and management over these issues shaped the circumstances under which the boy entered the mine as a labourer and under which, on maturity, he became a miner.

As the coal industry developed in British North America, distinct markets for child labour developed in the major nineteenth-century coalfields of Nova Scotia and Vancouver Island (see Table 3.1). On Vancouver Island, boys accounted for no more than 2 or 3 percent of mine workers until the late 1880s, when employers removed Chinese workers from underground employment in the Nanaimo-area mines and legal restrictions on child labour were loosened; and no more than 5 percent afterwards. In Nova Scotia, in contrast, boys consistently accounted for 15 to 20 percent of the coal-mining labour force over the last decades of the nineteenth century. The coal-mining industry of the western interior, developed late in the nineteenth century, based largely on single transient workers, never employed more than a handful of boys.[1] Nor were many boys ever employed in the small mines of New Brunswick.[2] By the early twentieth century, while over one thousand boys remained employed in Canadian mines, their numbers failed to keep pace with the rapid growth of the coal industry, even in Nova Scotia. By 1914, child labour in coal mines was in eclipse throughout Canada.

DEVELOPMENT OF THE COAL INDUSTRY

As early as the middle of the seventeenth century, coal was mined on Cape Breton Island for personal use or for very small local markets. Outcrops of coal were worked more regularly after 1720 to supply Louisbourg with domestic fuel. Commonly found in Europe, coal was not a desirable staple product for developing colonial societies. Only limited trade was established with the West Indies, where the coal was used in sugar refineries, as well as with Quebec and France. After the fall of Louisbourg in 1758, British authorities placed restrictions on the mining of coal because of a fear that extensive development of colonial coal mines would harm the domestic industry. But soldiers mined coal for the garrison's use, and during the American Revolutionary War, Halifax was also supplied.[4] From the turn of the nineteenth century, colonial authorities authorized a succession of limited-term leases in Cape Breton and in Pictou County to defray the cost of local government. But only once during this period did the annual output of Cape Breton's mines exceed ten thousand tons.[5] Output was even smaller in Pictou County, where never more than a couple of thousand tons were lifted per annum.[6]

Table 3.1
Boys' Participation in the Coal Mining Labour Force, Nova Scotia and Vancouver Island, 1866–1914[3]

Year	Nova Scotia Total Number of Boys	Percentage of Mine Labour Force Comprised of Boys	Vancouver Island Total Number of Boys	Percentage of Mine Labour Force Comprised of Boys
1866	449	14.8		
1868	395	15.1		
1870	372	14.3		
1872	489	13.9		
1874	542	13.8	No boys recorded	
1876	531	17.3	18	3.1
1878	531	17.5	23	3.3
1880	600	18.0	15	1.8
1882	703	17.0	No boys recorded	
1884	806	16.5	15	1.2
1886	738	16.3	18*	1.4*
1888	746	16.3	42	2.1
1890	897	17.0	58	2.2
1892	No statistics published		92	3.2
1894	774	13.2	137	4.7
1896	803	13.5	143	5.2
1898	630	14.3	131	4.6
1900	794	12.7	143	5.0
1902	820	10.5	132	4.4
1904	907	8.0	109	3.6
1906	900	7.5	152	5.0
1908	999	7.8	173	5.0
1910	938	8.5	168	4.0
1912	829	6.3	166	4.1
1914	936	6.4	52	2.2

Note: Official statistics on the employment of boys from both Nova Scotia and Vancouver Island are available from the mid-1870s (the first British Columbia *Mines Report* was published in 1874); they are reported until the First World War, when collection of statistics on the employment of boys in Nova Scotian mines ceased. Absolute numbers also reflect the much greater level of mining activity in Nova Scotia. Statistics for boys were not kept in other provinces, where their numbers were in any case small.
* Figure includes boys and aboriginal workers.
Sources: NSMR, 1866–1914; BCMR, 1874–1914.

By the 1820s, demand for coal was strengthening in the growing towns and cities of the Maritime colonies, where firewood was scarce and expensive. But it was New England, where urbanization was rapid and local coal in short supply, whose markets made colonial merchants and officials increasingly anxious to expand Nova Scotia's coal production. The Imperial government opposed this aim until 1828, when the London firm of Bridge, Rundell and Bridge – transformed as the General Mining Association (GMA) – came into possession of a monopoly of mineral mining in Nova Scotia. The GMA searched unsuccessfully for precious metals, but turned to coal as an acceptable substitute, petitioning the government in London for a long-term lease on coal reserves. Within a short time, it acquired existing short-term leases and negotiated a fifty-five-year monopoly lease over all coalfields in the province.[7] Soon the GMA was operating mines on a vast new scale and vigorously developing markets for Nova Scotian coal. It met with mixed success in the United States, the start of its operations coinciding with substantial new American tariffs on coal.[8] Even in regional markets, the GMA faced competition, notably from lumber ships importing British coal as ballast into New Brunswick.[9]

Increasingly over the 1840s and 1850s, the GMA's British-granted privileges were challenged by colonial politicians seeking to extend the local autonomy promised by the winning of responsible government in 1848. The GMA monopoly, one of Nova Scotia's central political issues, was all the more hotly contested after 1854 because of the removal of American tariffs on British North American coal under the Reciprocity Treaty and the rapid expansion of markets in the United States.[10] When the GMA monopoly was finally ended in 1858, dozens of new mines were developed and demand for mine labour increased sharply.[11] On the abrogation of the Reciprocity Treaty in 1866, Maritime exporters faced not only escalating tariffs, but competition in their traditional New England markets from American coal from Pennsylvania and Ohio that benefited from subsidized freight rates. Confederation with the Canadas was welcomed as a means to compensate for lost American markets.[12]

Demand for coal emerged more slowly on the Pacific coast than on the eastern seaboard of North America. By 1836, the presence of coal deposits on Vancouver Island had been brought to the attention of the Hudson's Bay Company (HBC), which made use of the small quantities exchanged by its Native trading partners in its blacksmith shop at Fort Victoria. In an effort to discourage any trade in coal between Vancouver Island and the United States, the Royal Navy opposed any further development at that time, and the Hudson's Bay

Company, holder of a trading monopoly until 1859 in most of what would become British Columbia, showed little interest in any case. But when declining profits from fur-trading activities led the HBC to look to new sources of income and when strong markets for coal developed in California following the gold rush of 1849, coal mining was reconsidered. An enquiry from an American shipping firm prompted the HBC to begin to mine coal at Fort Rupert, located on the northeastern tip of Vancouver Island.[13]

Fort Rupert coal, of poor quality, failed to win that contract with the Pacific Mail Steamship Line. But the HBC pursued commercial mining when exploratory work elsewhere on Vancouver Island revealed more promising deposits. In 1850 the company acquired two hundred tons of coal mined by Native peoples at Nanaimo, and shifted all its mining activity there at the end of 1851.[14] Mining remained on a limited scale: to 1863, the greatest single-week output was 120 tons. State-of-the-art steam engines were used with a primitive, horse-drawn, wooden-railed surface railway.[15] Company directors were reluctant to invest further large sums of money after the mid-1850s, restricting the development of the Nanaimo mines.[16] The HBC could report the export of only six thousand tons of coal over its first decade.[17]

As on Vancouver Island, coal was mined in Canada's western interior from an early date. Long prairie winters and a scarcity of readily available wood encouraged small-scale mining of accessible seams for local markets. Four men were employed in November 1863, for instance, digging coal to heat Fort Edmonton.[18] The first commercial coal mine in Alberta was opened the following decade at Coalbanks (near the site of what is now Lethbridge). The coal from this small mine was transported by horse and wagon and used to heat both dwellings and North-West Mounted Police posts in the area.[19] By the 1880s, the HBC, as it had earlier on Vancouver Island, was contracting with local Native peoples to dig coal for local use at a number of posts.[20]

One of Confederation's primary goals was to integrate the economies of the British North American colonies. Railways, which served as major year-round consumers of coal and, just as importantly, as economical carriers to emerging urban markets, were key to this project. The Intercolonial Railway, linking the Maritimes and Montreal, was quickly constructed. The Springhill mine in Cumberland County grew rapidly in the 1880s, as a consequence of the markets provided by the Intercolonial and by burgeoning industrial towns throughout the region. By 1885, Springhill boasted the largest output attained in Canada to that time, averaging fifteen hundred tons daily.[21] Similarly, the small New Brunswick coal industry was boosted by the completion of a rail link to the Intercolonial Railway in 1904.[22]

Demand for coal in the emerging industrial markets of Ontario grew rapidly over the middle decades of the nineteenth century, but continued to be met largely from the Ohio Valley, while British coal brought out in ballast dominated markets in Montreal and Quebec City.[23] Only with the adoption of the National Policy of protective tariffs in 1879 was Quebec opened to Nova Scotia's coal (the tariff level was never high enough to displace American coal in Ontario). Regional markets for coal were also stimulated by the success of protective tariffs in fostering industrial development in the Maritimes.[24]

Federal tariffs were of far less immediate consequence on Vancouver Island, where coal was produced principally for export in the nineteenth century. Between 1849 and 1891, three-quarters of Vancouver Island's coal sales were in the United States.[25] Markets only shifted to Canada after the turn of the century, with the development of railway and urban demand for coal. On the eve of the First World War, 70 percent of Vancouver Island coal raised was consumed in British Columbia, 20 percent in California, and 10 percent elsewhere, mostly in Mexico.[26]

In the western interior, railway construction drove the development of the coal industry. As the Canadian Pacific Railway (CPR) was pushed across the prairies during the early 1880s, a series of mines opened along its route. Among them, the mine at Lethbridge, with a capacity of 160,000 tons per annum by 1898, was the largest.[27] CPR branch lines extended throughout the western interior. After the arrival of the rail line from Calgary in 1891, mining in Edmonton boomed, supplying the railway market as well as local consumers.[28] More significant was the Crow's Nest Pass Railway, extending from MacLeod, Alberta, to Kootenay Lake, British Columbia, completed in 1898. Major new coalfields were developed as the railway advanced. The largest, owned by the Crow's Nest Pass Coal Company, operated mines in British Columbia at Fernie, Morissey, and Michel.[29] On the Alberta side of the Crowsnest Pass, small mines opened at Frank (in 1901), Coleman (1903), and Hillcrest (1905).[30] In 1902 the extension of the Great Northern Railway opened American markets to Crowsnest Pass coal.[31] Subsequently, commercial mining began in the inland British Columbia coalfields of Nicola (in 1907) and Similkameen (in 1910). Their output was also destined for the Crow's Nest Pass and Great Northern Railways.[32]

The construction of the two new transcontinental railways early in the twentieth century provided a further impetus to coal mining in

the western interior. The Grand Trunk Pacific built the Coal Branch
Railway in 1911 to tap the bituminous coalfields of west-central
Alberta. In 1914 the Brazeau Collieries southwest of the Coal Branch
were opened by the German prospector Martin Nordegg to supply
the Canadian Northern Railway.[33] While the major mines were linked
to railways, small quantities of coal were mined at dozens of sites
throughout the western interior for local consumption as western
settlement boomed at the turn of the twentieth century. Coal output
in Alberta increased tenfold between 1900 and 1910.[34]

LABOUR SUPPLY

Large steam-powered mines, often called collieries, required skill
levels unnecessary at the earliest, primitive mines. Both the General
Mining Association and the Hudson's Bay Company recruited experienced miners in the United Kingdom. Initially, the GMA brought
coal miners from northern England and South Wales.[35] Over the
1830s, it continued to draw its labour supply from these "distressed
districts" of England; by the 1840s, however, "the more skilful among
the miners [were] almost wholly from Scotland."[36] Into the 1850s,
skilled work at Nova Scotian collieries was limited to experienced
immigrant miners from Great Britain. "A great part of the miners in
Nova Scotia are from Scotland," an American observer reported in
1850, "some from the north of England, and a few from other parts
of Britain. Small numbers of native Nova Scotians are engaged about
the mines, chiefly as fillers and other labourers above ground."[37] On
the Pacific coast, the HBC brought in a number of groups of miners
and their families beginning in 1849. Most were Scottish, although
the last contingent arrived from South Staffordshire in 1855. British
immigrant miners provided the basis of the early mining communities of both Nova Scotia and British Columbia.[38]

   These immigrant miners brought with them their traditional means
of organizing work. In early-nineteenth-century Great Britain, the
miner contracted independently with coal companies, offering "the
labour power of himself and his family."[39] The family-based organization of labour committed the miner "to the ideal of the hereditary
closed shop" – an ideal reinforced by the isolation of many coal-
mining communities.[40] He sought to restrict access to the mine to his
sons, to whom he taught the craft.[41] In practice, the miner was less
successful. Only intermittently did contemporary mine managers
recognize the value of the boy's apprenticeship to the mine. One of
the most prominent among them, John Buddle, would claim no more
than that boys should start young. He and fellow managers were

"decidedly of [the] opinion that if [boys] are not initiated before they are 13 or 14 – much less 16, 17 or 18 – they *never will become Colliers.*"[42]

The GMA went to considerable trouble and expense to bring colliers from Great Britain. His monopoly of recognized skills allowed the immigrant miner, familiar with what was often a very formal initiation of the sons of miners to the mine, to continue traditional practices in British North America.[43] Following a plea from the GMA for lower royalties, a provincial commissioner was sent to investigate the operation of the Albion Mines in 1841.[44] George Wightman observed: "[T]he colliers are considered as tradesmen and as such paid high wages. They fix their prices and will not consent to admit any other persons into the works. Two-thirds of their work can be done by common labourers and yet they insist on doing the whole themselves at wages of from eight to twelve shillings per day besides privileges in rent and fuel to the value of twelve or fifteen pounds annually. In the same pits labourers perform services equally severe for three shillings per day; but these men are not allowed to touch the work of the miners. Sometimes the miners take an apprentice who by the payment of a fee obtain the standing of a miner, but the employer cannot send a single man among them."[45] The experienced collier enjoyed considerable authority in early GMA mines.[46]

When the Hudson's Bay Company recruited in Great Britain for its Vancouver Island mines, it acknowledged not only the collier's skills but also the family-based organization of the mining workforce. The first contingent of HBC miners was a small party, led by John Muir, consisting of his four sons, two nephews, and wives and young children. A nine-year-old son of Muir's was the youngest to receive a contract. As further groups were recruited, the company continued to bring families of miners to Vancouver Island. John Muir, as Chief Factor James Douglas reported from Fort Victoria in 1852, "calculates that each head of a family is to have the assistance of two or three boys each of whom he supposes capable of performing half a man's work."[47] Accordingly, when the company's mining agent in Scotland, David Landale, was asked the following year to recruit a further contingent of forty colliers, he was instructed that "[t]hey should all be married men, but not with numerous families … it is desirable that none of the children should be very young. Families in which there are boys, two of whom can do work equal to that of one man are to be preferred."[48] Miners on Vancouver Island employed the traditional Scottish tactic of restricting their output of coal (on the assumption that this would maintain both coal's price in local markets and their level of pay). An HBC official complained from Fort Rupert shortly after the Muirs' arrival that the miners "play half the day." James Douglas raised this point again in 1852.[49] As late as 1868 a visitor to Nanaimo observed that miners restricted their output to keep their pay high, rarely working "full days."[50]

Despite the care these early British North American mining companies had taken to recruit experienced miners, the fragility of miners' claim to "skill" ensured that their position was rapidly compromised whenever employers enjoyed easier access to labour.[51] Employers, recognizing the value of the miners' skills, sought to ensure that local conditions of work did not drive skilled colliers away. Their expert judgment and practised dexterity enabled them to produce the largest pieces of coal most efficiently. They were also needed for the difficult work of developing new mines or the dangerous work of closing districts of existing mines by mining the last accessible coal. But at the same time, employers did not want to leave control over mining and the mining workforce with miners. Mine operators actively sought to broaden their supply of labour and their control over mine work by sending inexperienced workers into the pit. As Don MacLeod has observed, "almost anyone could mine coal, if only inexpertly."[52]

The lower productivity of inexperienced miners was only of limited concern to coal companies, because the major bottleneck to coal production in the nineteenth century was generally *not* miners' output, but the capacity to take coal out of the mine. A higher quantity of "smashed" coal, too, was no great obstacle – if the coals were not of a sufficient size, the novice miner was fined or not paid at all for the coal he sent up.[53] And with the development of substantial markets for small coal for coking towards the end of the century, there was a reduced premium on the skill required to mine large lumps of coal.[54] The miner's most crucial asset, the ability to recognize danger by the noise, odour, "feel" of the coalface, was of far more value to him than to his employer. Coal companies could tolerate a higher incidence of mine accidents so long as inexperienced mine workers alone bore their price.

Mine operators aimed to retain their skilled labour as much as possible year-round, yet be able to expand their workforce rapidly at periods of peak demand for coal. Their task was made more difficult because of the sharp seasonal peaks and troughs in demand for coal to which all nineteenth-century Canadian coalfields were to some extent subject. In an era when coal was used primarily as a domestic fuel, it was mostly consumed in winter. In Nova Scotia, difficulties in meeting seasonal demand were compounded by the seasonality of shipping. The Northumberland Strait was closed for four winter months, seriously limiting the output of Pictou's collieries. Operations virtually ceased at Cape Breton mines with the freeze-up of harbours in January, not to resume before March. Nature also closed access to the growing markets in the St Lawrence for at least three or four months each year. In Cape Breton in 1880, only 1.5 percent of production occurred in the winter quarter, increasing to 20.3 percent in the spring, peaking at 49.1 percent in the summer, and dropping to 29.1 percent in the autumn.[55] Only at the turn of the twentieth century did winter and summer coal output on Cape Breton begin to balance with the emergence of a local iron and steel industry.[56] The coal industry of the western interior was also marked by strong seasonal rhythms. Those mines dependent on domestic coal markets were most active from November to April, when people were burning coal to heat their homes. Those mines supplying railway markets generally worked more steadily, although output in the Crowsnest Pass peaked in the summer as railways stockpiled coal for fall grain shipments.[57] On Vancouver Island, by virtue of year-round ports adjacent to the coalfields, the construction of the Esquimault and Nanaimo Railway in 1886, and the range of export markets, seasonality was least marked, although demand weakened in the spring and summer.[58]

Although the development of the railway network helped to integrate continental labour markets, the workforces of the widely separated Canadian coalfields were distinct. In Nova Scotia, the growing demand for mine labour – notably after the end of the GMA monopoly in 1858 – coincided with an out-migration from the rural districts of the province, particularly the "backland" farms of Cape Breton.[59] Mines Inspector Edwin Gilpin subsequently identified two "classes of miners," those resident year-round at the mines and those who came to the mines to work for a few months each year. Many seasonal mine workers had small farms, others were fishermen from Newfoundland, for whom the twenty or thirty dollars brought home after a season in the mines bridged the gap between failure and subsistence. In Cape Breton, where until the twentieth century colliery work slowed sharply during the winter, migrant workers departed in the autumn.[60] Similarly, the small New Brunswick mines depended on the seasonal influx of workers from the rural areas of the province.[61]

In the western interior, nineteenth-century mines drew to some extent on existing sources of skilled mine labour in Nova Scotia.[62] They also relied on the cross-border migration of young transient workers.[63] Most importantly, they drew on the seasonal labour of homesteaders. Wintertime demand for labour in the mines dovetailed neatly with pioneer farming. In January 1917, 8,550 were employed in Alberta mines; in June, 3,091; and in December, the workforce had shot up again to 9,812.[64] Even at the large Lethbridge mine, seasonal swings in the demand for labour were sharp. In the typical December, over 400 workers could find work six days a week. In May, perhaps 200 workers worked only three days a week. Consequently, "[o]nly a small percentage of the Lethbridge work-force made a long-term commitment to the company or the community."[65]

On Vancouver Island, sources of unskilled mine labour were wider still. The Hudson's Bay Company relied initially on the aboriginal peoples. At Fort Rupert, the Kwakwaka'wakw (Kwakiutl) told local HBC officials that "they would not permit us to work the coal as they were valuable to them, but that they would labor in the mines themselves and sell us the produce of their exertions."[66] Coal was produced as another commodity of trade. Despite the objections of Vancouver Island's original inhabitants, the HBC soon employed "whites, half-breeds, and Kanakas [natives of the Hawaiian Islands]" to mine coal at Fort Rupert, and was encouraged enough by potential markets to bring the first group of Scottish miners out to Vancouver Island in September of 1849.[67] Coal was mined at four sites at Nanaimo during the 1850s, at two pits by British miners and at two outcrops by Island Natives.[68] Subsequently, aboriginal workers were also employed by Europeans. Their labour, rather than commodities, was exchanged for trade goods.[69] They were employed in 1861, for instance, to load coal into the lighters that brought it to the ships in which it was exported.[70] But mine managers felt aboriginal labourers were both scarce and irregular workers. "The want of Indian labor is certainly a great inconvenience of the miners," observed HBC Chief Factor Douglas in 1857, "but really they must learn to be independent of Indians for our work will otherwise be subject to continual stoppage."[71] As the scale of mining grew, Vancouver Island coal companies looked increasingly to alternative sources of unskilled labour.

Wretched social and economic conditions in their native provinces in southern China helped draw Chinese workers to the Pacific coast of North America.[72] They first migrated to British Columbia during the Gold Rush of 1858 and were first employed in colonial coal mines in 1867, as surface labourers at Nanaimo.[73] They displaced aboriginals rapidly, very few of whom worked in local mines after 1880.[74] More than one-quarter of the Vancouver Island mining workforce in the 1870s was Chinese, a figure that moved above 40 percent by the early 1880s. Over the last years of the century, even after restrictions had been placed on their employment underground, the Chinese still accounted for between 10 and 20 percent of provincial coal workers (see Table 3.2).[75]

Table 3.2
Chinese in Vancouver Island Coal Mines,
1874–1902

Year	Absolute Number Employed	Percentage of Labour Force
1874	121	28.2
1878	230	33.0
1882	353	40.4
1886	530	41.8
1890	490	18.4
1894	539	18.4
1898	399	14.0
1902	499	16.5

Note: Official statistics *understate* until 1886 the extent of
Chinese labour because they exclude helpers hired and
paid by miners directly.
Source: BCMR, 1874–1902.

MINERS' UNIONS AND CHILD LABOUR

Miners first organized unions late in the nineteenth century to offset
their eroding power at the colliery.[76] Early unions lobbied the state
in efforts to gain formal recognition of the collier's skills as the
groundwork for satisfactory pay and working conditions, issues that
were closely linked and bitterly contested. The first enduring miners'
union was formed in Nova Scotia in 1879 under the name the Provincial Miners' Association (changed the following year to the Provincial Workmen's Association [PWA]). The PWA, which won wide
recognition among coal companies and within the government at
Halifax as the representative of provincial miners, was led for its first
twenty years by an articulate Scottish Presbyterian immigrant, Robert
Drummond. A one-time miner and mine official, Drummond played
a leading role in the 1879 strike at Springhill that led to the PWA's
formation. He subsequently became its head as grand secretary and
its most prominent spokesman as editor of its official newspaper, the
Trades Journal. An outspoken Victorian liberal, Drummond affirmed
the virtues of self-help, thrift, temperance, and respectability. He was
a firm advocate of negotiation and compromise as means of addressing industrial disputes. The PWA was most distinguished by its success as a political pressure group. In the view of Ian McKay, "its
lobbying achieved a record of political and social reforms unparalleled in nineteenth-century Canada."[77] The PWA remained the union
of choice among Nova Scotian miners until the first decade of the

twentieth century, when the United Mine Workers of America (UMWA) began to organize in provincial coalfields. By 1919 it had supplanted the PWA in Nova Scotia.[78]

Union recognition was far more elusive on Vancouver Island, where two employers dominated coal production. The Dunsmuir family, which operated collieries at Wellington, Cumberland, and Extension, refused to recognize organized miners in any form, a policy continued by the subsequent owners of their mines (from 1910), Canadian Collieries (Dunsmuir) Limited. Miners at Wellington formed the Miners' Mutual Protective Association in 1877, which did not survive a strike in 1883.[79] Organized miners were first recognized on Vancouver Island in 1891, when S.M. Robins, manager for the New Vancouver Coal Mining and Land Company at Nanaimo, successor in 1862 to the Hudson's Bay Company mines, signed a collective agreement with delegates of the Miners' and Mine Labourers' Protective Association. Founded in 1890, this union sought unsuccessfully to organize throughout the coal mines of Vancouver Island.[80] International unions, despite a series of attempts, were even less successful. A short-lived Knights of Labor chapter was formed in Nanaimo in 1883.[81] Efforts by the Western Federation of Miners (WFM) in 1903 and the UMWA from 1912 to 1914 to strike for recognition failed.[82]

In the western interior, a local of the WFM was organized at Lethbridge in 1897.[83] After an unsuccessful strike in the Crowsnest Pass in 1903 involving fifteen hundred mine workers, the WFM was abandoned in the region in favour of the UMWA, which formed its first locals in 1903 in southeastern British Columbia, and early in 1904 in Alberta.[84] In 1906 the UMWA won the first of a series of contracts at the large Lethbridge mines.[85] In 1907 and 1908 they successfully organized at mines in Saskatchewan.[86]

Union efforts on behalf of boys differed sharply. In Nova Scotia, the question of control of entry to the mining workforce was subsidiary to the issues of union recognition and pay, although the PWA persistently lobbied for legislative protection for boys. In the western interior, the employment of boys was not an issue – there were few to be found in the mining camps and developing coal communities of the region. On Vancouver Island, in contrast, the displacement of boys – and at times, of skilled colliers – by Asians united concerns about loss of skills, entry to the workforce, and family income. It was of central importance as a strike issue.[87]

In Nova Scotia, the entry into the mines of inexperienced labourers from the mid-nineteenth century underlined miners' weakening control over the production of coal in the mine.[88] Although early in the

1880s at least eighteen months' experience in the mines was normally required before employment as a miner (at least on the Nova Scotian mainland), during periods of sharply expanding demand for labour managers did not discriminate closely as to whom they hired to mine coal.[89] This practice generated intense concern among experienced colliers. "Spring Hill will be able to boast of having produced more coal smashers than any other district in the province," complained one miner. "Men fresh from the back woods are being given the picks."[90] Miners repeatedly told the federal Royal Commission on the Relations between Capital and Labour that coal companies employed "[t]oo many men for the capacity to take the coal out of the mine."[91] The hiring of "outsiders" was linked to the failure to promote boys. It was reported in 1884 that "at one of the mines lads verging on manhood and who had been brought up in the mine and were capable of mining were denied the picks, while those about whom the officials knew nothing were given them."[92] Similar concerns were raised frequently. Robert Drummond claimed in 1888 that "under the present system an inexperienced stranger will be given the better paid work of cutting in preference to a trained boy."[93]

Miners' control over the helpers they employed was similarly eroded. Until well into the twentieth century, many miners hired and paid a helper to assist them to load their coal into the tubs used to transport it from the mine.[94] Even so, by the end of the nineteenth century, control over hiring was clearly migrating to coal companies. A delegate to the PWA Grand Council complained in 1880 that miners even encountered obstacles in employing their sons as helpers.[95] Much of the activity of early unions was directed to the resolution of such local disputes.[96] The minutes of the Springhill PWA lodge describe a delegation to the mine manager to appeal the refusal of a junior official to allow a boy to enter the mine as a loader because "he considered him to[o] small." Manager Hall promised the delegation, which included the boy's father, "satisfaction."[97] Control over hiring remained contested. The clause in the major contract of 1920 (the so-called Montreal Agreement) between the corporate giant the British Empire Steel Company and the United Mine Workers of America whereby the right to hire and discharge was "vested entirely in the company" was bitterly opposed by rank-and-file miners.[98]

In Nova Scotia, even as miners' authority in the workplace deteriorated, boys enjoyed one basic advantage over other claimants to their positions in the mines: they would accept lower wages than adults. As a consequence, boys' access to work in the mine was never seriously challenged during the nineteenth century. The situation in western Canada was altogether different: in the interior, mining workforces were based on transient unskilled labour; there was little by way of an indigenous mining population to contest the employment of poorly qualified workers at the numerous small mines in Alberta or Saskatchewan, nor was there a local supply of miners' offspring seeking employment in the mine.[99] On Vancouver Island, where an established mining population had emerged, employers' access to a large alternative supply of unskilled labour seriously curtailed boys' opportunity to work in local coal mines. While immigrants from continental Europe also laboured in Vancouver Island mines, contemporaries referred repeatedly to Asian workers' domination of unskilled work at local mines.

Chinese were first employed at Nanaimo in 1867, earning a dollar a day, over the objections of European miners, who were locked out for seven weeks. A compromise was reached whereby miners reluctantly tolerated the presence of Chinese labourers on the mine surface.[100] But "[t]he colliers threaten with violence," reported the Victoria *Daily British Colonist*, "the first Chinaman who forgets his Celestial origin so far as to descend to the 'bottomless pit' of a coal mine."[101] Nonetheless, through the 1870s Vancouver Island miners began to employ Chinese helpers underground, at far lower rates than they would white workers. A clearly segmented labour market developed: Europeans monopolized the work of the miner, while Chinese were employed underground to load coal into tubs and to assist in bringing these tubs to the mine surface.[102] The availability of Chinese labourers for work underground enabled the exclusion by law of most boys from provincial mines in 1877.[103] By the early 1880s, at mine owner Robert Dunsmuir's West Wellington Mine, European miners "employ[ed] each of them a Chinese labourer." Similarly, at the Nanaimo colliery, "the miners [were] white men, with Chinese labourers."[104]

The *modus vivendi* on the question of Asian labour on Vancouver Island was shattered in 1883. When miners at Wellington struck for an increase in pay, Dunsmuir employed Chinese labourers to mine coal in a successful effort to break the strike. The colour bar was crossed. Having lost their monopoly of skilled mine work, white miners resolved to exclude the Chinese altogether from the mines. Their sense of urgency was almost certainly heightened by the presence in British Columbia of thousands of Chinese navvies, to be released onto the labour market with the completion of the Canadian Pacific Railway.[105] Consequently, Chinese exclusion was a key element of major strikes throughout the 1880s: at Wellington in 1883, at both Nanaimo and Wellington in 1888, and at Cumberland in 1889. White miners won a major strike victory in 1888 when both the New Vancouver Coal

Mining and Land Company at Nanaimo and Robert Dunsmuir and Sons at Wellington agreed to withdraw the Chinese from underground employment. This followed serious explosions at Nanaimo in 1887 and at Wellington in 1888, which Europeans succeeded in blaming on inexperienced Chinese workers. Asians continued nonetheless to be employed on the surface at the Nanaimo-area mines, as well as underground at Dunsmuir's large new Union Colliery at Cumberland, where they comprised a majority of mine workers.[106]

By the mid-1880s only mine managers indicated satisfaction with the presence of the Chinese in Vancouver Island coal mines. The manager of the Wellington colliery, John Bryden (a Dunsmuir in-law) praised the Chinese in 1885 as "industrious, sober, economical and law-abiding, more so than the same class of white laborers." "I have not the slightest doubt," claimed another Dunsmuir manager, G.M. Little, in 1902, "that if left to their own choice the white miners would retain the Chinese as helpers. It enables them to work easier and they can make more money."[107] Miners nonetheless took a clear position in favour of Chinese exclusion after 1883. This view was acknowledged by certain mine managers; and it appeared in the platforms of organized miners; it was expressed by individual miners. Nanaimo mine manager S.M. Robins, recognizing that "the labouring population [was] always strongly averse to their introduction," advocated in 1885 the gradual exclusion of the Chinese from the mines.[108] The Knights of Labour, organized in Vancouver Island coalfields by Samuel Myers, was fervently exclusionist.[109] From its formation in 1890, the Miners' and Mine Labourers' Protective Association adopted a policy to exclude Chinese from the mines.[110] Another miners' group, the Miners' Protective Union, also supported Chinese exclusion.[111] "I would be willing to have my wages reduced," asserted miner Richard Hodson in 1902, "rather than employ Chinese."[112] No public official ever thought to query the Chinese themselves.[113]

Links between the extensive use of Chinese workers at Island mines and the relatively low incidence of boys in the mines were repeatedly drawn. Robert Dunsmuir argued in 1883 that existing legislation was "a hardship on miners who could not employ their strong, lusty boys, but were compelled to employ Chinese, while their boys idled away time that might be profitably employed."[114] Two years later, the Nanaimo Local Assembly 3017 of the Knights of Labor reported that because of the Chinese "our boys have very little chance to be employed in the mines ... our boys grow up to near manhood without an opportunity to earn any part of their living such as they might have were there no Chinese, and such as boys have in other parts of the world."[115] Under such circumstances, a miner at Nanaimo

Table 3.3
Labourers' Daily Wages at Nanaimo, 1875–1900

Year	Boys	White Adults	Chinese Adults
1875	Not given	$2.00	$1.125–1.25
1880	Not given	2.00	1.000–1.25
1885	$1.50	2.00	1.000–1.25
1890	1.00–1.75	2.50	1.000–1.25
1895	1.00–2.00	2.37	1.000–1.25
1900	1.00–2.00	2.50	1.125–1.25

Note: The lowest end of the pay scale for white adults is given here.
Source: BCMR, 1875–1900.

observed, "a race of practical miners, trained from their childhood to the difficulties or dangers of mining, can hardly ever arise."[116]

This view was expressed repeatedly before the Royal Commission on Chinese and Japanese Immigration in 1902. "Chinese keep boys out of employment," claimed one miner.[117] S.M. Robins, sympathetic to the traditional British patterns of initiating boys to the mine, emphasized that the use of the Chinese discouraged the employment of white youths, noting both boys' disinclination to perform what they labelled "coolie labour" and managers' attraction to low-wage Chinese workers. "[M]anual labour – that is labour that is not usually regarded as skilled – is looked upon as humiliating by the white population, because of the presence of the Chinese ... The younger generation here seems ashamed to do the work that the Chinese do." He acknowledged that "[he] employ[ed] Chinese above ground, financial grounds forcing it upon the company."[118] The commissioners concluded that the employment of Chinese "on the surface and in the mines ... excludes white labour and distinctly promotes idleness among the youth and young men of the villages and towns adjacent to the mines."[119]

The employment of Asians as mine labourers undercut the workplace authority the family-based organization of labour gave miners. It fractured the labour force and helped to frustrate efforts to organize trade unions on the Pacific coast. It also fulfilled a need for labour on Vancouver Island. The lower corporate wage bill associated with the use of Chinese workers added considerably to their attractiveness as employees. Wage statistics indicate a persistent differential between European and Chinese workers. Over the last decades of the nineteenth century, Chinese workers earned a daily rate of $1.00 to $1.25; white *boys* earned up to $2.00 daily (see Table 3.3).[120]

THE STATE IN THE COALFIELDS

The state's role in the coalfields extended back to the beginning of the industry. The Imperial government had fostered coal mining by granting monopolies of production and trade in Nova Scotia and on Vancouver Island. Subsequently, colonial government scientists, notably the Geological Survey of Canada from 1843, explored, mapped, and surveyed potential coalfields.[121] Over the latter third of the nineteenth century, the growing importance of coal mining drew increasing attention from the state, whose role expanded from attracting investors, to subsidizing the railway construction that opened new coalfields, to regulating the industry in the interests of expanding output. Immigration policies sought to ensure ample supplies of workers, and repressive labour legislation guaranteed their discipline by making provision for military intervention during conflicts between coal operators and miners.[122] At the same time, coal royalties came to contribute substantially to provincial revenues.[123]

Unable any longer to enforce at the pit their control of access to the mine, miners turned to the state late in the nineteenth century. Their major concern was to secure restrictions on workforce supply from both the federal and provincial governments. Nationally, they lobbied for limits on immigration. Provincially, their object was to heighten qualifications for mine work. The Provincial Workmen's Association, while strongly supportive of the tariff on coal instituted by the federal Conservative government in 1878–79, made clear that its support for the National Policy was not unqualified. Why, asked the *Trades Journal*, was there protection on coal, yet "free trade in labour"?[124] Of some concern to Nova Scotian miners, but not nearly as consequential an issue in Atlantic as in western Canada, was the question of Chinese immigration.[125] British Columbian miners, in seeking restrictions on immigrants from Asia, met with widespread sympathy within the province. The critical decade for the exclusionist movement was the 1880s, as the influx of thousands of Chinese railway navvies prompted a nativist reaction. The British Columbia legislature passed laws in 1884 and 1885 seeking to ban further Chinese immigration to the province. Following federal disallowance of this legislation and the province's persistent calls for federal action, a two-man royal commission was appointed. Subsequently, Ottawa instituted in 1885 a "head tax" of $50 on every Chinese immigrant to enter Canada, restricting at the same time the number of immigrants that vessels were entitled to carry. Widely seen within British Columbia as inadequate, the tax was raised to $100 in 1902 and to

$500 in 1903. Whatever the impact these provisions had on the immigration of Chinese workers, they did not prevent Chinese already in the province from seeking employment in the mine.[126]

Both Nova Scotia and British Columbia had drafted their first Mines Acts in the 1870s. Mines were growing in size, and mine safety emerged as a public concern. "The mines were now about to assume great importance," argued the responsible minister when the Nova Scotia bill was presented, "and it was high time that stringent laws should be put upon the statute book to enforce their proper working." These colonial assemblies followed clear British precedents. The Nova Scotia bill was "mainly taken from the English Act of 1872."[127] In British Columbia, the proposed legislation was "almost a copy of the English Mining Bill."[128]

The British Columbia Mines Act was first amended to exclude the Chinese from underground employment in 1890, largely on the strength of the European miners' claim – given credence in the wake of explosions at Nanaimo and Wellington – that the Chinese were a threat to safety.[129] It never obtained legal force. Although unanimously upheld by the Supreme Court of British Columbia in 1897, this act was ultimately declared *ultra vires* by the Judicial Committee of the Privy Council in 1899. Annual amendments to the Mines Act to exclude by various means Asians from work underground (Japanese workers first worked in Vancouver Island mines in the 1890s) followed over the first years of the twentieth century. All this legislation was either disallowed by the federal government on constitutional grounds or fought in the courts, especially by the Dunsmuirs. It was never effective as a weapon of Asian exclusion.[130] At the outbreak of the First World War, Asians continued to be employed underground at the Union collieries and on the surface elsewhere on Vancouver Island.[131]

Provisions for miner certification, in contrast to strictly exclusionist legislation, addressed the common interest of miners and provincial governments in mine safety, whose regulation clearly fell to provincial jurisdiction. Miners also saw certification as a means to restrict access to the mine. In British Columbia, Asian exclusionists often appealed to the requirements of workplace safety: illiterate (at least in English), inexperienced workers, they claimed, put the lives of hundreds of co-workers in jeopardy.[132] In 1894 the inspector of mines was empowered to examine and remove from the mine "any person who, by reason of want of understanding or owing to mental or physical incapacity or incompetency for the performance of the particular task or duty upon which he is engaged, is a source of danger to his co-labourers or to others who may be in the mine, and whose presence and employment threaten or tend to the bodily injury of any person." An amendment to the Mines Act in 1901 established a five-man Examination Board to grant "certificates of competency" to miners and minor officials. While requiring miners to have one year's experience in the mine and to be knowledgeable about the Mines Act and mine safety, this amendment also stipulated that candidates be "sufficiently conversant with the English language." Widely viewed as a weapon to exclude Chinese from skilled mine work, these amendments failed to receive support in provincial courts and were not adequately enforced until after the First World War.[133]

The government of the North-West Territories made limited efforts to regulate the new coal mines in its jurisdiction. A mining ordinance, introduced in the territorial legislature in Regina by the member from Lethbridge, was passed in 1893. By 1897, it required mine officials to be certified.[134] More comprehensive Mines Acts were not passed until after Saskatchewan and Alberta were created as provinces in 1905. In Alberta, the first Mines Act, in 1906, only required that the mine manager and mining supervisors be certified.[135] Alexander McCulloch, a Crowsnest Pass miner, argued in 1907 to the Alberta Royal Commission on the Coal Industry that miners needed at least two years' experience "by working with another competent miner."[136] But in a province with hundreds of mines, often operated on a small scale, there was considerable pressure not to introduce certification provisions for miners.[137] A similar situation applied in Saskatchewan.[138] In New Brunswick, few mines operated, and again these were generally on a small scale. Weak certification legislation was only introduced there in 1933.[139]

The question of certification arose at an early date in Nova Scotia, where the first provincial Mines Act empowered the mines inspector to enforce a number of regulations governing mine safety.[140] Although this act was passed without consultation with miners, the PWA soon gained a role for them in determining the safe operation of a mine.[141] Key for miners was the need to restrict the unqualified from mining coal. Ex-miner Patrick Neville, a deputy mines inspector, outlined in 1884 the consequences of the seasonal influx of rural workers into Nova Scotian mines: "It often happens that a young man from the country starts to work as a loader with a miner for a summer. [He returns home in the autumn when mining slackens for the season, then returns in the spring with his own loader.] The result is this inexperienced man and his loader make dust of the coal, and are not capable of taking care of themselves." Neville advocated, as a means to improve mine safety, a provincial law stipulating that three years' experience in the mine was required to get a place as a

miner.[142] Edwin Gilpin, the senior provincial mines inspector, recalled
later in the century that "when the rush of business came in the
summer, men were employed in coal-cutting, even in gaseous mines,
who were certainly not experienced miners, nor likely to become so,
as they looked upon their underground work merely as an interlude
in their home employment."[143]

The PWA lobbied intensively for legislation requiring the certification of miners. It sought unsuccessfully at the same time to win legal
recognition for the *de facto* apprenticeship that miners' sons were
continuing to enter at the beginning of the twentieth century. Robert
Drummond, PWA grand secretary, argued before the federal Royal
Commission on the Relations between Capital and Labour in 1888
that "[t]o learn mining takes three or four years." Legal requirements
for apprenticeship would orient the recruitment of mine labour to
the male offspring of miners, while protecting miners' jobs from
colliery newcomers, who threatened the local mining community's
monopoly of colliery work. In Drummond's expression, legal apprenticeships to the mine "would exclude people from other places."[144]
He also felt that certification would improve the public's opinion of
miners: "If we can get a law passed, ordaining that miners must hold
certificates it will have a tendency to keep uneducated men out of
the mines, and thereby raise the status of miners."[145]

The principle of miner certification was first recognized at law in
Nova Scotia in 1881, whereby underground mine officials were to be
licensed by a provincially appointed Board of Examiners. In 1884
managers at mines employing more than thirty workers also required
certification. In 1890 minimum qualifications for a certificate of competency for mine officials were set at three years' experience of mine
work underground, and for a manager's certificate, at five years'
experience. Candidates also had to pass an oral examination.[146] By
1891 the PWA fought successfully to extend the principle of certification to include miners, a step which colliery operators disputed
bitterly. "It is difficult," Don MacLeod has observed, "to overstate the
hostility the certificates aroused among mine managers and owners."[147] By this law, a worker needed two years' experience in the
mine before receiving charge of a working place; one year's experience was necessary to be entitled to cut coal.[148] To this extent, the
boy's experience in the mine was recognized by law in Nova Scotia.[149]

Provisions for certification were made in the absence of adequate
administrative machinery to ensure compliance, which was to be
contingent on the strength and vigilance of miners. Although a
"prominent colliery manager" criticized PWA efforts "to make as [if]
it were a guild and prevent the employment of strangers at a time
when labor below may be required," the union was far from resolute.[150]

Indeed, the PWA permitted flagrant non-compliance with certification provisions for the operators of mechanical coal cutters when they were introduced in the 1890s. If the union did not insist that the law be observed, mine managers would certainly not either. Over the turn of the twentieth century, a time of rapid expansion in Nova Scotia's coal industry, mine operators rode roughshod over the law. Qualifications for certification became an additional source of conflict between miners and mine operators.[151]

As provinces began to make stipulations for miner certification, they attempted to provide appropriate training facilities, often in cooperation with coal companies, concerned by a potential shortage of qualified officials.[152] Nova Scotia, where seven men were hired in December 1888 to teach mining classes in colliery towns, was the pioneer in this area. These instructors, generally mine officials, gave courses in mine safety and rudimentary mining engineering.[153] These efforts were supported by miners, who recognized that despite their work experience they often lacked the "book-learning" necessary to pass the certification exams.[154] The following year, in recognition of the limited formal education of many miners, instruction was also offered in basic reading, writing, and arithmetic. "[I]t was evident," mines inspector Edwin Gilpin observed, "that the pitboy's education, often finished as he entered his teens, was not a good ground for the instructor to work upon."[155] Initially oversubscribed, the men for whose benefit the classes were offered were soon displaced by younger students, often boys who had recently left public school. Robert Drummond felt that "[t]he lads were quicker in the 'up take' than their elders who, partly through pride, became discouraged and ceased attending."[156] Efforts continued. Nova Scotia's Technical Education Act, passed in 1907, provided for upgraded local mining schools, special courses of instruction in preparation for officials' and managers' certificates, and basic classes in reading, writing, and mathematics.[157]

Daniel McDougall, president of UMWA District 26 (Nova Scotia), explained how the boy's informal apprenticeship to the mine had acquired formal aspects by early in the twentieth century. "Boys generally go to work in the mine as [horse] drivers or door-keepers [underground], and after a while get with somebody as a helper, and then after working a certain time at the face of coal, they go before the examiners appointed from the working miners, and after examination get first a [coal] loader's pass, then a miner's pass, then after a certain time they can get a pass for what is called examiner or deputy [minor officials] in a mine. That is all the passes the boy gets … If a boy gets a good show he would be a miner in two or three years." McDougall said that he "did not know of any case where drivers are younger than 14, but the law now is that a boy must be in the 6th grade at school before he is allowed to work in a mine."[158] Organized miners' commitment to formal schooling for their offspring was certainly linked to the increasing onus on credentials in the coalfields.

Boys were a focal point of the struggle between miners and mine operators to control labour markets and coal production. Managerial efforts to discipline their labour force, all the more significant with the growing investment of capital in the mines late in the nineteenth century, focused on "open-door" employment practices, which clashed with miners' efforts to maintain control of mine labour recruitment and promotion. If the appropriate pattern of initiation to mine labour was contested terrain, it was a battle waged in circumstances increasingly unfavourable to miners. The essence of the miner's skill was the ability to produce large coals efficiently and safely, but this was not good enough to maintain recognition from employers of the boy's apprenticeship to the mine.

Employment practices varied from mine to mine and from province to province, but to the extent that mining at a given pit was sufficiently developed technically to call for skilled labour and that this labour was scarce (and likely had to be recruited in the United Kingdom), miners were able to have their qualifications recognized. This was reflected in high wages, but more importantly in the recognition of the miners' authority within the workplace: the decisions they made as they mined coal and the control they exercised over other mine workers. Negotiated rules for hiring and promotion were established at each mine in response to local circumstances. But as the supply of labour expanded, assisted by the same railway network that stimulated the expansion of the coal industry, miners found these rules increasingly unfavourable to them. Over the last two decades of the nineteenth century, miners began to organize, and they enlisted the support of the state in reaction to declining levels of control at the mine. Using the powerful lever of mine safety concerns, miners won a limited success in formalizing certification requirements. This in turn represented a very tentative step towards legal recognition of boys' apprenticeship to the mine. But even after province-wide standards nominally governed access to mine work, the actual rules of mine labour recruitment and promotion were set in confrontation at the pit. The low wages paid boys allowed familiar British patterns of informal apprenticeship to continue in Nova Scotia. On Vancouver Island, in contrast, immigrant mining families were comparatively unsuccessful. Asian adults, rather than European boys, dominated unskilled work. And in the interior of western Canada, where mines developed much later, boys only rarely found a place in the pit.

CHAPTER FOUR

Coal Mining Technology
and Child Labour

"It may be truly said, that this is the age of improvement."
James McKeagney, Nova Scotia Inspector of Mines, 1859

The methods used to mine coal created distinct demands on the workforce. Two events marked watersheds in coal mining technology in Canada. The early introduction of steam engines, in Nova Scotia in the 1820s and on Vancouver Island in the 1850s, allowed the development of the first large mines in British North America. Because many jobs in these new mines did not place large demands on individual strength, skill, or experience, they encouraged the employment of considerable numbers of boys. The heavy investment in mining at the turn of the twentieth century, particularly in Nova Scotia, revolutionized mine work through new divisions of labour and heavy mechanization. These new techniques of mining coal eroded corporate demand both for the traditional skills of the collier and for pit boys.

From their arrival, European colonists in North America mined available outcrops of coal with simple tools.[1] By the early nineteenth century, the largest mines, like Sydney Mines in Nova Scotia, extended underground. Coal was cut and pried from the seam with handpicks and crowbars, then loaded in tubs that were placed on sleds and dragged along a roadbed of logs to the base of the shaft. The tubs were raised out of the mine by the "gin-wheel," a system of rope and pulleys powered by horses. When underground haulage roads became too long, a mine was abandoned and another shaft was sunk at some convenient spot along the outcrop. Coal could generally be extracted to a depth of perhaps fifty metres. Little attempt was made to ventilate these mines; some effort might be made to drain

---

Note: An earlier version of this chapter was published as "'Grotesque Faces and Figures': Child Labourers and Coal Mining Technology in Victorian Nova Scotia," in *Scientia Canadensis* 12, no. 2 (Fall/Winter, 1988): 97–112.

pit water by drilling "adits" (tunnels) when possible. Coal was carried by wagon to the nearby shore, where it was loaded aboard small skiffs and brought to waiting vessels for shipment to market.[2] Only a handful of experienced coal miners arrived from Great Britain to oversee these shallow mines, whose workforces were small and overwhelmingly unskilled.[3] Few boys were employed.[4]

The steam engine was first introduced to British North American mines by the General Mining Association during the 1820s.[5] The Hudson's Bay Company introduced the steam engine to the Vancouver Island mines in the 1850s, although mines there remained small until the 1870s.[6] In the western interior, mines were generally smaller, but steam engines were introduced at the large Lethbridge mines in the 1880s.[7] The adoption of steam was closely linked to capital investment. Relatively large sums were needed for steam engines, for sinking the deeper shafts associated with them, for surface rail lines and buildings, and often for worker recruitment and dwellings. Steam's repercussions on the industry were profound. By removing existing constraints on mine size, the steam engine encouraged the systematization of mining and an extensive division of labour. In creating a range of mine jobs that children were competent to perform, the door was opened to their extensive employment. In fact, at Victorian mines where "expansion and technical progress" were most evident, child labour was most extensive.[8]

Problems of drainage and in removing coal from underground had placed strict limits on the size of early mines. The development of the steam engine in Great Britain over the eighteenth century began to remove these constraints. Newcomen's engine had been tested by 1720, but before the end of the century, the far more efficient Boulton and Watt engine was available to the mining industry.[9] Powerful pumps were required to remove the water that flowed steadily into mines both from underground springs and from the surface. Similarly, methods of hoisting coal from the pit were vastly improved when steam power replaced the gin-wheel. Shafts penetrated far deeper underground. In Nova Scotia, one was sunk in 1830 to 200 feet (61 m), a second in 1834 to 320 feet (98 m), and another in 1837 to 455 feet (138 m). The Foord Pit was sunk in the late 1860s to 900 feet (275 m).[10] The No. 1 shaft of the Esplanade colliery at Nanaimo, drilled in 1881, extended 628 feet (over 190 m) underground before first striking the coal seam.[11] The limits on the extent of mining were redrawn by the successful application to mining of the steam engine as a pump and as a hoist.

These deep new coal mines, called "collieries," grew to be vast workplaces, among the largest in Victorian Canada. At the Nanaimo mines alone, nearly 1,500 workers were employed in 1890, in sharp contrast to the few dozen who laboured there during the 1850s.[12] The Sydney Mines employed only 52 men at the time of the arrival of the GMA in 1827; but 174 in 1832; 372 men and 73 boys in September 1838; and 323 men and 70 boys in December 1858. The workforce grew to slightly over 600 in 1890 and to nearly 2,000 in 1906. At the Springhill mines, 451 were employed in 1882, roughly 1,200 in 1890, and 1,700 in 1906.[13]

Each coal mine was unique, reflecting the nature of the coal deposits. Seams could extend from a few centimetres to dozens of metres in thickness. They could rest close to the surface or dip to depths of thousands of metres. Coal basins often had a number of overlying seams, so that, at a given mine, coal might be extracted from more than one seam simultaneously. Alternatively, coal could be mined at different levels from the same seam. Difficulties of mining coal were compounded by geological quirks. Seams could be uneven or broken. They might also dwindle away abruptly. Each coal mine called for the distinct application of technology.[14]

Collieries required a considerable degree of planning.[15] Ian McKay has labelled the mine the "most historical of workplaces," where every development decision taken remained as a constraint on future mining at a given colliery. There was no starting again from scratch. Mine managers, even if they had little day-to-day role in supervising miners in the nineteenth century, provided a basic direction to the progression of mining.[16] Development work at a new mine began with the sinking of a vertical shaft, or a diagonal slope, depending on the location, size, and nature of the seam of coal to be mined. From the base of the slope or shaft, the major underground passageways, the levels, extended into the seam; at larger mines, several levels might be used, each intersecting with the slope or shaft at a different depth underground. Off each level, a variety of auxiliary roads led at right angles to the working places, or "bords," each of which was separated from the next by a solid pillar of coal. Rooms were driven at an upward incline to drain water from the coalface and to aid underground haulage. This method of mining, labelled "bord and pillar," was the standard technique in Victorian Canada (see Illustration 1).[17] Coal was mined in two distinct phases. In a first round of mining, pillars were left standing to support the roof of the mine while adjacent coal was removed. In a second round, the pillars themselves would be removed by careful cutting with the handpick, leaving the mine ceiling to settle against the floor.

These expanded and systematized workplaces encouraged increasing subdivision of the labour force and the specialization of mine workers. Four principal tasks were performed. These included, first, the actual mining of the coal in the various bords; second, the transportation of the coal out of the mine; third, the maintenance of the mine; and fourth, on the mine surface, the preparation of the coal for shipment to market. Miners were the key mine workers.[18] Often lying prone, dependent on the weak illumination provided by the safety lamp, the miner used a handpick to "undercut" the coalface to a depth of approximately one metre. He then "sheered" the sides of the coalface to create a mass of overhanging coal. His experience enabled him to exploit "cleats," natural fractures in the seam, as he broke down this remaining coal by hammering iron wedges into it.[19] After the adoption of gunpowder, the miner dislodged coal by blasting. Hand-held augers were used to drill a hole in the overhanging coal, into which the charge was placed. The quantity had to be gauged carefully. Too little powder, and the miner failed to dislodge the coal. Too much, and the coal turned to dust. The miner's skill was measured by his ability to send large chunks of coal rapidly and safely to the mine surface.[20] The mining of pillars – the second phase of bord-and-pillar mining – called for particular skill. Only the most experienced miners were employed at this task, as they could listen for signs of the imminent collapse of the roof. As one miner explained, "in pillars you have to watch the roof and one of the guides is to listen to the roof. You can tell by the sound if it is reaching the dangerous stage."[21]

The use of bord-and-pillar techniques allowed the miners to work in dozens, even hundreds, of separate working areas. Underground transportation systems had to keep pace with the output from these numerous bords. As mines grew larger, this task became more difficult, and miners complained regularly about the inadequate supply of tubs they received to be filled with coal.[22] Generally these systems contained two distinct elements. Underground haulage refers to the movement of coal from the bords to the landing at the base of the mine shaft or slope (the "bottom"). From this point, a hoist brought the coal to the mine surface. The "bottomer" assembled "rakes," trains of coal tubs to be pulled by a hoist up a slope to the mine surface (see Illustration 13). If the mine had a vertical shaft, "cages" (a frame with one or more platforms for receiving tubs) were loaded by the "onsetter" or "cager." The "brakeman" operated the hoist that raised the coal from the pit.

The infrastructure essential to the maintenance of a mine included track laying and roadway maintenance, roof support, and the moving of supplies into the mine. Two others were especially significant.

Ventilation systems functioned to bring fresh air to the mine workers and to dissipate noxious and explosive gases. Pumps removed the water that accumulated continuously within mines. For every ton of coal extracted from Nova Scotia's mines in 1885, three tons of water were pumped out.[23]

Coal was removed from the mine directly into the large surface structure called the bankhead (see Illustration 2), where it was prepared for shipment to market. Tubs laden with freshly mined coal were first brought to the "tipple," a mechanical device that served to upend and unload the coal tubs. Originally operated by hand, from the 1870s the task became automated.[24] The coal was then sorted by size and cleaned. For Victorian mining companies, coal quality was almost as important as quantity. Coal was passed over different-sized screens for grouping into various sizes, then over mechanical picking tables for removal by hand of impurities such as stone. By the end of the nineteenth century, coal was also commonly washed. Finally, it was loaded onto the ship, cart, or railway car that brought it to the consumer.

Steam-powered railways to move coal short distances were introduced in British North America by the GMA. Rails were laid between mines and nearby waterside loading docks in both Pictou and Sydney Mines, where it was shovelled on board smaller skiffs to be loaded into ships. Coal was handled several times between its initial extraction and its arrival at its final market, a process that diminished its value, as the preferred lump coal crumbled further at each stage. At the largest collieries, mammoth docks were constructed later in the nineteenth century, allowing ocean-going vessels to be directly loaded with their coal by the use of a series of chutes (see Illustration 15).

BOYS IN THE STEAM-POWERED COLLIERY

It was in steam-powered collieries that thousands of boys mined coal in Canada. Relatively few boys worked on the mine surface, but in a wide variety of occupations.[25] As general labourers, some boys distributed miners' handpicks or greased coal tubs, changed batteries and otherwise serviced lamps, filled powder cans, loaded timbers and cordwood on to flatcars, or pushed and assembled empty tubs for return trips into the mine.[26] The tally boy kept track of the amount of coal each miner sent to the surface; he did this by removing the identifying tally the miner placed on every tub he filled and reading the number to the checkweighman, who credited the coal to the miner.[27] Other boys drove horses or tended mules. Some worked as

helpers to the tradesmen employed at the colliery, including blacksmiths, boilermakers, and foundry men. Others operated pumps.[28]
When steam-driven hoists replaced the gin-wheel, boys continued to
be employed as their operators.[29] Boys worked as wharf hands,
helping to dump coal cars.[30] More rarely, a boy might be taken on
for work in the mine office.[31]

Many boys were employed on the mine surface to clean coal. A
number of impurities were inevitably raised from the mine; dirt,
slate, other rock, even slack (dust-like) coal had to be removed before
coal was shipped. At earlier, smaller mines, miners were responsible
for cleaning coal before sending it to the surface. They or a helper
passed coal through a "riddle" (sieve) before loading it into tubs.[32]
As mines grew larger, part of the task of cleaning was removed above
ground. On picking "tables" or "belts," the coal was conveyed slowly
in front of a line of "pickers," giving them time to remove impurities
by hand.[33] Boys were employed as pickers from the 1870s on Vancouver Island, but by the twentieth century they had been displaced
by Chinese adults.[34] In Nova Scotia, boys and older men dominated
work at the picking tables from the time of their adoption after the
1870s. Those tables installed at numerous collieries by Dominion Coal
were praised by the *Canadian Mining Review* in 1897 for "distribut[ing
the coal] over the belt area, giving the boys and men every opportunity to pick out the impurities."[35] Into the 1930s, it was at the picking
tables "where practically all of the cleaning of Nova Scotian coals
takes place."[36] Bill Johnstone started work at a picking table at the
age of thirteen. He recalled it as "the most mind-stifling occupation
that can be imagined. Our job was to pick out the pieces of shale
from the coal as it passed on a conveyer. The boredom of watching
a slow-moving conveyer passing one's eyes for eight hours a day, six
days a week, was enough to drive one crazy."[37] Boys preferred to
work underground. Most did.

BOYS UNDERGROUND

As mines grew larger, an ever greater proportion of the colliery
workforce was employed underground. In Nova Scotia, for example,
58 percent of colliery workers laboured underground at the time of
Confederation; 74 percent in 1896; and 79 percent in 1911.[38] Underground, boys generally worked at one of three tasks: the youngest
helped to ventilate the mine (as door-tenders or "trappers"); older
boys worked at underground haulage, the onerous task of transporting freshly cut coal to the mine's surface; and the oldest boys worked
in the bords as helpers to miners.

Table 4.1
Percentage of Underground Workforce Comprised by Boys, Selected Nova Scotia
Collieries, 1866–1911

	Sydney Mines	Springhill	Albion Mines	Cape Breton South
1866	24.7	–	26.6	15.9
1871	22.2	–	17.4	18.0
1876	27.6	14.4	19.5	18.0
1881	23.3	17.7	16.0	21.5
1886	26.9	16.1	17.7	18.8
1891	26.8	14.0	12.2	16.8
1896	19.0	11.8	11.7	14.1
1901	17.3	12.8	10.3	6.7
1906	4.6	11.3	9.7	6.8
1911	9.9	5.5	10.5	5.9

Note: These figures indicate the percentage of the underground workforce comprised by boys. The Springhill collieries were not developed until the early 1870s. From 1891, statistics under the heading "Albion Mines" include all the mines operated in Pictou County by the Acadia Coal Company, formed by the amalgamation of the companies operating the Albion Mine, the Acadia Mine in Westville, and the Vale Mine in Thorburn. Statistics under the heading "Cape Breton South" are for all Cape Breton mines south and east of Sydney Harbour, consolidated in 1893 as the Dominion Coal Company.
Source: NSMR, 1866–1911.

THE VENTILATION OF MINES

The first mines were so limited in extent that ventilation had posed few difficulties. But to permit seams to be exploited deeper into the earth, some means of ensuring adequate supplies of oxygen and of removing undesirable gases was required. Some early mines relied on "natural ventilation." If two shafts were sunk on the side of a hill, the differential air pressure would create a current through the mine. This method had its disadvantages. It was not entirely reliable: in certain seasons, when the air temperature outside equalled that inside the mine, circulation would cease. And mines could not always be placed on a hillside.[39]

Natural ventilation came to be supplemented by the use of underground furnaces. These were placed at the bottom of the "upcast" shaft and, by heating the air, created an artificial current. This system had its drawbacks, not the least of which was the danger of the furnace itself igniting fires or explosions. If the same shaft was also used for hoisting, the furnace was damaging to hoisting equipment and objectionable to mine workers entering and leaving the pit.[40] As mines grew in extent, an innovation in mine ventilation systems popularized in Great Britain by John Buddle early in the nineteenth century, labelled "compound ventilation," was adopted. By dividing (or "splitting") the air current at a number of points, the mine was subdivided into a number of independent ventilating systems. No longer did a single current ventilate an entire mine. This shortened the aircourses and helped to keep air velocity at a maximum. Gases could be more easily dispersed and better levels of oxygen for miners and horses maintained. Mining could extend far further underground.[41]

By the last decades of the nineteenth century, "the rapid extension of the workings" of Canadian collieries "render[ed] a more efficient ventilation power imperative."[42] Mechanical fans provided that more efficient power. These were employed successfully in the United Kingdom from 1850, either to push air down the downcast shaft or to pull it up the upcast shaft.[43] The GMA introduced one of these fans at the Albion Mines in 1871.[44] By the 1880s, fans were also in use at the largest collieries on Vancouver Island, the No. 3 mine at Wellington and the No. 1 Esplanade colliery at Nanaimo. Mines extended yet deeper underground.[45]

In larger mines, ventilation doors, or "traps," situated along the mine's main haulage roads, were introduced to channel the air currents throughout the mine. "Trapping" was an area of mine work almost monopolized by boys into the twentieth century. "Trappers" (also called "door-boys") kept these doors closed to prevent the short-circuiting of the air current, and opened them to allow the passage of horses and drivers. The trapper's work was simple: "When he hears the sound of a footstep or wagon approaching his door his duty is to pull on a string, one end of which is attached to the door and the other secured where he can grasp it in a moment, when the door will open. After the passengers or cars have safety passed, by slacking the rope, the door shuts of its own accord."[46]

Other methods were employed specifically to remove gas. Mines in Pictou County were particularly gaseous. Small boys were employed at the Acadia colliery in 1866 to operate fans in areas that produced especially large quantities of gas.[47] Later that year one of these boys, Alexander McLean, whose "duty was to drive a fan for the purpose of ventilating a working place in which gas was made," was killed at the Albion Mines by an explosion of gas "fired at his naked light."[48] Hand-driven fans continued to be used into the twentieth century to aid ventilation in awkward areas.[49] "If you stopped for a minute and changed hands," recounted an elderly miner to Ian McKay, "they'd yell, 'Turn that fan.' And they didn't call you sweetheart, neither."[50] Another recalled that he "started in coal mining when he was nine, cranking a fan by hand for ten hours a day. He'd fall asleep on the job until a miner would come down and rap him on the head with a pick handle."[51]

Attempts were made to dispense with ventilation doors, but only when bord-and-pillar techniques of mining were abandoned were they finally removed from the mine. Caleb Pamely's late-nineteenth-century textbook for mine managers included a description of a self-acting ventilation door used in conjunction with a rope haulage system.[52] Mechanized colliery doors were advertised in the *Canadian Mining Review* in 1899.[53] Even in the middle of the nineteenth century at a British colliery, "swing doors without trappers" were employed, although they were unpopular with miners because they were prone to be knocked off their hinges.[54] Canvas curtains rather than door-boys were in use at the Coal Creek Colliery in 1901.[55] At most mines, trapper boys remained on the payroll into the 1920s. Mine managers were not pressed to replace them. They were not costly to employ.[56]

UNDERGROUND HAULAGE

The movement of coal from the areas it was mined to the colliery surface, as the major constraint on increased coal production, was a persistent area of concern for mine managers. It was also where boys were most numerous. The potential boost to mine productivity that steam power allowed would only be realized if the bottleneck represented by antiquated means of transporting coal underground was removed. Improvements were particularly pressing because gunpowder, just coming into general use in Great Britain, was introduced into British North American mines at about the same time as steam. The use of gunpowder to help dislodge coal increased the miner's productivity by perhaps 40 percent. The burgeoning output of coal in the bords threatened to overwhelm existing haulage systems.[57]

The use of animals to haul coal underground was a first step in removing this bottleneck. From their introduction in British collieries in the eighteenth century, horses (or, less often, ponies, mules, or donkeys) had been used underground to pull carts laden with coal.[58] The General Mining Association adopted on its arrival what was generally perceived as the best mining practice of the day when it introduced horse haulage underground, supplemented wherever possible by a variety of labour-saving techniques. Initially horses pulled sleds, but by 1852 these had been gradually displaced by wooden tubs or boxes, bolted to an iron frame and designed to run over underground rails.[59] By 1871 the GMA had in place several miles of light underground railway.[60] At Nanaimo, underground passage-ways were enlarged to allow horses to be used to haul coal because of a shortage of aboriginal labourers in 1856.[61] Coal companies increased or reduced their complement of horses as their coal production fluctuated. The ease with which this was done accounts for the attractiveness of horse haulage for mine managers.[62]

Although horse haulage remained the principal means of transporting coal underground until the twentieth century, there were a number of ways in which it was commonly supplemented in steam-powered mines. Where seams pitched steeply, use was made of gravity. If the grade was sufficiently steep, freshly cut coal would be brought down to the travelling roads by the use of slides or "shoots," a narrow, inclined passage used in a mine for moving coal by gravity to a point at which it could be loaded into tubs. By lifting a door at the mouth of the shoot, the driver filled a tub with coal.[63] If the grade was not steep enough, boys were employed to "pull the rag." "We used to pull them long rags of canvas," one boy recalled, "about 25 feet long, hook it into your belt and haul it up to the chute there, where the miners were digging and shovelling their coal back. And we loaded up those rags and rode them down – tipped them all up like a sack of oats, only twice as long, and went down those sheets. We used to have a bar about 40 feet from the bottom, and when we hit that bar – we used to have a lamp hanging there – we'd grab that bar and let the thing go on without us."[64] Alternatively, there was the work done by boys called "shovers-down." They used their feet to shove coal down the chutes. "You'd wear out a pair of overalls in about a week," one claimed.[65] Shovers-down were extensively used at Springhill, where sixty-eight appeared on the payroll in August 1901.[66] They remained in the mine until after the First World War.[67]

A device called the "back-balance" also made use of gravity (see Illustration 3). Two mine cars, one of which carried ballast, were joined by a rope run around a pulley placed at the top of an inclined underground road. By the use of a lever, the empty car was brought to any point along the inclined road, where it could be removed to the bords. When filled with coal, the car was reattached to the back-balance. Gravity would lower the car to a principal underground road, where it could be attached to a horse.[68] A back-balance was in use at the Albion Mines in 1865, where it was estimated that one boy, over a ten-hour shift, could "brake down" 275 to 300 boxes of coal, each of which weighed fifteen hundred pounds.[69] By the early 1870s these were also in use at Cape Breton mines.[70] "Two boys," explained Mines Inspector Edwin Gilpin in 1888, "can transfer the coal from a dozen bords to the level, without any assistance from horses, etc."[71] One boy, who started in a Vancouver Island mine operating a winch, recalled: "You couldn't see. You had to go by sound. You watched your rope too. You knew if you was comin' near the bottom or near the top by the coils on your rope. You could hear the cars comin'; after the loads would pass the empties, the sound would be more clear. And then you would stand up and hold on the brake and watch the trip comin'."[72]

But these techniques of moving coal simply supplemented horse power, the basic means of underground haulage until the twentieth century. Most boys spent at least some time as a horse driver, collecting tubs laden with freshly cut coal, transporting them to a point where they could be hoisted above ground, and returning empty tubs to the working places. Because the work called for both finesse and strength, it was not the youngest boys who worked as drivers, but adolescents. Perched between the horse and the tub it pulled, with "his foot against the horse's rump to hold back the tub," the driver led the horse along dark underground travelling roads, labouring by the faint illumination of the pit lamp.[73] "We went more by instinct than light," one former driver recalled.[74] Where tunnels doubled as pathways for mine workers, as at Springhill in 1888, boys were employed "at each end to call to one another when the road [was] in traffic."[75]

A critical aspect of the driver's work was to ensure the horse's safety when travelling down an incline along underground roads. If the wheels of a mine car were not braced with "sprags," short pieces of hardwood, drivers risked breaking their horse's leg. Sand was also used to slow the movement of mine cars.[76] Generally the driver laboured alone. At Sydney Mines some drivers, those "not as strong" as most or who drove "bad horses," had a second boy to assist them.[77] Fifteen-year-old William Terrance complained that when empty coal tubs derailed he had to replace them himself. Only if full tubs were derailed would the "roadsman" (responsible for the upkeep of the underground roads), swearing at Terrance for blocking traffic, agree to assist him.[78]

A diligent horse greatly eased the driver's exertions. An attentive horse might save a boy's life, as horses were reputed to sense danger, particularly from imminent rockfalls.[79] In these circumstances, as a retired mine worker reported, "some of the drivers were very attached to their horses."[80] Dan J. McDonald recalled that "[t]he drivers in the mine built up a great pride in their horses, and woe and behold to anyone who came along and said anything bad about a man's horse. He'd probably find his teeth down his throat. I saw a fella come along, and spit tobacco on a driver's horse once, and the driver just hit him as fast as he did the spittin', and he wound up minus a few teeth."[81] Experienced boys took care in selecting their horse: "a good driver always looked for a horse that had some spunk about him, some temper, you know, that would be cranky and that. Because if he got a nice, pleasant, easygoing horse, when that driver'd put his horse in the end of the shift, maybe some driver would come out and take that horse out and work him by night. Well then, when the driver would come out the next day, his horse would be tired and couldn't stand up to the work. Because they really worked hard. So that's why some of the good drivers looked for the horses that were cranky and that would give you a little bump. His horse would always be fresh."[82]

A retired miner characterized driving as "one of the toughest jobs in the mine and you had to be careful all the time."[83] Horses were unpredictable. In 1890 William Dunbar was "severely hurt" when kicked by a horse in the McGregor Pit in Pictou County.[84] Another boy had his nose split a few years earlier.[85] Mules, alleged to be less temperamental, more sensible, less likely to bolt, were the beast of choice on Vancouver Island,[86] but in the Extension mine, Lewis Mackenzie, "the unfortunate victim of the mule's kick," was badly shaken when struck in 1901. "The uncertainty of the mule is proverbial," editorialized the Nanaimo *Free Press*, "and in that instance a little too much confiding trust was violently repaid with the usual compliment."[87] Sometimes accidents were much more tragic. A mule driver was killed at Nanaimo in 1887 "by falling off a run of cars drawn by a mule, the cars running on top of him."[88] Another boy died at Sydney Mines after a horse bolted in 1867. "The horse he was driving, from some cause, ran off and upset the tub in which [he] was riding. Being unable to extricate himself, he was unfortunately jammed between the tub and the timbers by the way-side, and was found in that position. Although no bones were broken, he appears to have suffered internal injuries, which caused his death."[89]

It was an easy matter for an angry or frustrated boy to maim or kill a horse deliberately, although there are few such acts on record. One such driver was brought before a court in Sydney Mines in 1895 by the local Society for the Prevention of Cruelty for "torturing a horse under his charge." Neil Boutilier was found guilty, but "in view of his youth" his fine was small.[90] A retired Vancouver Island miner spoke frankly about his frustrations as a boy with one particular horse:

I didn't like horses. They were finicky. For instance if you're going in a low place and the horse touches its neck or collar on the roof, bang, it goes and darts whereas the mule would just go down and bend. A horse will go just like a bullet. The same way if you try to get through between a load and an empty in a narrow place. The mule will just pull its tummy up and walk through. A horse will go crashing through. Sometimes I used to get mad at them horses. I killed one of them in South Wellington Number Five mine. Well, I had to do all the work. He shouldn't have been working at all. I'd practically be pushing the cars and his tail chain would be just hangin' slack, not pullin'. So I worked like that for a few days and then I says, "That's enough." So I clubbed it across the ears and it went down. I went outside and I says to the boss, "Mr. Martin," I says, "my horse passed away."[91]

Over the nineteenth century, underground haulage remained a major concern of mine managers. The potential growth in mine size that steam-driven pumps, hoists, and ventilation fans allowed threatened to be throttled by inadequate means of underground haulage. Horses were exhausted by ever-lengthening distances; expenses associated with the maintenance of underground roads increased steadily. Efforts had to be made to keep them well drained, because pit water, particularly corrosive in Cape Breton because it was saltwater, aggravated any cuts in the base of the horse's hoof.[92] "Roof-brushing" – raising the level of the roof to permit the passage of horses – became increasingly costly in lengthy underground roads, as did roof-buttressing, the placing at regular intervals of wooden props. The rails had to be well ballasted, otherwise horses, not to mention their driver, risked injury. As late Victorian mines grew to a considerable size, underground roadways lengthened and mine managers looked both to supplement and even to replace horse haulage.[93]

THE BOYS IN THE BORDS

The miner commonly hired a helper, often a younger relative if not his own son, to assist him in the bord he worked.[94] "When I started working first," recalled an Alberta miner, "I commenced right in with my father loading."[95] A helper relieved contract miners of a variety of unremunerative but essential tasks: cleaning coal, running errands as necessary, maintaining the miner's tools and safety light, ensuring an adequate supply of wooden props, and setting these props to buttress the roof. He also assisted in laying track. Helpers were most valued to the extent that they relieved the miner of two especially onerous tasks, loading tubs with coal and pushing loaded tubs to the nearest collection point on the underground haulage system. "As a boy we loaded coal for 10 and 12 hours without ever seeing the coal on the shovel," one miner recalled, "The only means of knowing when your mine car was full was to pass your hand over the box to discover if it were full."[96] If the height of the seam did not permit the use of horses, the miner or his helper had to push the fully laden coal tubs to the nearest underground road.[97] Even young boys were useful. In New Brunswick, boys thirteen to fifteen years of age laboured into the 1920s as "wheelers," pushing boxes out from the bords.[98]

Because those employed directly by miners as helpers often did not appear on company payrolls, the extent of the use of boys in the bords is unclear. Accidents occasionally disclosed their presence. In 1872, for instance, an inexperienced "lad" working as a loader at the Intercolonial Colliery was crushed to death while helping to replace a tub on the underground railway.[99] A seventeen-year-old pusher had his leg broken in a Cape Breton mine in 1914.[100] On the Pacific coast, a Victoria newspaper reported another mishap in 1867: "A man named James Hamilton, and his son, a young lad, were very badly burned about the face and body … at Nanaimo, from the effects of an explosion of gunpowder, which Hamilton had taken with him for use in the coal pit. He fancies that a spark from a light which he held in his hand ignited the powder."[101] Another boy employed to push boxes at Nanaimo in 1895 "got his arm broken by being jammed between two mine cars."[102] Work in the bords was the most onerous work performed by boys. For this reason, it was the biggest boys, on the verge of physical maturity, who were most commonly employed there. For boys aspiring to become miners themselves one day, it was where they learned the craft directly – by watching, by doing, by talking with miners.[103]

COAL AS KING: THE COAL INDUSTRY
AT THE TURN OF THE TWENTIETH CENTURY

By its nature, mining had discouraged major technical innovation over much of the nineteenth century. Because it involved a series of interdependent systems – that of cutting the coal from the seam, of removing it from the mine (which involved, in turn, loading the coal onto some means of conveyance), and of maintaining the mine (drainage, ventilation) – the mine functioned only as well as its weakest link. Improvements in one area of mine activity were of limited value in the absence of innovations elsewhere. The uncertain profitability of technical change was compounded by the steady exhaustion of mine properties – available coal would ultimately run out – and by geological quirks (such as faulting), which discouraged, on the one hand, extensive fixed investment and, on the other, attempts to mechanize mine work. No technical innovation dislodged the skilled collier – and the associated division of mine labour – from his central place in the production of coal until the twentieth century.

The two great companies of the British colonial era, the Hudson's Bay Company and the General Mining Association, were incapable of reaping the fullest benefits of their monopolies. Because mines had to be maintained year-round, considerable costs were associated with seasonally idle mines that had to be absorbed in the final price of coal. Mine profitability was also restricted by a poor local supply of skilled labour, small regional markets for coal, and dependence on export markets in the United States. After the dissolution of the GMA and HBC monopolies, dozens of companies emerged to exploit the extensive reserves of coal in Nova Scotia and British Columbia. Growing markets for coal could not offset the financial weakness of many of these companies, which had to bear heavy carrying charges for the fixed assets needed to run collieries. To the 1890s, despite large investment in steam-based technologies, most mines remained very undercapitalized. Only with the growth of investment and the consolidation of industrial ownership and control at the turn of the twentieth century, following the emergence of expanded and year-round coal markets, did a corporate structure emerge capable of supporting more modern mining techniques.[104]

At that time, however, the technical means to step up coal production sharply were coupled with the rapidly expanding markets for coal that were necessary to attract large new investment. Demand for coal increased greatly from industrial and domestic consumers in growing urban centres, from railways and ocean steamers, and from the developing metallurgical sector. The development of steel works in Pictou County during the 1880s, and a decade later at Sydney and Sydney Mines, was of immense importance in expanding and stabilizing markets for coal. The steel industry, with its huge demands for coking coal, increased the market for colliery output considerably by creating demand for coke, manufactured from previously discarded smaller pieces of coal and (dust-like) slack.[105] By 1911 the local steel industry was taking more than half of the total coal output of the largest Cape Breton mines.[106]

Rapidly expanding markets encouraged heavy turn-of-the-century investment and corporate concentration within the industry on Vancouver Island, and even more so in Nova Scotia. In the coalfields of the western interior, ownership remained diverse and its numerous mines – Alberta had 316 and Saskatchewan 53 in 1926 – remained considerably smaller on average than those in Nova Scotia and on Vancouver Island.[107] On Vancouver Island, strong export markets in the 1870s drove production up tenfold. Local mine owner Robert Dunsmuir bought out a number of smaller rivals, developed the Union collieries at Cumberland after 1888, and became the second

major regional coal operator. At the end of the century, control of the
Vancouver Island mines was shared between the Dunsmuir Company, with mines at Wellington, Cumberland, and Extension, and the
New Vancouver Coal Mining and Land Company (as it was known
after reorganization in 1889) at Nanaimo.[108]

Corporate concentration was even more evident in Nova Scotia.
The Nova Scotia Steel and Coal Corporation had emerged by 1900
as a major integrated producer of finished and semi-finished steel,
coal, and iron ore.[109] The Dominion Coal Company (DOMCO) brought
the important southern Cape Breton coalfield under a single corporate umbrella in 1893.[110] The Dominion Iron and Steel Company,
established at Sydney in 1899, gained control of DOMCO in 1910, the
same year it acquired the large mines of the Cumberland Railway
and Coal Company at Springhill. When the Nova Scotia Steel and
Coal Company, which had purchased the GMA properties at Sydney
Mines in 1900 and the Acadia collieries in Pictou County in 1919, and
the Dominion Steel and Coal companies were amalgamated as the
British Empire Steel Corporation (BESCO) in 1921, a corporate monopoly of Nova Scotia's coal mines, with a few small exceptions, was
complete.[111]

BEYOND STEAM: LONGWALL MINES
AND THE MECHANIZATION OF MINING

Large investment heightened pressure to increase the extent and
regularity of coal production and to reduce the considerable labour
costs at the mine.[112] Two means were adopted. Both called for the
radical reorganization of work, and both compromised the authority
of the collier. The first technical revolution in Canadian coalfields
brought the skilled collier and steam power to British North America;
the second, at the turn of the twentieth century, brought mine mechanization and the longwall method of mining coal. New forms of
power, compressed air and electricity, were introduced to Canadian
collieries. A range of machinery – mechanized underground haulage
in the 1880s, mechanical undercutters and pneumatically driven
machine drills in the 1890s – began to appear. The "modern" underground mine emerged slowly.

In contrast to bord-and-pillar systems, where coal was mined in
two distinct phases, the longwall method of mining allowed the
removal of all the coal in a single operation. In "retreating longwall"
mining, two parallel roads were driven from the level to the edge of
the seam; the coal was then mined along a continuous face back to
the level, the roof being allowed to settle behind the face workings.

In "advancing longwall," the coal was mined from the level to the edge of the seam, travelling roads being built and maintained in the refuse left after the collapse of the roof (see Illustration 4).

There were a number of technical grounds on which managers preferred longwall. At a certain depth, bord and pillar became impracticable. At this level – for instance, approximately 300 metres underground in Cape Breton and 450 metres on Vancouver Island – the overlying strata could no longer be supported by any feasible size of pillar.[113] Longwall also called for less mine infrastructure. Because longwall mines required two roadways per wall, while bord and pillar might demand seven or eight over an equivalent area, it was especially suited to narrow working areas, where workings extended rapidly and the cost of constructing and maintaining travelling roads was high. Ventilation was also much simplified, air no longer having to be coursed through the honeycomb workings of bord and pillar. Most importantly, longwall called for less-skilled and more easily supervised workers.[114]

Longwall was adopted unevenly. On Vancouver Island, a large supply of unskilled, often Asian, labour encouraged the use of numerous longwall faces late in the nineteenth century. These were most evident at the Dunsmuir collieries, where they were used extensively at both the Union mine and at Wellington.[115] In the western interior, small mines and irregular coal seams discouraged longwall's introduction.[116] In Nova Scotia, longwall trials occurred in Pictou County as early as 1899, although its use remained "experimental" in 1928.[117] Longwall was adopted at Springhill after 1925 as a means of avoiding "bumps," the periodic violent buckling of the strata that afflicted its mines.[118] Although experiments with longwall in Cape Breton began in the late nineteenth century, only towards the close of the First World War were trials considered to be successful.[119] The transition was rapid. In 1925, 2.6 percent of Nova Scotia's coal was mined by longwall; in 1930, nearly one-third; in 1935, nearly one-half. In 1935, 97 percent of coal mined by the Nova Scotia Steel and Coal Company was mined by longwall, often in workings extending far under the ocean.[120]

Commonly associated with longwall was the mechanization of elements of mining, a process closely tied to the adoption of two alternative new power sources coming into use by the 1880s. Considerable improvements were made in the efficiency of compressed-air engines, but problems remained in transmitting power over long distances.[121] Electricity, not handicapped in this manner, was defined as the motive power of the future in mines; it was introduced in the 1880s in United States mines and somewhat later in Canada.[122] The

Nanaimo mine of the New Vancouver Coal Mining and Land Company may have been the first colliery in Canada to use electricity as a source of motive power, in 1891.[123] That same year the successful use of electrical coal cutters was reported at the Union mines of Cumberland.[124] Although safe methods of electric power transmission had been developed by the 1890s, electricity was for many years to be viewed with deep suspicion owing to the threat of sparks causing explosions. For this reason, when Dominion Coal embarked upon an extensive program to mechanize its mines shortly after it was organized in 1893, it selected compressed air to power its machine cutters and drills underground.[125] Debate would continue among mining engineers for many years about the relative merits of electricity and compressed air.[126]

Although a British invention, having been tested as early as 1861 at a colliery in West Yorkshire, the mechanical coal cutter was most widely adopted in North America.[127] The Newcastle seam was opened at Nanaimo No. 1 Colliery in the 1890s on longwall, where "extensive use" was made of coal-cutting machines at least as early as 1893. First used in 1891, by 1894 four electric cutters were employed at the Union Colliery.[128] The Galt mines at Lethbridge experimented with compressed-air cutters in the 1880s and used them regularly the following decade.[129] By 1913, 22.5 percent of Alberta's coal was machine-cut; by 1924, 40.6 percent.[130] Nova Scotia adopted mechanical cutters particularly rapidly. In 1902, 76 percent of Dominion Coal's output, and 49 percent of the province's, was machine-cut. In the United States, the figure that year stood at 25 percent; in the United Kingdom, 2 percent.[131] The laborious task of undercutting coal by handpick might have taken the miner up to several hours, before the coalface was prepared for a charge of gunpowder. By machine, perhaps one-quarter of this time was needed and the production of coal in the bords increased sharply.[132] But because pillars could not be undercut by machine – "the noise of a machine drowns [the] sound" of the imminent collapse of the room – mechanization encouraged the gradual abandonment of bord and pillar in favour of longwall mining.[133]

For coal companies to reap the benefits of mechanization at the coalface, better means of underground haulage were also required, although the pressure was muted somewhat by the bottleneck produced by the continuing need to load coal tubs by hand. The first important innovations in this area, once again pioneered in Great Britain, were based on the systematic use of steam. While steam engines had been used to a limited extent underground in Britain from the turn of the nineteenth century to haul coal tubs up inclines, their wider use underground was restricted principally because of problems of transmitting power. With the introduction of wire ropes underground in the 1840s, these problems were largely overcome.[134]

A number of new haulage systems were developed in Great Britain at this time. Three varieties of mechanized rope haulage came into widespread use. With "main rope" (or direct) haulage, steam power was used to pull loaded tubs up an underground railway sufficiently steep to allow the empty tubs to run back by gravity. "Main and tail" haulage was identical except that "trips" (groups) of tubs could be pulled up a road and also, by virtue of a pulley at the end of the line opposite the engine, back down. This was necessary, for instance, where roads undulated up and down. The third system of underground haulage developed at this time, "endless rope," required half the manpower of the other two rope systems, under which a worker stood idle until a trip returned to him. Its principal drawback was that it required a double track, because the rope, to which trips could be attached at any point, travelled "endlessly" around a narrow, oval-shaped course. For this reason, endless rope was most commonly used on the major underground roadways, the levels.[135]

Although means of mechanizing underground haulage were available and familiar to the British-educated mine officials of nineteenth-century Canada, these techniques were only adopted slowly. Steam engines were first used underground in British North America during the 1850s to hoist coal tubs up underground inclines.[136] But mechanized haulage was costly: to the expense of the machinery had to be added the cost of preparing the roadway. To a greater extent than with horse haulage, mechanized haulage demanded straight and well-ballasted roads. Existing systems of underground haulage were generally perceived by managers to be adequate to the demands placed on them. Indeed, in Great Britain itself, debate over the relative advantages of horse and mechanized haulage continued over the second half of the nineteenth century, although it became increasingly apparent that on main underground roads rope haulage was to be preferred. As a rule, the larger the quantity of coal to be moved, the longer the distance, and the steeper the inclines, the more evident the advantages of mechanized haulage. At the same time, even in Great Britain auxiliary roads were seldom mechanized. In some instances, thin seams required that coal tubs be pushed by a young worker; more often, it was simply more economical to continue to use the flexible horse haulage.[137]

In Canada, long underground roads first encouraged the use of mechanized underground haulage; the adoption of mechanical cutters hastened the mechanization of haulage. The first system of mechanized rope haulage in the province was introduced in the early 1880s at the GMA colliery at Sydney Mines, where the longest levels extended for over a mile; at all other provincial mines, coal continued to be hauled on the levels by horses.[138] By the early 1890s, however, rope haulage was commonly used in larger provincial mines. On the mainland, these included endless-rope systems on the main levels at Springhill and at the Drummond Colliery in Pictou County.[139] By 1896 Dominion Coal, as part of its heavy capital investment, had introduced endless-rope haulage at half a dozen Cape Breton mines.[140]

Rope haulage, in displacing horses, also displaced their adolescent drivers. On one level at the Intercolonial Coal Mining Company at Westville, a tail-rope system "with 22 boxes on each trip" was in use by 1891. As described by one mines inspector, it "has proved an economical feature in underground haulage, and from the success obtained in its use I would wish to draw to it special attention, as with it in this district one boy can alone do the work that hitherto 8 horses and as many drivers were required to do."[141] Springhill's endless-rope system "[did] away with a large number of horses"; at the Drummond Colliery, "the management has curtailed boy and horse labour very much by a system of endless rope haulage underground which gives great satisfaction."[142] The mechanization of underground haulage at Sydney Mines, noted engineer John Johnson, "has altogether done away with the necessity of employing horse drivers."[143] By the 1880s rope haulage had also come into use on the slope at two Vancouver Island collieries.[144] It was the system of choice in Alberta from the start of mining in that province until well into the twentieth century.[145] The mechanization of underground haulage from the 1880s eroded labour requirements in the major site of boys' employment. Some indication of its impact can be gauged from the fact that, while mine employment more than doubled and coal production increased sixfold over the years between 1867 and 1900, the number of horses employed at Nova Scotian mines increased only slightly.[146]

The gradual mechanization of underground haulage continued well into the twentieth century. Like other aspects of technical change in mining, it was a slow and uneven process. At the smallest pits, the older techniques of horse haulage remained in use on even the main underground roads. Although horses had been entirely removed from three pits at Sydney Mines by 1910, such mines were exceptional.[147] More typical of the larger collieries by that time was a three- or four-part system of underground haulage, by which coal was removed from the colliery in a series of discrete steps. At the No. 1 Esplanade mine at Nanaimo, long underground roads encouraged the installation in 1892 of an electric trolley locomotive (which displaced mules). Within a year, three locomotives were in use on the two main levels. For secondary haulage, self-acting inclines were employed; mules and drivers moved the coal tubs from the workplaces to the inclines. This system was largely intact as late as 1923, except that mechanical hoists had replaced self-acting inclines.[148]

After the First World War, rope haulage came into increasing disrepute. It was considered to waste power to friction and inertia, and also to involve considerable trouble and expense in maintaining ropes and roadways, especially in wet mines.[149] Debate was all the more pointed because underground haulage was recognized as the most likely area for cost reduction in mine operations. New systems of underground haulage were introduced. The practicality of underground locomotives had been debated as early as the 1880s and tested during the 1890s, although they were not in common use until after the First World War.[150] By 1928 "conveyor pans" (a variety of conveyer belt) were used behind the mechanical cutter at Sydney Mines to move the coal from the working area back to the haulage roads, where it was dumped into boxes, still pulled by horses. Subsequently, a main-and-tail rope brought the boxes to the main level, where another rope system brought them to the surface.[151] Although at certain American mines conveyor systems extending from the coalface to the surface were in place by the 1930s, Canadian collieries were less successful in adopting such systems.[152] If in 1936 horses were still used at certain mines for gathering the boxes from the working faces, they were "disappearing as fast as coal won by longwall is replacing room-and-pillar coal."[153] In their place, the use of conveyors had expanded. In certain Dominion Coal mines, conveyors had been introduced as early as 1925 to transport the coal to the main roads.[154]

The new techniques of mining were most extensively adopted where child labour had been the greatest; western Canadian mines, particularly those in the interior, were mechanized far less than Nova Scotia's, because of lower levels of capitalization, irregular seams, and, on Vancouver Island, the presence of low-wage Asian labour.[155] By 1914 mechanical cutters were only in use in one district of one Vancouver Island mine.[156] In 1926 Nova Scotia and Alberta both had two and one-half times the coal production of British Columbia.[157] Yet 1,500 men operated mechanical cutters in Nova Scotia, only 384 in Alberta, and 38 in *all* of British Columbia.[158] Nova Scotia had 1,435 workers employed with mechanized means of haulage and 723 with horse haulage. In western Canada, non-mechanized haulage remained predominant. Alberta had 696 employed with horse haulage and 328 with mechanized means of haulage. British Columbia had 401 and 324 respectively.[159]

If mine mechanization was particularly extensive in the province where boys had been most heavily employed, two factors mitigated its impact on boys' jobs. First, the process of mechanization was at best partial. "[Into] the 1920s," David Frank has observed, "despite the advance of machinery and adjustments in the division of labour, the Cape Breton mines [among the largest and most mechanized in Canada] remained largely hand powered, labour intensive, and tradition bound in organization."[160] Jobs traditionally held by boys persisted at the most advanced Canadian collieries until after the Second World War.[161] The last horse was not out of the Cape Breton mines until about 1960.[162]

Second, mine mechanization did not necessarily exclude boys, who were more than capable of manning mechanized systems. Into the twentieth century, boys operated steam engines to hoist coal up underground inclines, worked with rope haulage systems as "chain-runners" and "rope-riders," coupling and uncoupling tubs from ropes, accompanying the trains used in underground mechanized haulage, and helping to maintain the mechanized haulageways. As "bottomers" and "cagers," they were employed to assemble trains of coal cars for haulage up a slope or to roll coal tubs onto the hoist, signalling the hoist operator when to start or stop a trip.[163] Fourteen-year-old Ralph Larner started at the No. 2 mine at Coal Creek in 1910, trapping. His next job, at which he spent four years, was "bell-rapping to make the hoist go up and down."[164] A coal-cutting machine introduced in 1904, touted to do "the work of five pair of men," was "operated by one man and one boy."[165]

To the extent that these new mining techniques were adopted, however, their effect was to reduce boys' usefulness in the colliery. Longwall mines were far simpler to ventilate and curtailed sharply or eliminated the use of trappers. More significant were innovations in underground haulage diminishing the need for labour in this sector. Technical changes eroded employment levels in jobs traditionally performed by boys.

The new techniques of mining presented miners with a dilemma. Larger, far more heavily capitalized collieries promised more regular work and a considerable improvement in living standards. The United Mine Workers of America's District 26 president, Robert Baxter, expressed the hope in 1920 that technical improvements, in leading to better remuneration for miners, "will make it unnecessary for boys to seek jobs at 13 or 14 years of age."[166] But at what price? From the 1890s, a conviction grew among miners that their status and skills were threatened by new divisions of labour and new kinds of machinery.[167]

The specialization of function that mine managers instituted in order to maximize mine productivity eroded considerably the sphere of a collier's control, even where bord-and-pillar mining persisted. As larger numbers of datal workers (paid a daily wage by the company) entered the mine to maintain underground roads, do timbering, or perform dozens of ancillary mine tasks, miners took responsibility for an ever-narrower range of tasks. Shot-firing, for instance, came to be performed over the last decades of the nineteenth century by specialized workers rather than by the collier.[168] Discrete tasks were often spread over two or three shifts of workers.[169] By 1920 there were three hundred distinct job classifications in the Cape Breton mines.[170] The proportion of men underground who were actual coalface miners decreased sharply. Miners had comprised half the workforce underground at Cape Breton pits in 1880; by 1920 they accounted for fewer than one-third.[171] While the miner of the past was "an artisan skilled in all the branches of his calling," his twentieth-century counterpart could boast a far narrower range of ability.[172]

The extension of mechanization in cutting, drilling, and haulage also had a considerable impact. The workplace became noisier and dustier – a more disagreeable environment.[173] Mechanization also impinged directly on the traditional liberties of colliers. As mines grew in size, miners found their right to come and go as they pleased restricted. "Men are their own masters," it was reported from Glace Bay in 1888, "and come up when they like."[174] But as mines deepened and lengthened, trains of boxes (called "riding rakes") were used to transport mine workers into and out of the pit. Managers would refuse to send these down before they felt a day's work had been put in. Miners were faced with the lengthy walk out of mines or a dangerous ride on top of a tub filled with coal if they wished to dispute this stricter definition of managerial time.[175]

Mechanized systems began to dictate the miners' pace of work in other ways. The organization of mining underground was increasingly the task of trained mining engineers responsible for coordinating the installation of different mechanical systems designed to mine coal more efficiently. In highly mechanized mines, apart from those employed to operate and maintain the new machines, "the work [was] done by unskilled labour."[176] Electricians and mechanics were increasingly to be found underground, making claims to the management positions that had previously been the objective of working miners. Miner Frank Wheatley, underlining the need for miners trained from boyhood, argued that "[i]f the industry is going to be successfully run, it cannot be run successfully by transient labour." Edmonton businessman Harvey Shaw riposted: "If we are going to cut this coal electrically by machinery, we don't need to have such efficient men."[177] Mechanized systems were frequently implemented in tandem with longwall techniques of mining, further subordinating the miner. Teams of workers, readily supervised, their work planned and closely directed by mine officials, mined a single coalface in unison.[178]

In Nova Scotia, although the PWA exercised recognized power, its liberal leadership endorsed wholeheartedly the mechanization of the industry spearheaded by the corporate behemoth, the Dominion Coal Company, on account of its promise of steady work and pay.[179] In western Canada, a transient, ethnically divided workforce hampered workers' ability to resist the reorganization of labour. Canadian mine operators adopted the new techniques of mining as they saw fit.[180] At the turn of the twentieth century, a Nova Scotia mine manager and former provincial inspector of mines reflected on the changes in mining over the previous eighty years. Despite the variety of mechanical improvements, H.S. Poole could not help but express his sense of loss. In his words, earlier in the century "[c]oal cutting was an art, the collier took pride in his ability to handle the pick, to cut a straight and narrow shearing, to make a low holeing deep." Now, Poole felt, "[a] neat wall is only seen in old workings; rough, ragged and irregular sides are accepted with the urgent demand for large outputs."[181]

When the federal Labour Commission visited Nova Scotian coal communities in 1888, boys were following their fathers into the pits.[182] By 1908, when the Commission on Miners' Old Age Pensions and Relief Societies toured provincial coalfields to gather testimony from Nova Scotian miners, miners' sons were not following, to the extent they had in the past, their father's occupation.[183] Miners hesitated to initiate their sons into a craft they felt was declining.[184]

CHAPTER FIVE

The State and Pit Boys

"[T]he employment of children of very tender years injures the health, stunts the growth and prevents the proper education of such children, so that they cannot become healthy men and women or intelligent citizens."
Royal Commission on the Relations between Capital and Labour, 1889

"[The pit boy] is looked upon as a peculiarly privileged chap with boundless opportunities for plenty of mischievous fun, which he never fails to embrace."
Halifax *Morning Chronicle*, 4 December 1890

Traditionally, children worked. Their early initiation to work, if remarked on at all, was most commonly considered as salutary, as "good" for the child, as teaching him or her the virtue and necessity of labour in preparation for a lifetime of labour. Concern was far likelier to be expressed regarding the unemployment or idleness of children than over the fact that they laboured productively.[1] But among a broad coalition of social reformers, in which the participation of the organized working class was evident, the legitimacy of child labour was brought into question from the middle of the nineteenth century. Reformers envisaged the universalization of childhood, whereby all children were to benefit from minimum rights to education, health, and play. All children were to be "protected" from wage labour (to at least a certain age); all were to receive a minimum level of schooling.

On account of this pressure, the state began to develop a model of appropriate childhood, which it first defined in an array of legislation and then proceeded to extend by progressively lengthening the period of legal minority. Because the model for childhood was developed within the affluent classes of urban Canada, working-class childhood was closely scrutinized. By early in the twentieth century, most boys and girls were no longer legally entitled to work for wages. The few analyses of the decline of child labour undertaken in Canada, while citing a variety of factors, have been unanimous in discounting the role both of compulsory schooling laws and of legislation restricting children's employment – despite evidence of the generally upward trend of children's level of school attendance and their steady withdrawal from the paid labour force. Rather, research has emphasized that the level of school attendance was subject to the possibilities for work: the greater the employment opportunities, the fewer the number of children going to school.[2] Consequently, both world wars had the effect of diminishing levels of school attendance; the Depression raised attendance levels.[3] Similarly, compliance with labour legislation hinged on improved wages for adult males[4] or on labour market changes that reduced the demand for child labour[5] or on a mix of both.[6] The orthodox view is clear: legislation had little impact on children's employment. But among nineteenth-century legislation restricting child labour, the first British Columbia Mines Act was exceptional: it had a direct role in excluding boys from the collieries on Vancouver Island as early as the 1870s.

VICTORIANS VIEW CHILD MINE LABOUR

Journalists and writers of travel literature often visited coal mines, among the most impressive of nineteenth-century workplaces. Their views reflected those of the urban centres where they resided. Boys' presence in the pits was generally unquestioned. Indeed, it was depicted as picturesque. "Tyro," touring the Albion Mines on behalf of a Halifax periodical, remarked in 1852 on "a black-faced, but cheerful looking little fellow of some twelve years old" who worked at a door underground.[7] The Montrealer Andrew Spedon, visiting the same colliery in 1862, described "a half dozen of black, little gabby imps – not printers' devils [errand boys, often the youngest apprentices] – but a class of a similar 'type' only a degree *lower*, who seem to think like them that *little* favors should merit *great* rewards, and that 'coal visitors' should have *long* purses and *short* payments." When the boys quit the mine for the day, Spedon noted "the grotesque faces and figures of the let-loose imps, the unearthly yells and gestures."[8] In 1867 a second journalist from Montreal described the passage of coal tubs in this mine "driven by a young looking imp with a black face and shining eyes, with a lamp flaring from his cap, who, as he passed, was shouting most lustily to warn approaching boxes of his approach." Alexander Gilbert noted with equanimity the presence of an eight- or nine-year-old trapper in the mine: "At this door stands another imp, whose duty it is to attend the door from morning to night, and see that it is immediately shut on any one passing through."[9] Nearly two decades later, a correspondent of the *Scottish American Journal* visited these same mines: "The boys seem happy enough, and were bright little fellows from 11 to 15 years of age; the men were respectful and small in stature, but they appeared dull and phlegmatic by contrast with the younger generation."[10]

An extended account of the pit boy was published in the Halifax *Morning Chronicle* in 1890:

The pit boy occupies a foremost position in Springhill to-day, and is causing not a little anxiety [boys were prone to strike]. As a rule he is a bright, interesting little fellow. Let me try to describe him. Long before your city boys are astir the pit boy is awakened by the steam whistles, which blow three long blasts at half-past five o'clock every morning, thus warning him that it is time to get up. Breakfast partaken of, he dons his pit clothes, usually a pair of indifferent-fitting duck trousers, generously patched, an old coat, and with a lighted tin lamp on the front of his cap, his tea and dinner cans securely fastened on his back, he is ready for work. He must be at his post at 7 o'clock. Off he goes, and in a few minutes with a number of others he is engaged in animated conversation, and having a high old time generally, as he is lowered on a riding rake to the bottom of the slope ... At twelve years of age and upwards, working down in the dark pit all day, a boy expects to have his outing in the evening ... When the pit boy attains to years of discretion he settles down and begins to evince an interest in many things. But previous to that he is looked upon as a peculiarly privileged chap with boundless opportunities for plenty of mischievous fun, which he never fails to embrace.[11]

The youngest "imps" were "cheerful," older boys were "happy," "bright," "interesting," and "animated." Mine visitors agreed that the colliery boy was colourful: he was content with his work; his place was in the mine. Brash and self-confident, boys insisted on tips from one mine visitor. Indeed, Spedon's account of their "grotesque" appearance and "unearthly" demeanour suggests they may have intimidated the visiting journalist.

Even tragedies in the mine left child labour unquestioned. Journalist R.A.H. Morrow lamented the dead trapper boys at Springhill in 1891, describing them in terms that contrasted sharply with the account in the *Morning Chronicle* the year before. "Sitting so long alone in the darkness they become thoughtful, sober, sometimes melancholy. They go silently to their homes when they leave the mine; they do not stop to play tricks or joke with their fellows; they do not run, nor sing, nor whistle. Darkness and silence are always depressing, and so much of it in these young lives cannot help but sadden without sweetening them."[12] Similarly, Robert Drummond described in 1907 the onset of "after-damp," the deadly gas released in mine explosions. His saccharine prose does not entirely obscure the horror of the event: "[T]he men see the little boys fall upon their knees and mumble that they are sleepy. Fathers take their sons up in their arms to carry them home to their mothers. But fathers and sons lie down together in the dust. The mysterious, invisible, after-damp has crept into their lungs, and they are sleeping peacefully with the little boys in their arms. Only God can wake them!"[13] Although the comments of these journalists point to the sentimentalization of childhood more characteristic of the twentieth century, in neither instance were they coupled with a call for the exclusion of boys from the mines.[14]

The few dissenting voices in Victorian Canada focused on very young pit boys. When Nova Scotia established in 1873 a minimum age of ten for work underground in coal mines, the responsible minister argued that "[t]he effect of employing boys of tender age in the mines under ground was to make them stunted and demoralized by shutting them out from the influences of the free air and sunshine."[15] Federal commissioners, reporting fifteen years later on "the employment of children of very tender years," claimed that it "injures the health, stunts the growth and prevents the proper education of such children, so that they cannot become healthy men and women or intelligent citizens." They observed of the Nova Scotia Mines Act that "[i]t is very certain that children removed from schools at the age of ten cannot acquire education sufficient to fit them for the duties of life in a civilized community."[16]

Efforts of the Victorian state to define a qualified workforce reflect the radical redefinition of children over the nineteenth century, from competent economic contributors to the household to individuals emotionally, intellectually, and physically disqualified from labouring. In reviewing the constitutionality of the Chinese exclusion clauses of British Columbia's Mines Acts, for instance, provincial Supreme Court judges underlined that legislated restrictions on child labour reflected views of both children's special need for protection and their incompetence to perform mine work (therefore endangering other workers). In the words of Justice George A. Walkem, "the exclusion of boys is for their benefit on account of their youth, as well as for the protection of others, who might suffer from their inexperience."[17] G.S. Montgomery, an Alberta mine manager, spoke in 1919 to the view, by that time commonplace, that children were unfit to make their own decisions. He complained that the legislated eight-hour day for miners "treats them as children, making us pull them out at the end of eight hours."[18] This growing view of their unsuitability for labour had the effect of creating a secondary status in the labour market for children.

WOMEN AND MINE LABOUR

As with children, appropriate roles for women were recast radically over the nineteenth century, making them, too, unfit to labour.[19]

Whereas women were not defined as incompetent – they were not seen, as children were, to constitute a safety threat to other workers – they were portrayed as both physically and morally unsuited for the mine. Justice Walkem justified female exclusion from work underground in British Columbia mines by arguing that it was "in their interests, as it is evidently done on moral grounds." And he observed that there were limits on the hours they could be employed above ground "so as to save them from being overtaxed."[20] Yet women's ability to do mine work was demonstrated clearly in Great Britain, where women and girls laboured underground until well into the nineteenth century in many coalfields and above ground into the twentieth century. In fact, Angela John has argued that British women's exclusion from mine work was associated with new techniques of mining that *lightened* the workload.[21] Women's capacity to do mine labour was also evident in colonial British Columbia, where the earliest mine workers, the Native peoples of Vancouver Island, gave women the arduous task of transporting coal by canoe from shore to ship.[22]

With these rare exceptions, women never worked at British North American mines.[23] The explanation is found in the United Kingdom, from which the first immigrant miners imported their views and practices.[24] British women were first excluded from work underground by the Mines Act of 1842, even if its provisions were reportedly evaded into the 1860s. This legislation was closely linked with the efforts of Lord Shaftesbury and other reformers to bring to wider attention practices in the isolated coalfields of the nation which they labelled immoral and which they felt brutalized women. When accounts of the conditions of women's and girls' labour in the mines were published in the reports of the Children's Employment Commission in 1842, the Parliament at Westminster rapidly passed corrective legislation. "An enormous mischief is discovered," Shaftesbury announced to the House of Lords, "and an immediate remedy is proposed."[25] Robert Colls identified a "metropolitan-bourgeois" public animated by "a new sensibility of womanhood and motherhood and their proper refinements" as the force behind this legislation. In need of "special protection," the youngest children were barred from all mine work, and women from labour underground.[26]

But to attribute female exclusion simply to this legislation fails to account for wide evidence that the employment of women underground was clearly declining well before the controversy of 1840–42. By 1780 women were no longer employed underground in the important Northumberland-Durham coalfield; indeed, by the third or fourth decade of the nineteenth century – the approximate period of the earliest emigration of skilled colliers to British North America –

female mine workers were restricted to coalfields in Scotland, York-shire, Lancashire, and South Wales.[27] The role of male miners in the removal of women from the mine is ambiguous. But it must be recognized that the traditional labouring household was dependent on economic contributions from all its members. Under the family system of labour by which much early mine work was organized, male miners employed women, directed and supervised their labour (and that of children), and appropriated their wages. Male miners – as workers – had no interest in female exclusion. In testimony given before the Children's Employment Commission, in coalfields where females were employed, male miners did not support exclusion. Nor, for that matter, did women.[28]

If women's gradual removal from the mines predated parliamen-tary action, and if mine workers were hostile to female exclusion, then the initiative to exclude women from the mines necessarily lay with employers. Certainly a number of mine owners, labelling female labour underground as barbaric, unilaterally undertook to remove females from the mine.[29] But more than moral outrage was at issue. Historians have recently drawn a useful distinction between tradi-tional and "improving" mine operators. Opposition to female labour was strongest in coalfields where very heavy recent capital invest-ment and its requirement for regularity of output prompted concern among employers over workforce discipline. Improving operators were united around the need to undercut the miner's power in the mine. The exclusion of women "would cut across the control over the labour process which the family system of labour gave to the male hewer."[30] Female exclusion was an aspect of the struggle over mastery in the workplace between miners and mine operators.

The disruption of the traditional organization of mine labour recast women as threats to miners. Early trade unions consequently advo-cated their exclusion. One of the first colliers' unions, in Lanarkshire, Scotland, was instrumental before its demise in the 1830s in tempo-rarily excluding women from the mines. When the Miners' Associa-tion of Great Britain and Ireland was founded in 1842, it saw female exclusion as a means to restrict the supply of mine labour (and ultimately, to increase wages). Male workers, interested in protecting their position in the labour market, only adopted exclusionary tactics in British coalfields after the demise of the traditional, family-based organization of labour.[31]

Ultimately, the urban middle-class model for the family came to be widely assimilated within British society. The working class itself set about restructuring family life to these standards by excluding women (whenever practical) from wage labour. Of course, the more women's labour underground came to be associated with archaic techniques of mining, the more anachronistic the practice itself appeared (in the coalfields of eastern Scotland, for instance, women and girls traditionally carried coal from the pit on their backs using a type of basket called a "creel").[32] Consequently, as major mines opened in British North America during this period, women's right to work underground was never at issue: it was accepted by both workers and mine operators that they were not to be employed. The question remains as to why, at British North American collieries, European women failed to find a place on the surface, where they continued to work at British mines. In part, it is because little that is considered surface work, involving the preparation – sizing and cleaning – of coal for market, was done at the surface at early British North American collieries; rather it was done underground. There was little enough even in the United Kingdom. Large numbers of jobs on the mine surface emerged only in the last decades of the nineteenth century, with the extensive differentiation of markets for coal and the removal of cleaning to above ground. Women, having never established a claim to labour in Canadian mines, were unable to get access to this work.[33]

The deliberations of the British Columbia Legislative Assembly in 1877 on women's right to work were recounted in the Victoria *Daily British Colonist*:

Mr. Milby did not wish to see women working in the mines.

Hon. Mr. Elliott – We must not interfere with women's rights.

Mr. Walkem [the future b.c. Supreme Court justice] would like the women to have a chance to work above ground if they wished.

Mr. Milby asked whether it would look well for a woman to be shovelling coal and her husband drinking lager beer and playing cards in a saloon? (Cheers.)

Mr. Smith – The moment you tell a woman she mustn't do a thing she wants to do it. (Laughter.) If you say women shan't work in the mines they will drop their pianos and their crochet-work and crowd into the mines three deep looking for work. (Great laughter.) Don't you tell a woman she shan't do anything if you don't want her to do it. Tell her she may and then may be she won't. (Roars of laughter.)[34]

Premier A.C. Elliott upheld women's unqualified right to work, while George Walkem, at that time leader of the opposition group, sought to restrict their access to colliery work to the surface, as was the case in contemporary Great Britain. One member, William C. Milby, echoed a frequent comment among bourgeois Victorians by linking women's labour with male malingering. The patronizing claims of another member, Robert Smith, which poke fun at women's wage work, evidently resonated well within the Assembly. Among middle-class Victorians – and within the more affluent portions of the working class – women's wage labour had become ridiculous.[35]

THE STATE AND CHILDHOOD

Similar themes are evident in children's exclusion from the workplace: because of emerging views of their incompetence, their employment was redefined as a focus of public concern requiring remedial legislation.[36] Laws restricting child labour, however, as with those that addressed women's employment, were generally responsible to only a limited degree for exclusion, in part because the nineteenth-century state employed limited powers to enforce legislation, and in part because of other factors at play in removing children from the labour market. The first product of state efforts to restructure childhood, and the one whose impact was ultimately most profound, was the common school. Growing state interest in children's education produced particular criticism of coal-mining communities. The British Columbia inspector of schools noted in 1876 (before the first provincial Mines Act) that "[a] disposition on the part of many parents to send their children into 'the pit' at an early age is exercising a prejudicial influence on the rising generation by depriving them of the advantages of free school education."[37] As late as 1908, Nova Scotia's mining towns were qualified as "notorious as communities where the boys leave the public schools just as soon as they get the opportunity."[38]

Yet organized miners supported compulsory schooling legislation. J.S. Hurt observed that British miners "formed the industrial group that has probably the longest tradition of making this demand [compulsory education] on behalf of their children."[39] Miners in British Columbia agreed at Nanaimo in 1877 "on the necessity of educating boys" and proposed a mechanism for ensuring school attendance.[40] Neil Nickerson, a collier at the Albion Mines in Nova Scotia, told members of the Labour Commission that "no boy should be employed who could not read and write, and that [legislation] might be the means of getting careless parents to get their children a proper education."[41] When the PWA debated legislation restricting child labour in 1890, one miner expressed the view that "parents sent boys to work at too early an age." He had known of "a father [who carried] his boy to work, the little fellow being unable [to manage] the long journey." Miners agreed that "boys must be protected by the public if their parents neglect them."[42]

The period of time a child was to spend in school was debated for decades. Increasing calls for formal certification encouraged interest in schooling within the mining community. Former PWA grand secretary Robert Drummond argued in the Legislative Council in 1902 that "it takes away a great many advantages from a boy going so early to a mine."[43] A delegate to the PWA Grand Council in 1906 spoke of the need "to abolish a system of parents sending their boys to work before they have been fitted in any way by education."[44] UMWA District 26 President Dan McDougall observed in 1912 that "I don't think any boy should be sent to work until he is 16, more particularly to the pit."[45] He added that "there is great neglect sometimes on the part of parents in [not] sending their children to school."[46] McDougall's successor, Robert Baxter, told a federal commission in 1920 that "if you could see some of the small boys coming from those Mines you would realize that they are not equipped for the future, they have not the advantages they should have in the way of education."[47] Coal miners, like other organized workers, believed that a common school education would benefit their children. And, parental prerogatives notwithstanding, organized miners supported legal restrictions on child labour. To be sure, reservations existed. Robert Drummond, for instance, uneasy about such extensions to the state's authority, groped for a definition of the legitimate extent of parents' prerogatives: "[t]he parent, or the guardian of the child has surely certain rights which should not be interfered with."[48] Drummond was nonetheless instrumental in tightening the child labour clauses of the provincial Mines Act; he was also a tireless booster of the merits of schooling.[49]

School legislation, particularly provisions calling for compulsory school attendance, first restricted younger children's right to work. In Nova Scotia, the Free Schools Act of 1864 established the framework for a common school system and an 1865 act made this system viable by providing for compulsory assessment of property owners for the upkeep of schools. A child's formal education was not necessarily ensured by the mere existence of a school system, and no provision was made in the 1860s for compulsory attendance outside of Halifax. In 1883, however, local school boards were permitted to require children between seven and twelve to attend school for at least eighty days per year, and to fine parents who did not send their children to school. In 1895 the Towns' Compulsory Attendance Act was passed by the province. At local option, school boards could require every child aged between six and sixteen, resident in an incorporated town, to attend school at least 120 days per year. At the same time, provision was made for truancy officers authorized to arrest children absent from school. Their parents were subject to fines; the child, in certain circumstances, to detention in an industrial school. Exemptions from school were granted to children over twelve with at least a Grade 7 common school education and to any child whose income was indispensable to the family. In 1915 attendance between the ages of six and sixteen was made compulsory in all urban areas province-wide.[50] Because many mining communities remained unincorporated until well into the twentieth century, their school boards remained subject to the provisions of the Education Act pertaining to rural areas: the regulations of 1883, whereby at local option seven- to twelve-year-olds could be compelled to attend school, remained in force. The House of Assembly did not inaugurate province-wide compulsory school attendance (for those seven to fourteen) in rural areas until 1921. In 1923 rural school boards were authorized to require attendance by all children between the ages of six and sixteen.[51]

In British Columbia, the Public School Act of 1872 was followed by the School Amendment Act 1873, which empowered local trustees to require all children aged seven to fourteen to attend school, and to levy fines in cases of non-compliance. This was soon found to be ineffective. The provincial superintendent of education reported in 1875 that local trustees shirked their responsibility to institute compulsory schooling, pleading that they were "desirous of living peacefully with their fellow settlers."[52] The province enacted its own provisions for compulsory education in 1876 whereby all children aged from seven to twelve were compelled to attend school for at least six months annually. In 1901 urban children in this age bracket were required to attend throughout the school year; in 1912 rural boards were given the authority to make the same requirement. Province-wide compulsory attendance to the age of fourteen was enacted in 1920; the following year the school-leaving age was raised to fifteen.[53] Compulsory schooling was introduced by an ordinance of the North-West Territories in 1888, whereby seven- to twelve-year-olds were to attend school at least twelve weeks a year, of which at least six had to be consecutive.[54] By 1898, children in these age range were compelled to attend school at least sixteen weeks annually.[55] The province of Alberta raised the requirement to full term attendance to the age of fourteen in 1910, and to fifteen in 1915.[56] In Saskatchewan, these thresholds were legislated in 1917 and 1922 respectively.[57] In New Brunswick, as late as 1929, attendance was compulsory in the rural districts (where provincial coalfields were found) only at local option, only for 60 percent of the term, and only for children between the ages of seven and twelve.[58]

MINES LEGISLATION AND BOYS

Mines legislation was the first to place restrictions on children's employment in the new industrial workplaces in Canada. The child labour clauses of the initial provincial mines legislation in the 1870s drew on a number of principles established in the United Kingdom. Most significant among these were minimum-age provisions, restrictions on the hours of labour and the kinds of jobs boys might occupy, discrimination on the basis of sex, and educational requirements. The first British legislation restricting employment in mines had been passed in 1842, when all females, and boys under the age of ten, were prohibited from employment underground. The requirement for a minimum level of formal education before children were permitted to work was introduced in 1860, when legislation was enacted stipulating that ten- and eleven-year-old boys could only be employed in British collieries if they had earned an educational certificate or if they attended school at least two days a week for at least three hours per day. In 1872 the minimum age for boys' employment underground was raised to twelve (with provision for ten-year-olds to labour part-time where seams were especially thin). At the same time, surface work was regulated, a minimum age of twelve being required for both boys and girls for full-time employment (and ten years for part-time work).[59]

Most of these principles were reflected in the Nova Scotia Mines Act of 1873. This act, as Don MacLeod has observed, "was almost entirely the product of pressures exerted from within the government."[60] Age restrictions were introduced: the employment of boys under ten in or about coal mines was prohibited. Women lost the legal right to work in provincial collieries, although there is no evidence they were ever able to exercise this right. Boys were prohibited from operating steam-hoists, and a minimum age of twelve was required to operate a horse-gin. The act also limited the hours of work of boys under sixteen years to ten daily and sixty weekly (fifty-four hours weekly for boys under thirteen). There was no requirement that pit boys would have had to have ever attended school.[61]

Subsequent revisions to the child labour clauses of the Nova Scotia Mines Act were largely attributable to the efforts of organized miners. The topic of educational requirements for pit boys was raised at the annual meeting of the PWA Grand Council in October 1890, a number of delegates speaking to this question. Robert Drummond produced a resolution to be submitted to the provincial legislature, whereby no boy under twelve years of age was to be employed underground, and that "a boy before being permitted to work should be able to

read, write and count, as far as fractions." This resolution was passed
virtually *verbatim* by the House of Assembly in 1891.[62] Amendments
in 1908 made the educational requirements for boys more explicit,
stipulating that boys under sixteen years of age had to produce
certificates "of having satisfactorily completed the prescribed course
of study up to the end of Grade seven."[63] Only in 1923, when boys
had largely withdrawn from the mine for other reasons, was the
minimum age of employment raised to a point, the age of sixteen,
where it would have excluded large numbers of boys from Nova
Scotia's mines. This followed once again on an initiative from organized miners.[64]

A formidable obstacle to legislative restrictions on the employment
of boys in Nova Scotia was the resistance of mine operators. In Nova
Scotia, the clause of the 1873 Mines Act limiting boys under twelve
years to sixty hours of work weekly had raised objections from
several mine managers.[65] The 1891 legislation was labelled both
ambiguous and discriminatory in the industrial publication the *Canadian Mining Review*. The clause "to 'count to fractions' made too
indefinite an x on the school book to please the managers, who feared
suits at law for possible inattention to the Act's numerous requirements." It was also pointed out that "[t]he eight hour movement
found expression in the limitation of boys' employment to 48 hours
a week ... which met ... a vigorous opposition from Cape Breton
men, whose shipping season is short and who desire to make the
most of that season for trade with the St. Lawrence," and that "no
similar legislation has yet been introduced with reference to child
labor in factories, where the atmosphere and the monotony of work
are much more injurious to health than in mines."[66]

Although as a rule mine managers resisted protective legislation
for boys, even in the nineteenth century dissenting views were
expressed. The passage of a law to restrict child labour, one correspondent to the *Canadian Mining Review* argued, "would do a great
work for the sons of miners. Under its operation every father would
be compelled, by self-interest, to send his sons to school."[67] In the
twentieth century, mine operators more universally endorsed restrictions on child labour. A New Brunswick mine owner, who prided
himself on his paternalist views, indicated "that a boy should not be
employed in a mine under sixteen years of age, and even then, unless
he has passed some stated grade [he suggested the eighth] in the
public schools, he should not be given any employment."[68]

In British Columbia, the child labour clauses of mining legislation
did not reflect the expressed wishes of miners. When the provincial
Legislative Assembly debated its first Mines Act in 1877, miners met

in Nanaimo and agreed on "the necessity of educating boys, and limiting the time they should be underground." They passed a resolution recommending a minimum age of twelve for a boy to work underground to a maximum of eight hours daily. This resolution dovetailed with the provincial educational requirements enacted the previous year, and the minimum age accorded with contemporary British legislation.[69] Despite the government's claim that the bill had "the sanction of the Nanaimo miners," the subsequent act curtailed child labour far more sharply than the miners wished. Legislators inserted quietly, with little debate, a clause that barred most boys from work in coal mines. It was so restrictive – no boys under twelve were permitted to work; boys under sixteen were limited to six hours of work per day underground and thirty hours of work per week; special approval from the province (on the grounds of thin seams) was required to hire boys under fourteen – that mine managers had little incentive to employ boys. The act was clearly an effort to legislate boys out of the pits.[70]

In other coalfields, mine proprietors would have been up in arms over these restrictions to their labour supply. As British Columbia Supreme Court Justice George Walkem observed, employers protested any such limitation, "as it materially lessens competition in labour, and thereby increases the expense of the production of their coal."[71] On Vancouver Island, the powerful local mine owners petitioned vigorously against the act, calling for a select committee or commission "to enquire as to the necessity for such a measure."[72] They also supported the lobby that emerged rapidly within local coalfields against the act's stringent child labour clauses, although the vigour of their objections was certainly muted by the presence of a plentiful alternative supply of unskilled mine labour, the Chinese. Even the provincial mines inspector observed that "[m]any complaints have been made to me in regard to Section 5, 'Coal Mines Regulation Act, 1877.' It is felt to be a great hardship by many parents that boys of from 14 to 16 years of age cannot get work in these mines on account of this section. The fact is, that although this section allows them to work, yet it is only for 6 hours a day, and then only 5 days in the week; therefore the employers will not engage them at all, as they can get Chinamen to do the same work for the same price, and work the full shifts. I think it would be a great boon to many if this section was amended so that boys of 14 years of age were allowed to work the same hours as a man."[73]

In light of strong opposition to these child labour clauses – and in a rare instance of a backward step in the extension of protective legislation for children – the Mines Act was amended in 1883 to make

fourteen-year-olds eligible for full-time employment. Robert Dunsmuir suggested that he would replace Chinese men with white boys.
"The parents of the children were in favor of the change," he argued,
"as it would prevent the employment of many Chinese." The provincial press agreed. "The law as it stands makes 16 the minimum
age; and it is found that in consequence of that restriction Chinese
get employment that would otherwise fall to white youths," the
Victoria *Daily British Colonist* observed. "The bill seems to be a good
one."[74] Although boys remained marginal in Dunsmuir's collieries,
their numbers increased slightly in Vancouver Island mines from the
late 1880s (see Table 3.1).

While the old coalfields of Nova Scotia and Vancouver Island were
the major sites of child labour in Canada, other coal-producing provinces also ultimately drafted child labour clauses into their Mines
Acts. The North-West Territories passed an ordinance in 1899 stipulating that no females or boys under twelve years of age were to be
employed underground at mines.[75] The Alberta Coal Mines Act of
1906 maintained this requirement and added that no boy, until he
reached the age of sixteen, could be employed at a mine "unless he
is able to read and write and is familiar with the rules of arithmetic
as far as and including division."[76] Nonetheless, members of the 1907
provincial Royal Commission on Coal Mining heard miner after
miner advocate tighter restrictions on child labour. Edward Holmes,
a miner at Coleman, was typical of these voices. He had started to
work in the mines in England at nine years of age. He felt, however,
that boys should not be employed in any capacity at mines until the
age of fourteen, and that they should be sixteen before working
underground. Other Alberta miners felt likewise: Reese Evans, a
miner at Bellevue, argued that pit boys should not start before fourteen or fifteen years of age; George Cunningham, a pit boss (a minor
official) at the Morinville Coal Company, advocated a law prohibiting
boys from non-gaseous mines until fourteen and from gaseous mines
until sixteen; James Sutherland, a miner at Morinville, felt that fourteen was the proper age for a boy to begin to work in a mine, although
he had started at twelve years of age.[77] In 1913 the Alberta Mines Act
was amended to reflect such concerns: it fixed a minimum age of
sixteen for underground employment and of fourteen for employment on the mine surface. Women were limited to jobs in mine
offices.[78] Although mines had operated in the province on a small
scale for over two decades, Saskatchewan only passed legislation
restricting child labour in mines in 1917. The law prohibited boys
under the age of fourteen and all women and girls from mine employment.[79] New Brunswick, the last coal-producing province to pass

legislation restricting the mining workforce, fixed a minimum age of sixteen for underground mine workers in its Mines Act of 1933.[80]

Few were as sanguine about the effectiveness of early legislation – or as dismissive of the extent of child labour – as the first federal deputy minister of labour. "I am of the opinion," wrote William Lyon Mackenzie King in 1902, "that the question of the employment of children has never been a serious one in this country. Where it has the laws of the several Provinces have been speedily framed to meet possible abuses."[81] King failed to appreciate the considerable distance between the passage of legislation and its adequate enforcement, let alone compliance.[82] The impact of legislation depended very much on local circumstances and the enforcement mechanisms employed.[83]

Yet with respect to the child labour clauses of the British Columbia Mines Act, King was at least partially correct. Armed with clear legislation, the power to fine, and at least the toleration of provincial coal operators, mines inspectors were able to enforce the act effectively. If a small number of boys worked illegally, as in the case of the Wellington miner who employed his underage son in 1891, one inspector was more than adequate to supervise the handful of pits on Vancouver Island.[84] Legislation curtailed child labour in that province as early as the 1870s.[85]

In contrast, Robert Drummond claimed in 1902 that managers in Nova Scotia were not even aware of the existence of minimum-age provisions.[86] Reports of the employment of underage children were not infrequent. The *Trades Journal* noted in 1882, for instance, that an eight-year-old labourer, "a very precocious little chap," was employed at the Halifax Company's mine in Pictou County. Naming the boy's father, the report stressed that the boy "will make a bright scholar if he has a fair chance of education."[87] But the minimum-age clauses of the Nova Scotia Mines Act were almost certainly widely observed, if only because few workers below the age of employment stipulated in the act (ten in 1873 for underground work, twelve in 1891) could be usefully employed in the mine. Alberta boasted one of the few instances of a coal company being prosecuted for the employment of underage workers. When the young boy Michel Angelo Valpiola, employed as a brakeman on a compressed air locomotive, was killed underground at Bellevue in February 1910, mines officials prosecuted Western Canadian Collieries Limited under the provincial Mines Act, both because the lad was under sixteen while employed underground and because he had been employed above ground in 1908 while under twelve years of age. The company pleaded guilty to both charges and was fined $20 and costs on each.[88]

The effect of school legislation was both slower and more profound. If the first steps towards compulsory education were tentative,
by early in the twentieth century they were having some effect in
placing those labelled "children" in the classroom. In the nineteenth
century, attendance was irregular and to some extent seasonal. Work
and school could be intertwined. Twelve-year-old Robert McTagarth
of Springhill recounted that "when on the night shift I used to go to
school too."[89] In Cape Breton, attendance was relatively good in the
winter, when mine work was scarce. And at other times of the year
colliery boys might attend school on days when there was no work
at the mine. Alexander McEachren, a mine manager who had started
to work in the pit as a trapper boy, declared he had attended school
on days the mine was not worked.[90] The manager at Glace Bay
claimed in 1888 that "the boys who work in the mine when they are
idle attend school too"; the colliery accountant affirmed that "[i]n the
winter months they frequently attend school."[91]

Statistics for attendance were maintained from the advent of free
and universal public education in the major nineteenth-century
coalfields of British Columbia and Nova Scotia. In British Columbia,
local statistics were published. On Vancouver Island, boys' enrolment
at Nanaimo Public School increased over 50 percent from 1876–77 to
1877–78 (from 93 to 133), potentially in response to the 1877 Mines
Act. That same year, boys' enrolment at Wellington rose from 25 to
40.[92] But concerns persisted. Of a school-age population of 300 at
Nanaimo, only were 248 enrolled, and the average daily attendance
was only 154. Teachers, in the view of school officials, were "hindered
in their good work by local peculiarities."[93]

In Nova Scotia, data were published at the county level, which
unfortunately reduces their usefulness. These statistics offer nonetheless a broad picture of school attendance patterns. They indicate that
compliance with school legislation, embracing increasingly older
children for longer stretches of the year, gradually improved. If
during the 1870s and 1880s perhaps 50 percent of registered children
actually attended school on any given day, the figure rose to over
60 percent by the 1890s and to over 70 percent by the end of the
1900s. The attendance of children in the mining counties followed
this trend. Cape Breton County attendance remained just a few percentage points lower than the provincial average until 1906; by 1910
it consistently exceeded the provincial figure. More stringent legislation was evaded less often as children were gradually removed from
the world of work and seated in the classroom.[94]

By the twentieth century, debate over school attendance had
shifted from universal compulsory education (that children should

attend school for at least a certain period of their lives) to the appropriate school-leaving age. The mine manager at Springhill told the federal Labour Commission in 1888 that boys generally quit school at thirteen, but that "some go till 14 or 15."[95] Nationally, the average age at which children left school increased from 14.38 in 1911 to 16.25 in 1931, although mining towns remained a special focus of concern among education officials.[96] "If boys felt that the public school fitted them for life," one miner argued, "they would stay longer, and teachers must be competent to attract young men, who feel they ought to be earning."[97] Practical mining courses were introduced in public schools in Nova Scotia's mining communities after Grade 7 to encourage boys to remain in school.[98] Nonetheless, the provincial director of technical education, F.H. Sexton, felt that the compulsory attendance legislation (at that time, to the age of fourteen) was "not enforced in the industrial districts of Nova Scotia nearly as stringently as it should be."[99] Dr. James H. Bingay, superintendent of schools for Glace Bay, claimed in 1922 "that in mining centres boys dropped out of school early and in grade ten the girls outnumbered the boys at the rate of two to one."[100]

Although in the twentieth century schools came to have a profound impact on children's experience, compulsory schooling legislation, the most comprehensive, most coercive expression of the reconstructed childhood, had a limited role in restricting child labour in Canadian coal mines. Implemented gradually and often indifferently enforced, especially in the nineteenth century, compulsory attendance regulations at best put pressure on mining families to delay boys' entry into the mine. In Nova Scotia and British Columbia, where most pit boys laboured, province-wide compulsory attendance even to the age of fourteen was not legislated until after the First World War. Mines legislation was a different matter. While nineteenth-century legislation in Nova Scotia curtailed the employment of only the youngest pit boys, it had a role in excluding most boys from employment in the mines on Vancouver Island.

CHAPTER SIX

The Mining Family

The miner who "get[s] comfortable is a man that has a number of boys."
Nova Scotian mine manager, 1888

Although the new industrial workplaces emerging in the nineteenth century vastly altered the circumstances in which children laboured, the rationale for their employment remained unchanged. Children worked as part of a collective response within working families to the insecurity of their lives.[1] Any study of the mining family has to be sensitive both to its economic vulnerability – breadwinners died regularly in coal mines, or became disabled, or became sick, or became unemployed, or were underemployed – and to its long-term strategic concerns, notably the pressure to put by for old age. All members of the family laboured at tasks that reflected physical ability and cultural assumptions.[2] Men and older boys worked outside the home, for wages. Women and younger children did not. In the nineteenth century, the wages earned by boys gave the Nova Scotian mining family a precious measure of security. Pressure within the family to place boys in the mines was not reduced until adults' wage income increased from the mid-1890s and insurance and pension programs improved in the early twentieth century.

The industrial working-class family, Bettina Bradbury has underlined, was a complex institution. Family members were "bound together by bonds of kinship, marriage, and cultural tradition, by their past history, and often by present circumstances and economic need." Yet, she adds, "families also contained individuals of different ages and sexes, with unequal power and legal rights within the family."[3] While elements of family decision-making may have been negotiated, the preponderant voice within the family belonged to the

Note: Portions of this chapter were published previously as "The Family Economy and Boy Labour in Sydney Mines, 1871–1901," *Nova Scotia Historical Review* 13, no. 2 (1993): 87–100.

adult male breadwinner. The freedom of choice boys had within the family depended largely on their age. Older boys, closer to economic independence, enjoyed greater latitude in crucial areas such as their entry into the mine, the disposition of their earnings, and their residence within the parental home.

The slow withdrawal from the land and its resources that accompanied the transition to an urban and industrial society gave wage labour a central place among family survival strategies. Research on the major urban centres of Montreal and Toronto has emphasized that for all but a narrow and privileged segment of the working class, the adult male's wages were inadequate to support a family, at least not until well into the twentieth century.[4] Sheer survival, let alone the "degree of comfortable independence" Chad Gaffield has underlined as a basic goal, was beyond the reach of families employing the prescribed strategy of limiting wage-earners to adult males.[5]

Working-class families, in seeking this "comfortable independence," necessarily adopted a range of responses to supplement uncertain wage income, responses whose staggering variety testifies to these families' resourcefulness. Even in urban areas, gardens, pigs, cows, and chickens were kept; outside of cities, hunting and fishing were widespread. Food produced domestically could be consumed, bartered, or sold. Income was also generated through other petty sales and through services such as washing clothing, cleaning houses, or taking in lodgers.[6] Families also turned to secondary wage-earners. Women's paid labour has been explored in a growing literature.[7] Relatively limited attention has been paid in Canada to the place of child labour in the family. Historians of the working class, noting that the use of child labour was greatest among families headed by labourers or semi-skilled workers, have tied the practice closely to family need. Some have simply noted that the poorest segments of the working class were most likely to place their children on the labour market. At other times a stronger claim is made, that children's wage earnings were required for family subsistence.[8] Given the gender-based division of labour in mining communities, secondary wage-earners were necessarily boys.[9] But how necessary were boys' wage earnings to the mining family?

Springhill manager William Hall readily acknowledged in 1888 that family need had a role in determining when boys started to work in the pits. "Those who can afford to do it keep their boys [in school] as long as they can; it is only those who cannot afford to keep them that put them to work at a younger age." He observed that all children spent some time in school, but that they generally ceased to attend at thirteen years of age. In families where economic pressure was less, children were able to attend school to the age of fourteen or fifteen.[10] By the twentieth century, as child labour came to be viewed as illegitimate, it became far more contentious. Miners and mine operators argued the issue in 1920, a period by which children were expected to spend considerably more time in school, before the federal Commission on Coal Mining Conditions in the Maritime Provinces. Miners linked child labour with poor adult wage earnings. UMWA District 26 President Robert Baxter observed: "[W]e find there are boys working at 13 and 14, and the only conclusion we can come to under those circumstances is that the conditions of supporting a family are so hard that it is necessary for the parents of that family to get the wherewithal in one way or another, and they put their children in the mines so they can get the wages of those children to give the other children some of the comforts they desire to give them."[11] Miners made appeals to the commissioners on behalf of their families: "[I]f you decide in favor of the workers you will give them better things for their families and homes and give them an opportunity to educate their children and clothe them in respectability."[12]

Mine operators were dismissive of miners' claims. W. Benton Evans, owner of the mid-sized Rothwell Colliery in New Brunswick, testified that "when the miners are given an increase of wages they work less time. It is a matter with a good many of them of working just enough to make enough money to live on, and when they have got that they stop."[13] He went on to review his experience of boys in the pits:

[S]peaking for our own Company only, we have had but very, very few cases in recent years where boys have worked. We had one case just recently of a boy about 12 years of age working with his father a few weeks. They had quite a large family, undoubtedly; but the fact that he worked with his father wasn't because his father couldn't make sufficient wages; it was because his father didn't want to work, because he only worked three or four or five days a week – generally three or four. If he worked as some other miners work he could easily have made money enough to keep his family without any trouble. In fact that man has left our employ, and when he came to me and said he was going I offered him a job on the surface, where he wouldn't be overworked, at $25.50 a week, and he said, No, he was going to the Marysville Cotton Mills. I said, "You can't get that money there!" "No," he said, "but when I go up there my wife can work and my boy can work."

We had another case of a boy in the vicinity of 14 years of age. We put him in a place where the top was good, and he worked by himself under a man who had a contract. As far as I could make out in his case he has simply got to earn his own living, as his father doesn't seem to want to keep him.

In a sentence, employers argued that whatever the reason children laboured, it "isn't because the father can't make money enough."[14] These conflicting claims reflect the late-nineteenth- and early-twentieth-century discourse over child labour. On the one hand, it is portrayed as a necessary response to working-class subsistence needs because of poor adult wage levels. On the other, working-class parents are condemned as idle and exploitative.[15]

Within the working class, the adult male's wage income was always of critical importance to family survival strategies.[16] The miner's nominal earnings were relatively high, comparable to the daily income of the skilled urban worker.[17] In Nova Scotia, they averaged from $1.25 to $2.00 daily over the last decades of the nineteenth century.[18] But two factors depressed the miner's earnings, making his take-home pay by the last decades of the nineteenth century approximate far more closely that of urban unskilled labourer, with whom child labour was generally associated in late-nineteenth-century Canada, than that of the urban skilled worker to whom the miner likened himself. First, while irregular work was a common feature of working-class life, the miner's labour was subject to particularly acute seasonal rhythms.[19] Until the late nineteenth century, even large Nova Scotian mines operated irregularly – on average only 193 days in 1880. On Cape Breton Island, where ports were closed by ice during the winter months, the average was lower.[20]

The second factor increasing the gap between a miner's nominal and take-home earnings was the number of deductions to which his pay packet was subject: for powder, oil, tools, the school, the colliery doctor, even to support local clergy. These might amount to $30 or $40 from a gross wage income that might not reach $300 or $400 annually in late-nineteenth-century Nova Scotia, at a time when the average working-class male in Ontario brought home roughly $450 annually.[21] In addition to these negotiated deductions, the miner was also subject to fines, levied if the tubs of coal he sent up contained too many impurities.[22] His nominal daily wage could also disguise deductions for a loader, notably in western Canada, where there was less opportunity for a miner to bring a son or young relative into the mine to assist him.[23] Among late-nineteenth-century workers, the miner was not exceptionally well paid.

Families, in developing their economic strategies, had to account for the modest level of adult male wage earnings. They also faced two inalienable threats: the daily possibility of the death, disability, or illness of the adult breadwinner; and his ultimate infirmity in old age. The mine was an exceptionally dangerous workplace: mine accidents occurred with tragic frequency. The major explosions –

Springhill in 1891, Nanaimo in 1887, Hillcrest, Alberta, in 1914 – seized newspaper headlines; but over the years it was the small accidents, commonly falls of rock from the mine roof, that took the greater toll of mine workers.[24] More difficult to establish today was the price in men's lives exacted by mining-related illnesses such as blacklung, a debilitating respiratory condition. In the absence of appropriate provisions, disabled miners faced a shameful loss of independence: "Men have been maimed for life, and the burden of their future maintenance thrown on their relations and friends."[25]

Varieties of limited insurance did exist. Fraternal orders were a common means of insuring against accidents or doctor's fees or the costs of a funeral.[26] Miners might also subscribe to a benefit society. A "widows and orphans" fund was in existence at the Drummond Colliery as early as 1873; it provided one dollar weekly for boys under the age of thirteen and girls under fifteen (these ages suggest when children were considered capable of earning their keep). More local societies emerged during the 1880s in Nova Scotia, including one at the Albion Mines in 1881 and another at Bridgeport by 1883.[27] After a number of earlier attempts, a relief fund was in operation at Springhill by mid-decade (orphan children received benefits to the age of twelve).[28] These societies were not universal, being open only to those who could afford to pay the regular subscription fees. Nor were they comprehensive. They commonly provided against short-term illness or accident and offered benefits for widows and orphans, but they did not offer pensions and did not necessarily provide insurance against total disability. Many miners were not affiliated with them.[29] The characteristic means of insurance in the nineteenth century remained the informal collection at the pit-head taken on behalf of a needy community resident.[30]

Families also had to take steps against the ultimate infirmity of the adult male breadwinner, whose working life was not simply dangerous – it was also short. The miner was typically a young man. Fifty-five percent of Nanaimo miners in 1891 were under thirty years of age.[31] The proportion of youthful miners was even greater in Nova Scotia, where, in 1908, 35.7 percent of mine workers were under twenty years of age and 67 percent were under thirty. Only 6.4 percent were over fifty years old.[32] "One is impressed, first of all, by their extreme youth," wrote a journalist in describing striking Cape Breton miners in 1925.[33] By the age of forty or forty-five, reported union official Dan Livingstone in 1919, a miner was considered old.[34]

Small savings societies were organized in the coalfields as early as 1868, when the Sydney Mines Industrial and Provident Society was

Table 6.1
Occupations of Elderly Men, Sydney Mines, 1901

Age in Years	Collier	Other Mine Work	Other Occupation	None	Total
Over fifty	23.8 (43)	37.6 (68)	25.3 (46)	13.3 (24)	100 (181)
Over sixty	12.5 (11)	39.8 (35)	30.7 (27)	17 (15)	100 (88)
Over seventy	10.3 (3)	27.1 (8)	41.9 (12)	20.7 (6)	100 (29)

Note: Percentage figures are given first, followed in brackets by the number of individuals falling in a given category. For example, of the 181 men over fifty years of age in Sydney Mines in 1901, forty-three, or 23.8 percent, gave the occupation of collier to the census taker. Most men occupied under the category "other mine work" were labourers, but the category includes a handful of mine officials.

Source: NA, Records of Statistics Canada (RG 31), Sydney Mines, Mss Census, 1901.

incorporated with the declared aim of providing "a safe and profitable investment [in real estate] for the small savings of the working man."[35] However, in coalfields where coal companies permitted privately owned dwellings, the most characteristic form of investment was the purchase of a house. It could be used to generate revenue from boarders; if necessary, the elderly could mortgage their home in their "declining years."[36]

In the absence of a pension or adequate savings, mine workers were compelled to continue working. A man could find work at the mines to almost any age: the miner no longer capable of work at the coalface moved back to the lighter work of boys. As one elderly mine worker explained, "an experienced miner in his old age can work on the surface when [he gets] too old to work at the face."[37] "[T]he miner is like an old horse," explained another miner in 1919, "he works until he is done and then they pull him away out in some other place."[38] "I know of old miners who are working in the mines who should be at home," reported T.J. Brown, general superintendent of the Nova Scotia Steel and Coal Company, in 1908.[39] John McDonald was still working at the age of seventy when he was mortally injured by an empty trip of mine cars in 1890.[40] A seventy-two-year-old deputy manager was employed at Sydney Mines in 1905, having entered the mines at the age of thirteen.[41] In 1906, seventy-five-year-old Joseph Maddison, calling himself the oldest miner in the world, still laboured at Springhill. He claimed to have started work at the age of six and a half in Durham, England.[42] A visitor to Nanaimo in 1898 noted that "[a]mong the workmen returning to the town are several showing the signs of advancing age."[43] In Sydney Mines, only 17 percent of men over sixty years of age, and not quite 21 percent of men over seventy, did not report an occupation in 1901 (see Table 6.1).

When an elderly miner was incapable of working and had no savings, the support of family and friends was sought. The federal Royal Commission on Industrial Relations heard frequently of this concern in 1919: "I know," one miner stated, "that when a man gets old he cannot earn sufficient money to keep him, and then he falls back on his sons and daughters, or if he has no sons and daughters who are willing to share their lot with him, he must go to the Poor House, and when a man works hard all his life and there is nothing ahead of him but the Poor House I think it is a disgrace, and I think that we, as voters, should hang our heads with shame to see our old men going under."[44] Working-class parents were necessarily sensitive to the need to make provision against old age. The threat of the loss of independence, to be thrown on the uncertain means and patience of family, friends, or a wider community, was a powerful preoccupation.

Excluded from the mine, women in coal communities were poorly placed to contribute wage earnings to the household. Only a small number may have found work as domestic servants, retail clerks, seamstresses, schoolteachers, or office help.[45] Even in Nanaimo, rare among mining communities for its economic diversity, only 10 percent of women in the census area were "gainfully employed" in 1891.[46] Most women were raised in mining communities to be wives and mothers. Others faced spinsterhood in the home of relatives. The rest left mining towns in search of a job.[47] "[Y]oung men grumble a good deal at this," the *Trades Journal* reported in 1885.[48]

The miner's wife took charge of all domestic labour, to the schedule set by the mine. If the miner went down the pit at six or seven in the morning, his wife arose considerably earlier, to light the stove and prepare his breakfast. She also made lunches, placed in metal containers called "piece cans" to frustrate the rats in the pit.[49] When family wage-earners were employed on different schedules, as was common with the growth of shift work at collieries in the early twentieth century, these tasks were repeated throughout the day. "The double shift system," one miner testified in 1920, "makes for dissatisfaction and trouble in the home. Perhaps the husband is coming in in the morning, and the children going to school, the boys may be on day shift. They come and go at all hours, and meals have to be served night and day. The house is in an uproar the whole 24 hours."[50] Mine workers returned home, exhausted and hungry, their body and clothing filthy with perspiration and coal dust, expecting a warm bath and hot food ready for them. Because of the labour required in fetching and heating water, the establishment of pit-head showers at many mines from the 1890s was more of a boon to his wife than to the miner.[51]

At other times, women cleaned the house and washed clothing – coal dust was a particular problem. They sewed. They minded young children. They shopped and baked and canned food. They fetched fuel and water. "Look, I don't know what you'd call her," one elderly miner recalled of his mother. "She cuts my hair, she used to half sew my shoes, she used to make my clothes. I don't know if she's a tailor, a shoemaker, or what she was – or a breadmaker. You had a big family and that's what you had to do in those days."[52] The large size of the typical mining family increased the burden carried by the miner's wife. Relatively high earnings at a young age encouraged early marriage and its consequence, a higher birth rate. In Great Britain and the United States, mining families had at least one more child than the national average, if not more.[53] John Belshaw has undertaken the only detailed examination of family size in a Canadian coalfield. In 1891 the average age at first birth of the Nanaimo miner's wife was 20.7, several years younger than the Canadian average.[54]

Housing in coal communities was commonly substandard and overcrowded. A traveller to Wellington described the community in 1898 as "very wretched and poverty stricken."[55] The Chinese on Vancouver Island inhabited "wretched hovels."[56] "The mining towns, as a rule, can only be described in one way," reported Nova Scotian commissioners in 1910, "they are ugly."[57] The Quirk Commission on Mining Conditions in the Maritimes noted in 1920, *before* the distress associated with the industrial strife of 1922–25, that "the Housing, domestic surroundings and sanitary conditions of the [Cape Breton] miners are absolutely wretched."[58] Cape Breton trade unionist Silby Barrett noted in 1919 that "[t]he woman here has to do all her work and look after her children in one room downstairs."[59] In Minto, New Brunswick, one-half of the mining workforce inhabited "jerry-built tar-paper and beaver-board shacks" provided by the company.[60] These conditions had their consequences. Eugene Forsey observed in 1926 that Glace Bay had the highest infant mortality rate in Canada.[61]

Wives were in charge of the family purse. Their careful management of the family budget helped to stretch modest and irregular wage earnings. Miner Murdock McLeod had no idea of the cost of groceries. "I let my wife manage the house and buy things," added Springhill miner Elisha Paul, also in 1888, "and I don't know much about that business."[62] Miner Arthur Petrie told the Duncan Commission in 1925 that miners' wives were best placed to testify to the inadequacy of the wages the British Empire Steel Company paid its miners.[63] To a limited extent, women also brought earnings into the household: from the sale of garden produce, from taking in washing from local managers or professionals, or from taking in lodgers.[64]

Sophia Anderson supported herself and her daughter on the basis of ten lodgers in South Nanaimo in 1891.[65]

Non-wage-earning children assisted to the best of their ability with cleaning, shopping, supervising younger siblings, running messages, laundry, fetching water.[66] They could also be useful foragers, notably in ensuring a good supply of domestic fuel. It was work not without peril. In an incident at the Drummond Colliery in 1889 a mine official set a boy on a youngster sent to scavenge coal, applying "the finishing touches" himself.[67] At Glace Bay in 1911, two coal "thieves" were brought before the stipendiary magistrate and fined one dollar apiece.[68]

If "pigs, cows, and boarders" were crucial to family survival strategies in late-nineteenth-century Montreal, they played that much more important a role in the semi-rural coal districts. Miners fished, hunted, and raised domestic animals.[69] Other mining families kept boarders.[70] Most importantly, miners traditionally kept a garden. Montreal journalist A.G. Gilbert commented in 1867 on the number of miners' houses with gardens in Nova Scotia.[71] Their access to non-wage forms of income was precious to mining families. For many in Nova Scotia, their gardens – and some fishing – allowed them to stave off famine during the coal depression of the mid-1870s. The Nova Scotia *Mines Report* for 1876 remarked on "the wisdom of the many [in Cape Breton] who sought to eke out a livelihood by such planting and fishing as they could command." Two years later, when the mines at Springhill operated for 223 days, those in Pictou Country averaged only 171 days. On Cape Breton, where mines only operated on average for 135 days, the miners "suffered from a scarcity of work; and had it not been that many of them were able on idle days to fish, or to plant potatoes, and to thereby lay in a small store of provisions, they would be poorly off indeed."[72] Even in the early twentieth century the Nova Scotian miner's house always had "a plot of ground attached, suitable for a good-sized garden."[73]

Coal companies encouraged gardening by providing seed and fertilizer: gardening reduced necessary wage levels and also helped to tie the miner to a given community by fostering a sense of proprietorship. In Nanaimo, the colliery company leased five-acre properties called "crofts" where miners were encouraged to grow food. Some mining families put agricultural produce on the local market.[74] When subsistence became the issue of industrial disputes, as it did in Cape Breton in the early 1920s, employers complained of the inadequacy of miners' efforts to plant gardens. The owner of the British Empire Steel and Coal Company, Roy Wolvin, grumbled in 1925 that miners had failed to take advantage of his offer in 1921 of free plowing and fertilizer, with seed potatoes at cost.[75] At the same time, non-

Table 6.2
Boys' Daily Pay, Nova Scotia, 1888

Occupation	Cape Breton	Mainland
Trappers	$.32–.40	$.50–1.00
Drivers	.60–.85	.50–1.00
Boys on balances		.80–1.00
Loaders		1.20–1.30
Labourers	.85–1.00	

Note: The *Trades Journal* had earlier (16 June 1880) published wage scales for mainland Nova Scotia: trappers earned thirty-five to fifty cents daily; drivers, fifty to seventy cents daily; and chain-runners, sixty cents to one dollar a day.
Source: Gilpin, "Coal Mining in Nova Scotia," 377.

wage forms of income were a two-edged sword for employers: at times of lengthy strikes, Allen Seager has observed, "it became difficult, if not impossible, to starve a community into submission."[76]

The nineteenth-century mining family faced considerable insecurity arising from uncertain adult male income, the possible disability or death in the mine of the adult male breadwinner, and his ultimate infirmity. Non-wage forms of income provided a partial response. Many mining families also chose to multiply the number of their wage workers.[77] A family's ability to do this was contingent on its stage in the family life cycle. Baskerville and Sager have noted that in Canadian urban centres, per capita family income in 1901 was highest when couples were young and without children.[78] With little access to female wage earnings, mining families' income cycle differed from that of the urban working-class families, which lost female earnings with the arrival of children. Like other working-class families, a brief period of relative affluence was enjoyed by mining families during the working years of co-resident children.

Boys' wage contribution to family income could be substantial.[79] In the 1880s, the youngest boys started at between thirty and fifty cents daily in Nova Scotia. Older boys could earn up to a dollar daily, the wage level of the mine labourer (see Table 6.2). If compared with the average pay packet of the adult miner, boys' earnings were a considerable supplement to family income. Over the last third of the nineteenth century, the miner averaged between one and two dollars daily. Two adolescent boys in the mine might double family income at a time when the miner's wage earnings, dependent on his output of coal, may have begun to decline as his strength waned with middle age. A Bridgeport (Cape Breton) miner claimed in 1891: "A few years ago myself an' son could only make three hundred dollars a year, an' that I thought was not so bad. Last year meself an' two boys made over nine hundred. I have a nest egg in the Co-operative Store. My family is well rigged fer the winter. I have plenty of grub laid by fer the next three months."[80] The miner who "get[s] comfortable," as the federal Labour Commission was told in 1888, "is a man that has a number of boys." Added H.S. Poole, at that time manager of the Acadia Coal Company, "I am under the impression that a man who has a large family of boys, when they are large enough to act as drivers and loaders, is the man who makes the money as a rule."[81] In late-nineteenth-century Nova Scotia, the economic incentive to bring boys into the mine was powerful.

Boys in the pit also contributed to family income in other ways. As helpers in the bord to their father or an older brother, they spared him the expense of paying a non-family member. Moreover, at some pits a boy as helper entitled the miner to an increased "turn" of coal tubs, allowing him to boost his production of coal. It was a persistent complaint of miners that they did not receive an adequate supply of coal tubs because underground haulage failed to keep up to the coal they could cut and load.[82] Also, parents knew that if a boy did not choose mining as an occupation, he was likely to have to leave the community in search of alternative work. If they did go into the mine, in contrast, sons were likelier to be at hand later to take infirm or elderly parents into their homes if the need arose. The crucial place of boys' earnings in family survival strategies was evident in parents' attempts to go to court to seek compensation after a boy's death in the pit. John O'Henly, for instance, took action against the Acadia Coal Company in 1888 after the death of his boy, also John, in the Vale Colliery.[83] Far from "sordid profiteering," Ian McKay observed, it was "more likely motivated by the desire of families to survive after the loss of an important breadwinner."[84]

The youngest boys, such as twelve-year-old Robert McTagarth and fifteen-year-old William Terrance, handed over their entire earnings to their parents, possibly receiving a small allowance in return.[85] As long as boys remained at home, at least some of their pay packet continued to be given to their parents. Yet as boys entered late adolescence, it became increasingly unlikely that all of their earnings were disposed of in this way. Boys' economic power was simply too great. Rather, boys "boarded" at home, contributing a portion of their earnings towards their maintenance.[86]

The obverse of the situation in late-nineteenth-century Nova Scotia, where mine work was available for boys, was the frustration over its lack encountered on Vancouver Island, the only other major contemporary coal mining region in Canada. Their inability to put their boys into the pits was "felt to be a great hardship by many parents."[87] It contributed to the rapid departure from Vancouver Island of a sizeable group of Scottish immigrant miners recruited by the Dunsmuirs in 1900–1901.[88] "[A]lthough nominal wage rates for white miners were in some cases as much as treble what was earned in British coalfields," John Belshaw has argued, "the difficulty of finding employment for more than one breadwinner per household in certain years and the slightly higher cost of living reduced and could even eliminate this advantage."[89]

Because of the large non-wage component of family budgeting, a statistical basis for family need for children's earnings can not be established by comparing adult male income levels with estimates of the cost of living. Incalculable, non-wage forms of income vitiate any attempt to establish family need for boys' wage earnings in this manner. But family need for child labour can be examined quantitatively by comparing those families that sent boys out to work with those families that did not. Whatever its imperfections as a historical source, the manuscript census – detailing information about every Canadian citizen – is a unique tool to enter the working-class household.[90]

Sydney Mines, perhaps the oldest mining community in Canada, is located on Cape Breton Island, on the north side of Sydney harbour. Drawing its livelihood from the collieries of the General Mining Association, the only employer of note in the community, Sydney Mines was a major site of mining and child labour throughout the nineteenth century. By 1871 the GMA employed 460 workers, who supported a population of 2,300 in the Sydney Mines area. Rapidly expanding demand for coal swelled the mines workforce to 700 and the local population to 3,200 by 1901.[91] In this single-industry coal town, there was very little work for wages available to women. But the colliery offered many opportunities for the employment of boys. Until the 1890s, boys accounted for approximately 25 percent of the underground workforce at Sydney Mines (see Table 4.1). There were 101 families with boys eligible to work for wages (aged from thirteen to seventeen inclusive) living in Sydney Mines in 1871, 138 in 1891, and 131 in 1901. Over the last thirty years of the nineteenth century a consistent (approximately) 60 percent of these families sent at least one son in this age range out to work (see Table 6.3).[92]

Were there features about families with boys in the pit that distinguished them from families that did not send boys into the pit? Attempts were made to correlate child labour with family dependents (those listed to be without an occupation). If family need was a prominent motive for boys to be sent to work, presumably more boys

Table 6.3
Sydney Mines Families with "Eligible" Boys,
1871–1901

Year	Total	Percentage Employing Boys
1871	101	59.4
1891	138	63
1901	131	60.3

Source: NA, RG 31, Sydney Mines, Mss Census, 1871–1901.

Table 6.4
Boys' Labour and Employed Adults,
1871–1901

Year	One	Two	Three
1871	56.1 (41)	64.0 (25)	66.7 (21)
1891	61.5 (65)	72.3 (47)	66.7 (18)
1901	51.1 (47)	66.7 (36)	66.7 (24)

Note: Percentage of families in each category (i.e., with one, two, or three
employed adults) that employ at least one eligible boy. The absolute number of
families follows in parentheses. The small number of families with no employed
adult, or with more than three, are excluded from this table. Unless noted
otherwise, figures are presented similarly in subsequent tables.
Source: NA, RG 31, Sydney Mines, Mss Census, 1871–1901.

would be working within larger families. But no clear trends emerged
from the data. Boys' labour was also correlated with the number of
employed adults (eighteen years of age and over) in the household
(see Table 6.4). If need was a strong motive for boy labour, we could
expect that the greater the number of employed adults residing within
a household, the lower the likelihood that boys were employed. In
Great Britain, the youngest children in working-class families frequently benefited by longer periods in school by virtue of the earnings of their older siblings.[93] In contrast, in Sydney Mines the
likelihood of the family employing at least one eligible boy increased
with the number of employed adults (to three). This data fails to indicate that younger siblings enjoyed longer periods of schooling. It does
support anecdotal evidence, as an Alberta miner affirmed, that "[c]oal
mining was more or less for family. If your father was a miner, you'd
go down to the office every morning before they started and look for
a job."[94] The large number of adults in Sydney Mines households is
likely attributable to youths' lengthy co-residence within the parental

Table 6.5
Marital Status of Men in Sydney
Mines, 1901

Age	Married	Single
18	2	38
20	1	26
23	8	26
26	25	16
29	19	11

Note: There was also one twenty-six-year-
old widower.
Source: NA, RG 31, Sydney Mines, Mss
Census, 1901.

Table 6.6
Boys' Labour and Income of Household Head, 1901

Under $350	$351 to 450	Over $450
66 (53)	52.2 (46)	62.5 (32)

Source: NA, RG 31, Sydney Mines, Mss Census, 1901.

home, where they generally resided – if they remained in the community – until marriage. In Sydney Mines, only when men were in
their mid-twenties were more married than single (see Table 6.5).

Because mine work was closely linked to specific families, which
at a certain phase of their life cycle would characteristically be sending two or three men and boys into the mine, major pit disasters such
as that at Springhill in 1891, in decimating the mine workforce, could
annihilate the male portion of mining families. Reid Carter, father of
the thirteen-year-old boy mortally wounded in the explosion, was
also killed. The McVeys lost sons David, sixteen, and James, fourteen.
The Ross family lost Philip and Murdock, also sixteen and fourteen.
The Beatons were more fortunate. Fifteen-year-old Dan Beaton was
able to carry his injured younger brother out of the mine.[95]

The interrelation between family need and child labour can be
most closely examined for 1901, when the census recorded individual
income for the previous year. By examining the income of the household head (almost always the father), it can be seen that boys were
almost as likely to be employed by households whose heads were in
the highest income bracket as by those in the lowest. Sixty-six percent
of households whose head earned less than $350 annually, with boys
aged between thirteen and seventeen, employed at least one of them;
but so did 62.5 percent of households where the head earned more
than $450 annually (see Table 6.6). If boys had been brought into the

Table 6.7
Boys' Labour and Total Household Income, 1901

Under $700	$701 to 1300	Over $1300
51.7 (60)	64.4 (45)	73.1 (26)

Source: NA, RG 31, Sydney Mines, Mss Census, 1901.

Table 6.8
Religion of Household Head and Boys' Labour,
1871–1901

Year	Presbyterian	Catholic
1871	59.1 (44)	57.5 (40)
1891	61.2 (49)	64.8 (71)
1901	48.8 (41)	63.0 (73)

Source: NA, RG 31, Sydney Mines, Mss Census, 1871–1901.

mines for immediate financial considerations, the incidence of child labour would be considerably lower in the highest income category. Indeed, the evidence indicates that the families enjoying the greatest aggregate income were those that made the most use of boys' labour. In families earning over $1,300 annually, 73.1 percent of eligible boys were employed; only 51.7 percent of eligible boys laboured in families whose aggregate income was under $700 annually (see Table 6.7). The pattern of use of boys' labour in Sydney Mines challenges conventional links between family need and child labour. At the same time, it appears to lend weight to the views of the advocates of the reconstructed childhood – harsh critics of child labour – who were quick to condemn working-class parents for their alleged exploitation of their children.[96]

What of "cultural" factors? We can begin by considering religion. In Sydney Mines two creeds predominated, Presbyterianism and Roman Catholicism. If there is little to choose between the disposition of household heads of either faith to employ their boys in 1871 and in 1891, by 1901 a clear difference had emerged. There was some movement away from wage labour among boys on the part of Presbyterian fathers by the turn of the twentieth century, whereas in Catholic households the pattern of use remained constant (see Table 6.8). The ethnic origin of the household head is also a potential variable, but it is of no use for Sydney Mines because its residents were overwhelmingly Scottish.

Literacy figures were collected by the census enumerators in 1871, when literate (defined here as the declared ability to write) household

Table 6.9
Literacy of Household Head and Boys' Labour, 1871–1891

Year	Head Able to Write	Unable
1871	64.4 (45)	55.4 (56)
1891	59.3 (91)	70.2 (47)

Source: NA, RG 31, Sydney Mines, Mss Census, 1871–1891.

Table 6.10
Boys' Labour by Household
Head Occupation, 1871–1901

Year	Miner
1871	73.3 (30)
1891	73.7 (38)
1901	56.4 (55)

Source: NA, RG 31, Sydney
Mines, Mss Census, 1871–1901.

heads were in a minority, and in 1891, when they accounted for two-thirds of all heads. If in 1871 literate heads were more likely to employ their boys, by 1891 the situation has reversed (see Table 6.9). In 1871 boys' labour retained a legitimate place among the educated working class; later in the century, signs of its rejection were evident, likely accounted for by the portion of the mining community most committed to the emerging public school systems.

The relation between the occupation of the household head and the incidence of child labour is also revealing. Focusing on households headed by a miner, we see that into the 1890s nearly three-quarters of miners employed at least one eligible son (see Table 6.10). But the decline in the use of their boys' labour by miners at the end of the century is striking and may reflect miners' efforts, discussed in Chapter 4, to steer their sons away from the mines.

This examination of Sydney Mines families during their most affluent years, when co-resident wage-earning sons were potential contributors to the family purse, challenges conventional links between child labour and subsistence. In Sydney Mines only 60 percent of families employed any of their "eligible" boys in any census year over the last three decades of the nineteenth century. At the same time, fewer than one-half of all boys eligible to labour (i.e., aged from thirteen to seventeen) were reported to be employed. Clearly, labouring families in Sydney Mines coped in the absence of their boys' earnings. Those families most likely to have sons employed in the mine have been identified. A clear relation between immediate family need and boys' employment in the mines does not emerge.

Were boys sent to work, or did they choose to enter the mines? In the absence of immediate family need (to the extent that conclusions drawn from Sydney Mines apply to other coal communities), there was presumably scope for a certain freedom of choice on the part of the boy and his parents. The lengthiest nineteenth-century discussion on this question occurred when members of the federal Royal Commission on the Relations between Capital and Labour toured the Nova Scotian coalfields in 1888. Mine managers were unanimous in their claims that parents requested them to find work for their boys; all witnesses – managers, miners, boys – reported that this request was made at boys' prompting. Recognizing the commissioners' preoccupation with child labour, managers were at pains to minimize their role in hiring boys. The manager of the Drummond Colliery, Robert Simpson, maintained both that he had "never heard of boys being forced to come; it is their inclination," and that parents encouraged boys to seek work at the mine "to get [them] to know what it is to work."[97] "[T]heir parents are their guardians," observed the Little Glace Bay manager, "and when they ask for work we give it."[98] Springhill miner Henry Rea testified that his boys had started work at twelve or thirteen years of age: "[T]hey felt as if they would sooner work than go to school; they were not doing much at school, so I let them go in."[99] Twelve-year-old Robert McTagarth was asked if he would not prefer to be in school. "I would rather work in the pit," he responded.[100]

One may wonder if the boys felt free to express their true views before their parents, mine managers, and royal commissioners, but elderly retired miners interviewed by Ian McKay in the 1970s also reported that as boys they had taken the initiative in going to work in the mine. One recounted his boredom with school and the attractions of the mine. Another boy "recall[ed] putting on two overcoats to convince a mining manager that he was 14, when in fact he was only 12."[101] Yet another retired miner boasted of convincing a manager he was sixteen, when he was actually far younger.[102] A retired Vancouver Island miner claimed: "They couldn't keep me out of the mines. I was bred a coal miner. My father was eight years old when his father was killed and he was diggin' coal when he was eleven. He was workin' on the face and he worked in the mines all his life. I left school on my own accord to work in the mines. They wanted me to keep going to school but I said, 'No dice!'"[103] Archie Mac-Donald started work at the age of fourteen in 1918 in a Cape Breton mine: "It was a big day when I went to the mine. It was the first job in which I made money. In other words, it meant I had my foot in the threshold of being a man – I would be somebody. I would be something on my own."[104] Nova Scotia's director of technical education, F.H. Sexton, noted unhappily in 1912 the eagerness of boys in colliery towns to leave school and enter the pit.[105]

In the mining family, boys learned not simply that certain work was women's; they learned also that men's work warranted both women's respect and the lion's share of the available food, drink, and leisure time.[106] Evidence from Great Britain points to a clear demarcation within the family between dependents (females and the youngest boys) and wage-earners (most other males). At the turn of the twentieth century, wives of Fife miners "oriented themselves round the men, leaving them the best chairs, filling their pipes on demand, getting their meals but never joining them at table … all the time the men were at home … the women would hover about ready to be instantly commanded for the most menial services."[107] Durham miner Jack Lawson recounted his experience of starting to work in his autobiography published in 1932: "I was a man and I knew it … I was entitled to as much meat as I wanted, and others were cleared out to make a seat for me. Even mother slightly deferred to me." He also expressed his satisfaction that he would receive no more "hand-me-downs."[108] The testimony of Nova Scotian women, who reported having waited as girls on their brothers at table, suggests that similar practices extended to Canada.[109] "The day of entering the mine was usually a happy one," Ian McKay has observed. "It represented a declaration of independence for the boys, and caused a wonderful change in their status at home. Now their sisters waited on them and they were treated like men."[110]

If by the turn of the twentieth century, the period from which most of the evidence is drawn, most families were not confronted with an insistent need for boys' earnings, there was latitude regarding if and when boys entered the mine. But it is doubtful that the boy whose father carried him to work, "the little fellow being unable [to manage] the long journey," or those who entered the pit still believing in Santa Claus, or who cried bitterly for their mother in the wake of the Springhill explosion in 1891, were of an age to choose freely to enter the mine.[111] Some boys were thrust into the mine by family crisis. Allie McKenzie "went in" at the age of nine after the death of his father.[112] One factor that delayed the age of entry into the mine was the scarcity of jobs for very small boys, who were confined to trapping and a handful of other positions.[113] Only when a boy reached a certain size and intelligence – perhaps at the age of twelve or thirteen

Table 6.11
Age of Entry into Labour Force, Sydney Mines, 1871–1901

Age	1871	1881	1891	1901
12-year-olds	1 (28)	0	2 (23)	6 (40)
13-year-olds	1 (25)	0	9 (42)	7 (33)
14-year-olds	7 (24)	0	15 (32)	14 (37)
15-year-olds	14 (25)	26 (37)	31 (40)	21 (36)
16-year-olds	25 (28)	30 (38)	28 (36)	24 (31)
17-year-olds	21 (24)	17 (20)	30 (39)	27 (35)

Note: These figures give the proportion of employed boys as recorded in the manuscript census for the Sydney Mines subdistrict for the "employable" age brackets. Thus, in 1871, of twenty-eight boys aged twelve, one was reported as employed. Although the use of children intensifies (with a greater proportion of employed children in the employable age brackets) as the century approached its close, documented child labour below the age of twelve remains very rare. An eight-year-old and an eleven-year-old were recorded as employed as general labourers in 1891; a ten-year-old was employed as a mine stable keeper in 1901.
Source: NA, RG 31, Sydney Mines, Mss Census, 1871–1901.

– was he able to drive a horse, let alone perform more onerous work. At the same time, the relatively low pay the smallest boys received may have encouraged families to defer sending them into the mine. Drivers earned twice the amount that trappers did (see Table 6.2). For these reasons, only at the age of fifteen were a clear majority of boys in Sydney Mines employed (see Table 6.11).

Lengthy co-residence within the parental home appears to have been common. There are only a handful of accounts of pit boys leaving home. The *Trades Journal* reported in 1887 that a number of boys had left the Albion Mines on account of the higher wages paid at Springhill. "It is said some of the boys [at the Albion Mines] are paid five cents a day less than paid them two years ago. This [erosion in pay] is reversing the natural order of things with a vengeance."[114] Similarly, in 1899 pit boys from Springhill, "twenty-five turbulent spirits," were alleged to have been the ringleaders of strikes in Cape Breton.[115] Parents exercised most control over the movements of their youngest children. When Vancouver Island miners walked away from their contracts with the Hudson's Bay Company in 1850, the only workers remaining of the small initial party brought out on contract from Scotland were its leader, John Muir, and his youngest son, a lad of nine or ten years. Muir's adolescent sons left Fort Rupert with the other workers.[116]

Notwithstanding their relatively large earnings as very young men, miners did not generally marry until the age of twenty-four or twenty-five (see Table 6.5). Bill Johnstone, who was to emigrate to western Canada within a few years, recalled his situation as a young man of twenty in the north of England: "I suppose I could have left home and searched for work in other parts of the country, but mining was the only thing I knew. This, and my fear of the unknown, held me back. I was also held by bonds of family loyalty. The extra few pounds that I contributed to the household were sorely needed."[117] This evidence underlines family success at arriving at mutually satisfactory compromises with respect to control over the earnings of resident sons and the deferral of sons' departure to start their own family. It also suggests that paternal authority was widely seen by boys to have been exercised legitimately. To paraphrase Katz and Davey's remarks about industrializing Hamilton, youths continued to live at home because they wanted to.[118]

The most basic measure of family need is the food, housing, and fuel absolutely necessary to survive. Because of the large numbers of families whose boys did not work for wages, it is clear that subsistence in nineteenth-century Nova Scotia did not depend on child labour. But mining families aspired to more. PWA Grand Secretary John Moffat described the miner's goal as "a good, comfortable home, education, music, good literature, [and] insurance with sufficient wages to lay by to help out in old age."[119] All family members wanted creature comforts; all benefited from insurance against the death, disability, or old age of the principal breadwinner. This modest standard of living involved considerably more expense, perhaps twice the outlay, than did subsistence.[120]

Given the gender-based division of labour, which excluded women from wage labour, and the evident ability of many mining families to keep eligible boys off the labour market, what was the place of child labour as a family survival strategy? Family subsistence was not contingent on boys' work in the mines; rather it was one of many tactics to which families resorted in the coal communities of industrializing Canada in their search for some modest degree of security.[121] That brief period of relative affluence during which the family had wage-earning co-resident sons was when provision had to be made for life's contingencies. In the short term, it was a buttress against the illness or accidental death of the principal breadwinner. In the long term, it helped parents meet the challenges of ageing. In the absence of immediate need, other variables were prominent in shaping family decision-making, as was evident in Sydney Mines. Parents, in sending their sons into the mine over the last decades of the nineteenth century, helped to gain a limited independence at the same time as they introduced their sons to their adult occupation.

Only in the twentieth century did the situation change for Nova
Scotian mining families: increased adult income, more formal insurance programs, and the introduction of pensions attenuated financial
pressure. Miners' income improved sharply at the turn of the twentieth
century, owing to higher daily earnings and, more importantly, more
regular work available in the mine.[122] By 1907, Nova Scotian miners'
income averaged from $630 to $860 annually; men operating mechanical cutters earned even more.[123] Higher wages permitted improved
access to insurance. Provincial contributory funds were strengthened;
many were amalgamated as the Dominion Coal Employees' Benefit
Society in 1910.[124] Provinces began to organize programs of insurance
against workplace accidents.[125] They also established pensions for
women with dependent children and without a male breadwinner.[126]
A Nova Scotia commission of inquiry in 1908 strongly urged that a
pension scheme be established for miners.[127] The Dominion Coal Company inaugurated a non-contributory pension scheme in 1923.[128] Traditional financial motives within the family for sending their boys to
work in the pit, if not removed, were weakened.

CHAPTER SEVEN

Boys in the Mining Community

Boys in coal towns are "particularly rough and uncultivated."
Nova Scotia teacher, 1886

At the centre of the boy's life in coal towns and villages was the mine. He was raised within sight of it; the smell of coal dust was as familiar to him as the sounds of steam pumps and hoists. The boy may have seen for years his father and older brothers leave for the pit. For most boys raised within these communities, the day arrived when they too surrendered their childhood to it. In the nineteenth century, boys raised in coal-mining towns and villages were expected to enter the mine. The class, gender, and cultural identities the community defined for boys encouraged them in this aim. But as childhood was reconstructed in the urban centres of late-nineteenth-century Canada, reservations over child labour filtered into coal communities. Teachers and school and mines inspectors arrived to enforce the new laws reflecting emerging views of childhood. Although they were seldom numerous, they helped to constitute a respectable, reforming middle class in coal towns. Organizations dedicated to the reconstructed childhood also entered coal towns and villages: the Woman's Christian Temperance Union (WCTU), Bands of Hope, Boy's Brigades, and the YMCA in the nineteenth century; in the twentieth, the Scouting movement, Children's Aid Societies, and public health nurses. More importantly, early trade unionists were also drawn to the emerging new standards of appropriate childhood. Advocates of compulsory education and restrictive mining legislation, they were instrumental in enforcing the legal redefinition of childhood in the coalfields. By the early twentieth century, the mining community was clearly ambivalent about boys' presence in the pit.

The coal community was marked by the mine, literally overshadowed by the prominent bankhead at the top of the pit housing its hoisting, dumping, and screening equipment. In close vicinity were pump and winding-engine houses, their large smokestacks and engines "blowing and snorting away most furiously," the lamp cabin, the fan house, stables, carpenter's and blacksmith's shops, and mine offices.[1] Various storehouses were also distributed about the mine surface, the one for explosives at a distance from the rest. Huge mounds of coal, awaiting shipment out, were adjacent to the bankhead, as were the substantial mounds of waste removed from the coal at the picking table. Piles of lumber to buttress the roof of working places and underground roads were collected prior to transport into the mine. A pond or reservoir to supply water for the steam engines was in the vicinity, as was a waste pond to collect the water pumped out of the mine. Also on the mine surface was the transportation infrastructure to ship coal out: rail lines inland, loading wharfs at the seaside. By the turn of the twentieth century, compressor sheds, coal-fired electrical generating stations, with their large chimneys, and wash houses for miners had been added to the colliery landscape.

Never far from the mine were the community buildings: churches with their adjacent cemetery, a schoolhouse, the company store, possibly independent retailers beyond company property, the temperance hall, and drinking establishments. Other community halls were erected by fraternal societies or trade union locals. The manager's residence, commonly on a hill overlooking the community, was a prominent landmark. The miners' far more modest dwellings clustered closer to the pit. Larger communities would have a town hall, hotels and restaurants, a bank, a post office, a variety of merchants, perhaps even a newspaper office or a small hospital.[2]

The earliest coal-mining communities in British North America were typically camps, with perhaps only a few dozen inhabitants, generally young, single, transient men. At Sydney Mines, until the arrival of the General Mining Association in 1827, the entire workforce of eighty or ninety men was accommodated in two log cookhouses; as well there were half a dozen log-and-sod huts for mine officials and craftsmen, a framed house, and a couple of storehouses. The men slept in bunk-beds along the cookhouse walls.[3] Nearly a century later, the primitive mining community remained unchanged. The mining camps of the Alberta Coal Branch were notorious for their fetid, overcrowded bunkhouses.[4]

Even once mining was well established, the population of the typical coal community was small. Coal was dug to be shipped out: little secondary industry developed at the site of mining. The towns and villages along the Cape Breton coast east of Sydney, developed around mines opened after the end of the GMA's monopoly, typically had 700 to 1,000 inhabitants in the 1880s: Victoria, Bridgeport, Reserve, Caledonia, Blockhouse, and Gowrie. Glace Bay was exceptional, with about 2,400 inhabitants at that time, the same number that inhabited Sydney Mines, north of Sydney harbour. Both towns grew rapidly with their surrounding collieries: Sydney Mines to 3,191 and Glace Bay to 6,945 in 1901. On the Nova Scotia mainland, the principal community in Pictou County, Albion Mines (later Stellarton), had 1,881 inhabitants in 1881, 2,410 in 1891, and 2,335 in 1901. Springhill, in Cumberland County, had 900 residents in 1881, but grew very rapidly over the decade to reach 4,813 in 1891, when it was briefly the largest coal town in Nova Scotia, before declining to 4,559 in 1901.[5] In western Canada, the coal camps and villages of the interior had typically just a few hundred inhabitants. Lethbridge, with a population of 2,326 in 1901, was particularly large.[6] Nanaimo, on Vancouver Island, was rare among coal communities because it was also the site of secondary industry. Numbering 151 European inhabitants in 1851, Nanaimo grew to a population of 1,645 in 1881 and 6,130 in 1901, on the strength of lumbering, sawmills, a tannery and brewery, the fishery, a cannery, and a small shipyard – in addition to the local mines.[7]

The ethnic character of the early coal-mining communities in both Nova Scotia and on Vancouver Island was shaped by their first inhabitants, Scottish and English immigrant miners. The British influence was reflected throughout the Canadian mining industry: in the dominance of the English language, in workplace techniques and terminology, in customs, leisure activity, fraternal and cooperative institutions, even in preferred food and drink.[8] Over time, greater ethnic diversity emerged, particularly in western Canada. In Nova Scotia, the British complexion of mining communities remained strong, fed into the twentieth century by a continuing "trickle" of new British immigrants.[9] Mine workers, if not born within local coal towns and villages of British immigrant parents, arrived from (equally British) rural areas of the province. In late-nineteenth-century Cape Breton, two-thirds of the residents of mining communities were of Scottish origin, and the balance were largely Irish or English. Similarly, the Nova Scotian mainland retained its strongly British complexion, although Scots did not predominate to the same extent. From the 1880s, some immigrants arrived in Nova Scotia from continental Europe – Belgians, Italians – but never in large numbers.[10]

In western Canada, non-British immigrants were far more prominent. From the 1860s, hundreds of Chinese in-migrants flocked into the coal settlements of Vancouver Island. Subsequently, newcomers arrived from continental Europe, comprising 20 percent of Nanaimo wage-earners by 1891.[11] The new coalfields of the western interior had even greater ethnic diversity. At Frank, in the Alberta Crowsnest

Pass, only one-third of the 150 miners employed in 1907 were English-speaking (others spoke French, German, Finnish, or an eastern European language).[12] At Fernie, in the British Columbia Crowsnest Pass district, 43.5 percent of mine workers in 1911 were from continental Europe.[13]

New districts on the resource frontier – pre-GMA Sydney Mines, Nova Scotia; Wellington and Cumberland on Vancouver Island for a period later in the century; the Crowsnest Pass at the turn of the twentieth century; the Alberta Coal Branch in the 1910s – were marked by a sharp sexual imbalance. They drew transient men, confident of finding work, but not women, for whom employment was scarce. Rapidly growing communities could exhibit similar imbalance. The population of Nanaimo increased rapidly after the completion of the Esquimault and Nanaimo Railway in 1886. Even excluding the almost uniformly male Asian population, the ratio was 1.2 men for every woman in Nanaimo in 1881; 1.98 to one in 1891; and 2.07 to one in 1901.[14] Sexual imbalance was reflected in household structure. Of the 150 men employed at the new mine of Wellington in 1874, only 8 resided with their family.[15] In Nanaimo in 1891, only 29 percent of mine workers were members of a household with a resident spouse. Nearly half of mine workers were lodgers. In Wellington that year, two-thirds of mine employees were lodgers and only 14 percent headed a household.[16]

Western Canadian coal towns and villages were also marked by high levels of transience, both geographic and occupational. Alberta mine owners, operating seasonally, lamented their dependence on unskilled migrant workers, commonly farmers, alleging that these workers left a legacy of smashed coal and damaged company dwellings.[17] English-born Frank Wheatley, an official of District 18 of the United Mine Workers of America and president of the Alberta Federation of Labour, underlined that this "isn't a proper basis as to the way of training miners. They haven't any intention of making it a life industry like the miners where I was brought up at home, where men worked in the mines from boyhood and gave their life to it. This isn't being developed in Alberta."[18] Transience was similarly evident in British Columbia. Of the 323 miners on the Nanaimo voters' list in 1886, only 72 (22 percent) were found on the 1891 census rolls.[19] Mining also functioned for many men on Vancouver Island as an occupational way-station. Small businesses, artisanal occupations, and especially farming drew many miners from the coal pit. By one estimate, of the miners employed on Vancouver Island in 1880–81 and still resident there in 1899, fewer than half had been consistently employed in mining over this period and a further 14 percent had returned to the mine after a stint in another occupation.[20]

In contrast, the coal communities of Nova Scotia were far better established than their western Canadian counterparts: in-migrants either brought their family with them or established one rapidly. Men from rural Nova Scotia would return home during a slow period at the mine to find a wife; less commonly, they married a woman raised in the mining community.[21] These towns contained a better balance between men and women. Sydney Mines, for instance, was home in 1901 to 1,617 men and 1,574 women.[22] Nova Scotian coal towns consisted overwhelmingly of single family dwellings. In late-nineteenth-century Sydney Mines, 80 percent of households consisted of nuclear families.[23] Despite very rapid growth over the turn of the twentieth century, large boarding houses were absent from Cape Breton. Single men lodged with a surrogate family that, as Del Muise explained, "was probably related in some way, either by blood or through association."[24]

To at least to the end of the nineteenth century, boys were raised in these coal towns with the strong expectation that they would enter the pit at some point in their life. Far more than elsewhere in Canada, boys were bred to the mine in Nova Scotia. Coal mining was a way of life, a lifelong occupation. Dan J. McDonald recalled: "I was just a boy when I first went down in the pits. I never thought much about it one way or another because it was natural for all the miners' sons in those days. You just followed on."[25] As late as 1927 a Springhill miner complained to the UMWA local that "he got three boys laying around and eating every thing and the Company won[']t give them work."[26] Coal companies made a practice of hiring on a preferential basis men and boys inhabiting company dwellings – and indebted at the company store – for mine employment.[27] F.C. Kimber, manager at the Reserve Mine on Cape Breton Island, indicated in 1888 that he took boys when they reached the age of thirteen – "They are always our own boys who live in the place."[28] Of the 937 boys twelve years of age and older resident in Dominion Coal–owned housing in 1907, an estimated 811 were working in the mines.[29] These coal towns and villages were generally able to reproduce the mining labour force, although in periods of rapid growth, such as from 1900 to 1914, demand far outstripped the local supply of boys.

CLASS IN THE COAL COMMUNITY

Class profoundly marked coal towns and villages. In single-industry coal communities, there were few merchants, professionals, or clergymen to form an intermediate class between mine management and mine workers. Coal companies exercised wide authority within the community, as employers, as landlords, and as merchants. "Everybody in Glace Bay," reported the *Canadian Mining Journal* in 1908, "is either the servant of the Coal Company, or the servant of the servant of the Coal Company."[30]

Considerable investment in community infrastructure was required to draw and retain a workforce, particularly if the mine was located in an isolated or remote district. Companies built and maintained schools and encouraged the construction of churches by providing free land.[31] Most importantly, coal companies built houses. The General Mining Association erected company housing on a large scale, setting a pattern for Nova Scotia, where the construction of company houses continued throughout the nineteenth century, particularly in Cape Breton. By the turn of the twentieth century, the Dominion Coal Company owned twelve hundred houses.[32] In the isolated mining communities of the western interior, companies typically erected bunkhouses.[33] On Vancouver Island, single-family dwellings were built by coal companies from the time of the Hudson's Bay Company.[34] James Dunsmuir was so wedded to the company town that when he opened the Extension mine a few miles south of Wellington in 1897, he insisted that miners employed there, many of whom had built houses in the vicinity, move (at their own expense) to the company village of Ladysmith, better isolated from unionized Nanaimo.[35]

The class gulf was clearly expressed in housing. Mount Rundell, a two-storey building constructed by the GMA for its manager at the Albion Mines in 1827, contained twenty-two large rooms. Situated on a seventy-five-acre property overlooking the mine and entered by a long curved carriage drive, the estate had a cricket pitch, a fruit orchard and gardens protected by a wooden palisade, stables, servants' quarters, and out-buildings for guests.[36] The slightly smaller Beech Hill was built at Sydney Mines in 1829 for manager Richard Brown.[37] Miners, in contrast, inhabited tenements.[38] Typically, these were brick houses built in one-storey terraces on an English model. The smallest houses had one room and a kitchen, the largest two or three rooms, a kitchen, and sleeping space in the attic. The backyard would usually have an outhouse and large garden, with perhaps a cow, pigs, and chickens.[39] Although by the twentieth century "miners' rows" were no longer built, having been supplanted by "cottages" comprising two homes, company houses were reputed for their dilapidation and overcrowding (see Illustration 12).[40]

Whatever its quality, company-owned housing was an effective tool of corporate control. In a sequence of events frequently repeated in coal communities throughout Canada over the years, a strike at Sydney Mines in the spring and summer of 1876 was followed by evictions from company-owned houses. The arrival of strikebreakers at the end of July led to violence along the picket lines and the arrival of militia units.[41] The coal operators most likely to employ these tactics were the Dunsmuirs, on Vancouver Island. Participation in a strike led to prompt eviction. And efforts to resist eviction led to prompt calls for the militia.[42]

In addition to owning housing, coal companies frequently operated retail outlets. Company stores were originally established to offer merchandise to miners that might otherwise have been unavailable; to offer credit to miners to carry them over periods (during winter especially) when there was little work at the colliery; and, crucially, to ease financial pressure on coal companies by paying workers in goods rather than cash. A store was established at Sydney Mines as early as 1809.[43] GMA manager Richard Brown alleged that the early mine owners on Cape Breton Island "made more profit by the sale of their stores than of their coal."[44] The Hudson's Bay Company operated what was effectively a company store, but its successor, the Vancouver Coal Mining and Land Company, instead encouraged independent merchants to establish themselves at Nanaimo.[45] Alberta mining camps, in contrast, typically contained a company store.[46]

Where they persisted, company stores emerged as a lightning rod for controversy. A slow mining season could rapidly inflate the extent of a miner's indebtedness to the company store and deepen his subjection to the coal company.[47] As a resident of Cape Breton observed in 1881, company stores "are a fertile source of disease. It is true they keep on hand all articles the men require, but the prices are most exorbitant. Such being the case, when work is slack, the workmen, especially if they have large families, are soon head and ears in debt, hopelessly I might add, and completely under the will of the agent [manager], who uses the men as one uses a football. Under these circumstances if the workman sees a chance of bettering his position and pay, he requires to ask permission of his lord and master, which request is often met with a point blank refusal, or a declaration to the effect that he *may* leave *when* the store debt is paid."[48] The requirement to pay wages in currency – rather than, for instance, in credit at the company store – was not legislated in Nova Scotia until 1899. Company stores persisted into the twentieth century.[49]

The nineteenth-century manager wielded wide power in the community. He ruled on access to company housing and to consumer goods in the company store; he determined the nature of local services, including streets (frequently named after corporate officials), policing, and schooling.[50] Small wonder that Pictou County boys doffed their caps when the manager of the Acadia Company drove by in his carriage or sleigh.[51] As late as 1946, the Royal Commission on Coal condemned closed camps in the western interior, where "the local coal operator controls all land within convenient distance of the mines, owns all housing and controls all stores, hotels and service facilities."[52]

The power of the colliery manager was tempered by the authority that miners retained underground, for at least as long as bord-and-pillar mining continued, and the need for ongoing negotiation of working conditions in the mine. It was also mediated by paternalism: a relationship marked by mutual obligations whereby the powerful offer protection and direction; the weak, obedience and loyalty. Even at the largest nineteenth-century mines managers knew all employees by name. R.H. Brown noted in his diary in 1874 that the "[b]oy Alex McAskill [was] hurt in pit today, driving tubs on No. 1 Level. One tub got off road and jambed [sic] his leg. [N]o bones broken."[53] Similarly, when a boy broke his leg at Springhill in 1890, manager Henry Swift reported this event in his regular correspondence with company officials.[54] Reinforcing paternalist relations were the ties of family, which frequently bound miners and mine officials. Into the twentieth century, the majority of mine officials were former working miners.[55]

Paternalist overtures gave mine managers a more compliant work-force. As one correspondent wrote in 1881, "I know of no instance where an employer has displayed a concern for the social well being and improvement of his workmen, in which he has not been amply repaid, by their increased respect and zeal on his behalf."[56] Paternalism offered employees a range of benefits. Companies might provide coal free or at cost to employees.[57] The Hudson's Bay Company offered miners at Nanaimo in 1862 a house, fuel, and medical attendance.[58] In Pictou County, the General Mining Association purchased uniforms for a volunteer rifle company in the 1860s.[59] Boys at the Caledonia Mine received a traditional Christmas treat, which they forfeited in 1888 when one of their number inadvertently broke a piece of mine machinery.[60] In the twentieth century, coal companies commonly provided sports fields and open-air rinks.[61]

Paternalist gestures in the mining community extended to a contest run by the Provincial Workmen's Association in 1884 for the most popular mine manager in Nova Scotia.[62] Respected officials could expect periodic tokens of the miners' regard. G.M. Appleton, engineer at the Vale Colliery, was presented in 1885 with "a very valuable box of Drawing Instruments and a Writing Desk." Shortly before mine manager Leckie left Springhill it was suggested that "[o]n the eve of his departure there should be a big meeting of the workmen and the presentation of something tangible that he might take away with him – as a memorial of the good wishes of the men – and be able to show his friends."[63] As Ian McKay has pointed out, gift-giving carried significance both as a "gesture of subordination" but also as reflecting notions of "reciprocal rights and obligations."[64] Paternalism placed limits on the powerful by embodying expectations about how power could legitimately be exercised.

Only gradually was corporate strength within the company town eroded. Fraternal orders, whereby miners combined to provide mutual death, disability, or medical benefits in exchange for the payment of dues, carved out a niche for mine workers outside of the ambit of the company (although members of the lodge of Freemasons formed at the Albion Mines in 1860 asked permission of the local manager before they marched through the town).[65] Miners also established cooperatives. As early as the 1860s, cooperative retail stores were organized in the Nova Scotian coalfields. A store established at Albion Mines (later Stellarton) in 1861 may have been the first in Canada. Some, including stores at Stellarton and Sydney Mines, enjoyed considerable longevity.[66] The British Canadian Cooperative Society in Cape Breton, with nearly thirty-five hundred members and $1.5 million in annual sales by the 1920s, was a significant counterweight to the extensive chain of company stores operated by the Dominion Coal Company in Cape Breton.[67] Retail cooperatives were also formed in western Canada: at Nanaimo before the end of the nineteenth century and in the Crowsnest Pass in the first decade of the twentieth.[68]

Miners also organized for electoral politics. They formed political clubs, including one in Stellarton in 1882.[69] In 1886 the PWA entered provincial politics, unsuccessfully running two candidates for the House of Assembly.[70] The incorporation of mining towns from late in the nineteenth century and the extension of the franchise to miners in company housing in Nova Scotia in 1889, encouraged political organization.[71] But the political education the PWA attempted to provide only slowly overcame a tradition of deference to the company in mining towns. "For a long time," David Frank quoted a former miner, "the miners themselves wouldn't vote for a miner. They'd figure he wouldn't know enough." It was not until the 1910s that numerous trade union municipal councillors were elected, determined to restrict company police and evictions from company housing and to review the modest levels of municipal taxes paid by mining companies. A miner was elected mayor of Glace Bay in 1918.[72] During the 1920s, four Farmer-Labour candidates were elected to the provincial legislature from Cape Breton County.[73] Paralleling the changing political orientation of Nova Scotian miners, a Socialist Young Guard emerged in provincial coalfields in the early twentieth century.[74] Coal miners enjoyed more success in electoral politics in western Canada. In Alberta, they were represented in the provincial legislature between 1909 and 1913, and from 1921 to 1930.[75] And in British Columbia, labour candidates were repeatedly elected: in fact, with the exception of the years 1894 to 1898, miners were represented in the provincial legislature continuously from 1890 to 1930, a unique accomplishment, as Allen Seager observed, for working-class constituencies of the period.[76] Nanaimo even sent miner Ralph Smith to Parliament in 1900.[77]

Most importantly, corporate domination was challenged by the growth of unions in the coalfields.[78] Trade unions allowed mine workers to carve out a margin of manœuvre. As part of this process, they allowed them to re-examine child labour in light of class, to question its value to the boy, and to explore options, such as the acquisition of formal education that would open broader opportunities, both within and outside of coal communities, for their sons. Organized miners, we have seen, were strong advocates both of compulsory education provisions and of laws restricting child labour in the mines. Mine owners, in contrast, resisted these legislative initiatives.[79]

Boys raised in coal towns and villages learned their class identity in various ways. During the UWMA recognition struggle of 1909–11 in Nova Scotia, few non-union children ventured to attend school, where they were subjected to scorn, even blows.[80] At the same time, children boycotted one of Glace Bay's Sunday schools because it was led by a Dominion Coal manager.[81] Similarly, the UMWA recognition strike on Vancouver Island produced a boycott of school classes in 1912.[82] Two boys were among those jailed after the riots of 1913 at Nanaimo.[83] At the times of greatest industrial conflict, class identity was most keenly felt.

GENDER IN THE MINING COMMUNITY

If class was the basic social division boys encountered in coal towns and villages, gender also divided the residents of coal communities. Manhood was defined most fundamentally against women. A miner unhappy about his pay, yet not voting for a labour candidate, was told to give his wife "the pants" and "go home with the children and wear the skirt."[84] The sexes were distinguished in other ways. Men were rugged. Women were not. A manager at Springhill, Henry Swift, remarked favourably on a badly cut young boy: "He never flinced [flinched] ... being a smart, handy little fellow."[85] Sydney Mines manager R.H. Brown recorded in his diary that his wife was "bled in the right arm by the Doctor for her giddy head."[86] Men fought. Women swooned. "The excursion of the athletic association [at Springhill] ended in a row. I believe the boys had the best of it although some of the women fainted."[87] Most importantly, men worked for wages in the mines; women did not. A man was a breadwinner.

Masculine identity, based in men's work, shifted over the turn of the twentieth century. In the nineteenth-century coalfields, the model for manliness was the craftsman, an independent contractor, paid on the basis of the quality and quantity of coal he produced. He took pride in his ability to produce large coals efficiently and safely. Victor Belik, a Crowsnest Pass miner, observed: "You know, a coal miner is just like a fisherman with his fish tales. In the bar, we dig more coal than in the mine, because everyone brags about what they do."[88] But masculinity, when defined around craftsmanship, was exclusive.[89] Thomas Keating, a British immigrant miner, considered the mine labourer "in the light of the weak brother, unskilled, requiring all our aid."[90] Similarly, the elderly mine worker, no longer capable of work as a miner, was no longer a complete man. An expression current in the anthracite coalfields of Pennsylvania at the turn of the twentieth century held that "twice a boy and once a man is a poor miner's life."[91]

Boys learned that their masculine identity – their integrity as men – hinged on their ability both to acquire a craft and to earn a living. To linger at school was effeminate – even disreputable. Boys looked forward to their start in the mine as a mark of approaching manhood, assuring them added respect in the family and within the community. Their initiation to the mine consisted largely of "pit-hardening," the acquisition of the required toughness. The *Springhill News and Advertiser* wrote admiringly about a "young lad who walked uncomplainingly for a good mile from the mine with a severe scalp injury, which was ultimately treated with 11 stitches."[92] After the explosion at Springhill in 1891, only a handful of survivors were able to stagger out of the stricken pit unaided. Two boys particularly distinguished themselves in the eyes of journalist R.A.H. Morrow. Fifteen-year-old Dan Beaton, "on hearing the explosion, immediately ran to the place where he knew his younger brother was working, and found him burnt, wounded, and his clothes on fire. After extinguishing the fire he put him on his shoulder, and would not give up his charge to any one who offered assistance until he had taken him out of the mine and laid him on a lounge in his own home."[93] Fourteen-year-old driver Dannie Robertson only survived the explosion because his horse, Jenny, absorbed the brunt of the blast, which threw Robertson back into a box. Momentarily dazed, he was aroused by the noise of timber cracking as the roof collapsed. Almost delirious, with bad burns on his head, face, arms, and side, he started to make his way out of the pitch-black mine. Hearing the cries of twelve-year-old trapper Willie Farris, he groped his way to his side. Because of his burns, Robertson could not take hold of the boy to assist him out. Instead, he instructed Farris to climb on his back, and supporting him as best he could, he ran out of the mine. Once on the surface, Robertson asked the men carrying him home on a sled "that he be allowed to walk into the house, so that his mother might not be alarmed."[94]

The craft-based definition of manliness – hard-working, respectable, bread-winning, reasonable – was challenged in its day by "rough" behaviour in the coal towns – hard-drinking, gambling, improvident. But it was also under increasing stress as the transformation of mine work and skills lessened miners' autonomy and scope for independent judgment, and as the crisis in the coal industry threatened miners' livelihood. If one pillar of manhood in nineteenth-century coalfields was the miner's skill, a second was his ability to bring home a living family wage. A resident of Glace Bay underscored to the Nova Scotia premier in 1924 the humiliations of economic distress "that rob a man of his last ounce of self-respect he possesses."[95]

The transformation of the skilled miner's work from the 1890s and the decline of the coal industry after the First World War, produced a crisis in the definitions of masculinity carried over from the nineteenth century. The new basic "test of manhood" was reconstructed less around skill than around class loyalty.[96] Trade unions built support by appeals to manliness. Strikebreakers were excoriated as effeminate (or female-dominated).[97] But long strikes created a dilemma for the miner, torn between his loyalty to fellow workers and his responsibilities as the family breadwinner. As one New Waterford miner pointed out in a letter to the Sydney *Post* during the lengthy Cape Breton strike in 1925, "The miners can stand the gaff [strain] far better than their wives and little children can."[98] Employers were quick to apply pressure to this tender point. "As between the wives and families on the one hand and the Western Federation of Miners on the other," Vancouver Island miners were lectured in 1903, "I should think the families have the highest claim upon the husband."[99] Likewise, a striking Glace Bay miner was told by the mine manager in 1909 that if he "thought more of the United Mine Workers than he did of his wife and family, then he had better pack his traps and leave the country."[100]

Unlike the male role, women's place in the community did not change. Girls were raised to be wives. The miner's wife's status was based on her ability to "make do," her demonstrated capacity to maintain a home. Within this sphere, women could exercise considerable influence.[101] In addition, women were the mainstay of the community's social and religious networks, as Bill Wylie has observed, "keeping up the ties within families and with neighbours, ensuring the observance of religious traditions, and pulling together with other women in times of crisis."[102] Women shared the stress of uncertainty, the possibility faced daily that their husband and sons might not live to return home from the mine.[103] They also bonded together to support male trade unionists in women's auxiliaries, where they organized dances, dinners, picnics, excursions.[104] They also embarked on limited self-organization through participation in Women's Labour Leagues, which sponsored educational programs.[105]

Women also learned of wage-earners' superior entitlements. Unequal consumption patterns within mining communities are most clearly illustrated with respect to alcohol. Like mine work, alcohol consumption was gendered. If accounts of drunken men and boys were common in mining communities, there were none of women.[106] These reports are emblematic of more than merely the rough aspects of the colliery town; they also illustrate males' superior access to leisure and drink.[107]

Corporate challenges to family livelihood forced women into unusual roles. At times of industrial conflict, they paraded, demonstrated, and appeared on picket lines. During a strike at the Albion Mines in 1842, miners' wives and children attacked the mansion of the company agent, smashing kitchen windows, hurling insults at him.[108] At Wellington in 1877, women "discouraged" strikebreakers, meeting them at the pit with their infants, jeers, and missiles.[109] A generation later, miners, their wives, and their children collectively harassed strikebreakers at Nanaimo.[110] Women took a prominent part in the riots of 12 August 1913 on Vancouver Island, shouting "Drive the scabs way," throwing stones, urging others on.[111] On Cape Breton Island, women participated in the riots and looting that followed decisions on the part of company stores during the major strikes of the early 1920s first to suspend the sale of anything but basic foodstuffs and then to cut off credit sales altogether.[112]

Women's public role was recognized very reluctantly. Their voices were seldom if ever heard before the numerous government commissions of enquiry that toured the coalfields.[113] Newspapers hesitated to report their role in riots, preferring to depict women (and children) as victims. The police did not arrest or charge women, and consequently the courts did not try them.[114] Miners too may not always have accepted a public role for their wives. Striking miners at Minto, New Brunswick, for instance, distanced their wives from the conflict in 1937 by failing to inform them of picket locations.[115]

Women did not share the intimate relation with the mine that their menfolk had. Marking the distinction within the family between those who earned wages in the mine and those who did not was "pit talk," conversation about the experience of the mine which – to their frustration – excluded women.[116] There is some evidence to suggest that women were the first to resist boys' entry into the mine.[117] Alberta miner Frank Wheatley, for instance, acknowledged in 1919 that although he advocated boys' traditional apprenticeship to the craft, his wife was "keen that [their sons] don't go into the mine."[118]

CULTURE IN THE COAL COMMUNITY

Nineteenth- and early-twentieth-century coal towns and villages were also marked by a cultural divide that reflected contested views of class and gender identity. In these communities, a traditional culture characterized by irregular work habits, tolerance of disorder, superstition, and questionable leisure activities – such as the "rum-hole" and fist-fights, the brothel, gambling and blood sports – had become the target of an emergent liberal ethic, one that found the coarse, turbulent behaviour within the coal community abhorrent.[119] Early trade unionists, who congregated at the "respectable" end of the cultural spectrum, devoted considerable energy to hectoring miners to counter a public perception that they were "[r]ough in speech, in mind and in manners; reckless of reason and right; regardless of law, of order, and morality."[120] Traditional, rough culture in coal towns and villages tolerated child labour. Respectable culture grew increasingly intolerant of boys' early start to work in the mines.

Most characteristic of traditional culture – and a target of early trade unions – was miners' irregular mode of working.[121] "What our miners should aim at," the PWA urged in Nova Scotia, "is to be steadily industrious."[122] Sydney Mines manager R.H. Brown, searching for means of "making them work steadily," noted in 1874 the number of occasions when the majority of mine workers were absent, severely curtailing or even stopping coal production: on the twelfth night of Christmas "many men and boys were off work," on St. Patrick's day "not half the men [were] out," on Good Friday, and on May 1st, when the "Queen Pit night shift [was] idle, [because] only 9 pair men and no boys came out."[123] Because "the pits were very frequently idle owing to the number of holy days or saints days that were celebrated," mine managers requested the assistance of the PWA. Robert Drummond suggested that they enlist the aid of the clergy, "telling them that commemoration days were abused and offering to collect church dues through the office in return for their intervention." The clergy was amenable and was rewarded with the check-off.[124]

Absenteeism was also related to superstition. Arbitrary death in the pit, while spurring organized miners to lobby for safety measures, including miner certification, also encouraged folk beliefs. At Springhill, it was held that a life was lost whenever company owners visited.[125] Madame Coo, an aboriginal Nova Scotian credited with predicting the explosions at the Foord Pit in 1880 and at Springhill in 1891, wielded influence with many Nova Scotian miners.[126] On one occasion, even the pits at distant Sydney Mines were closed, as their manager complained, "on acc[oun]t of [a] prophesy [of a mine disaster] of [an] old woman at New Glasgow."[127] This manager protested a few years later to the local Roman Catholic and Presbyterian clergy about their superstitious congregations after a very low turnout at work one day because "one foretold for an explosion."[128]

There were other causes of absenteeism. When a death occurred in the mine, work ceased immediately and did not resume until after the deceased was buried. Companies resisted these pit closures, and by 1887 the tradition of suspending work from death to burial was not always respected.[129] In 1909 C.O. MacDonald observed that whereas miners might remain idle on the day of an accident, they would be at work on subsequent days "unless the number of men desiring to actually attend the funeral prevents its being worked on that day."[130] But the tradition of closing a pit for a funeral continued at least into the 1920s.[131]

The lure of pleasant weather also took mine employees from work. Spring led to a "picnic scourge," when high levels of absenteeism were "not unusual."[132] "The miners are strong on picnics," reported the trade publication the Canadian Mining Journal, "preferring a day's picnicking to a day's pay at any time, and this year the month of August was prolific in picnics."[133] Much absenteeism was closely linked to the traditional "idle spell" after payday to attend to chores around the house, in the garden, or to do some shooting or hunting.[134] The lure of a circus or a game of baseball also periodically drew enough boys away from smaller mines to force a temporary closure.[135]

Absenteeism was also the child of a binge. According to a report from Westville, Nova Scotia, in 1883, "Things were lively round the streets on pay Saturday. All the Rumholes were in full blast."[136] A Stellarton correspondent observed that "[a]ny stranger coming into our village last Saturday night would have said 'Well I've heard that miners were rough and thriftless, but I never thought they were quite so bad.'"[137] A description of Joggins in 1885 included "one general store ... and twenty grog shops."[138] Nearby Springhill boasted forty rum-holes.[139] Neil A. McDonald, a PWA official from Glace Bay, wrote candidly in 1882: "Work is very brisk and there is plenty of Shipping, but the output is often very short of what it should be. Too much rum the cause."[140] The issue of absenteeism began to be raised with greater insistence by mine managers in the twentieth century. An industrial publication claimed in 1914 that on post-payday Mondays up to fifteen hundred Nova Scotian miners were absent from work.[141] Senior British Empire Steel Corporation officials condemned miner absenteeism, which they alleged to reach 10 percent on Mondays, before the Duncan Royal Commission in 1925, linking it with drinking.[142]

Drink produced irregular work habits. It also led to violence. Although the claim of local Salvation Army converts that Westville was "the worst place this side of Hades" was likely exaggerated, coal towns and villages were notorious for their rough behaviour.[143] In one account, "The first public pugilistic exhibition, for a long time, was held on the street [in Westville] last Friday night, and some say it was splendid, and I'm sure it must have been refreshing after such a long interval of quiet; and especially after so much Scott Act [prohibition by local option] talk. What would the village, or in fact any place, be without the 'wee drop' that gives us more than school or college, that wakens wit, and kindles lore, and bangs us full of knowledge."[144] A correspondent sent this report from Springhill in 1883: "Last Saturday, pay day, there was considerable drink and noise. Quiet drunks before dark, raging ones after dark ... Big bloody fight in Rogues corner [a popular local gathering point]."[145] Druggist John D. Higinbotham, newly arrived in Lethbridge from Ontario in 1885, remarked of payday brawls that "[i]t was a surprise ... that any of the eighteen saloons were still standing."[146] Drink also led to domestic violence. An immigrant to Nanaimo from Scotland early in the twentieth century remarked that "a lot of the men would get drunk to drown out their troubles and come home and sometimes would beat up the wife and kids."[147] On occasion it drew a public response. The *Trades Journal* referred in January 1885 to a "wife beater [who] got quarters in the jail."[148] More commonly, domestic violence was privately endured.[149]

Drink and disproportionate numbers of young single men encouraged other coal town vices. Efforts in one Nova Scotian coal town to close a brothel were recounted in the *Trades Journal*: "There is one house that has a very questionable name, and which a large number of the young men visit. It is kept by a fair charmer and goes by the name of 'Over the Garden Wall.' It is a pest to the neighborhood."[150] When a citizens' vigilante group assembled to destroy the Garden Wall, its female proprietor threw a brick, striking the leader of the group bent on tearing it down. Her assailants withdrew.[151] Informal mechanisms for the maintenance of propriety were more successful in Springhill. A disreputable house at "Rogues' Corner" was raided between four and five one Sunday morning. The crowd "horse-whipped a temporary lodger up the street to his boarding house." The residents of the house were told to leave town.[152] Prostitution flourished less in the settled communities of Nova Scotia than in the frontier camps of western Canada.[153]

Gambling was a popular leisure activity.[154] One PWA lodge meeting in Springhill was particularly poorly attended because of the number of miners "having to at[t]end the preformance [sic] of a Card Sharper and patent med[icine]s hack."[155] Races of all varieties also drew wagers.[156] So did traditional blood sports. "The barbarous custom of dog fighting prevails largely at present," reported one indignant coal town journalist. "When people are coming from Church on Sunday, it is common to see large crowds running madly hither and thither to witness a dog-fight."[157] Cock-fighting was also reported.[158]

For boys, the cultural divide in coal communities revolved on school attendance, increasingly the badge of youthful respectability. By the late nineteenth century, if the family had money for appropriate clothing and books, children were spending some time in school. Nineteenth-century schools were generally of poor quality and teachers of uncertain qualification.[159] Information was drawn from textbooks, memorized by sing-song chant, and reproduced on demand in overcrowded primary classrooms that grouped several dozen children in perhaps six or eight grades.[160] The harassed teacher, increasingly female, soon discovered that if she could keep children in their seats and teach them to read, "she would be safe from interference on the part of parents and trustees."[161] The relevance of the curriculum to working children was unclear and the lasting legacy of the school years uncertain.[162] While Robert Drummond claimed that of the hundreds of pit boys in Nova Scotia "we would be surprised, if told that more than a dozen could not read or write," the federal labour commissioners repeatedly encountered illiterate boys in 1888.[163] A Cape Breton miner, testifying that the youngest pit boys were nine or ten years of age, was asked if they could read and write. "I think they have a small chance," he responded.[164] The experience of the mine distinguished the pit boys of the mining community from those boys who did not work. Hostility between pit and school boys was embodied in an event as innocuous as a snowball fight. When "missiles" broke school windows in the course of an exchange of snowballs between pit and school boys at Stellarton, the responsible pit boys were brought before a justice of the peace and fined fifty cents apiece. Such was the price of the pit boys' probable triumph.[165]

Pit boys' participation in rough culture demarcated them from schoolchildren. Wage-earning relieved them from the domestic chores that had previously had the first call on their time outside of school. It also liberated them of the more circumscribed behaviour required of the schoolchild. Once boys started to work, parental control of their leisure activities was substantially diminished. "Now that I was a wage-earner," recalled one English pit boy in writing his autobiography, "I could go out at night for as long as I liked and where I liked."[166] The community offered a range of attractions. A Halifax journalist observed of Springhill's pit boys that "they meet in little groups on street corners or wherever there happens to be an attraction, and make things as lively as possible."[167] They would lounge, exchange news, chew tobacco, stare at girls and women, and observe other street activity. Street-corner idling was free and, as Lynne Marks has underlined, one of the few alternative leisure pursuits to uncomfortable, overcrowded homes.[168]

Other sites of boys' activity included the bowling alley (when Springhill's burned down, the *Trades Journal* reported that "mothers of boys ... are heartily glad") and the shooting gallery.[169] Although the youngest pit boys' leisure activity did not generally involve girls, older boys might be drawn towards them. One censorious journalist noted in 1885: "Dance-Halls are the rage. Morality is at a discount."[170] The ubiquitous rum shops led to frequent accounts of intoxicated boys[171] – "Last Saturday there were quite a number of drunks to be seen on the streets, a few of whom were boys."[172] In 1888 two particularly "drunk and disorderly" boys aged twelve and fourteen were jailed in the course of their merry-making.[173] Similarly, a year later, "[s]everal small boys not more than ten to twelve years, were seen paralyzed through drink."[174] "[T]he rum fiends," complained the *Canadian Mining Review* in 1894, "serve the devil by dispensing liquid poison to the miners, boys as well as men."[175] When driver Malcolm Ferguson was asked if boys were "generally sober," he responded, "Some of them."[176] The drunken and blasphemous boys reported at Springhill in 1887 were the despair of Robert Drummond.[177]

By the 1880s, the charivari, a mock serenade to a couple on their wedding night, belonged to the young.[178] "Of all the forms, kinds, species and degrees of blackmail," complained one writer in 1884, "certainly the worst kind of all is that which goes by the name of charivari." He told of a couple on their wedding night "being bombarded by tin tea kettles, bake pans, old dinner horns, bone crackers and old horse pistols." He advised: "Boys give it up once and for ever. Don't be a charivarist."[179] His advice was unheeded. One charivarist rashly used a two-dollar bill as wadding for a gun salute later in the decade. "After the salute had been successfully fired, he recovered consciousness and bethought him of the bill. Parts of it were found but the glory of the whole had faded."[180] Hallowe'en demanded its rituals of youth also. The *Trades Journal* commended boys on their behaviour on that evening in 1887: "They contented themselves with waving torches and doing a little shouting."[181]

Boys' views of organized religion were evident when they disrupted church services. "Young Rowdies" disturbed a Primitive [Methodist] service in 1870; and another service at Stellarton in 1885.[182] Two lads were fined two dollars apiece and costs after disturbing a Salvation Army meeting in 1888.[183] Three boys were fined the following year in Springhill for the same reason.[184] "Unruly" boys attempted to burn the Presbyterian Mission at Nanaimo in 1900.[185] Temperance groups were similarly targeted. The *Trades Journal* complained in 1889 that boys in Sydney Mines "make what they think great sport by tearing away [the] doorsteps" of the new temperance hall.[186]

Lynne Marks has observed that, in late-nineteenth-century Ontario, regular church attendance and participation in church organizations were the "central focus of local respectable culture." She also noted that this culture – in contrast to local rough culture – was dominated by women, who had far higher rates of church attendance than men.[187] Church groups and temperance associations were further hallmarks of respectability in the coalfields. Associated with the Protestant churches were a great range of temperance societies. The Sons of Temperance, the Church of England Temperance Society, the Cadets of Temperance, the International Order of Good Templars, and the Juvenile Templars were all active in coal communities.[188] In the 1880s, an active Vigilance Society prosecuted liquor-sellers in Springhill.[189] The PWA, a strong advocate of temperance, denied membership to anyone engaged in illicit liquor-selling.[190] It readily acquiesced in the allotment of punishment by mine managers to mine workers for liquor offences.[191] Robert Drummond repeatedly urged that miners be paid on some day other than Saturday, in light of the ensuing drunkenness.[192]

Fraternal societies, with some reservations on account of the alcohol consumed on certain occasions, were deemed respectable. Commonly organized on ethnic lines, they were the most popular form of voluntary association. Major ones included the Masons, the Loyal Orange Lodge, the Odd Fellows, the Knights of Pythias, and the Ancient Order of Foresters. Using the Masons as the model, these groups developed elaborate rituals and degrees of hierarchy, and their rhetoric centred on a brotherhood of male virtues such as independence. Initiation into a fraternal order was seen as a rite of passage into manhood.[193] Fraternal orders had a significant place as means of working-class self-help, sponsoring a variety of insurance programs.[194] They also encouraged occasions of community sociability: parades, balls, dinners, and picnics. Although women were not members of fraternal orders, much of the activity these groups sponsored – unlike "rough" pastimes within the mining community – included women. The Orange Society of Westville, after parading through the town behind the lodge banner, retired to a supper and ball in November 1882.[195] Fuller Lodge, of the Independent Order of Odd Fellows, marked the arrival of the New Year of 1885 with a "Supper and Ball" – described in the local press as "a most recherché affair."[196] On other occasions, the activities of fraternal orders could be marked by heavy drinking. The revelry associated with the Orangemen's Glorious Twelfth picnic in 1904 led to considerable absenteeism in Pictou County the following day.[197]

Many coal operators' and early miners' unions encouraged access to good literature, considered a guarantee of regular work habits and thrift. The Nanaimo Literary Institute was founded in 1862, its "news and reading room" provided by the colliery company.[198] A proposal in 1882 that a reading room be established in Springhill came to fruition in 1885.[199] Albion Mines opened its reading room in 1883.[200] At Sydney Mines, a "Reading Room and Debating Society" was founded with the explicit intention of diverting miners from the rum shops on winter evenings and on days when the pit was idle.[201] The sale of the stock of the Fidelity Lodge reading room at Stellarton in 1885 indicates that the PWA encountered setbacks in delivering its improving message.[202] Springhill miner Elisha Paul told members of the federal Labour Commission in 1888 that the reading room at Springhill was "now closed up."[203] Two representatives of the Reading Camp Association spent the summer of 1914 in tents in the Glace Bay area so as to teach English and "supply suitable literature." They reported that, in Nova Scotia mining towns at that time, there were no reading rooms and no free libraries.[204]

Music was a popular alternative form of respectable leisure activity. The union hall in Stellarton was the venue for songs performed by the Taylor Quintette Club in 1885; Miss Tweedie gave "first class renditions of music" there two years later.[205] Fondness for brass bands and male choirs reflected British immigration.[206] The Springhill band, organized in 1879, recruited boys as young as thirteen years of age; complaints were made that its clattering disturbed Sunday church services.[207] The *Maritime Mining Record* claimed in 1906 that every Nova Scotian colliery had its own brass band.[208] Within two decades of its first settlement, Nanaimo boasted a Philharmonic Society and a Concert Band.[209]

Professional entertainers also made their way to coal communities. An itinerant acrobat at Stellarton offered gymnastics, a trapeze show, and "some vocal music in the bargain."[210] In July 1889, the first Italian organ-grinder of the season arrived in Stellarton.[211] By the early twentieth century, a new commercial culture was emerging in large towns. Glace Bay had a theatre that would present a repertory of plays or, by 1911, short movie clips and vaudeville shows.[212]

Sport, reflecting male pride in physical prowess, acquired a growing place in respectable behaviour within coal towns and villages. Track and field events, frequently associated with picnics, were popular. The first anniversary of the formation of the PWA was marked by hundred-yard, six-hundred-yard, and half-mile races, vaulting, a standing-jump competition, and contests involving throwing large and small stones.[213] Among British immigrants, soccer remained a favourite sport.[214] A ball game called "rounders" and cricket were played in the nineteenth century. They gradually gave way to baseball.[215] Organized sport emerged and was widely followed. The Sydney Mines *Star* was delighted to announce in October 1905 that the local team had recently defeated one from the Reserve Mines at rugby football.[216] Boxing was also popular in the Cape Breton coalfields.[217]

At the same time, organizations dedicated to reconstructing child-hood assumed a growing presence in the coalfields. The Sons of Temperance was forming "youthful temperance societies," including Bands of Hope and the Cadets of Temperance, in Nova Scotia as early as 1873. Later in the nineteenth century, the Woman's Christian Temperance Union took a major role in temperance work among children, establishing Bands of Hope.[218] A visiting temperance lecturer in Springhill led to the formation in 1887 of a local branch of the WCTU.[219] The first branch of the WCTU in Cape Breton was organized at Cow Bay in 1888.[220] Throughout this period, churches organized youth groups. The YMCA was active in Stellarton in the 1880s, sponsoring lectures such as "Fifty Years of Progress in Pictou County."[221] It had erected a building in Springhill by 1905.[222] Four members of the Boys' Brigade of the Presbyterian Church died in the Springhill explosion of 1891.[223] The Boys' Brigade was in Nanaimo by 1900.[224] Boy Scouts in Glace Bay spent a day in May 1911 on a trail exercise, learning to follow tracks.[225] A Children's Aid Society was organized in Springhill in 1912; a chapter of the Imperial Order of the Daughters of the Empire opened there in 1916.[226] The first Well-Baby Clinic in Nanaimo was established in 1927 after lobbying from the Local Council of Women and the WTCU.[227]

Into the twentieth century, a traditional view of boys dominated coal communities: they were competent to labour, their early initiation to work was valuable to them and their families, schooling was of uncertain worth. Gainful employment was fundamental to male respectability: to remain a schoolchild was effeminate, even disreputable. C.W. Lunn, a railwayman, journalist, and labour advocate, contributed a serialized story to the Halifax *Herald* over several months in 1905 about a young boy, Tommy Barnes, who entered the mine at the age of ten as a trapper to support his widowed mother. Diligent in his studies at home in the evening, a fine sportsman, organizer of a boys' junior PWA lodge while still an adolescent, committed to "wise councilling and clever negotiating," Barnes was distinguished as a youth who was going "to make a mark."[228] The pit boy was not offensive to the respectable mining population.

But shifting notions of respectability and the new views of appropriate childhood led to changing commentary on the pit boy. A growing commitment to children's schooling among the mining population put into question a boy's early start to mine work in coal towns and villages. Their behaviour, as child wage labour was defined ever more commonly as a social problem, led to frequent claims that the mine brutalized boys. While O.R. Lovejoy offered an extreme opinion in claiming that the pit boys of his experience were "so tainted by vicious habits that an almost insuperable obstacle to a maturity of virtue and intelligence is presented," his views were widely shared within the urban reforming classes.[229] Boys in coal towns and villages were "particularly rough and uncultivated" claimed a teacher in 1886; another educator affirmed in 1912 that pit boys were "chiefly interested in learning how to chew tobacco and in acquiring an extensive vocabulary of picturesque profanity."[230] With increasing frequency, pit boys were defined as violating liberal society's new and universal prescriptions for childhood.[231] Respectable society was increasingly hostile to the employment of boys in the mines.

Within the mining community, new views of class interest led organized miners to scrutinize boys' early start to work at the mine. At the same time, women began to raise doubts about sending their boys into the pits. Concern also arose among men about the integrity of their craft, about whether it was a suitable basis of earning a livelihood. The redefinition of respectable culture in coal communities also undermined the popular view that local boys' appropriate place was the mine. By the early twentieth century, the expectation had weakened that boys raised in coal towns and villages would work in the mines.

CHAPTER EIGHT

Boys in the Pits

"Summed up, it amounts to this: the boys holding the position they do
in the mine, the management will of necessity – if for no better reason –
have to consider their rights."
Resident of Springhill, Nova Scotia, 1891

If the world that pit boys encountered was overwhelmingly shaped
for them – by class relationships and the technology of mining; by
constraints of gender and legislation; by family survival strategies
and the expectations of the mining community – boys' response to
their experience affirms that they remained in their own way historical agents. Although the control they enjoyed over their lives was
small, it was tangible. The boys' world was defined principally by
their experience of the colliery. This chapter focuses on Nova Scotia,
where most Canadian pit boys laboured, during the period between
1880 and the First World War.

Boys did not simply serve an apprenticeship to the techniques and
operations of the mine; more importantly, they were initiated into a
set of relationships that defined their experience of the mine and
generated a distinctive pit boy culture. Everyday life in the mine
wove a "web of solidarity" among pit boys, a set of attitudes and
practices marked by a high level of collective loyalty.[1] Their solidarity
gave boys a clear margin of manœuvre, helping them to negotiate
the demands of family, the community, older mine workers, and mine
officials. At the same time, in rapidly giving the boy an identity, it
helped him to cope with his early initiation to the intimidating environment of the colliery.

The child's first descent into the mine was memorable. The environment was harsh and frightening, David Frank observed, defined
by "rough footing, steep grades, a low roof, dripping water, narrow
passageways, pools of stagnant water and mud, cold rushing air
currents, clouds of bitter smoke and choking coal dust, falling stone
and coal overhead, fatal pockets of methane gas embedded in the
seams, and ... an almost universal darkness."[2] The absence of light
accentuated sounds underground: the clatter of coal tubs against

underground rail lines, the scurrying of rats, the dull retort of distant explosions.[3] The distance that had to be travelled underground could be considerable. Archie McIntyre, who started in the mines at the age of eleven in 1912, recalled that "[m]ost of the miners had to walk to their place of work in the mine and I remember the first day I worked I had to walk three miles underground before I got to my work and three miles back after I finished my twelve hours."[4] Miners would tell of the boy who refused to return after the first day. "I first went down as a winch boy [related a Vancouver Island miner] and I was with another young fella. The first day in the mine, the first trip I pulled up from the face was a dead mule that had been killed on the shift before. The other young fella was workin' farther up and I would pull one trip up and he picked it up and took it up to the next winch. The second trip I pulled up there was a man sitting in the box of the car and he had been hit in the head with a fall of coal. He was quite a mess with black face and blood running down and the other young fella when he pulled that man up, he left the mine. Quit right there. He just couldn't take it."[5] Another young trapper recalled the day he was sent to a door on another level: "I got a couple of hundred feet up the travelling road when this groaning started … I heard moans and groans – I said to myself, 'That's a ghost.' I kept going up and going up. A great big grey cloud started down. Boy, when I seen that, down the hill I went." An impatient official explained to the lad that he had witnessed a pump starting up, emitting exhaust.[6]

The various rites of initiation accompanying the boy's entry into the mine labour force sharply demarcated boyhood from childhood. Dan J. MacDonald recalled that when he was a young trapper, passing drivers routinely spat tobacco juice at him. At fourteen years of age, he was considered old to trap. Drivers told him: "Get away from there, you big bastard, and get a horse." MacDonald continued: "And there were lots of tricks played on you by the older fellows. Someone would send you to pick up a 'roofing-down-taker' or some foolish thing like that which didn't exist. They would send you to some old cross fellow. Well, he'd chase you out if he was in a cranky mood, but if you met some jolly fellow who understood the game he'd hand you something big and heavy and you'd take it back, and then you'd be directed somewhere else … This was your introduction into what was called mining sense."[7]

The warm rhetoric of reminiscence should not entirely mask the capacity of hazing to intimidate and bewilder. Robert Drummond complained of a particularly brutal assault in 1891. "Four or five half grown up boys set upon a quiet loader as he was going to his work along the level of the West slope. They used him roughly, kicking and striking him. If this is the initiation given to strangers or green-horns, it is high time the matter was looked into and stopped."[8] This account describes a transient's experience, someone new to the local mining community who may have frustrated the promotion of a local boy. Nonetheless, even local boys could expect to be the butt of often cruel practical jokes from older boys. The practice at Springhill was described in 1890 by a Halifax reporter: the newcomer's "face is painted with black oil and other handy colors … If his hair happens to be long the boys step up behind, burn off the long ends, blow out his lamp and disappear in the darkness."[9] The noises of the mine, the utter darkness, the descent underground were unsettling. The abuse from older boys was upsetting. Then followed the tedium, discomfort, and isolation of what was commonly the boy's first job in the mine, trapping. The child, instructed to keep to his door, was left alone in the dark with his fears.[10] Yet well-informed observers generally agreed that boys matured rapidly in the pit.[11] In a short time, trappers' greatest struggle was to resist sleep.[12]

Boys expected to rise gradually though the workforce hierarchy as they grew. The youngest boys performed light work such as trapping. Bigger boys would soon be driving a horse. The passage from frightened, bullied trapper boy to the self-confident driver could be rapid. Jack Lawson recalled that when he first entered the mines, drivers, often only a few months older than he was, seemed "old and experienced … I was a butt for them and the subject for jokes."[13] Boys on the threshold of adult strength performed the most arduous of boys' jobs: loading and unloading tubs from mechanized hoists, or filling tubs with coal in the bords. On reaching physical maturity, pit boys expected to become miners. Members of the federal Labour Commission heard in 1888 of the variety of work that the boys performed in the course of their informal apprenticeship to the mine. Robert McTagarth, a veteran of the mine at twelve, had started work at the age of ten. He had recently started to work as a driver. William Terrance, fifteen, had first worked at the age of ten turning a fan and had also recently started driving. Murdock McLeod, a twenty-nine-year-old miner, had entered the pit at nine as a trapper; he had "worked [him]self up," spending many years as a driver before becoming a miner. Elisha Paul's path to coal cutter was even more varied. Employed first as a trapper, Paul had graduated to the position of driver within a few months. His next occupation was on a balance, operating a pulley-based system that moved empty boxes up to the miners' workplaces and boxes filled with coal down to the levels. By sixteen he was a cage runner: he placed full boxes on the hoist and took empty ones off for the return trip to the miners. Later he was employed as a loader: he filled the boxes with the coal freshly cut by the miners. It was in the bord that Paul learned a "great deal as to how to work the coal from seeing the men he [was] working for and how they [did] it." At nineteen, Paul too became a miner.[14] A minority of boys rose to become mine managers.[15]

While far less pervasive, boys' informal apprenticeship also extended to western Canada. On Vancouver Island, despite the obstacles mining families faced, miners did bring their sons into the pit.[16] This practice also extended to the newer mines of the western interior, as members of the Royal Commission on the Coal Mining Industry in Alberta discovered in 1907. An adult mine worker at Lethbridge, William Davis, explained to the commissioners: "Q[uestion]. There is a time in the life of every miner when he is not a practical man? A[nswer]. Take this mine for instance, a little lad of twelve or thirteen years of age goes down to do trapping. During his term he learns … driving and such like. When old enough they put him driving. Well when he gets driving he is going into working places and learning all the time and every day's work brings him near the practical miner."[17] To be sure, much of the boy's experience of mine work did not contribute directly to acquiring the technical skills of the miner. Rather, it taught the boy how to work safely in the pit; it also consisted of "pit-hardening," the development of qualities of "toughness, manhood and fatalism" needed by the miner.[18]

The work day started at 6:00 or 7:00 a.m. Because boys' work was dependent on miners' production of coal, the length of time they spent in the pit on a given day was irregular. A Springhill official claimed in 1888 that boys were "supposed to work ten hours," but that generally they laboured for no more than eight or nine. In fact, the length of the working day might be much longer. Malcolm Ferguson of Sydney Mines explained that drivers left the mine "whenever you get the men's coal out," in his case any time between 2:00 and 6:00 p.m. Because the mine surface might be more than an hour's journey away, breaks were taken in the mine. Boys, like adult miners, would pause in their work to rest, talk, drink tea, eat, or chew tobacco.[19] Trappers necessarily remained in the mine as long as there was traffic on the underground haulageways, although the tedium of work could be offset by informal job exchanges.[20] From the 1890s, some use of the double shift was made, particularly at the Dominion Coal Company mines in industrial Cape Breton. In those circumstances, boys laboured "week about" – a week on days followed by a week on nights.[21]

Like older mine workers, boys were prone to absenteeism. Of course, until the turn of the twentieth century, many Canadian mines operated very irregularly – mine workers listened for the whistle blown in the early evening to indicate whether the mines would operate the following day.[22] To the days that coal companies decided not to operate the mine were added those days individual mine employees decided not to work the mine. The few surviving time sheets help to establish the extent of irregular work more clearly. At Sydney Mines in August 1839 twenty-four drivers and seven trappers were employed. Most drivers worked approximately nineteen days that month, but the range extended from a minimum of six and three-quarters days to a maximum of twenty-four and a half days. The range was far narrower among trappers, from twenty-two to twenty-five days. In January 1858 forty-three drivers and twenty trappers were listed on the Sydney Mines time sheet. If most drivers laboured between fifteen and twenty days that month, the range extended from nine to twenty-two and three-quarters. Among trappers, days worked extended from a minimum of five to a maximum of twenty, with an average between eleven and twelve.[23] At Springhill, in the first half of February 1891, nineteen drivers were listed on the company payroll. Most worked from nine to eleven days: at one extreme, Adolphus Landry worked seven and a quarter days; at the other, John Conway, son of the underground manager, worked fourteen. Among the twelve trappers, thirteen-year-old Willard Carter worked six and a quarter days, while sixteen-year-old Murdock Ross worked twelve and three-quarters (both boys were to perish in the explosion later that month). Most trappers laboured from ten to twelve days that pay period.[24]

BOYS AND MINE ACCIDENTS

Death in the mine came suddenly, violently, seemingly arising, Ian McKay argued, "from an unknown logic, capriciously assigning rewards and penalties arbitrarily."[25] The ever-present threat of death in the mine instilled a fatalism in miners, who at the same time recognized that their odds were improved by skilled and harmed by inexperienced co-workers.[26] A hallmark of the miner's skill was his ability to distinguish a safe from an unsafe workplace. Pit workers tell of "'getting a feeling' that makes them stop and investigate," wrote Stuart McCawley: "it may be a change in the air pressure, a queer odour, a crack or creep in the rock."[27] Hazards underground were difficult to detect, even for the most experienced miners who knew how to sound the roofs and walls of their workplaces frequently.[28]

If the small accidents killed and maimed more boys over the years, it was the great explosions, killing hundreds of mine workers at a stroke, that seized public attention. In Nova Scotia's Cumberland County over the years 1873 to 1927, explosions accounted for fewer than one-half of mine fatalities (46 percent), despite the carnage of the explosion at Springhill in 1891. Twenty percent of deaths were related to underground transportation, occurring on mine slopes and travelling roads. A further 19 percent ensued from falls of rock and coal. Five percent of deaths took place on the mine surface.[29]

Disaster was marked by "short sharp insistent blasts on the colliery whistle," triggering a rush to the pit-head by community residents (see Illustration 5).[30] As mines deepened, became larger, and employed more people, explosions increased in number and severity. The first major mine explosion in Canada was at Pictou's Drummond Colliery in 1873. According to one description, "The noise was terrific, the bank-head and other buildings over ground were shattered, impeding attempts at rescue. A cage in a shaft with its living contents was shot up into the air [cages were like elevators, used to bring workers and supplies into and workers and coal out of mines]. Smoke came rolling out the slope mouth in great dense volumes. Explosion succeeded explosion. The houses in the villages were shaken at intervals well on into the night. The explosion was caused by a fire, originating from a shot, which was uncontrollable, though heroic attempts were made to extinguish it." Fifty-nine men and boys died.[31] The following decade, major explosions occurred on Vancouver Island: in 1887 at Nanaimo, leaving 150 dead; and at Wellington the following year, killing 77.[32] Hillcrest, Alberta, was the site of the worst mining disaster ever to occur in Canada, in 1914. Sparks from falling rocks ignited coal dust, sparking an explosion which killed 189 mine workers. Reflecting boys' limited role in the mines of the western interior, the two youngest killed were seventeen years of age.[33] One of the last major coal mine explosions occurred at New Waterford, Nova Scotia, on 26 July 1917. It left 65 dead, including a boy of fourteen.[34]

A basic test of boys' ability to work in the mine is the extent to which they were killed in the smaller accidents endemic to the industry. The evidence is mixed. On the one hand, boys' accidents were attributed to their irresponsibility. "Two boys went into a place where they had no right to go," claimed the manager at the International Coal Mine in 1888, "and there was a slight explosion which burnt their faces."[35] Managers were criticized after two boys were "seriously hurt" after a runaway cage crashed at Springhill in April 1889: "it must be loose work on their part, when two and three little fellows can ride on a cage."[36] On the other hand, adult negligence could lead to a boy's death. In June 1889, at Sydney Mines, two boys laboured one night hauling timber into rooms. An accumulation of gas, which should have been checked by a mine deputy, ignited. Fourteen-year-old George Jones, leading the horse, was killed, and his brother James was badly burned.[37] At a small mine in the Nicola Valley of British Columbia, a fan-boy was killed in 1911, along with two miners, as a result of an explosion after a defective shot.[38]

If boys were incompetent to work in the mine, this would be most evident with young trappers. To pull a cord when asked to open a door was not beyond the capacity of a ten- or twelve-year-old boy. But because the mine environment was dangerous and the work tedious, lasting ten hours a day or longer, their inexperienced judgment could be expected to lead them to a disproportionate number of accidents. One mines inspector labelled as "familiar" accidents where "the 'trapper boys' [were] either jammed by boxes, or trampled on by horses. The cause is in many instances leaving their doors to gratify their curiosity, or in visiting the next trapper, but more frequently by going to shift points [on the rails, to move trips from one rail line to another] or some other duty for the driver." Rather than calling into question the presence of these boys in the mines, this mines inspector called for management to impose "strict discipline and [to] rigidly enforc[e] the laws."[39]

Yet very few trappers died in the mines, even if injuries were more frequent. As the inspector noted, accidents almost always occurred away from the door: "Edward Jones was employed to keep a door [at the Albion Mines] at the foot of a slope up which the coal was drawn by horse-gin. On the last tub of the day having passed, he followed behind, and the rope breaking, the tub came upon him, and crushed his leg so severely that it had to be amputated."[40] A trapper boy at Nanaimo "was injured about the head by a kick from a mule" in 1891.[41] Thomas McLeod, who died in November 1867 at Lingan, was less fortunate. "McLeod was employed in the Lingan Colliery as a door-keeper. It appears he had left his door for the purpose of having a ride in the empty tubs, one of which on his attempting to get into it, had ended up and got off the way; it had then come in contact with the props by the wayside, which were knocked out, and a portion of the roof falling upon him crushed him to death."[42] Albion Mines trapper Robert Harvey "left his post, and was injured" in 1882.[43] James McClellan was killed at the same mine in January 1884 when he "[l]eft his door and was killed by the rake striking him." Even though, complained the mines inspector, "[McClellan] was provided with a safety hole, and with a rope to open the door ... he had left his post."[44] The youthfulness of trapper boys was not perceived by mines inspectors as a problem. Rather, careless individuals made bad decisions.

Evidence from the United Kingdom and the United States indicates that boys were more prone to accidents. Owen Lovejoy claimed that they were up to three times as likely to be hurt at Pennsylvanian mines as adults. John Benson, examining the South Wales mines in the 1850s, calculated that boys were twice as subject to accidents as adults.[45] The *Canadian Mining Journal* observed in 1923 that a disproportionate number of Nova Scotia mine accidents occurred in "narrow, unlighted roadways, from the high speed of trips and from the still higher speed of mine cars breaking away from haulage roads and rushing down heavy grades," an area of mine work dominated by boys.[46] Despite this evidence, statistics from Cape Breton, by far the principal Canadian coal district at the turn of the twentieth century, do not indicate that mine accidents took a greater toll of boys. Over the period from 1889 to 1909, 217 deaths were recorded. Boys accounted for twenty-four of these, or 11 percent, a figure not far removed from their share of the mining workforce. Only four of these deaths involved the youngest boys, those under fourteen years. All occurred during the 1890s. These included two twelve-year-olds, an errand boy run over by an empty trip and a spragger, caught between a full trip and a roof prop; and two thirteen-year-olds, responsible for oiling tubs and mechanical underground roadways, both of whom fell under trips. But the rarity of boys' deaths in the mine is striking. By this stark measure, boys were no less capable than adults to work in the mine.[47]

BOYS AND OLDER MINE WORKERS

Studies on the relations between older and younger workers in other nineteenth-century workplaces such as textile mills have focused on the tensions that arose between them. There, adult male union members exercised enough control in the workplace to have younger workers labelled "unskilled," thereby excluding them from the most prestigious and best-paid jobs in the mill. Even though boys might have sufficient strength and experience to do work labelled "skilled," they were obliged to serve lengthy and increasingly, as boys matured, futile apprenticeships. Frustration with such systemic discrimination led to boys' strikes directed against older workers.[48]

In the mines, there were grounds for conflict between pit boys and older workers. The boys were paid at lower rates; they were ranked lower in the mine hierarchy. The distribution of authority in the mine, where boys were supervised more commonly by their older co-workers than by mine officials, led to friction. A boy's work in the bord throughout this period was organized and supervised generally by his father or another older relative; elsewhere in the mine, boys were subject principally to the authority of older mine workers, although the managerial presence increased after the turn of the century. The work was arduous and the hours long, boys being subject to the work rhythm of adult workers. Boys left the mine at the discretion of older workers. There existed moreover, in Daunton's expression, a "functional tension" between miners and haulage workers; until well into the twentieth century this would largely have been a generational schism in Nova Scotia. Continual pressure was placed on haulage workers to hasten to provide empty tubs to, and to remove full tubs from, the bords. Miners' earnings depended on the speed with which haulage workers laboured. Finally, boys' informal apprenticeship to the mine did not contribute directly to the acquisition of the technical skills of the miner; it simply developed experience of the mine.[49]

Nonetheless, miners never enjoyed the rigid rules of apprenticeship that Lancashire cotton spinners, for instance, did and were never able to buttress their position within the labour hierarchy at boys' expense. Credibly, given the strong family links among mine workers, older mine workers emphasized their paternal regard for pit boys. As trade unionist J. Morrison explained in 1906, "To help the boy is our bounden duty."[50] This concern may have been reflected in small considerations enjoyed by boys. At the Joggins mine, for instance, they were entitled to leave first at the end of each working day.[51] At times of disaster, older mine workers viewed boys to be in particular need of protection. Adult miners had made a point of sending boys up first when the explosion occurred at the Drummond Colliery in 1873.[52] As the pace of mine work accelerated with technical innovation at the turn of the twentieth century, adult miners expressed particular concern for boys. As early as 1906 the PWA Grand Council heard complaints regarding the use of multiple shifts. One delegate claimed that "[t]he injurious effect of night work on the human system is seen in the physique of our young boys." Added A.J. McDonald, "It is unfair and almost inhuman to have a boy of tender years go into the coal mine to be stunted in physical growth and in intellect, or else be injured, possibly fatally as sometime occurs. Large corporations care not what age boys are so long as their work is done." Another complained that Dominion Coal had "forced many of our young men to leave their homes and go elsewhere to work at an age when the boy should still be under parental care."[53]

If boys recognized that the basic division in the mine was not between them and older workers, this was easily obscured in its day-to-day operation.[54] An early editorial in the *Trades Journal* remarked

on the boys' general lack of respect for their elders and their readiness
to abuse them verbally – in the expression of the day, their "saucing."[55] One miner complained in 1888 about a pick-boy "having a
tendency to be a boss."[56] Later that year Springhill boys were criticized for "shoot[ing] the crow," removing ladders that miners used
as shortcuts out of the colliery.[57] The PWA lodge at Joggins dispatched
one of its members in 1906 "to see the Boys" about the noise they
made underground.[58] In 1891 a Caledonia miner went so far as to
enlist the help of mine officials in controlling pit boys: "Men working
by night are left to the mercy of a few boys, while there are four
bosses by day. Would it not be better for one of these officials to step
down by night?"[59]

The PWA leadership was never easy about unilateral actions by
boys. In Robert Drummond's expression, "Boys should be taught to
respect their bosses, and leave the saucing to their parents or to the
[Trades] Journal."[60] This, emphatically, boys refused to do, generating
considerable concern among adult miners. A Springhill resident
wrote that pit boys "won[']t be driven; they won[']t be ignored. They
have the whip hand in every sense. The men know this. The management ought to know it. But they are boys after all and can be kept
in their places by judicious and fair treatment. They will, however,
resent unjust dealing more promptly than men, and with entire
disregard of consequences. Considering all the circumstances is it not
perfectly right to have them combined where they can all be reached
by good advice from older heads."[61]

The mechanism chosen to pacify boys was to organize them within
the union. The PWA insisted on a minimum age of seventeen for
membership, but made provision for the establishment of boys'
lodges with the sanction of the existing adult lodge at a given pit.
The PWA saw boys' lodges as a means of moderating boys' actions
by making them more subject to the control of adult trade unionists.[62] The earliest boys' lodge on record was founded at the Reserve
Mines in 1883. "A new institution at the Reserve Mines is a 'union'
among the pit boys. They meet regularly for the transaction of
business. It is said you cannot put an old head on young shoulders.
Yet is to be hoped that the boys, will at all times conduct themselves
wisely."[63] A second juvenile lodge was reported in Pictou County
two years later, when mine workers met to discuss the question. "It
was pointed out, that the boys in a sense, were at present in a
'Union'; that if a supposed injury was done any boy then the boys
without due deliberation might strike; that there being no system,
the boys were likely to fall into grave mistakes [ie. they would
strike], and that, therefore, it would be better for all were they

properly organised and in some way under the control of [the PWA's] Cameron Lodge. The boys were unanimous in favor of forming a lodge and they are to meet again on Thursday evening to organize, having first obtained the consent of their parents."[64] At Springhill, where boys' strikes were frequent, a boys' lodge had been formed by the autumn of 1890, after a walkout by boys had compromised the efforts of adult workers to initiate a case under the province's new arbitration legislation.[65] At its formation, a correspondent to the *Trades Journal* outlined the adult miners' aim. They wanted "some method of controlling the youngsters ... What better way could be thought of than inviting them under the wing of the P.W.A. ... The numerous disputes that arose between the boys and the bosses occasioned much loss of time to the men, generally ... To prevent this – and render them more amenable to the wishes of the men – after a thorough consideration of the question in all its bearings, they were organized as a branch of the union, and the result was beneficial."[66] But with the exception of the lodge at the Reserve Mines, which appears to have been in existence at least intermittently from 1883 to 1907, boys' lodges were invariably short-lived. Generally, their existence was simply recorded once. Indeed, much of the initiative in their organization appears to have been taken by adults. Boys' lodges represented the vain attempt of adult unionists to subordinate boys' actions to the agenda of older workers.[67]

Surviving minutes for PWA lodges at Springhill (1882–86, 1899–1901) and at Joggins (1894–98, 1904–6), as well as for the UMWA at Springhill (1917–26), indicate, however, that boys' grievances were also heard by adult unionists. The nature of this relationship is unclear. At the funeral of a boy killed by a roof-fall at Little Glace Bay in 1882, PWA members turned out in their regalia.[68] Was this to mark the death of a co-worker, or of the son of a lodge member? Did the initiative lay with boys in lodging a grievance with the union local, or did fathers act on their sons' behalf? The evidence is mixed. In 1904 the Joggins lodge took up the case of a boy, Elie Downie, who had been promoted from driving to shoving on in a balance, yet continued to be paid at the (lower) driver's rate.[69] In 1905 the lodge struck a committee to establish a scale of wages for boys, and heard Tom Livingston request that a delegation approach the mine manager to reinstate his son Joseph, dismissed because he did not get along with "Coleman the overman." In 1906 it demanded a full day's pay for boys on days when the pit closed at 3:00 p.m.[70] At times of boys' strikes, adult unionists might act as mediators, such as at Springhill in 1895.[71] A committee of the PWA also helped to settle boys' "differences" with the manager at Sydney Mines in 1900.[72]

Unlike the PWA, the UMWA did not discriminate on the basis of age, but boys did not as a rule hold union office.[73] Concern for boys was evident. The minutes of the Springhill local refer in 1922 to a standing "Boys' Committee"; they record also regular efforts to have dismissed boys reinstated.[74] Through the UMWA, boys also had access to conciliation boards. A board that was formed in 1916 to adjudicate a dispute at the Acadia Coal Company, for instance, heard among other union grievances "a complaint from the boys employed by the Company that there are frequent shortages in their pay."[75] Yet the more formal the negotiation procedure, the more it excluded boys. The 1920 Montreal Agreement between the British Empire Steel Corporation and the UMWA, which based grievance procedures on the three-man pit committee and negotiated avenues of appeal, further formalized collective negotiations.[76]

BOYS AND MINE MANAGEMENT

Boys were restive under the tutelage of organizations of older workers and demonstrated this in a variety of ways. But despite boys' disputes with older mine workers, their most serious clashes were with mine officials. Colliery managers emphasized corporate paternalism. In Pictou County, H.S. Poole, in protesting against provincially set minimum-age provisions, emphasized officials' "fatherly regard" for boys. Yet the threat of violence was ever present in nineteenth-century industry. Why? In one view, because "corporal punishment increased the productivity of child labor."[77] In statements before the federal Labour Commission in 1888, mine officials were unanimous in claiming that boys were well treated. Commissioners doubted their sincerity. William Hall, the manager at Springhill, claimed that he had no objection to foremen whipping boys. Perhaps taken aback at the commissioners' expressions, he elaborated: "Because I think a whipping does him more good than discharging him or turning off the work; at times it does not look well, but many a good lashing and a good whipping I got in the pit, and I believe in it, though we do not do it, as I stated." Similarly, R.H. Brown, manager at Sydney Mines, testified that there was no current abuse of boys. "Before my time," he added, "there was a man who it is said did it."[78] Rumours of the physical abuse of boys arose at Springhill in 1889. "If officials are in the habit of beating the boys," warned the *Trades Journal*, "they should at once desist."[79]

But there are ample grounds for assuming that the treatment of boys within the mines did not diverge widely from community standards. Boys appearing before the Labour Commission acknowledged no more than that they had been "scolded."[80] Kinship, the presence in the mine of the pit boys' older relatives, who included mine officials, limited the potential for victimization.[81] The PWA saw the protection of boys to be one of its functions, boasting that it had put a stop to the beating of boys by mine foremen.[82] There also existed protection in law. After a mine official in Pictou County thrashed a boy in 1873, he found himself brought before a magistrate.[83]

Most important was boys' clear ability to defend themselves. While evidence of beaten boys is sparse, boys' unruliness in their relations with mine managers was well documented. In Springhill in 1887, a boy was ordered by a mine official to travel through a section of the mine the boy considered dangerous. He refused. "Harsh words passed between them," reported the *Trades Journal*, "the boy using the harshest it is said." Later, complained the official, the boy puffed smoke in his face while he was on his way to church.[84] "When Boys are Kept Working [together]," affirmed one manager in 1890, "they are always Combin[e]d for some Mischief."[85] Similarly, complained another in 1906, "if an examiner or deputy or road boss [all minor officials] wants a driver and his trapper to haul a load inside after he has hauled his coal out, he is just as likely to be told to go to hell as not, and then to be called all the names possible, as I can testify to."[86] When a chainrunner's lamp was stopped (when a boy was suspended) at New Waterford in April 1924, "the boy [clearly a good size], on hearing of this, disputed with the overman, knocking him down."[87]

Boys negotiated their conditions of work for the most part individually. A boy approached the responsible official to bargain over his pay or seek a promotion. Elisha Paul saw the promotion of boys within the mine workforce to be largely a function of intelligence and size. The graduation from trapper to driver, it was customarily understood, "is according to whether he is smart or not, or whether he is a big boy or not." When the fifteen-year-old driver William Terrance wanted his daily earnings of fifty-five cents increased, he approached Springhill mine manager Henry Swift, who agreed to raise the boy's pay to seventy cents.[88] A boy's quick-wittedness was no liability. "In the early days, you wouldn't get a raise, you had to go and see the general manager," a retired miner recounted to Ian McKay. "You wouldn't go in a crawl, you know. I went down to see him one day for a raise – I was only getting 61 cents – 'Oh,' he says to me, 'You're pretty small,' and he took and picked me up on the desk. And I said, 'The money's pretty small, too.' 'Oh,' he says, 'All right,' and he wrote me out a paper."[89]

At other collieries, the wage structure was more formal. Robert Simpson, manager at the Drummond Colliery, paid trappers a standard rate of fifty cents per day. He had established three grades of drivers, paid respectively sixty cents, eighty cents, and one dollar daily.[90] The season had a bearing on wages. Malcolm Ferguson earned eighty-five cents daily as a driver in summer at Sydney Mines, but only eighty cents in winter, when work at the mine slowed and labour was more plentiful.[91] By the twentieth century, wage structures were formalized in collective agreements. At the Dominion Coal Company, boys were paid a certain rate up to the age of seventeen, and from seventeen to eighteen an "augmented" boys' rate. "After that, [a boy] will either have to quit the job or go to a job that calls for a man's rate."[92]

Building on a common experience of work and their crucial place within the workplace, boys collectively exercised some control over the conditions in which they laboured in the mine. When boys did not find satisfaction individually, they approached mine officials collectively with *ad hoc* delegations – they had little interest in formal organizations. Henry Swift, manager of the Springhill collieries (and future victim of the explosion of February 1891), commented on a series of negotiations with boys in 1890. As Swift recorded in his journal:

Had a Committee of Boys to the house this evening about rates of wages[.] Refused to treat with Boys and told them to send either the Pioneer Committee [of the adults' PWA lodge] or their parents. [Swift subsequently faces a boys' strike after dismissing a boy named McDonald.] Boys Came down in the afternoon and asked Me if McDonald was going to get his work again I told them NO they went of[f] again have heard of nothing since[.] They are evidently backed by a large Majority of the Men[.] Something will have to be done towards weakening their power[.] Kindness and steady work do not seem to be of any use or have any desired effect[.] The More we do and the More we can do for them [and] the steadier the work, the greater their independence[.] In the afternoon about 2 P.M. the So Called Committee of Boys Came into My office – asked them what they were after this time ... I told them not to come to me again as a committee [because I] Never intended to recognize them again[.] I Gave them a downright Good talking to – told them that their actions were a disgrace to them their parents and in fact all Springhill. One McMullen[,] who has very little home restraint[,] replied[, "]well Mr. Swift the men transact their own business and we thought we could do ours[,"] which I considered a very frank acknowledgement as to the old [adage] "Cock Crows the Young one learns."[93]

Swift's initial response, which lends weight to the *Trades Journal*'s claim in 1887 that officials considered boys' grievances beneath their notice, was to refuse to meet a boys' committee, asking instead for their parents.[94] The boys persisted, striking with the support of older mine workers, as Swift recognized. He was forced to meet a committee of boys. His efforts to intimidate the delegates was unsuccessful, one lad asserting the boys' right to negotiate. Swift's account is particularly striking for its illustration of the independent initiative of mine boys, their refusal to channel their grievance via older mine workers.[95]

If both the PWA and the UMWA were willing to hear boys' grievances and to raise them with management, the dozens of strikes that boys waged independently of adult miners over this period testify to the shortcomings of negotiation and to the boys' impatience with adult trade unionists. The strike was the most powerful weapon the boys wielded against their employer, although it was by no means their sole means of protest. It was simply the most visible and regularly documented. Boys' strikes were a continuous irritant to mine management. Boys demonstrated repeatedly their willingness to walk out of the mine; in fact, they may have struck more often than older mine workers. A.S. MacNeil, general superintendent of the British Empire Steel Corporation's mines, testified to the Duncan Royal Commission that "a boy if he was disciplined in any way, or did anything wrong, he was liable to go home and would cause a strike in that part of the mine, or the whole of the mine, or two or three mines."[96] John Moffat underlined in 1924 the frequency of these strikes. "There are nearly always small incipient strikes among the boys," noted the former PWA grand secretary, "but they don't last long."[97]

Among boy mine workers, those who worked in underground haulage, among whom drivers constituted a majority until well into the twentieth century, were the most likely to initiate strikes. Drivers were "a very troublesome element to manage," complained mine engineer John Johnston in 1910.[98] American drivers were "strike-prone," particularly in the 1880s.[99] In England, "haulier lads" were a similarly "strong and independent force" in the period from 1888 to 1914.[100] In the Ruhr, "the particular strike-proneness of the young hauliers" was well documented.[101] Far more was involved than the "youthful impetuousness and the lack of family responsibilities" that one historian has identified.[102] "The great power of the haulage workers," observed Dave Douglass, "was that it only needed a five minute strike by them to bring the whole pit to a standstill as tubs clogged up waiting to be removed."[103] Boys' militancy is ascribable to the strategic position they occupied within the mine and their willingness to exercise the power they collectively possessed to their own ends. "And the drivers were a contrary lot," recalled ex-miner Archie MacDonald, "a lot of them, and they pretty well ran the pit."[104] When boys "want to control the output of the mine," complained another miner, "they can do it at will." The same miner, clearly speaking from

personal experience, observed that drivers were well situated to
bring sanctions against miners who engaged in strikebreaking
against boys. Afterwards, "they cannot get their coal taken away, as
the boys will only take as little as possible from them."[105]

A variety of motives prompted boys to strike. At issue most often
was the determination of a fair day's work and a just level and mode
of pay. Boys also struck over questions of hiring, promotion, and
wrongful dismissal. As well, boys struck to protest unwelcome
changes in working conditions. One of the earliest boys' strikes on
record stemmed from a dispute over pay at Stellarton in 1880.[106] Boys
again "showed their generalship" by going out in 1885 after a
number of them had their pay reduced by ten to twenty cents daily.
Their pay was restored to them by the mine manager, who claimed
ignorance of the original reduction.[107] When drivers at the Reserve
Mine struck for higher wages in 1887, the Trades Journal remarked
that boys were "apt to take offence even more quickly than men."[108]
At least twice in 1895 boys struck at Springhill to resist the company's
attempt "to cut some of the boys down in wages."[109] In 1900 drivers
at Sydney Mines struck successfully for higher piece rates, winning
"an extra half-cent per box on condition that they work steady."[110]
Robert Drummond remarked rather testily that they were "perhaps
the best paid of their class in the province," earning from $1.25 to
$2.00 daily.[111] Likewise, Dominion Coal drivers struck twice in Octo-
ber 1920 for a higher contract rate.[112]

The mode of pay was also disputed. Dominion No. 2 drivers
walked out to resist the replacement of contract pay by a daily rate
early in 1904. The company proposed to pay drivers a daily rate of
$1.38 and to find jobs on the surface for older boys at $1.65 daily.[113]
Robert Drummond recommended against the change: "[T]ampering
with contract driving is dangerous and not in the best interests of
either the companies or the miners. Drivers are generally diffident
about working on contract, but when they agree to do so, every one
interested is benefitted, strikes are less numerous among boys and
harmony reigns; the driver exerts his powers and skill to get as much
coal hauled as he possibly can, because it adds to his pay. In doing
so he adds to the output of the mine and the wage of the miner, and
fewer horses also are needed."[114] Drummond, by this point in his life
particularly interested in boosting coal production and the coal
industry, saw piece rates as an effective means to pacify boys. In
January 1922 drivers at Dominion No. 1 struck, with the support of
575 miners, when two of their number were transferred to jobs at a
daily rate. When officials promised that the boys would receive their
former jobs back, work at the mine resumed.[115]

The questions of pay and hours of work were often intertwined. Boys walked out of the mine at Springhill in June 1883 to object to a new managerial practice whereby, if work "got done" at 3:00 p.m. (perhaps one hour earlier than was customary), boys were sent home with three-quarters' time. "This was done five days in succession," reported the *Trades Journal*, "then the rebellion occurred and stopped it."[116] The issue arose there again in 1895:

Another strike has occurred at the Springhill mines this time it is the boys who have gone out on strike. It is stated that previous to [a fire which temporarily shut the mine] the men were working eight hours for a day, and the boys ten. Since the fire the men have been working six hours, three-quarter time, and the boys eight hours, as three-quarter time. The boys considered this was unjust, and demanded six hours as three-quarter time, and as this was refused they came out. The boys are an indispensable factor in mining, and as a result of their strike all the men were obliged to quit work. Things at present are at a standstill, and nothing will be done until the first of the week. [This account then describes the strike's resolution.] An agreement has been come to by which the strikers resumed work on Monday. Beginning with the first of April their demands will be acceded to.[117]

In July 1906 Springhill boys struck against dockage in their pay when work was completed early. Within a few days boys had been paid for the time docked and had "obtained a verbal agreement that a full day's pay would be given in the future under similar conditions."[118]

Boys at the Acadia Colliery launched an unsuccessful two-day strike in October 1901 for full pay on days when they were sent home early.[119] Results were more ambiguous after a week-long strike of boys at the Albion Mines in 1904. Triggered by the company's decision to lengthen the working day and to fine a boy accused of mistreating a horse, thirty boys struck one day, followed by ten more the next. The boys' position was compromised by the use of adult blacklegs (strikebreakers) – at adult rates of pay – as drivers.[120] Boys often sought a shortened workday on Saturday. Drivers at the Acadia Colliery struck in 1907 for riding rakes to be put on earlier on Saturdays.[121] Drivers at the Drummond Colliery struck on two successive Saturdays in May 1909 for a 3:00 p.m. quitting time and a twenty-five cents per day increase in pay.[122]

Boys' income was also affected by the common corporate practice of fining workers. Dominion Coal fined four drivers for an infraction against "company time" at New Waterford in 1921. At issue was what constituted a "fair day's work" – whether horses were to be stabled on the company's or the boys' time. After four drivers had stopped work at 2:30 rather than 3:00 p.m., they were each docked one hour's pay. This initiated a four-day general walkout, the drivers claiming that horses were to be unharnessed and stabled during the eight hours of working time.[123] The Sydney *Record* reported that "Foolish Boys Continue to Tie Up No. 12 and Keep Men Idle."[124] Companies also attempted to fine boys for the death of horses. At Sydney Mines, observed C.O. Macdonald in 1909, "if a horse is killed [the] boy in fault pays half value."[125] The question of fault was, of course, moot. When the mining company at Springhill threatened to deduct the value of a horse, $150, from the wages of driver William McLeod, blamed for its death when it was struck by a loaded box, boys struck the mine on McLeod's behalf. The company then dropped its plan to fine him.[126]

A second common motive behind boys' strikes was to protest dismissals. Springhill boys struck on behalf of fired fellow workers in 1887, when a boy was sent home after a dispute with an official, and in 1890, when a fourteen-year-old was discharged "for neglect of duty" and for "abusing" a horse.[127] At Glace Bay in 1902, boys walked out for a day to protest the firing of one of their number.[128] Particularly noteworthy was a four-day walkout in Springhill in July 1905. When a trapper boy named Foster was found absent from his door by an assistant manager, Hargreaves, an "exchange of heated words" passed between them. Hargreaves then suspended Foster. Subsequently, all 150 boys employed at Springhill walked out, putting 1,600 adult mine workers off the job. As journalist C.W. Lunn explained, "[boys] are very loyal to each other, and it is not an uncommon thing for them to sympathise with one of their comrades in trouble with the management, even to the extent of quitting work and walking out of the mine in a body."[129] After a two-day strike, a committee of boys negotiated a promise of an inquiry from mine managers. Boys struck again when mine officials were tardy in undertaking this inquiry. After a further two-day walkout, mine manager J.R. Cowans, while insisting that the boy be brought to trial on grounds of conspiracy, promised that Foster would be rehired, irrespective of whether or not he was fined by the judge. As it happened, Foster had been absent from his door for a legitimate purpose. As a trapper, in Lunn's account, "he was also supposed to attend [a point on the underground rail line] where the loaded and empty cars pass each other ... about forty feet from the door." From there he had been sent to get a trip-runner's lamp relighted (trip-runners tended trains of coal tubs on mechanized underground haulage systems): "it is claimed to be customary for the trapper boys to do that sort of thing for the trip-runners." Foster's replacement, a lad named O'Brien, had also been sent home after refusing to obey an order to leave his post to attend to a problem further along the underground road. "You discharged a boy for going away from his post," the lad told Hargreaves, "I'll not go."[130]

The following November, Springhill boys once again undertook a major strike, after a trip-runner was placed in an inferior job and a loader was discharged for not filling boxes fully. While the boys were eventually forced back to work, this did not occur before they had defied mine operators, middle-class opinion, and the PWA for ten days, tying up work at the mine entirely. Mine employees lost 16,500 working days.[131] The boys' "irresponsibility" was condemned by ex-PWA grand secretary Robert Drummond, who described the walkout as "probably the longest strike of its kind in the history of mining."[132] The situation remained unsettled for a number of weeks, the Amherst *Daily News* reporting in December a "rumor around town … that the boys had another grievance, and were thinking of going on strike again." Mine manager J.R. Cowans denied reports of unrest among the boys: "[H]e states that he doesn't know anything about it. He says that if there was anything in the talk, he would be likely to hear of it before this."[133] Less commonly, boys struck for the dismissal of unpopular officials. They struck unsuccessfully at Sydney Mines in 1901, for the dismissal of overman David Brown.[134]

Boys' frustration at the restrictions placed on their access to promotion gave rise to a third category of strike. The boys at the Drummond Colliery in Westville walked out for a day in June 1887 in protest against their obligation to perform boys' work, at a maximum of seventy-five cents per day, until the age of eighteen. Pit boys were unable to graduate to the position of loader, while workers new to the mine – "greenhorns" – were taken on for this task. Although the *Trades Journal* believed the boys to have "acted a little rashly," it acknowledged their "just cause of complaint."[135] Another strike was fought on this issue in 1906, at River Hebert. It stemmed from the refusal of the Minudie Coal Mining Company to allow a boy working in underground haulage to become a loader. Supported by the PWA local, work was halted for two weeks, the company eventually capitulating.[136]

The fourth category of boys' strikes stemmed from the desire to maintain traditional working conditions. Boys disputed undesired changes to their jobs. Following heavy investment by the Dominion Coal Company early in the twentieth century, work intensified. Drivers struck the Dominion No. 3 and No. 4 collieries in March 1901 to protest a decision by Dominion Coal "owing to the scarcity of boys" to reduce the number of boys employed with each horse from two to one. "The boys thought this would impose too much work on them and they decided to go out."[137] Dominion Coal also turned to extensive use of the night shift. Drivers at Dominion's No. 2 colliery struck in 1920, protesting that three of their number were working nights contrary to their wishes.[138] Boys jointly struck with miners at Springhill for a week in May 1920 against the replacement of 1,800-pound boxes with a much larger 2,300-pound box. Miners objected to pushing these far heavier boxes, and drivers to bringing them to the slope. The company soon undertook "to have more suitable boxes installed."[139]

Did boys pay a price for their willingness to walk out of the mine? The evidence is ambiguous. Elements such as local demand for boys' labour, the level of organization among boys, the support of older mine workers and their level of organization, and managerial idiosyncrasies determined the sanctions boys faced for striking. The claim of the Gowrie manager in 1888 that "[w]e have a great many applications from double the number of boys we want" must have sounded ominous to boys at that mine.[140] Similar circumstances may have prompted the *Trades Journal*'s claim in 1880 that boys were kept in dread of discharge at Springhill.[141] Nonetheless, of the dozens of boys' strikes of which there is record, only three involve clear instances of company reprisals against striking boys. In one of these cases, at the International colliery at Bridgeport in 1887, the colliery manager dismissed four boys as "ringleaders," placing them on a Cape Breton blacklist, after parents had forced striking boys to return to work.[142] In another instance, at Dominion No. 1 (Glace Bay) in 1899, seventy boys struck. The *Industrial Advocate* subsequently claimed that "[i]t is understood that half a dozen young men who engineered the movement have received notice of dismissal."[143] The drivers' strike at Dominion No. 3 and No. 4 in March 1901 "resulted in the discharge of quite a number of them."[144]

Boys also faced legal sanctions. While pit boys were not formally bound, and thus not subject to the sanctions of the law of apprenticeship for desertion of employment, employers had a variety of legal remedies in dealing with striking boys. Draconian colonial legislation passed in 1864 during a strike of adult miners at Sydney Mines carried a penalty of up to twelve months' imprisonment at hard labour for any worker who, in the judgment of any two justices of the peace, had coerced others to leave their employment. This law was never used against boys and disappeared from the provincial statute books within a few years.[145] The 1873 Nova Scotian Mines Act subsequently made provision for the establishment of "Special Rules" at each colliery "to provide for the safety and proper discipline of the persons employed in or about the mine." These rules were enforceable by law and, like the Mines Act, carried provisions for fining offenders.[146] Boys were tried at Westville for infractions against "the rules" in 1880. (The *Trades Journal* spoofed the judge as a liquor-seller.)[147] Boys were also tried at common law. Conspiracy was the charge to be brought against Foster, the trapper alleged to have precipitated the major boys' strike at Springhill in 1905.[148] In light, however, of the regularity of boys' strikes, it appears that legal sanctions were not an effective deterrent until the twentieth century.[149]

The mammoth Dominion Coal Corporation was far less tolerant: two cases in the summer of 1906 testify both to its willingness to use the courts and to the success it enjoyed there. In the first, a driver "was convicted and fined on a charge of endeavouring to persuade other drivers of the company to come out on strike" after a popular official was suspended. A few months later, two drivers at Dominion No. 3 who "embarrassed operations in the pit by persuading other drivers to quit work [for an increase in pay], and by forcing a few others to do so" were brought to court. One was fined sixteen dollars, the other, eighteen.[150] There are few subsequent boys' strikes on record at Dominion Coal until the intense and general industrial conflicts of the early 1920s, when drivers inaugurated use of the key tactic of the major 1922 Cape Breton strike, restriction of output.[151]

Boys received the respect and approval of older mine workers – their fathers and other older male relatives – if not as peers, then as co-workers and independent decision-makers. The broad approval boys enjoyed within mining communities was demonstrated most clearly by the support offered striking pit boys by adult miners. If, on the rare occasion, they would act to break a boys' strike, as a rule they tolerated the boys' actions. A few days after boys struck at Glace Bay in July 1899, "[t]he co[mpany] tried ... to get the men to do the work of the boys, but they refused."[152] The *Trades Journal* published a curious account of a strike at the Vale Colliery in 1881. The whimsical tone of this account is itself suggestive: "Quite a large number of men have lately left the locality on account of the temporary suspension or slackness of work. On dit [It is said] that the slackness arises not from lack of orders but from a strike among not the men, but among those who should not be guilty of such things. One wicked rumour hath it that the whole trouble is on account of some of the big fellows wishing, to put down and out the 'litter fry.'"[153]

Adult toleration is all the more noteworthy because of the work time miners lost as a consequence of boys' actions. Boys' strikes might throw adult mine workers off the job for one or two weeks. More commonly, as the *Trades Journal* noted in 1890, "the trouble was generally a local one. A slope or a district might be thrown idle

to-day, another slope or section of the pit tomorrow." But if boys
struck for simply a day or two at a time, they struck frequently.
"Summed up, the entire loss of time would make a very considerable
item to the run of a year."[154] Yet there are very few documented
instances of adult workers failing to support striking boys. In July
1887 drivers were on strike for four days over wages at Bridgeport,
Cape Breton. Because "the parents of the fractious youths considered
that the step was ill-chosen they took the culprits in hand and sent
them to work."[155] During a drivers' strike at the Albion Mines in 1904,
the management "put men to drive" at adult rates of pay.[156] In the
summer of 1909, boys at the Drummond Colliery struck for a shorter
workday on Saturdays. The PWA local pressured for a return to work,
and the boys saw some lodge members go so far as to blackleg.
Although after May 20 these men refused to continue to fill the boys'
places, members of Ladysmith Lodge, the PWA local, met on June 2
and agreed to assemble the boys and insist they vote to end their
strike. By the slim margin of 21 to 18, drivers submitted to the will
of older mine workers. They returned to work on June 4, not before
having received the wage increase they demanded.[157] These rare
exceptions underscore the point that, on the whole, adult mine workers were remarkably supportive of boys.

By their nature, boys' strikes were commonly undocumented; short-
lived, they were frequent enough to be unremarkable. They were also
generally successful. Of the forty-seven strikes that boys waged independently of adults between 1880 and 1926 in Nova Scotia for which
some evidence exists, the boys were clearly defeated in only seven.
Ian McKay calculated that of the fourteen boys' strikes to occur at
Springhill between 1879 and 1911, the boys were victorious in eleven.
Three ended in compromise.[158] If much depended on the relative balance of power at the colliery involved, and boys did face reprisals on
occasion, they achieved a remarkable level of success in striking.

Boys' response to mine work forces the reassessment of the sentimental view of the pit boy. Often small, frightened, and victimized
by pranks when they first entered the mine, boys matured rapidly.
Building on a common experience of mine work, they developed a
strong sense of mutuality. This collective loyalty was fundamental to
boys' efforts to shape the circumstances in which they found themselves. In managerial calculations of workforce discipline, productivity, and profit, boys were to be reckoned with. If they fell short of
creating the world they would have wished, pit boys did no worse
than other contemporary workers.

CHAPTER NINE

Conclusion

"I never again will go down underground."
Rita MacNeil, *"Working Man"*

Boys' participation in the Canadian coal mine labour force was in decline by the early 1880s – a reflection of early mine mechanization in Nova Scotia, the growth of mining workforces in the western interior based on transient adults, and restrictive legislation and alternative sources of low-wage labour in British Columbia – although their absolute numbers continued to grow because of the rapid expansion of the industry. At any given time between the turn of the twentieth century and the First World War, well over one thousand boys still laboured in Canadian collieries. But by the 1930s, they have virtually disappeared from mining workforces.

As major collieries were developed in British North America, in Nova Scotia from the 1820s and on Vancouver Island a generation later, English and Scottish immigrant colliers brought their familiar practices to these new workplaces. Boys, taken into the mine by their father or an older male relative, underwent an informal apprenticeship to the craft of mining. Aspiring to be miners, boys rose through a hierarchy of mine jobs: opening and closing ventilation doors, driving horses, assisting at the coalface. Working closely with older workers, boys assimilated mining lore as they acquired the technical skills of the handpick miner. Perhaps the most important lesson boys learned was that workers shared a common interest in safety: a mistake by an incautious or inexperienced mine worker could cost the life of everyone in the mine.

But the craft of mining faced threats. Miners had limited success in restricting access to the mine as the industry expanded rapidly over the last decades of the nineteenth century. All too frequently, the skilled collier found his room adjacent to another mined by an inexperienced "coal smasher." Appeals to the state to establish legal qualifications for mine work provided only partial recognition of pit boys' informal apprenticeship. At the same time, the development of larger, more highly capitalized collieries serving industrial markets forced managers to increase mine productivity. The introduction of cutting machines and mechanized haulage systems, and the associated turn to longwall techniques of mining, if adopted slowly and unevenly, reduced corporate demand for child labour. Subject to an increasingly mechanized work environment, the craft of the individual miner became more restricted in scope. Decision-making moved steadily from the domain of the skilled collier to mine managers and engineers. Miners steered their sons away from what they viewed as a declining craft.

Within the family, boys learned that everyone's welfare hinged on the collective effort of family members. Family strategies incorporated both non-wage forms of labour based on the household and the low and uncertain income that work in the mines yielded, continually threatened by seasonal fluctuations in demand for labour or by illness, disability, or death. Boys learned that at times even subsistence was elusive and that mining families had a strong interest in increasing the number of wage-earners. As boys, they assumed responsibilities for wage-earning that were denied girls. For the family, boys' income was a step towards an always tenuous security. Those few years when co-resident wage-earning sons contributed to the family purse were fleeting.

Families in Sydney Mines and other coal-mining communities sent their boys into the colliery in an increasingly inhospitable social environment. New ideological prescriptions for childhood were particularly hostile to child wage labour. Under pressure from a broad reform coalition, the state had gradually taken steps towards the "universalization" of childhood by setting standards for the treatment of children. From the mid-nineteenth century, provincial governments began to implement the legislative basis for a new and universal childhood. The primary target of these efforts was the labouring child. Two principal vehicles were employed against the pit boy. Mines legislation progressively raised the minimum age for mine workers and, on Vancouver Island, had a clear role in excluding boys from the mines. The compulsory attendance provisions of school legislation, while implemented gradually, embraced increasingly older children for greater portions of the year. If the initial impetus for these reforms was from outside the mining community (indeed, from outside the working class), organized miners, committed to schooling, were quick to demonstrate their support for efforts to restrict child labour in the mines. By the turn of the twentieth century, increasing numbers of boys raised within coal towns and villages no longer made mining their livelihood.

THE DECLINE OF COAL

While boys' place in the coal mine was diminishing from the late nineteenth century, the exclusion of all but a handful of older boys from mine work is linked to the decline of the traditional coal industry after the First World War. Though fundamental to the emergence of industrial society, underground coal mining entered a period of crisis after the war from which it never fully recovered. There were two dimensions to this crisis. One was short-term, largely a function of wartime disruption, and focused on the older coalfields of Nova Scotia and Vancouver Island. The second was far more ominous: a permanent loss of markets reflecting a secular trend away from the use of coal as a primary energy source.

The competitive position of older Canadian mines was weakened by the postponement of new mine planning and development work during the war. Wartime pressure for increased, uninterrupted output encouraged maximum short-term coal production. Despite these efforts, coal output declined significantly during the war years as many miners enlisted for wartime service. In 1913, 7.3 million tons of coal had been mined in Nova Scotia; by 1918, annual output had fallen by nearly 2 million tons. Difficulties in procuring shipping on account of the requisition of ships for wartime service by the British Admiralty, and delays in returning these ships to the coal trade, further hampered Nova Scotia's efforts to displace cheaper American coal that had entered St Lawrence markets during the war.[1] High wartime demand for coal and artificially inflated prices delayed the impact of increasing production costs, particularly severe in the older coalfields of Nova Scotia and Vancouver Island.[2] During the war, the centre of gravity of the Canadian coal industry began to shift to the western interior.

Far more damaging to the coal industry was the emergence of a secular trend away from coal as alternative energy sources came into use. From the turn of the century, coal was gradually displaced as the fuel of choice among a number of major consumers. As early as 1902, directors of the New Vancouver Coal Mining and Land Company warned shareholders that "[t]he competition of Fuel Oil is assuming a more serious aspect"; by 1921, petroleum was believed to displace over six hundred thousand tons of Vancouver Island coal annually.[3] The changing energy requirements of the shipping industry clearly illustrates petroleum's threat to coal. In 1833 the *Royal William*, the first vessel to cross the Atlantic by steam, had bunkered at Pictou, Nova Scotia, and inaugurated a major market for coal. In 1910 80 percent of the world's shipping continued to use coal. By 1924, as shipping converted to oil-fired diesel engines, the figures were reversed, and soon virtually all vessels were powered by the more economical oil.[4] Railways also abandoned coal. In British Columbia the switch to oil was under way even before the First World War.[5] Ultimately, coal would lose all railway markets in Canada when the last locomotives converted to diesel during the 1950s.[6]

The Great Depression of the 1930s made a bad situation worse. Declining industrial activity, particularly in the manufacture of pig iron and steel products, and in world trade generally, weakened traditional markets for coal.[7] Industrial consumers in Ontario and Quebec converted from coal to hydro-electricity wherever possible. Domestic consumers across Canada switched to electricity, natural gas, or oil.[8] The more energy-efficient use of coal eroded demand within remaining markets. Mining engineer T.L. McCall claimed in 1938 that "the average fuel efficiency of industry and railway transportation [had] risen by no less than 33 percent in the period 1909–1929."[9] In 1935 Canadian consumption of coal stood at 75 percent of its 1920 total. Per capita consumption had dipped far below pre–First World War levels.[10] The federal Royal Commission on Coal estimated that whereas coal had accounted for approximately two-thirds of total energy consumption in 1926, by 1945 it accounted for just over half of energy consumed in Canada.[11]

With reductions in demand, employment in coal mining also stagnated, particularly in older coalfields. On Vancouver Island, an industry that had employed 4,005 in 1911 provided jobs for just 3,150 in 1927.[12] Between 1910 and 1934, by one estimate, nearly 5,000 British Columbian coal miners lost their job.[13] Only 2,969 coal miners were employed in the province in 1939.[14] Underemployment could mask declining or stagnating employment levels. In Nova Scotia, 12,522 workers laboured 3,527,149 days in 1911; fifteen years later, 12,622 workers received only 2,988,281 days' work.[15] And in 1939, 13,208 workers had 3,009,025 days' work.[16] Among major coal-producing provinces, only in Alberta did employment levels grow appreciably after the First World War, although the 7,908 miners employed in the province in 1939 represented a considerable decline from the 9,324 employed in 1926.[17]

The crisis in the coal industry capped a trend whereby boys' place in the colliery workforce had been eroding for a number of decades. In Nova Scotia, it led adult heads of families to usurp boys' traditional access to certain categories of mine jobs. At Springhill, for instance, both management and the union adopted policies that gave priority to family breadwinners. By 1922 the company would only hire married men and the few boys who headed a household. The following year, the UMWA local announced that boys would not be hired "until such times as those that maintain a home gets work." During an era of industrial stagnation, these times did not arrive. Faced with the common resolve of coal companies and organized labour to exclude them from the mine, few boys were able to enter the colliery workforce after the First World War.[18]

BOYS IN THE PITS: AN EVALUATION

The new industrial workplaces in which children laboured in Victorian Canada – large, impersonal, marked by an unsettling pace and intensity of work – encouraged efforts to reconstruct childhood. But causal links can not be directly drawn between changing attitudes, increasingly reflected in restrictive and effective legislation, and the eradication of child wage labour. Child labour in the coalfields rested on fundamental props: employers' need for workers; the mine's role in training boys for their adult occupation; the long-term economic need of the family; community expectations; and boys' desire to enter the mine. Only as these props were undermined did child labour in the mines decline.

Employers needed a range of labour for their collieries. The lower the cost of this labour, the better they were satisfied. A key factor in the cost of labour was the level of organization among mine workers. Mine operators willingly undercut the older family-based organization of mine labour in favour of strategies that weakened worker unity while broadening the pool of available labour, be it on the basis of a seasonal influx of rural workers as in Nova Scotia, seasonal transient labour, as in the western interior, or Asian immigrant miners, as on Vancouver Island.

Boys' informal apprenticeship in the mine gave employers a supply of qualified miners – it also gave the boy recognized skills. Early initiation to the pit was distinguished from many other kinds of contemporary child labour because it had no negative impact on the boy's ability to find work as an adult.[19] Rather, boys' informal apprenticeship to the mine was a recognized path to his adult occupation as a miner. The alternative – prolonged school attendance – was of limited use to a future miner until the beginning of the twentieth century, when certification requirements for miners and mine officials gave formal schooling clearer value in the coalfields.

The economic need of families for child labour rested on the desire of mining families for a standard of living that allowed them modest creature comforts and some measure of security. Because the miner was threatened daily with illness, injury, or death, the prudent family widened its sources of wage income. Key to this goal were the savings accumulated during those few years when co-resident sons' earnings were put into the family purse.

For these reasons, into the twentieth century boys were raised in coal towns and villages with the expectation that they would one day start to work in the mine. Their class identity, their wish to be viewed as men, to make the transition from childhood to maturity, and their desire for the freedom gainful employment gave them encouraged them in this aim. A basic support for child labour in the coalfields was boys' well-documented willingness to enter the mine. Paid employment gave them status in the family and community, marked their maturity, and enfranchised them from the restrictions placed on the dependent. Children's wage labour, Neil Sutherland observed, was an absolutely key step "in the process of freeing themselves from the enormous power and authority of their parents."[20] Despite some individual testimony to the contrary, the weight of evidence is that boys entered the mine happily. In this context, there was no compelling reason in Victorian Canada to defer the start of a boy's apprenticeship to mine work: indeed, delay would have been perverse.

But when enough factors buttressing child labour were weakened, boys did begin to withdraw from the mines. Changing techniques of mining, based on higher levels of capital investment, diminished the employers' call for child labour, as the decline of the traditional craft reduced miners' interest in bringing their sons into the mine. Informal apprenticeship led no longer to a recognized lifetime trade. The introduction of certification and formal testing, encouraged by the changing technology of mining, placed a new premium among miners on picking up the rudiments of schooling. And for the more ambitious, the rising prominence of university-trained mining engineers and managers underlined the utility of secondary and postsecondary education. Whether the boy would ultimately enter the mine or not, by the turn of the century miners were placing increasing emphasis on at least some "book-learning" as the appropriate path in boys' education. At the same time, better adult wage earnings on account of more regular work lessened the economic pressure on mining families. And the introduction early in the twentieth century of new programs of insurance and pensions reduced the need among working families to make provision against the loss of the adult breadwinner. What is least clear is whether boys' desire to labour productively was in any way diminished. In the task of reconstructing childhood, their opinions were rarely sought. Work moved from the centre of boys' lives in coal communities to the margins.

Childhood was defined and redefined over the nineteenth and early twentieth centuries in light of competing views of what it meant to be a child. While never uncontested, the key elements of the modern definition had been identified by early in the twentieth century. The reconstructed childhood, premised on the emotional and psychological dependence of boys and girls, their vulnerability, corruptibility, and immaturity, was to be safer and less threatened than earlier childhoods. The child, deemed incapable of assuming adult responsibilities, was to be sheltered from the adult world.

These views took shape in an assortment of institutions, associations, and legislation designed to construct an appropriate environment for children. Fragmented, often with narrow aims and local in focus, an array of individuals and organizations all contributed piecemeal to the reconstructed childhood: the evangelical who was "rescuing" a child from a home she considered undesirable, the WCTU local enlisting children in a Band of Hope, the school reformer striving to make the system of common schools work, the factory inspector who advocated a Factory Act amendment raising the minimum age for employment, the Boys' Brigade leader, the lodge of a miners' local that passed a resolution that ten was too young an age for a child to enter a mine.

Within the coalfields, the nature of childhood was negotiated locally and differed from meanings articulated in the urban centres of power. In the nineteenth century, mine employers defined boys as potential mine labourers. The restrictive child labour clauses of the provincial Mines Act were only passed and effectively implemented on Vancouver Island because the local labour market, in giving employers an alternative supply of cheap labour, permitted such restrictions. Even the relatively lax requirements of Nova Scotia's Mines Act elicited protests from mine operators there. Organized miners defined boys as co-workers, valued helpers in the mine, and also as future miners until the transformation of mine work made the traditional skills of the handpick miner obsolete. Into the twentieth century, mining families defined boys as valued secondary wage earners and contributors to the modest family purse.

Most importantly, how did the pit boys define themselves? Emphatically, they did not view themselves as victims. Their actions reflect their self-respect, their pride in their identity, and their determination to assert their rights as they defined them. Pit boys rejected the reconstructed childhood. But in the clamour of voices raised redefining childhood in the pit towns and villages of late-nineteenth- and early-twentieth-century Canada, the boys' voices were ultimately the weakest. To the age of sixteen and beyond, boys were defined universally as schoolchildren – as non-productive members of the community – and institutionalized in schools.

Children's circumscribed freedom of action, relative to adults, is the result of more than any intrinsic dependence of the young. Those labelled children have been subject to further restrictions on their autonomy than their abilities might warrant. The pre-industrial household subordinated children to the demands of the household economy, in addition to customary, religious, and legal constraints. The child of today is subject to legal and other institutional controls, as well as to economic dependence. The level of scrutiny the child faces is taken for granted: "If an adult stays out late at night," Jocelyn Raymond has observed, "does a little gambling and drinking, or chooses companions unwisely, it usually evokes little comment. If an adult misses work he may lose his job, but it is most unlikely that he will be picked up by the police and required to explain his absence. Similar roustabout behaviour or simple truancy in a youngster, however, will very likely lead to great concern and perhaps intervention by a social agency or the courts."[21] The early phase of industrialization was unique in the access to economic independence it offered children. Traditional constraints on children were relaxed. Modern constraints had yet to be developed. To examine children as wage-earners is to catch glimpses of their potential.

Yet the most familiar view of child labour labels it as shameful: a record of blighted childhood. Certainly some coal miners, in reflecting back on their boyhood, emphasized its bleakness. One recalled "[c]oming home in the evenings and falling asleep while eating supper – the effects of rotten ventilation and damp. [I], in common with all boys, then obliged to work to eke out the family income, faced the prospect of a dismal and unhappy existence."[22] Another described the pit lad's life as "one of drudgery, work, and sleep, and little to look forward to."[23] In such a light, the history of the boy's labour in the mines is a tragic record of forfeited childhood.

A contrasting perspective has been developed here. The precocity of labouring children was widely observed by their contemporaries, and just as commonly deprecated, attributed to a premature association with adults.[24] Many codes were used to describe precociousness. J.J. Kelso complained of street urchins in Toronto that "[t]heir pinched faces were prematurely developed in vice, cunning and deceit."[25] Factory children, in the judgment of provincial inspectors, were "affected morally"; their "morality has been considerably contaminated"; they were "corrupted."[26] Bad language, drink, and the use of tobacco were depicted regularly as badges of this corruption.

The "latitude" of young boys left on their own without the "constant supervision of older heads," one late Victorian journalist argued, was harmful "morally and intellectually."[27] But far more consequential than their foul language or partiality to chewing tobacco was labouring children's evident competence. "When children become wage-earners and are thrown into constant association with adult workers," stated Margaret Mackintosh before the Canadian Council on Child Welfare in 1924, "they develop prematurely an adult consciousness and view of life."[28]

Boys' experience in the pits was sharply at odds with the new views of appropriate childhood. While the modern child was to enjoy a prolonged, cloistered period of dependence, pit boys mixed promiscuously with the world of (male) adults. They shared mine labour. To some extent, they shared leisure activities. Most vexingly for childhood's reformers, these boys commonly exhibited a preference for wage labour over the classroom. Maturing rapidly in the mine, they behaved like adults. Tough and self-reliant, their independence was transparent. Pit boys repeatedly demonstrated courage and initiative – a refusal to be the mere victims that historians have persistently labelled them. Their experience in the mines is a record of achievement. But viewed in light of the new prescriptions for childhood, these achievements were very disquieting. The independence of wage-earning boys and girls raised doubts that children were the dependent innocents they had been recast as, in need of segregation and protection, incapable of assuming adult responsibilities. As schoolchildren, pit boys were disenfranchised. Economically dependent on their parents, institutionally segregated, excluded from the adult world, boys remained children. They can be viewed as another kind of victim – of the prolonged institutional dependency that adults had redefined boys and girls to require. The workplace or the school? Children's proper place remains moot.

Notes

Abbreviations

BCMR	British Columbia Mines Report
CMJ	*Canadian Mining Journal*
CMR	*Canadian Mining Review*
LC	Canada, Royal Commission on the Relations between Capital and Labour
Mathers	Royal Commission on Industrial Relations
MG 20	Records of the Hudson's Bay Company
MG 28, I 10	Records of the Canadian Council for Social Development
MG 28, I 129	Records of the Montreal Society for the Protection of Women and Children
MG 28, I 25	Records of the National Council of Women of Canada
NA	National Archives of Canada
NSMR	Nova Scotia Mines Report
PAA	Provincial Archives of Alberta
PANS	Public Archives of Nova Scotia
RCTE	*Report of the Royal Commission on Technical Education*
RG 27	Records of the (federal) Department of Labour
RG 33	Records of Statistics Canada
TJ	*Trades Journal*

Chapter One

1 The principal accounts of this disaster are Morrow, *Springhill Disaster*;
   McKnight, "Great Colliery Explosion"; and Nova Scotia, *Mines Report*
   (hereafter NSMR), 1891, in Nova Scotia, House of Assembly, *Journals
   and Proceedings*, 1892. The *Mines Report* for any given year was published in the *Journals and Proceedings* dated the following year.

2 Morrow, *Springhill Disaster*, 39.

3 NSMR, 1891, i–xxvii.

4 Morrow, *Springhill Disaster*, 83.

5 McKnight, "Great Colliery Explosion," 10. Philip Ross was fourteen;
   his older brother, Murdock, sixteen, also died in the mine that day.
   NSMR, 1891, xxv.

6 Morrow, *Springhill Disaster*, 60–1.

7 Four were fourteen years of age; four, fifteen; five, sixteen; and four,
   seventeen. See NSMR, 1891, xxiii–xxvi.

8 For a brief introduction to child labour in agriculture, see Vernon,
   "Child Labour in the Country," 115–21. See also Jones, "'We can't live
   on air all the time,'" 185–202; and Sutherland, "'I can't recall when
   I didn't help,'" 263–88. "It's part of the farm heritage for children to
   work," explained federal minister of agriculture Eugene Whelan as
   recently as 1973. "We'd pay a hell of a lot more for food if it wasn't.
   Child labour is a fact of life." Quoted in Abella and Millar, *Canadian
   Worker*, 300.

9 A visitor to the Gaspé remarked in 1821 that "dès qu'un enfant est
   capable de marcher, il sert toujours à quelque chose d'utile dans la
   pêche." Cited in Mimeault, "Le capital industriel des pêches," 51–2.
   See also Sider, *Culture and Class*, 41–3; and Porter, "She Was Skipper
   of the Shore-Crew," 105–23.

10 See Neary, "Bradley Report on Logging Operations," 193–232; and
   Parenteau, "Bonded Labour," 108–19. Ian Radforth observed that a
   farmer's son accompanied his father into the bush as a rite of
   passage, "a sign of approaching manhood." See *Bush Workers and
   Bosses*, 44.

11 Lacelle, "Les domestiques dans les villes canadiennes," 181–207.

12 Hardy and Ruddel, *Les apprentis artisans*; Moogk, "Apprenticeship
   Indentures," 65–83.

13 On children as dock-workers, see Chisholm, "Organizing on the
   Waterfront," 52–5.

14 See Clark, *Of Toronto the Good*, 81–5. See also Houston, "Waifs and
   Strays," 129–42. On child prostitution, see Bullen, "Children of the
   Industrial Age," 147–9.

15 See Zucchi, *Little Slaves of the Harp*.

16 Kealey, *Toronto Workers Respond.*
17 Rouillard, *Les Travailleurs du coton.*
18 The single most comprehensive source on late-nineteenth-century industry in Canada is the *Minutes of Evidence* of the Royal Commission on the Relations between Capital and Labour in Canada, originally published in 1889. Extracts have been republished in Kealey, ed., *Canada Investigates Industrialism.*
19 Cited in Kealey, ed., *Canada Investigates Industrialism,* 16.
20 Cunningham, "Employment and Unemployment of Children," 115–50.
21 "There can be little doubt that when substantial numbers of working children were concentrated in the public view for the first time, and when the physical effects of labouring at a tender age were no longer buried in the family, conditions were ripe for a social reform campaign amongst the middle and upper classes." See Heywood, "Market for Child Labour," 49. A similar point is made in Pinchbeck and Hewitt, *Children in English Society,* vol. 2, 403.
22 Macdonald, *Address of the Honourable John A. Macdonald,* 94. A particularly attractive feature of factories for Macdonald was the opportunity they provided for useful employment during winter.
23 Sutherland, *Growing Up,* xi. It also reflects, as Joanne Burgess has pointed out, a perpetual biological relation: a child has birth parents. See Burgess, "Le travail des enfants au Québec," 28.
24 *TJ,* 21 January 1891.
25 Cited in Dobson, *Coal Industry of the Dominion,* 5.
26 The estimates on coal consumption are taken from Bartlett, *Manufacture, Consumption and Production,* 102; and the Dominion Bureau of Statistics, *Coal Statistics for Canada, 1927,* 27.
27 Production figures are taken from Canada [Carroll], *Royal Commission on Coal,* 61; and from NSMR, 1901, xv.
28 Employment figures are drawn from Brown, *Coal Fields,* 49; NSMR, 1867, 48; 1900, 71; and British Columbia, *Mines Reports,* 1874, 1900. The British Columbia, *Mines Reports* (hereafter BCMR), were published in British Columbia, *Sessional Papers.* The *Mines Report* for any given year is published in the *Sessional Papers* dated the following year.
29 NSMR, 1911, xxi; Alberta Coal Mines Branch, *Annual Report,* 62, in Alberta, *Annual Report of the Department of Public Works,* 1911; BCMR, K218.
30 Dominion Bureau of Statistics, *Coal Statistics for Canada, 1939,* 30.
31 See McKay, "Industry, Work and Community." On two smaller coalfields, see Samson, "Dependency and Rural Industry"; and Seager, "Minto, New Brunswick."

32 For an introduction to the Canadian coal industry, see Muise and McIntosh, *Coal Mining in Canada.*

33 Bartlett, *Manufacture, Consumption and Production*, 101; Canada [Carroll], *Royal Commission on Coal*, 61–73, for output by province from Confederation onward.

34 PANS, RG 21, series A, vol. 40, no. 10, "Particulars of Mining Operations in Cape Breton, 1832"; PANS, RG 1, vol. 463, nos. 32–3, "Statement of Men, Horses and Machinery Employed at Sydney Mines and Bridgeport Mines in September 1838," cited in Hornsby, *Nineteenth-Century Cape Breton*, 100–1.

35 NSMR, 1866–1910; BCMR, 1877–1910.

36 See the classic "pessimistic" account of industrialization, Hammond and Hammond, *The Bleak Age.*

37 One of the rare documents that recorded an age profile of pit boys is the list of individuals killed by the explosion of 1891 in the No. 1 Slope at Springhill. The average age of the boys killed was fifteen; more than three-quarters of these boys were aged between fourteen and sixteen years. See NSMR, 1891, xxiii–xxvi.

38 See *TJ*, 6 December 1882; LC, 294, 412, 454.

39 NA, Records of the Department of Labour (hereafter RG 27), vol. 142, file 611.04:6, "Proceedings of the Royal Commission appointed to inquire into Coal Mining Conditions in the Maritime Provinces at Meetings held in Fredericton, N.B., on August 17th and 18th, 1920," 42.

40 See Chrismas, *Coal Dust Grins*, 248, 269, 272, 294, 303.

41 Ibid., 256.

42 Popular definitions of a "boy" were commonly vague. A New Brunswick coal operator defined his mine workforce this way: "I think up to 14 or 15 years he is a boy. Up to 18 and 20 I think he is considered a man." NA, RG 27, vol. 142, file 611.04:6, "Proceedings of the Royal Commission appointed to inquire into Coal Mining Conditions in the Maritime Provinces at Meetings held in Fredericton, N.B., on August 17th and 18th, 1920," 42.

43 At least two published autobiographies were produced by Canadian miners. See Johnstone, *Coal Dust in My Blood*; and Labour Canada Library, Drummond, *Recollections and Reflections*. In both cases, though, their boyhood had been spent in the United Kingdom.

44 From 1874, the *Annual Report* of the federal Department of the Interior also carried brief descriptions of coal mining in the western interior. In New Brunswick, the limited mining in the province was reported in *Report of the Department of Crown Lands* and, from 1926, in *Report of the Department of Lands and Mines.*

45 Kealey and Warrian, eds., *Essays in Canadian Working Class History*; Kealey, "Labour and Working-Class History," 67–94.

46 As cases in point, see Palmer, *Working Class Experience*, 2nd ed.; Morton with Copp, *Working People*, rev. ed.; Heron, *Canadian Labour Movement*, 2nd ed.

47 The intense interest in coal mining in Canada is evident in the great variety of research it has attracted in graduate schools over the past twenty years. Recent theses and dissertations on the industry are indicated in the bibliography. Articles addressing pit boys include McKay, "Realm of Uncertainty," 3–57; and McIntosh, "Boys in the Nova Scotian Coal Mines," 35–50.

48 Sutherland, Barman, and Hale, comps., *History of Canadian Childhood*.

49 See, for example, Bradbury, *Working Families*.

50 See, for instance, Weissbach, *Child Labor Reform in Nineteenth-Century France*; Heywood, *Childhood in Nineteenth-Century France*; and Pinchbeck and Hewitt, *Children in English Society*, 2 vols.

51 McKendrick, "Home Demand and Economic Growth," 152.

52 See, for instance, Humphries, *Hooligans or Rebels*; Hendrick, *Images of Youth*; and Childs, *Labour's Apprentices*.

53 Parliamentary Papers, *Report of Select Committee on Factory Children's Labour*, 1831–32; Parliamentary Papers, Factory Inquiry Commission, Central Board of His Majesty's Commissioners appointed to collect Information in the Manufacturing Districts as to the employment of Children in Factories, *First Report*, June 1833, *Second Report*, July 1833; Parliamentary Papers, Commission of Inquiry into the Employment of Children and Young Persons in Mines and Collieries, *First Report*, 1842, *Second Report*, 1843. The Victorian coal industry was notorious as a large employer of children, in good part owing to the publicity surrounding the 1840–42 Royal Commission on the Employment of Women and Children and the commissioners' astute decision to illustrate their report with lurid images of half-naked children, harnessed as beasts of burden to wagons laden with coal, groping their way on their hands and knees through the total darkness of underground passageways. The repercussions of this royal commission are discussed in John, *Sweat of Their Brow*, and in Chapter 5 below.

54 Marx, *Capital*, 372–9; Engels, *Condition of the Working Class*; Hammond and Hammond, *Town Labourer*, 172–93.

55 Clapham, *Economic History of Modern Britain*, 414.

56 Trevelyan, *British History in the Nineteenth Century*, 157; Briggs, *Age of Improvement*, 61–2.

57 Thompson, *Making of the English Working Class*, 384

Chapter Two

1 See Sutherland, *Growing Up*.

2　See Lemieux, *Les petits innocents*; Lemieux, "Les Enfants Perdus et Retrouvés," 327–52; and Sutherland, *Childhood in English Canadian Society*.

3　Birth rates in Canada fell steadily from the mid-nineteenth to the mid-twentieth century. According to census data, the number of children under four years of age per one thousand women fifteen to forty years of age fell from 877 in 1851 to 536 in 1901 and to 397 in 1941. See Charles, *Changing Size of the Family*, Table I, 10.

4　Houston and Prentice, *Schooling and Scholars*, esp. Part One, "Interpreting Pioneer Schooling."

5　Those who bristled at this discipline could be punished harshly. Fathers in New France, for instance, had the right of "reasonable and moderate correction"; in practice, this allowed any corporal punishment that was not life-threatening. See Moogk, "Les petits sauvages," 17–43.

6　The "traditional family" was founded on the power of the father, whose authority was sanctioned by religion and long-standing practice, and reinforced by law. Mothers took charge of children's religious and moral education. In rural areas, women's productive activity centred on the house and adjacent garden; and men's, on market production and (seasonal) wage labour. See Cohen, *Women's Work*.

7　This is explored in Sutherland, *Childhood in English Canadian Society*; Gillis, *Youth and History*; and Kett, *Rites of Passage*.

8　Sutherland, *Childhood in English Canadian Society*, 6. Put starkly, "the mid- and late nineteenth century witnessed a transition from a view of children as wild creatures in need of frequent paternal whipping to a more tender view of childhood as an age requiring the compassionate nurturing only a mother was deemed fit to provide." Arnup, *Education for Motherhood*, 34.

9　A crude link between declining infant mortality and increasing value placed on individual children has been made. "People could not allow themselves," argued Philippe Ariès, "to become too attached to something that was regarded as a probable loss." Ariès, *Centuries of Childhood*, 38. A similar view is expressed in Pinchbeck and Hewitt, *Children in English Society*, vol. 1; and Stone, *Family, Sex and Marriage*. This view fails to stand up to close scrutiny. There was a clear shift in the valorization of children long before any significant decline in infant mortality became evident. In fact, levels of infant mortality remained tenaciously high in major Canadian urban centres into the early twentieth century. See Piva, *Condition of the Working Class*; and Copp, *Anatomy of Poverty*.

10　Hand in hand with this trend was the "social construction of the economically useless child." See Zelizer, *Pricing the Priceless Child*, 11–12.

A new appreciation of childhood as a special time in life produced a "cultural awakening to the value of children" at the turn of the twentieth century. See Comacchio, *Nations Are Built of Babies*, 17.

11 Charles Dickens was one of the first novelists to mark this transition. In writing of Little Nel, Jo the street-sweeper, Oliver Twist, and the young David Copperfield, he created characters calculated to appeal to his contemporaries on a sentimental level. See also Lemieux, *Une culture de nostalgie*.

12 Historians have remarked on the imprecision of the vocabulary defining childhood in New France. See Lemieux, *Les petits innocents*, 106–7. As late as 1890, the first three grades of primary school in Hamilton contained children as young as four and as old as fourteen. See Gidney and Millar, *Inventing Secondary Education*, 142.

13 In Great Britain, "special dress for children only began to appear at the end of the eighteenth century and even then was thought eccentric." See Pinchbeck and Hewitt, *Children in English Society*, vol. 1, 298. Gagnon, *L'apparition des modes enfantines*, dates the emergence of distinctive costume for children in Lower Canada to the same period.

14 This discussion of the redefinition of childhood is based on Schnell, "Childhood as Ideology"; and Rooke and Schnell, *Discarding the Asylum*.

15 The emphasis on environment over heredity, on the malleability of children, provided a rationale for action. Sutherland, *Childhood in English Canadian Society*, 10–21.

16 Traditional views of the inherent virtue of labour, in addition to the persisting need for their help, gave children a continuing role in domestic labour. See Bullen, "Hidden Workers," 163–87; and Sutherland, "We always had things to do," 105–41.

17 NA, Records of the Montreal Society for the Protection of Women and Children (hereafter MG 28, I 129), vol. 1, meeting of 25 January 1889.

18 Vernon, "Child Labour in the Country," 118.

19 NA, MG 28, I 25, Records of the National Council of Women of Canada, vol. 67, file 4, meeting of June 1912.

20 By the end of the nineteenth century, the view was widespread that the "prolongation and protection of childhood was essential to human progress." Bremner, ed. *Children and Youth in America*, vol. 2, 602. Educator G. Stanley Hall "celebrated the removal of the adolescent from the adult world as the crowning achievement of an enlightened civilization." Quoted in Gillis, *Youth and History*, 133.

21 See Valverde, *Light, Soap, and Water*, chap. 4.

22 "An Act Respecting Offences against the Person," 32–33 Vict., c. 20, s. 51, *Statutes of Canada*, 1869, prescribed the death penalty. Amendments in 1877 changed the sentencing provisions to a maximum of

life imprisonment and a minimum of five years in prison. See "An Act to amend the Act Respecting Offences against the Person," 40 Vict., c. 28, s. 2, *Statutes of Canada*, 1877.

23 "An Act further to amend the Criminal Law," 53 Vict., c. 37, s. 12, *Statutes of Canada*, 1890. This Act was confirmed in the *Criminal Code*, sec. 269, 1892. "An Act to amend the Criminal Code," 10–11 Geo. V, c. 43, s. 8, *Statutes of Canada*, 1920.

24 Sutherland, *Childhood in English Canadian Society*, 115, 130.

25 "Of the regulation of mines," c. 10, pt 1, s. 4, *The Revised Statutes of Nova Scotia, Fourth Series*, 1873; "An Act to amend Chapter 8, *Revised Statutes*, 'Of the regulation of coal mines,'" 54 Vict., c. 9, s. 3, *Statutes of Nova Scotia*, 1891; "An Act to Amend the Coal Mines Regulation Act," 13 Geo. v, c. 54, s. 38, *Statutes of Nova Scotia*, 1923; "An Act to Amend Chapter 1 of the Acts of 1927, 'The Coal Mines Regulation Act,'" 11 Geo. VI, c. 39, s. 7, *Statutes of Nova Scotia*, 1947; "An Act to Amend Chapter 4 of the Acts of 1951, 'The Coal Mines Regulation Act,'" 3 Eliz. II, c. 56, s. 14, *Statutes of Nova Scotia*, 1954.

26 The minimum age for girls remained at fourteen. Unlike compulsory school legislation, provincial factory acts commonly differentiated between boys and girls. See Department of Labour, *Employment of Children*, Table F.

27 The minimum age for girls remained fourteen until 1910. *Ibid.*, Table F.

28 Joyal, "L'évolution des modes de contrôle," 78.

29 See Gidney and Millar, *Inventing Secondary Education*, 9.

30 Pace Rooke and Schnell, *Discarding the Asylum*, 9–10; Bullen, "Children of the Industrial Age."

31 Sutherland, *Childhood in English Canadian Society*, 236.

32 Ibid., 241.

33 Grant, *Profusion of Spires*, 20–35.

34 Marshall, *Secularizing the Faith*, 26.

35 Ibid., 30.

36 Ibid., 20–1.

37 See Prentice, *School Promoters*, 26.

38 See Semple, "Nurture and Admonition of the Lord," 170–1; and Greer, "Sunday Schools of Upper Canada," 169–84.

39 This emphasis on the individual distinguished evangelical reform from the subsequent social gospel. See Parr, "Transplanting from Dens of Iniquity," 176.

40 On child-saving, see especially Rooke and Schnell, *Discarding the Asylum*.

41 The literature on juvenile emigration is extensive. See especially Parr, *Labouring Children*; and Rooke and Schnell, "Imperial Philanthropy

and Colonial Response," 56–77. Bagnell, *Little Immigrants*, is a popular account. A recent study, with a regional focus, is Harper, "Cossar's Colonists."

42 Its initial efforts to apprentice dependent children from Toronto soon expanded to encompass efforts to apprentice British juvenile emigrants with farm families. See Baehre, "Paupers and Poor Relief," 64.

43 For the various organizations sponsoring juvenile emigrants, and the numbers of children they sent to Canada, see Splane, *Social Welfare in Ontario*, 261.

44 Rutman, "Importation of British Waifs," 158–66.

45 See especially Harrison, *Home Children*. Doyle, "Emigration of Pauper Children," sharply criticized elements of the program.

46 See Warsh, *Drink in Canada*.

47 Shiman, "Band of Hope Movement," 49–74.

48 See Cook, *Through Sunshine and Shadow*; and "Educating for Temperance," 251–77. Making a useful distinction among WCTU objectives at the dominion level, legislative changes, and the local unions' focus on behaviour within the community, Cook uses the term "evangelical feminism" to describe the motives of WCTU members.

49 At the turn of the twentieth century, church surveys indicated that Sunday School attendance fell off sharply after the age of twelve. See Marshall, *Secularizing the Faith*, 151.

50 See Grant, *Profusion of Spires*, 173; and MacLeod, "Live Vaccine," 5–25.

51 See Marr, "Church Teen Clubs," 249–67; and Dirks, "Getting a Grip on Harry," 74–5.

52 Mitchinson, "YWCA and Reform," 368–84; Pedersen, "Keeping Our Good Girls Good," 20–4.

53 The CGIT was distinguished from Girl Guides (founded in Canada in 1910) principally by its Canadian nationalist, rather than Imperialist, orientation. Guides tended to be Anglican; the CGIT, Presbyterian and Methodist (and later United Church). Much emphasis was placed on developing leadership skills and progress in "the four-fold life": physical, intellectual, religious, and service. Prang, "Canadian Girls in Training," 161.

54 Gillis, *Youth and History*, 145.

55 The Boys' Brigades offered a blend of Christianity and patriotism. Companies, which numbered from thirty to one hundred, had to be affiliated with a church, mission, or other Christian organization. They were most closely associated with Presbyterians, but interest extended to Anglicans (although they also had their separate Church Lads' Brigade), Methodists, and Roman Catholics. See Hopkins, "Youthful Canada," 551–6.

56 These activities were in addition to the long-standing Sunday Schools. Marshall, *Secularizing the Faith*, 128.

57 Grant, *Profusion of Spires*, 196.

58 Ibid., 171–3.

59 Cook, *Regenerators*, discusses the secularization of Christian social reform.

60 Kealey, ed., *A Not Unreasonable Claim*.

61 Gouett, "Halifax Orphan House," 281–91.

62 Rooke and Schnell, "Childhood and Charity," 164–6.

63 See Bradbury, "Fragmented Family," 109–28; and Purvey, "Alexandra Orphanage," 107–33. POHS, like the later Children's Aid Societies, often functioned simply as a short-term shelter during family crises owing to illness, the death of one parent, or temporary unemployment. See Bullen, "J.J. Kelso and the 'New' Child-Savers," 107–28.

64 Rooke and Schnell, *Discarding the Asylum*, 137–80.

65 Buckley, "Ladies or Midwives?," 131–49.

66 See Strong-Boag, *Parliament of Women*; and Griffiths, *Splendid Vision*.

67 Comacchio, "Nations Are Built of Babies," 21; Le collectif Clio, *L'histoire des femmes au Québec*, 325–7; Ambrose, *For Home and Country*.

68 See Arnup, *Education for Motherhood*, 26–7; and Lewis, "Physical Perfection for Spiritual Welfare," 154–5.

69 Mitchinson, "The WCTU: 'For God, Home and Native Land,'" 162.

70 "Ontario Grammar School Masters' Association," *Journal of Education* 22 (1869): 138, cited in Robinson, "Child, the Family, and Society," 106. See *Christian Messenger* (Halifax), 6 November 1872, 357; 27 August 1873, 277; *Daily British Colonist* (Victoria), 14, 15 June 1900, on the dangers to small boys of smoking cigarettes. See also Robinson, "Child, the Family, and Society," 108–9.

71 Lizzie Wills, "True Education," *Educational Journal* 5 (1892): 631, cited in Robinson, "Child, the Family, and Society," 107.

72 Strong-Boag, *Parliament of Women*, 185.

73 "A Reading Age," *Journal of Education* 14 (1861): 22, cited in Robinson, "Child, the Family, and Society," 134.

74 See Moyles, "Boy's Own View of Canada," 41–56.

75 See Gillis, *Youth and History*, 104.

76 Cook, *Through Sunshine and Shadow*, 80.

77 See Howell and Lindsey, "Social Gospel and the Young Boy Problem," 78.

78 See "Common School Libraries," *Journal of Education* 6 (1853): 140; "Establishment of School Libraries," *Journal of Education* 27 (1874): 177, both cited in Robinson, "Child, the Family, and Society," 147.

79 See *Appendix to Women Workers of Canada*; Griffiths, *Splendid Vision*, 183–4; Bullen, "Children of the Industrial Age," 156–7; and Strong-Boag, *Parliament of Women*, 271–2.

80 "Youth and Crime in Montreal," *Journal of Education* 15 (1862): 40; "A Mechanic's Institute: The Mechanic's College," *Journal of Education* 6 (1853): 49, both quoted in Robinson, "Child, the Family and Society in Ontario," 131.

81 Mayor Howland of Toronto claimed that boys' street gangs were sufficiently well organized to have adopted "a regular process of electing a leader." They also waged regular turf wars. See Canada, Royal Commission on the Relations between Capital and Labour, *Ontario Evidence*, 164.

82 Strong-Boag, *Parliament of Women*, 184.

83 Ibid., 269.

84 These efforts built on earlier attempts. See Curtis, "Playground in Nineteenth-Century Ontario," 21–9. See also Jones and Rutman, *In the Children's Aid*, 123–4, on the Toronto Playgrounds Association.

85 Strong-Boag, *Parliament of Women*, 268–9. For reformers, the ideal playground was "supervised, sexually segregated and equipped with exercise equipment and game facilities." See Bullen, "Children of the Industrial Age," 158–9.

86 Bliss, "Pure Books on Avoided Subjects," 98.

87 Strong-Boag, *Parliament of Women*, 250; Valverde, *Age of Light, Soap, and Water*, 27–8.

88 See Cook, *Through Sunshine and Shadow*, 95.

89 National Council of Women of Canada, *Report of Sub-Committee on Laws for the Protection of Women and Children*. The NCWC repeatedly called for the raising of the age of consent. See the Women's Platforms of 1912 and 1920. Strong-Boag, *Parliament of Women*, 273, 429, 438.

90 See Fingard, *Dark Side of Life*, 171–6.

91 See NA, MG 28, I 129, vol. 1. See also Rooke and Schnell, *Discarding the Asylum*, 343–6.

92 Splane, *Social Welfare in Ontario*, 265.

93 See McLaren, *Our Own Master Race*. In 1914 the cadet movement, at 45,000, had three times the membership of the Boy Scouts. Morton, "Cadet Movement," 56.

94 See MacDonald, *Sons of the Empire*.

95 See Behiels, "L'Association catholique," 27–41.

96 The literature on education is vast. Useful studies of the development of the Ontario system, the model for English Canada, include Curtis, *True Government by Choice Men* and *Building the Educational State*; Houston and Prentice, *Schooling and Scholars*; Gidney and Millar, *Inventing Secondary Education*; and Gaffield, *Language, Schooling, and Cultural Conflict*.

97 See Sutherland, *Childhood in English Canadian Society*.

98 Designed as a laboratory school to study child development, it was
   headed by Dr William Blatz, whose influence was strengthened by
   his (brief) role with the Dionne quintuplets. See Raymond, *Nursery
   World of Dr. Blatz*.

99 Gleason, "Psychology and the Construction of the 'Normal' Family,"
   442–77.

100 See Hurl, "Overcoming the Inevitable," 87–121; Tucker, *Administering
   Danger*, 166–7.

101 "Report of Factory Inspectors," Ontario *Sessional Papers*, 1892, 19.

102 Ibid., 1906, 34–5.

103 Hurl, "Restricting Child Factory Labour," 93.

104 Forsey, *Trade Unions in Canada*.

105 See Labour Canada Library, Trades and Labour Congress of Canada,
   Annual Proceedings, 1883 *et seq*. The noteworthy exception is the Con-
   fédération des Travailleurs Catholiques du Canada, which resisted
   compulsory education legislation and other state efforts to restrict
   child labour, calling on employers to give children work suitable to
   their age. See Hamel, "L'Obligation scolaire au Québec," 83–102. The
   role of organized miners as advocates of schooling and mines legislation is outlined in Chapter 5 below.

106 Rooke and Schnell, *Discarding the Asylum*, 337–86.

107 Christie and Gauvreau, *Full-Orbed Christianity*, 20–1, 116; Allen, *Social
   Passion*, 13, 21.

108 Christie and Gauvreau, *Full-Orbed Christianity*, 212.

109 Ibid., xiv.

110 See Little, "Claiming a Unique Place," 80–102; and Strong-Boag,
   "Wages for Housework," 24–34.

111 Crowley, "Madonnas before Magdalenes," 520–47.

112 Copp, *Anatomy of Poverty*, 96–100; see also Comacchio, *Nations Are
   Built of Babies*, 46. The first Gouttes de Lait were established in France
   during the 1890s as depots to provide sterilized milk for women
   unable to nurse. They became models for milk depots in the United
   Kingdom and North America. See Arnup, *Education for Motherhood*, 19.

113 Dodd, "Advice to Parents," 203–30; see also Comacchio, *Nations Are
   Built of Babies*. One hundred and fifty thousand copies of *The Canadian Mother's Book* had been issued by the end of 1921, its year of
   publication; and 800,000 by 1933. Its successor, *The Canadian Mother
   and Child*, was first published in the autumn of 1940. Four years later,
   over 470,000 copies had been distributed in French and English.
   Arnup, *Education for Motherhood*, 52, 118.

114 See R.L. Schnell, "Children's Bureau for Canada," 95–110; see also
   Rooke and Schnell, *Discarding the Asylum*, 347–50; Arnup, *Education
   for Motherhood*, 29; and Dodd, "Advice to Parents," 210.

115 In the United States, the National Child Labor Committee was formed in 1904. See Trottner, *Crusade for the Children*.

116 24 March 1909.

117 In Nova Scotia, social reform groups, including clergymen, trade unionists, and temperance groups, united in 1909 under the auspices of "The Moral and Social Reform Council of Nova Scotia." See Halifax *Herald*, 22 January 1909, 6.

118 Halifax *Herald*, 24 March 1909, 3.

119 Shortly after its organization, the NCWC formed a Standing Committee on Female and Child Labour and a Sub-Committee on Laws for the Protection of Women and Children. See, for instance, the *Report of Sub-Committee on Laws for the Protection of Women and Children*, adopted at the annual meeting in May 1896. Halifax *Herald*, 24 March 1909, 9.

120 This campaign is documented in NA, MG 28, I 10, Records of the Canadian Council on Social Development, vol. 8, file 38. Lobbying within Canada for provinces to adhere to ILO standards was undertaken by Charlotte Whitton also in her capacity as chair of the Child Welfare Committee of the NCWC. See Griffiths, *Splendid Vision*, 183–4.

121 Bruce Curtis has linked state formation to the development of the Ontario education system. This insight could be explored further by examining subsequent state initiatives regarding children. See Curtis, *Building the Educational State*.

122 Pinchbeck and Hewitt, *Children in English Society*, vol. 2, 359.

123 Mill, *On Liberty*, 104.

124 Little attempt was made to categorize children beyond the concept of legal incompetence enshrined in the Quebec Civil Code. Children were legally subordinated to their father until the age of twenty-five. See Moogk, "Les petits sauvages," 21. In law in Quebec, the mother's role with regard to her children was merely supplementary to that of the father until 1977, when legislation provided for the joint exercise of parental responsibility. See Joyal et Chatillon, "La Loi québecoise de protection de l'enfance," 41; Lemieux, "Les Enfants Perdus," 333; and Joyal, "L'évolution des modes de contrôle," 73–83.

125 Lord Shaftesbury, replying to a letter canvassing his support for legislation to protect children from parental cruelty, wrote: "The evils you state are enormous and indisputable, but they are of so private, internal and domestic a character as to be beyond the reach of legislation, and the subject, indeed, would not I think be entertained in either House of Parliament." Only a generation later did two pieces of British legislation address the problem. The Children's Charter of 1889 and the Prevention of Cruelty to Children Act (1894) gave children legal protection against cruelty similar to that extended to animals

seventy years earlier. See Pinchbeck and Hewitt, *Children in English Society,* vol. 2, 622.

126 In Upper Canada, poor relief was administered by the same courts that tried criminal cases. See Murray, "Cold Hand of Charity," 180.

127 Baehre, "Paupers and Poor Relief," 57–80. District magistrates in Upper Canada would on occasion divert small amounts of public funds for direct poor relief. See Murray, "Cold Hand of Charity," 179–206.

128 See Splane, *Social Welfare in Ontario,* 40, 65–116. In Upper Canada, pauper institutions were not present until the arrival of the large influx of impoverished immigrants during the 1830s. The 1837 Houses of Industry Act, reflecting the influence of the English New Poor Law, was designed to encourage their construction throughout the colony. See Baehre, "Paupers and Poor Relief," 57–80.

129 Webber, "Labour and the Law," 127–30. In New Brunswick, boys could be bound until the age of twenty-one; females until eighteen or marriage. In Newfoundland, males could be bound until the age of twenty-four; females until twenty-one or marriage. See Rooke and Schnell, "Guttersnipes and Charity Children," 83.

130 In New France, dependent children were generally placed with relatives. For those without kin, expenses for wet nursing and/or apprenticeship were met by the Crown. Lemieux, *Les petits innocents,* 332. In Upper Canada, town wardens, with the consent of two justices of the peace, were empowered to apprentice any orphaned or abandoned child unless relatives were willing to support the child. Girls could be apprenticed to the age of eighteen, and boys to twenty-one. See "An Act to provide for the Education and Support of Orphan Children," 39 Geo. III, c. III, Upper Canada, *Statutes of Upper Canada,* 1799.

131 By 1850, it had placed 275 children. Splane, *Social Welfare in Ontario,* 223.

132 Whereas both apprenticing and binding out involved the use of the legal instrument of the indenture, apprenticeship generally suggested that a child was acquiring a trade. To bind out (or "indenture") was simply to enter into a contract whereby labour was exchanged for certain specified guarantees. The acquisition of a skilled trade was not necessarily involved. In practice, the terms were (and continue to be) used interchangeably.

133 *Mechanic and Farmer* (Pictou, N.S.), 2 February 1842.

134 Cited in Rooke and Schnell, "Guttersnipes and Charity Children," 83.

135 Jaffray, "A Day at the Waterloo Poor House," 72–8.

136 Rooke and Schnell, *Discarding the Asylum,* 36–7. See also Whalen, "Social Welfare in New Brunswick," 60, and "Nineteenth Century Almshouse

System," 5–27. Whalen points out that despite increasing efforts to differentiate the dependent, in many counties in New Brunswick children remained institutionalized with adults until well into the twentieth century. See also Splane, *Social Welfare in Ontario*, 68–70, 122–30. As late as 1889, there were 451 boys and 46 girls under sixteen years of age incarcerated in Ontario jails. See "Report of the Commissioners Appointed to Enquire into the Prison and Reformatory System of Ontario," Ontario, *Sessional Papers*, 1891, vol. 23, pt IV, no. 18, 19.

137 Houston, "Role of the Criminal Law," 42. In British Common Law, applicable in English Canada, children under seven were considered unable to distinguish between right and wrong. Those seven to fourteen were *prime facie* incapable, but if judge and jury distinguished otherwise, they faced the full penalties prescribed by law. Those over fourteen were fully responsible. See Sutherland, *Childhood in English Canadian Society*, 98.

138 "First Report of the Commissioners appointed to inquire into and report upon the conduct, economy, discipline and management of the Provincial Penitentiary, 16 March 1849," Province of Canada, Legislative Assembly, *Journals*, vol. 8 (1849), app. no. 3, B.B.B.B.B.

139 "Second Report of the Commissioners of the Penitentiary Inquiry, 16 April 1849."

140 See "An Act for establishing prisons for Young Offenders," 20 Vict., c. 28; and "An Act for the more speedy trial and punishment of juvenile offenders," 20 Vict., c. 29, *Statutes of Canada*, 1857. After Confederation, the "Act respecting the trial and punishment of Juvenile Offenders," 32 Vict., c. 33, *Statutes of Canada*, 1869, reconfirmed the earlier legislation, although for Quebec certain amendments were required in light of recent provincial juvenile offenders legislation.

141 Splane, *Social Welfare in Ontario*, 148–51.

142 In Ontario, a law was passed in 1890 prohibiting the incarceration of anyone under thirteen years of age in a reformatory. See "An Act respecting the Commitment of Children of Tender Years," c. 76, *Statutes of Ontario*, 1890. Ontario's reformatory was remote, with thick high walls and narrow cells. Boys wore drab prison uniforms. See Bullen, "Children of the Industrial Age," 248–50.

143 After 1880, dormitories were constructed and greater effort was made to school and reform children. See Jones and Rutman, *In the Children's Aid*, 104–5. See also Splane, *Child Welfare in Ontario*, 172–6.

144 The Penetanguishene reformatory was ultimately closed in 1904. See Sutherland, *Childhood in English Canadian Society*, 118.

145 Canadians followed British models for industrial schools. See Pinchbeck and Hewitt, *Children in English Society*, vol. 2, 477–89; and Neff, "Ontario Industrial Schools Act," 171–208.

146 Fingard, *Dark Side of Life*, 125–7.

147 Joyal et Chatillon, "La Loi québecoise de protection de l'enfance," 34;
Joyal, "L'Acte concernant les écoles d'industrie," 227–40. At the same
time, reform schools (*écoles de réforme*) were also established for juvenile delinquents. See Joyal, "L'Évolution des modes de contrôle," 75.
Joyal observes that this legislation, in permitting parents to send difficult children to an industrial school, served to buttress parental
authority.

148 The Industrial Schools Association of Toronto was formed in 1883 by
William Howland and the lawyer Beverley Jones to establish an
industrial school. On the Mimico industrial school, see Howland's
testimony to the Royal Commission on Capital and Labour, *Ontario
Evidence*, 159–69. See also Bennett, "Taming the 'Bad Boys,'" 71–96,
and "Turning 'Bad Boys' into 'Good Citizens,'" 209–32.

149 Neff, "Ontario Industrial Schools Act," 203–4.

150 Myers, "Revenge and Revolt," 104–13.

151 Sutherland, *Childhood in English Canadian Society*, 107.

152 See the "Report of the Commissioners Appointed to Enquire into the
Prison and Reformatory System of Ontario," Ontario *Sessional Papers*,
1891, vol. 23, pt 10, no. 18. Other recommendations included the
implementation of municipal curfew laws and the development of
supervised municipal playgrounds and gymnasia. The report also
advised the tighter enforcement of school attendance laws, closer control over pawnshops (to address the problem of juvenile thieving),
and better supervision of juvenile immigration.

153 If the late nineteenth century was characterized by efforts to remove
children from a natural family environment labelled unhealthy and
place them with an alternative family, the thrust of social work in the
twentieth century has been to support the natural family through
income supplements and counselling. See Rooke and Schnell, *Discarding the Asylum*.

154 The Ontario act clearly encouraged magistrates to send children
under fourteen years of age to industrial schools, rather than to a
reformatory or prison. See "An Act for the Prevention of Cruelty to,
and better Protection of Children," 56 Vict., c. 45, *Statutes of Ontario*,
1893.

155 See "The Juvenile Delinquents Act," 7–8 Ed. VII, c. 40, *Statutes of
Canada*, 1908. Sutherland gives individuals active in the Ottawa CAS
much credit for the passage of this act. See Sutherland, *Childhood in
English Canadian Society*, 119–20. The WCTU was also among those
organizations pressing for the establishment of juvenile courts. See
Cook, *Through Sunshine and Shadow*, 99. The federal Criminal Code of
1892 permitted separate hearings for children charged under federal

laws. In 1894, "An Act respecting Arrest, Trial and Imprisonment of Youthful Offenders," 57–8 Vict., c. 58, *Statutes of Canada*, 1894, required that children be tried separately from adults. See Trépanier, "Origins of the Juvenile Delinquents Act of 1908," 205–32. The cooperation of the provinces was essential, because most courts and places of detention fell under their jurisdiction.

156 At the judge's discretion, however, children over fourteen could be transferred for trial in an ordinary court if "the good of the child and the interest of the community demand it." In 1921 the threshold was raised to eighteen. See Sutherland, *Childhood in English Canadian Society*, 115, 130.

157 Children under twelve were not to be sent to an industrial school before an effort had been made to find them a foster home.

158 "Juvenile Delinquents Act," 7–8 Ed. VII, c. 40, s. 31, *Statutes of Canada*, 1908.

159 See Department of Labour, *Employment of Children*, 96. Public officials were always more confident about legislation's effectiveness than most Canadians.

160 Prentice, *School Promoters*.

161 Cited in Splane, *Child Welfare in Ontario*, 229.

162 Department of Labour, *Employment of Children*, 96–9.

163 Marshall, *Aux origines sociales de l'État providence*.

164 The Nova Scotia and British Columbia legislation will be discussed in more detail in Chapter 5. The Ontario and Quebec Mines Acts, in the absence of coal mines in those provinces, applied to hardrock mining. They prohibited women and girls from mine work, required boys to be at least fifteen years old to work underground, and limited fifteen-to seventeen-year-old boys to a maximum of forty-eight hours of work weekly. Department of Labour, *Employment of Children*, Table C.

165 See Roland, "Darby Bergin," 94–7.

166 "Report of the Commissioners appointed to enquire into the working of Mills and Factories of the Dominion, and the labor employed therein," 45 Vict., *Sessional Papers*, vol. 15, no. 9, 42, 1882, 2–3.

167 Forsey, "Note on the Dominion Factory Bills," 580–3. A lengthy discussion of the context in which federal and provincial legislators debated Factory Acts during the 1880s is found in Tucker, *Administering Danger*, chap. 4.

168 Ontario's and Quebec's first Factory Acts were limited to factories employing over twenty people, but subsequent amendments extended the acts' scope to smaller workplaces. Department of Labour, *Employment of Children*, Table F.

169 Department of Labour, *Employment of Children*, Table I. The Ontario act followed closely on testimony to the Labour Commission outlining

the harmful physical effects on young girls of standing ten or twelve hours daily. See Canada, Royal Commission on the Relations between Capital and Labour, *Ontario Evidence*, 1008–9, 1165–9.

170 Bullen, "Children of the Industrial Age," 152–4.

171 Goods such as pipes, door locks from vacant buildings, and other scrap metal were favoured. The distinction between gathering and stealing, of course, was often obscure. Bullen, "Children of the Industrial Age," 141.

172 "The Municipal Amendment Act," c. 33, s. 20, *Statutes of Ontario*, 1900.

173 This followed an act in 1886 prohibiting children under sixteen from billiard or pool rooms. Splane, *Child Welfare in Ontario*, 256–8. Toronto Mayor Howland created the Department of Morality in 1886 to attend to "all matters relating to the protection of women, children and animals." Bullen, "Children of the Industrial Age," 152. The chief constable of Toronto recommended in his *Annual Report* for 1907 that the age for boys in pool rooms be raised from sixteen to eighteen. Quoted in Bullen, "Children of the Industrial Age," 156.

174 Ibid., 128–59.

175 Municipalities failed to enforce their curfews. Kelso noted in 1906 that "even the WCTU has grown tired of its advocacy." Quoted in Bullen, "Children of the Industrial Age," 158.

176 "The Minors' Tobacco Sales Act," *Statutes of Ontario*, 1892, c. 52, prohibited the sale or furnishing of cigarettes, cigars, or tobacco in any form to a minor under the age of eighteen years, except for the purpose of filling a written order from a parent or a guardian.

177 The chief constable of Toronto recommended in 1909 that children under sixteen be banned from all theatres unless accompanied by their parents or a guardian. Cited in Bullen, "Children of the Industrial Age," 157. The subsequent *Theatres and Cinematographs Act*, 1 Geo. V, c. 73, s. 10, *Statutes of Ontario*, 1911, prohibited the attendance at moving picture shows of any child under the age of fifteen years unaccompanied by an adult.

178 These acts contained provisions for fining abusive adults. Any funds raised through fines were to be passed on to the local humane society. See "An Act to Prevent and Punish Wrongs to Children," 45 Vict., c. 18, *Statutes of Nova Scotia*, 1882. See also Veinott, "Child Custody and Divorce," 283–4.

179 "An Act for the Protection and Reformation of Neglected Children," c. 40, *Statutes of Ontario*, 1888.

180 See Sutherland, *Childhood in English Canadian Society*, 111.

181 Another clause of the act authorized municipalities to establish curfews. See "An Act for the Prevention of Cruelty to, and better Protection of Children," 56 Vict., c. 45, *Statutes of Ontario*, 1893.

182 Sutherland, *Childhood in English Canadian Society,* 112; Coulter, "Not to Punish but to Reform," 167–84; Rooke and Schnell, "Guttersnipes and Charity Children," 84.

183 Veinott, "Child Custody and Divorce," 299 n.42.

184 Joyal et Chatillon, "La Loi québécoise de protection de l'enfance," 35–6.

185 For a disturbing account of the twin role institutions played as asylums both for the insane and for orphan children, see Gill, *Les enfants de Duplessis.*

186 To give examples: reformers' views on prohibition were divided. There were tensions between amateur (philanthropic) reform and the emerging professionals. Institutionalization sparked growing controversy from the late nineteenth century. Unions protested against the use of public funds to assist orphan immigrants. On this last point, see Labour Canada Library, Trades and Labour Congress of Canada, *Annual Proceedings,* 1886, 24, cited in Seager and Baskerville, *Unwilling Idlers,* 163–4.

187 Sutherland, *Childhood in English Canadian Society,* 20.

188 As declared in Ontario, *Report of Committee on Child Labor.*

189 The current controversy over the Young Offenders Act indicates that the scope and length of children's period of lessened responsibility is in question today.

190 Vernon, "Child Labour in the Country," 115–6.

191 Parental authority over children was also eroded by the decline of the household as a place of work and the emergence of new industrial contexts of wage labour. It was further undermined by the decline of the skilled worker as a subcontractor; increasingly, he lost his responsibility for hiring and supervising his helpers (often kin). Employers, within the broad rules established by the state, assumed these roles. Much of the initial opposition to child wage labour in Great Britain, it has been argued, arose because it removed children from direct parental control. Chapter 3 addresses the erosion of miners' authority in the workplace. See also Smelser, *Social Change in the Industrial Revolution*; and McKendrick, "Home Demand and Economic Growth," 158.

192 On the extension of the powers of the state vis-à-vis parents, see Ursel, *Private Lives, Public Policy,* 114–16.

193 Backhouse, "Canadian Custody Law," 212–48 (the quotation is from p. 216); Veinott, "Child Custody and Divorce," 273–302.

194 Ontario, *Report of Committee on Child Labor.*

195 House of Commons, *Debates,* 1944, vol. 1, 27 January 1944, 2. See also Marshall, "Language of Children's Rights," 409–41. On the expanding international definition of children's rights, see Marshall, "Declaration of the Rights of the Child," 183–212.

196 The George Eastman Company had recently introduced the slogan that their cameras were so simple that "even a child" could "Push the Button" – they would do the rest. (This slogan is also a comment on contemporary views of the incompetent child.) See Schlereth, "Material Culture of Childhood," 5.

197 Cited in Clark, *Of Toronto the Good*. The article was in reaction to legislation restricting the access of minors to tobacco.

198 The Toronto *Globe*, 6 January 1881, protesting Bergin's first factory bill, observed "the less the state interferes ... the better." In Quebec, the Union catholique des cultivateurs, organized in 1924, resisted compulsory schooling, objecting to the tax on land used as the basis for school funding. It also pointed to the intrusion on parents' rights and underlined that the state had no role in education. See Hamel, "Obligation scolaire."

199 Cited in Thompson with Seager, *Decades of Discord*, 154. See also Chapter 5 below, on employers' reaction to Mines Acts restricting child labour at the colliery.

200 Eid, *Le clergé et le pouvoir politique au Québec*.

201 See Bradbury, *Working Families*.

202 See, for instance, early factory inspectors' reports from Ontario: "children are sent to work to allow parents to remain idle and live in laziness and in all the evils which follow" ("Report of Factory Inspectors," Ontario, *Sessional Papers*, 1892, 18); "The welfare of the child cannot be sacrificed to the short-sighted demands of parents, who, for their own apparent benefit, would doom their children to a life of toil and ignorance" (ibid., 1899, 22); "inhuman parents who would permit their offspring of tender years to work all night" (ibid., 1907, 23).

203 Cowles, "Juvenile Employment System of Ontario," 5.

204 See Sutherland, "We always had things to do," 105–41; Synge, "Transition from School to Work," 249–69; Coulter, "Working Young of Edmonton," 143–59; and Jean, "Le recul du travail des enfants," 91–129.

205 See Gaffield, "Schooling, the Economy and Rural Society," 69–92; Seguin, *La conquête du sol*; and Bouchard, *Quelques arpents d'Amérique*.

206 Doyle, "Emigration of Pauper Children," 271.

207 Quoted in Challinor, *Lancashire and Cheshire Miners*, 251.

208 Kelso, *First Report of Work*, 27.

209 See Barman, "Knowledge is Essential," 9–66. Despite expanding high school attendance, only 34 percent of fifteen- to seventeen-year-old English Canadians were still in school in 1923. See also Stamp, "Canadian High Schools," 78; and Heron, "High School and the Household Economy," 217–60. The domination of higher education by the offspring of today's "middle classes" testifies to the continuing

failure to extend this central aspect of the modern childhood to all young people. Ross, Scott, and Kelly, "Children in Canada in the 1990s," 15–45.

210 On this point see Marshall, "Reconstruction Politics," 261–83.

Chapter Three

1 In Alberta, reports on mining were published in the *Annual Report of the Department of Public Works* between 1905 and 1917 and, independently, in *Annual Report of the Mines Branch*, from 1918. In Saskatchewan, cursory reports on mining were also published in the *Annual Report of the Department of Public Works* between 1905 and 1915.

2 In New Brunswick, the limited mining in the province was reported in the *Report of the Department of Crown Lands* and, from 1926, in the *Report of the Department of Lands and Mines*.

3 These sets of statistics have to be used only as a very rough guide to employment patterns. First, they do not necessarily capture all workers. In the nineteenth century, those workers not on the company payroll (in other words, employed directly by the miner) are unlikely to be recorded. Second, although these statistics appear to indicate that employment levels for boys were very much lower on Vancouver Island, this observation must be qualified. The Nova Scotian *Mines Reports* clearly define the boy as under eighteen; those from British Columbia fail to define him. Almost certainly, though, because the first British Columbia Mines Act called for each coal company to maintain a registry of all employees under sixteen, this figure is entered under the "boy" category. See "An Act to make Regulations with respect to Coal Mines," c. 122, s. 8, *The Consolidated Statutes of British Columbia*, 1877. The Nova Scotia figures exclude workers employed in the development of new mines or of new districts in existing mines.

4 Martell, "Early Coal Mining," 41–53; Fauteux, *Essai sur l'industrie*, 22–4; Brown, *Coal Fields*, 32–44.

5 Brown, *Coal Fields*, 45–9; Martell, "Early Coal Mining," 43; Hornsby, *Nineteenth-Century Cape Breton*, 15–18.

6 On early mining in Pictou County, see Patterson, *History of the County of Pictou*, 398–9; Brown, *Coal Fields*, 147–9; Martell, "Early Coal Mining," 44–7; Cameron, *Pictonian Colliers*, chap. 3.

7 Crown officials were persuaded to transfer a long-dormant mineral lease in the name of the Duke of York, the profligate younger brother of King George IV, to a London-based jewellery firm in exchange for forgiving his debts. The lease was never taken up,

but neither had it ever been cancelled. Thus, the GMA received monopoly privileges granted directly from the Crown. On the origins of the GMA, see Muise, "General Mining Association," 70–87. On its subsequent history, see McKay, "Crisis of dependent development," 17–30.

8 Whereas most scholarship on the General Mining Association emphasizes its impact in terms of the scale of mining and extent of technical innovation, the most recent study underlines the harmful economic effects of its monopoly on coal development and its poor use of capital. See Gerriets, "Impact of the General Mining Association," 54–84.

9 Johnson, *Coal Trade of British America*, 34.

10 Muise, "General Mining Association," 70–87.

11 MacLeod, "Miners, Mining Men and Mining Reform," 316.

12 On Nova Scotia's politics of coal at Confederation, see Muise, "Forging the Bonds of Union," 13–47; and Tennyson, "Economic Nationalism and Confederation," 39–53.

13 Bowsfield, *Fort Victoria Letters*, xvii, 84; Gallacher, "Men, Money, Machines," 24–45.

14 Kemble, "Coal from the Northwest Coast," 123–30.

15 Hazlitt, *British Columbia and Vancouver Island*, 163–4.

16 Gallacher, "Men, Money, Machines," 90.

17 Half of the coal mined at Nanaimo to 1863 was extracted by European miners, the other half by Vancouver Island Natives. Robb, "Mineral Resources," 370–1.

18 Hamilton, "Historical Geography of the Coal Mining Industry," 31.

19 NA, RG 84, Records of the Canadian Parks Service, vol. 1399, file HS10–47.

20 Hamilton, "Historical Geography of the Coal Mining Industry," 35.

21 *CMR*, April-May 1885, 9.

22 Seager, "Minto, New Brunswick," 89.

23 Hornsby, *Nineteenth-Century Cape Breton*, 171.

24 Ibid., 172. See also Acheson, "Industrialization of the Maritimes," 3–28; and Muise, "Great Transformation," 1–42.

25 See Gallacher, "Men, Money, Machines," xiii. There had been complaints expressed in Nanaimo that the earlier Reciprocity Treaty had not been extended to Vancouver Island. Victoria *Daily British Colonist*, 11 May 1861.

26 *CMJ*, 1 November 1913, 672.

27 *CMR*, February 1898, 35.

28 *CMR*, February 1903, 30–1.

29 Report of the Royal Commission on Industrial Disputes in British Columbia, Canada, *Sessional Papers*, 1903, vol. 37, no. 13, 36a, 35.

30 On the development of the Alberta Crowsnest Pass mines, see Babaian, *Coal Mining Industry,* 3–38.

31 Sloan, "Crowsnest Pass during the Depression," 2.

32 Strachan, "Coal Mining in British Columbia," 70–2, 99–100.

33 Den Otter, "Railways and Alberta's Coal Problem," 89–90.

34 See Table 1.1. By the 1920s railways accounted for approximately one-third of Alberta coal markets. Alberta Coal Commission, *Report,* 120.

35 Hornsby, *Nineteenth-Century Cape Breton,* 101–2.

36 Martin, *History of Nova Scotia,* 112; Buckingham, *Canada, Nova Scotia, New Brunswick,* 362.

37 The same visitor also observed that the GMA no longer made much effort to recruit from Great Britain because "[a] native mining population is gradually growing up on the spot." See Johnson, *Coal Trade of British America,* 21.

38 Ralston, "Miners and Managers," 42–55. On the relative attractions and disadvantages of Vancouver Island for British miners, see also Belshaw, "British Collier in British Columbia," 11–36.

39 See Campbell and Reid, "Independent Collier in Scotland," 64.

40 Hair, "Social History of British Coalminers," 51.

41 Most British North American miners were from Scotland, where the major coalfields were marked in the first half of the nineteenth century by a highly structured system of apprenticeship. At eighteen a boy qualified as a miner after a ritualized "brothering" involving oaths, readings, and whisky. See Campbell, *Lanarkshire Miners,* 41–3. Many others came from the large coalfields of northeast England, where miners initiated their sons to the colliery in a variety of unskilled work before accepting them, on maturity, as miners. See Daunton, "Down the Pit," 589–90.

42 Buddle expressed his views in a letter to Lord Lambton, a major colliery owner, cited in Colls, *Pitmen of the Northern Coalfield,* 14.

43 Richard Brown, the first manager of the GMA colliery at Sydney Mines, linked the employment of inexperienced miners with the production of substandard coal prior to the arrival of the GMA. Brown, *Coal Fields,* 50.

44 Wightman, in addition to attacking the GMA for overuse of skilled labour, also accused the company of the mis-investment of capital. Gerriets, "Impact of the General Mining Association," 77–9.

45 Quoted in Martell, "Early Coal Mining," 52–3.

46 This authority translated into relatively high levels of pay. At approximately ninety pounds sterling annually, coal miners received an income equal to the "best mechanics." See Gesner, *Industrial Resources of Nova Scotia,* 273. An earlier observer defined the miners' standard of living as much by what was eaten (appropriate to a pre-industrial

context) as by what was earned, noting "two hundred well paid, beef-eating, and porter-drinking operatives" at Pictou. See Moorsom, *Letters from Nova Scotia*, 351.

47 Gallacher, "John Muir," 626–7; HBC Archives, A.11/73 fo. 652, Douglas to Barclay, 7 December 1852, cited in Burrill, "Class Conflict and Colonialism," 66.

48 NA, MG 20, Records of the Hudson's Bay Company, A.5/18 fo. 88–9, Barclay to Landale, 9 April 1853. HBC officials assumed also that married miners were more likely to settle permanently on Vancouver Island.

49 NA, MG 20, B/185/a/1, "Fort Rupert Post Journal," entry for 16 October 1849; Burrill, "Class Conflict and Colonialism," 76–7.

50 Brown, *On the Geographical Distribution*, 12.

51 On the question of miner skill, see McKay, "Wisdom, Wile or War," 29; McKay, "Realm of Uncertainty," 34–5; and Campbell, "Skill, Independence, and Trade Unionism," 155–62.

52 MacLeod, "Colliers, Colliery Safety and Workplace Control," 247.

53 On levels of dockage for slack in Nova Scotia, see McLennan, "Screening of Soft Coal," 82–96.

54 Macdonald, *Coal and Iron Industries*, 39; Galloway, *Annals of Coal Mining*, vol. 2, 362.

55 McKay, "Crisis of dependent development," 31.

56 CMJ, November 1911, 710.

57 Hamilton, "Historical Geography of the Coal Mining Industry," 115.

58 Belshaw, "Standard of Living," 46.

59 Muise, "Making of an Industrial Community," 76–94.

60 Edwin Gilpin explained that "cessation of work led to many men working their little farms or lumbering in the winter, and cutting coal during the summer. Other miners stayed at the mines, and received more or less work during the winter." See "Underground certificates," 5. See also Hornsby, *Nineteenth-Century Cape Breton*, 141. On links between seasonal mine work and (sub-)marginal farming, see Bitterman, "Farm Households and Wage Labour," 13–45; and Samson, "Dependency and Rural Industry," 105–49. On Newfoundland labourers in Cape Breton, see Crawley, "Off to Sydney," 27–51.

61 Seager, "Minto, New Brunswick," 104.

62 The Galt mines in Lethbridge sent recruiters to Nova Scotia in 1883. See Den Otter, *Civilizing the West*, 96.

63 See Schwantes, *Radical Heritage*.

64 CMJ, 1 May 1918, 57.

65 Den Otter, *Civilizing the West*, 273–4.

66 Cited in Lutz, "After the fur trade," 76.

67 Bancroft, *History of British Columbia*, 192–3; Kemble, "Coal from the Northwest Coast," 123–30. Muir's original party had also employed

Kanakas and aboriginals. See NA, MG 20, B/185/a/1, "Fort Rupert Post Journal," entry for 3 November 1849.

68 Hazlitt, *British Columbia and Vancouver Island*, 164.

69 Brown, *Geographical Distribution*, 12.

70 Victoria *Daily British Colonist*, 27 January 1861.

71 Cited in Burrill, "Class Conflict and Colonialism," 127. An editorial protesting the employment of aboriginal labourers anticipated an argument later directed against Chinese workers: that their low wages chased away white workers. Victoria *Daily British Colonist*, 19 February 1861.

72 Wickberg, *From China to Canada*, 19–20.

73 "Select Committee on Chinese Labour and Immigration," Canada, *Journals*, vol. 13, Appendix 4, 1879, 7; Victoria *Daily British Colonist*, 27 April 1867.

74 Natives were employed to at least 1912 as "trimmers," loading coal from the wharf on ships. See Burrill, "Class Conflict and Colonialism," 124–8.

75 BCMR, 1874–1902.

76 There were three means by which European miners sought during the nineteenth century to restrict access to the mine (*fermer le métier*): by systems of apprenticeship, by limiting mine work to miners' offspring, and by encouraging emigration. See Michel, "Politique syndicale et conjoncture économique," 65.

77 The PWA was also marked by grassroots militancy. Its lodges fought an estimated seventy-two strikes between 1879 and 1900. McKay, "Wisdom, Wile or War," 16–8, 60.

78 Relations between trade unions and boys are discussed in Chapter 8.

79 Phillips, *No Power Greater*, 6–8; Orr, "Western Federation of Miners," 39–45.

80 Mouat, "Politics of Coal," 6–13.

81 Phillips, *No Power Greater*, 12–16.

82 A UMWA local was formed at Nanaimo before the end of 1903 in the wake of the failed WFM strike. Phillips, *No Power Greater*, 38–40, 55–61; Norris, "Vancouver Island Coal Mines," 56–72.

83 Den Otter, *Civilizing the West*, 280.

84 "Report of the Royal Commission on Industrial Disputes in British Columbia," Canada, *Sessional Papers*, 1903, vol. 37, no. 13, 36a, 35, 46–7; 62; Macmillan, "Trade Unionism in District 18," 41–9.

85 Baker, "Miners and the Mediator," 89–117; Den Otter, *Civilizing the West*, 284–304.

86 Makahonuk, "Trade Unions in the Saskatchewan Coal Industry," 51–68.

87 See Belshaw, "British Collier," 34–6.

88 Don MacLeod observed that between 1858 and 1879 miners "lost a good deal of the control and independence they had exercised formerly." He linked this to the influx of unskilled workers during the mining boom of the 1860s. See MacLeod, "Miners, Mining Men and Mining Reform," 435.

89 Labour Canada Library, Annual Meeting of the PWA Grand Council, *Minutes*, April 1881, 21. At Bridgeport, miners complained: "It is scarcely fair to keep men idle five months in the year, and then swarm the pits in the summertime." *TJ*, 1 April 1885. Similar concerns were expressed that same summer at the Reserve Mines. *TJ*, 1 July 1885.

90 *TJ*, 11 May 1887.

91 LC, *Evidence*, 285–6.

92 Labour Canada Library, Annual Meeting of the PWA Grand Council, *Minutes*, April 1884, 59.

93 Macdonald, *Coal and Iron Industries*, 213. See also LC, *Evidence*, 366–7.

94 Later in the decade controversy arose over the amounts companies would deduct from contract miners' pay for loaders (effectively, over the sums miners paid their helpers). See *TJ*, 20 April 1880; *TJ*, 9 November 1887 (at Acadia); *TJ*, 30 October 1887 (at Springhill). The question concerned Drummond to the extent that he raised it before the Labour Commission. See LC, *Evidence*, 366. Loaders were paid directly by contract miners until after the First World War. See NA, Records of the Department of Labour (hereafter RG 27), vol. 142, file 611.04:6, "Proceedings of the Royal Commission appointed to inquire into Coal Mining Conditions in the Maritime Provinces at Meetings held in Fredericton, N.B., on August 17th and 18th, 1920," 56. See also Labour Canada Library, Royal Commission Respecting the Coal Mines of the Province of Nova Scotia, *Minutes of Evidence*, 1925, 3941.

95 *TJ*, 28 April 1880. The manager at Sydney Mines complained in 1876 of workers demanding to choose who was to be employed to haul coal. McKay, "Crisis of dependent development," 36.

96 Points of contention included rates of pay, hours of work, and miners' access to the riding rakes that brought them into and out of the mine; access to tools and lamps; the cost of gunpowder and fuel; and the fines levied when miners failed to remove impurities from coal. Extensive negotiations also occurred over where the miner worked: whether the seam was wide or too narrow, whether it was too wet, whether coal had to be shovelled an excessive distance to a tub, and whether tubs had to be pushed an excessive distance to the point where they were picked up by haulage workers.

97 Angus L. Macdonald Library, St Francis Xavier University, Springhill Minutebooks, Pioneer Lodge, PWA, entries for 24 April, 1 May 1884.

A boy complained during a lodge meeting on 28 August 1884 that "he would not be allowed to go loading although old enough."

98 Frank, "Contested Terrain," 103.

99 On the different mining communities, see Chapter 7.

100 Victoria *Daily British Colonist*, 27 April, 3 May, 8 May, 13 May, 24 May, 27 May, 15 June, 18 June, 24 June, 1 July 1867.

101 Ibid., 8 May 1867.

102 Ibid., 29 April 1879.

103 See Chapter 5 on the legislation excluding a large proportion of boys from British Columbian coal mines.

104 Watkin, *Canada and the States*, 70–2.

105 Roy, *White Man's Province*, 53–4. The potential use of Chinese as strikebreakers had been rumoured as early as 1871, during a lengthy strike at Nanaimo. Victoria *Daily British Colonist*, 20 January, 12 March 1871. Dunsmuir canvassed San Francisco for Chinese during the 1877 Wellington strike. While other strikebreakers were used, no Chinese appear to have been employed to mine coal during that strike. The Victoria *Daily British Colonist*, 24 February 1877, reported the presence in Wellington of American strikebreakers. See also British Columbia, *Sessional Papers*, 1879, 525–34.

106 Chinese strikebreakers were used again in 1903 and during the UMWA recognition strike of 1912–14. See "Report of the Royal Commission on Industrial Disputes in British Columbia," Canada, *Sessional Papers*, 1903, vol. 37, no. 13, 36a, 62; Canada, Royal Commission on Coal Mining Disputes on Vancouver Island, *Report*, 24. The explosion at Nanaimo in 1887 killed 150; that at Wellington the following year killed 77. See BCMR, 1887, 290; 1888, 324.

107 "Report of the Royal Commission on Chinese Immigration," Canada, *Sessional Papers*, 1885, vol. 18, no. 11, 54a, 110; "Report of the Royal Commission on Chinese and Japanese Immigration," Canada, *Sessional Papers*, 1902, vol. 36, no. 13, 54, "Chapter IX – Coal Mining Industry," 79.

108 "Report of the Royal Commission on Chinese Immigration," *Sessional Papers*, 1885, vol. 18, no. 11, 54a, 118.

109 Ralston and Kealey, "Samuel H. Myers," 637–9.

110 Mouat, "Politics of Coal," 13.

111 See "Report of the Royal Commission on Chinese and Japanese Immigration," Canada, *Sessional Papers*, 1902, vol. 36, no. 13, 54, "Chapter IX – Coal Mining Industry," 85–6.

112 Ibid., 88.

113 With the possible exception of an overture by the Western Federation of Miners at the Union colliery in 1903, miners' unions made no effort to organize Asian workers. See "Disputes in the Coal Mines of

British Columbia During 1903," Canada, *Sessional Papers*, 1903, vol. 37, no. 13, 36a, 60. The departure of the great majority (110 of 135) of a group of Scottish immigrant miners from Union was linked to the presence of Chinese workers underground at the mines there. "They learned that the only way to get a living at the business was to hire a Chinese loader." See Nanaimo *Free Press*, 1 February 1901.

114 Victoria *Daily British Colonist*, 27 February 1883.

115 "Report of the Royal Commission on Chinese Immigration," Canada, *Sessional Papers*, 1885, vol. 18, no. 11, 54a, 158. See also ibid., 119–20.

116 Ibid., 88.

117 "Report of the Royal Commission on Chinese and Japanese Immigration," Canada, *Sessional Papers*, 1902, vol. 36, no. 13, 54, "Chapter IX – Coal Mining Industry," 81.

118 Ibid., 72. See also S.M. Robins's testimony in Canada, *Royal Commission on Mining Conditions in British Columbia*, vol. 2, *Evidence*, 683.

119 "Report of the Royal Commission on Chinese and Japanese Immigration," Canada, *Sessional Papers*, 1902, vol. 36, no. 13, 54, "Chapter IX – Coal Mining Industry," 90.

120 BCMR, *passim*.

121 Canada [Carroll], *Royal Commission on Coal*, 525–7; Den Otter, *Civilizing the West*, 74–5.

122 In Nova Scotia, a "Combination of Workmen Act" was passed in a single morning sitting to enable the colony to send troops to Sydney Mines to evict striking miners from company houses in 1864. See Abbott, "Coal Miners and the Law," 26–7. On the use of the military during industrial conflicts, see Morton, "Aid to the Civil Power," 407–25; Silverman, "Military Aid to the Civil Power," 156–64; Silverman, "Aid of the Civil Power," 46–52; and Macgillivray, "Military Aid to the Civil Power," 45–64.

123 In Nova Scotia, for instance, coal royalties amounted to 35 percent of the federal subsidy (the single largest source of provincial revenue) in 1888, and to 64 percent in 1898. See *Journals and Proceedings of the House of Assembly of Nova Scotia*, 1889, Appendix 1, "Financial Returns," 121; 1899, 267.

124 *TJ*, 5 July 1882. On "assisted emigration" from Canada (the alleged consequence of government subsidies to immigrants to Canada), see *TJ*, 8 July 1885.

125 *TJ*, 15 July 1885. As late as 1917, fears regarding "Coolie Labour" were expressed by organized miners in Nova Scotia. See Labour Canada Library, Amalgamated Mine Workers of Nova Scotia, *Minutes of Second Annual Convention*, Sydney, 18–23 November 1918, 13. Only a handful of Chinese workers laboured at mines in the western interior. Some were employed, for instance, on the surface of the

mines at Anthracite (near Banff), Alberta, in 1899. See CMR, January 1889, 9.

126 Munro, "British Columbia and the 'Chinese Evil,'" 42–51. As early as 1892, the province was demanding that the head tax be doubled to $100. See British Columbia, *Sessional Papers*, 1892, 627–8; "An Act respecting and restricting Chinese Immigration," c. 32, s. 6, *Statutes of Canada*, 1900; and "An Act respecting and restricting Chinese Immigration," c. 8, s. 6, *Statutes of Canada*, 1903. See also Ryder, "Racism and the Constitution," 619–76.

127 Nova Scotia, *Debates and Proceedings*, 1872, 258. On the genesis of the act, see MacLeod, "Miners, Mining Men and Mining Reform," 404–5.

128 Victoria *Daily British Colonist*, 29 March 1877.

129 The initial act, in 1877, already offered a sop to the exclusionists in stipulating that "[n]o Chinaman or person unable to speak English shall be appointed to or occupy any position of trust or responsibility in or about a mine subject to this Act, whereby through his ignorance, carelessness, or negligence, he might endanger the life or limb of any person employed in or about a mine, viz.: A banksman, onsetter, signalman, brakesman, pointsman, furnaceman, engineer, or be employed at the windlass of a sinking pit." This clause was inconsequential: Chinese were not employed in these positions in the nineteenth century and no operator proposed that they would be. See "An Act to Make Regulations with respect to Coal Mines," 40 Vict., c. 122, Rule 33, *Statutes of British Columbia*, 1877.

130 See Roy, *White Man's Province*, 80–1, 134–42, 171–2; Grove and Lamberston, "Pawns of the Powerful," 3–31; and Lambertson, "After *Union Colliery*," 386–422.

131 BCMR, 1914, K429.

132 Asian mine workers, given no opportunity to speak on their own behalf, were accused of an inability to follow instructions or to read warning signs, as well as of a tendency to panic. See Lambertson, "After *Union Colliery*," 388.

133 "An Act to amend the 'Coal Mines Regulation Act' and Amending Act," 57 Vict., c. 5, *Statutes of British Columbia*, 1894; "An Act to amend the Coal Mines Regulation Act," 1 Ed. VII, c. 36, *Statutes of British Columbia*, 1901. See also Lambertson, "After *Union Colliery*," 386–422.

134 Den Otter, *Civilizing the West*, 270–1.

135 Mine managers were required to have five years' "practical experience" in a mine or a two-year "diploma in scientific and mining training" and at least three years' experience. A pit boss (in charge of underground workings) was only required to pass the certification exam. See "Act to make regulations with respect to coal mines," c. 25, secs. 13–25, *Statutes of Alberta*, 1906.

136 PAA, Royal Commission on the Coal Mining Industry, *Report and Evidence*, 9.
137 In 1913 a new comprehensive Mines Act did tighten the certification requirements for minor officials, establishing a minimum of three years' experience and fixing a minimum age (twenty-five years for an overman's certificate; twenty-three for an examiner's certificate). "An Act respecting Mines," c. 4, s. 20, *Statutes of Alberta*, 1913. The Alberta Coal Commission, *Report*, 282, recommended the establishment for a certificate of competency by means of a "special conference of operators and miners with the Government."
138 "An Act respecting Mines," c. 178, s. 4, *Revised Statutes of Saskatchewan*, 1921, contained requirements only for the certification of mine officials.
139 "An Act to Amend Chapter 35 of *The Revised Statutes*, 1927, Respecting Mines and Minerals," 23 Geo. V, c. 23, s. 130, *Acts of the Legislative Assembly of New Brunswick*, 1933.
140 Don MacLeod views the provincial mines inspector, H.S. Poole, disturbed by the level of accidents in provincial mines, as instrumental in seeing passed into law the first Nova Scotia Mines Act. A position labelled "inspector of mines" had existed in Nova Scotia as early as 1858, but its first incumbent treated it as little more than a sinecure. See MacLeod, "Colliers, Collier Safety and Workplace Control," 232–3.
141 PWA success at legislative reform has been underlined repeatedly as its "outstanding feature." See Logan, *Trade Unions in Canada*, 172; Forsey, *Trade Unions in Canada*, 346–63; and MacLeod, "Colliers, Colliery Safety and Workplace Control," 226–53.
142 NSMR, 1884, 19–20.
143 Gilpin, "Underground certificates," 5.
144 LC, *Evidence*, 366–7.
145 Labour Canada Library, Annual Meeting of the PWA Grand Council, *Minutes*, 1890, 221.
146 Officials were licensed after examination of their knowledge of "ventilation, gases, mines and mining" by a Board of Examiners consisting entirely of mine managers – over the protests of the PWA. Miners hoped that the requirement of work experience underground would improve their access to positions in mine management. See MacLeod, "Colliers, Colliery Safety and Workplace Control," 241.
147 Ibid., 252.
148 The exam for miners was oral, addressing subjects such as mine gases, ventilation, methods of working a coalface, timbering, safety lamps, and mining regulations. See ibid., 244–5.
149 Certification also inspired poetry. These verses, accompanied by laughter and applause, were read to Premier Fielding at a meeting of

the Mining Society of Nova Scotia. They reflect a traditional view of the value of schooling for work in the mines. See CMR, March 1894, 54.

"Our Certificate"

In learned professions, to carry more weight,
    An expert should have a good certificate.
Now, all sorts of miners must hold one as well,
    And how they regard it this chorus will tell.
I'm only a trapper and need no book lore
    To teach me to open and shot-to a door;
Still, I have to study and addle my pate
    Before I can pass for a certificate.
And I am a driver, I cannot go wrong,
    As o'er the gate roads I pass carelessly on.
A very poor scholar can drive a horse straight,
    Yet I must read up for a certificate.
And I work a windlass, it does not need brain
    To turn a crank handle again and again;
Still, I'm not exempted; I hear 'tis my fate
    That I, too, must pass for a certificate.
And I am a cutter, unpaid if I shirk
    (The strongest of motives to keep me at work),
But yet I must grind all new theories to date
    Before I can handle a certificate.
And I am an overman, high up the tree;
    Good practical mining is expected of me,
Which I learned, with much more, I now beg to state,
    Before I was crammed for a certificate.
And I'm an Inspector from [a] nondescript trade,
    Without special training, and fairly well paid.
I criticise freely, yet, strange to relate,
    I cannot produce a certificate.

150 CMR, February 1896, 30.
151 McKay, "Wisdom, Wile and War," 58; MacLeod, "Colliers, Colliery Safety and Workplace Control," 252. Robert Drummond, in explaining the PWA stance decades later, observed simply that "the miners were a reasonable class." Labour Canada Library, Drummond, *Recollections and Reflections*, 312. On the corruption of certification by 1907, see Samson, "Dependency and Rural Industry," 136–7. Miners testified in 1920 that certificates were granted to incompetents "simply because they have received recommendations from officials." See

RG 27, vol. 141, file 611.04:6, "Minutes of a Board of Investigation with representatives of Miners and Dominion Coal Company, Glace Bay, Nova Scotia: Proceedings of Conference at Glace Bay, 20 and 21 July 1920," 43.

152 MacLeod, "Colliers, Colliery Safety and Workplace Control," 242.

153 MacLeod, "Practicality Ascendant," 68–9.

154 I owe this expression to Del Muise.

155 See Gilpin, "Underground certificates," 3.

156 Drummond, *Minerals and Mining*, 351.

157 The act also established the Nova Scotia Technical College in Halifax to offer the last two years of a four-year program in engineering. Mining classes were underway in Sydney and Glace Bay as early as the autumn of 1907. MacLeod, "Practicality Ascendant," 86–7. See also Guildford, "Coping with De-industrialization," 70–4. On the technical schools, see RCTE, 1669–1706.

158 Ibid., 1706–7. McDougall is incorrect. An amendment in 1908 prohibited from the mine any boy between twelve and sixteen who had not completed Grade 7. "An Act to consolidate and amend Chapter 19, *Revised Statutes*, 1900, 'The Coal Mines Regulation Act', and amendments thereto," 8 Ed. VII, c. 8, s. 19, *Statutes of Nova Scotia*, 1908.

Chapter Four

1 Bourinot, "Cape Breton and Its Memorials," 277; Brown, *Coal Fields*, 35–44; Belshaw, "Mining Technique and Social Division," 53–4.

2 Brown, *Coal Fields*, 49–52; Gilpin, "Coal Mining in Nova Scotia," 395; Millward, "Model of Coalfield Development," 239; Patterson, "Early History of Mining," 116.

3 During one pay period in 1807, George Long, for instance, was paid for a variety of work that included cutting, hauling, mine development, and general labour. See PANS, RG 21, series A, 1/141 "Pay List of Persons Employed at His Majesty's Coal Mines," cited in Hornsby, *Nineteenth-Century Cape Breton*, 16–17.

4 "Gin–boys" operated gin-wheels to hoist coal from the pit at Sydney Mines and in Pictou County prior to the arrival of the GMA; even after the 1820s, three gin-boys were listed on company paybooks. Boys may have been employed as helpers underground, but no evidence of their presence there remains. Haliburton, *Historical and Statistical Account*, 439–43. Patterson, *County of Pictou*, 399, refers to the use of gin-wheels at early Pictou mines. See also CMR, July 1893, 116; PANS, RG 21, series A, vol. 40, no. 10, "Particulars of Mining Operations in Cape Breton, 1832"; and Martell, "Early Coal Mining," 156–72.

5 MacLeod, "Miners, Mining Men and Mining Reform," 306–7. Sympathetic contemporaries claimed GMA investment in Nova Scotia to stand at 300,000 pounds sterling before 1846, and at 400,000 pounds sterling by 1849. See Brown, *Coal Fields*, 77; and Gesner, *Industrial Resources*, 286.

6 There were two steam engines at Nanaimo by 1860. See Pemberton, *Facts and Figures*, 46.

7 Den Otter, *Civilizing the West*, 119–21.

8 Buxton, *Economic Development*, 27.

9 Millward, "Model of Coalfield Development," 239.

10 Brown, *Coal Fields*, 63–4; Gilpin, "Coal Mining in Pictou County," 175–6; New Glasgow *Eastern Chronicle*, 25 January 1868.

11 BCMR, 1883, 416.

12 BCMR, 1890, 392.

13 Brown, *Coal Fields*, 49; Hornsby, *Nineteenth-Century Cape Breton*, 100–1; NSMR, 1858, 377; 1882, 41; 1890, L; 1906, xiv.

14 Coal differed greatly in chemical and physical properties. The basic distinctions were among soft (lignite), medium (bituminous), and hard (anthracite) coal. The coal mined in Canada was generally bituminous. See Canada [Carroll], *Royal Commission on Coal*, 7–52.

15 A very detailed discussion of the technology of the steam-powered colliery is found in MacLeod, "Miners, Mining Men and Mining Reform," 299–428.

16 Managers made little attempt to oversee miners' work. At Springhill in 1891, for instance, there was one manager for every 140 miners. The difficulties of overseeing the work in hundreds of scattered workplaces (bords) are clear. But mine managers did have a role in supervising unskilled (datal) workers. See McKay, "Realm of Uncertainty," 11, 18–19. On a prominent early mine manager, see Frank, "Richard Smith," 730–1.

17 This technique was most commonly called bord and pillar in nineteenth-century Canada, but it was also known as room and pillar, stoop and room, breast and pillar, and stall and pillar.

18 Miners were also commonly called "cutters," or "colliers," or "hewers."

19 MacLeod, "Colliers, Collier Safety and Workplace Control," 246.

20 See also MacLeod, "Miners, Mining Men and Mining Reform," 314–15.

21 NA, Records of the Department of Labour (hereafter RG 27), vol. 141, file 611.04:6, "Minutes of a Board of Investigation with representatives of Miners and Dominion Coal Company, Glace Bay, Nova Scotia: Proceedings of Conference at Glace Bay, 20 and 21 July 1920," 43–4.

22 See ibid., 21.

23 See Gilpin, "Coal Mining in Nova Scotia," 371. In Cape Breton, where
    mining extended under the sea, an estimated seven tons of water
    were taken out for every ton of coal during the 1920s. See Frank,
    "Contested Terrain," 104.

24 MacLeod, "Miners, Mining Men and Mining Reform," 331.

25 The surface workforce at the large colliery at Sydney Mines num-
    bered 117 in 1858, of whom 17 were boys. See NSMR, 1858, 376–7.

26 Bowen, *Boss Whistle*, 33. At Springhill, the company agreed in 1885 to
    "put a boy to give out the picks." See Angus L. Macdonald Library,
    St Francis Xavier University, Springhill Minutebooks, Pioneer Lodge,
    PWA, entry for March 1885. Edwin Gilpin remarked in 1888 that auto-
    matic tub greasers were "more reliable" than boys. See "Coal Mining
    in Nova Scotia," 392.

27 Corless, "Coal Creek Colliery," 61.

28 See NA, RG 27, vol. 141, file 611.04:6, "Minutes of a Board of Investi-
    gation with representatives of Miners and Dominion Coal Company,
    Glace Bay, Nova Scotia: Proceedings of Conference at Glace Bay,
    20 and 21 July 1920," 41.

29 The manager at Sydney Mines noted in 1874 that a boy was injured
    while operating a winding-engine. See PANS, RG 21, series A, vol. 38,
    no. 10, Richard Brown diaries, entry for 10 August.

30 Cameron, *Pictonian Colliers*, 277.

31 A fifteen-year-old boy was employed in the office at Sydney Mines.
    See PANS, RG 21, series A, vol. 38, no. 10, Richard Brown diaries,
    entry for 23 April 1873.

32 Belshaw, "Mining Techniques and Social Division," 51; MacLeod,
    "Miners, Mining Men and Mining Reform," 312. In Great Britain, coal
    was typically cleaned underground to the 1850s. Only large coals
    were sent to the surface. Mitchell, *Economic Development*, 95.

33 MacLeod, "Miners, Mining Men and Mining Reform," 331.

34 Belshaw, "Mining Techniques and Social Division," 55.

35 *CMR*, June 1897, 219.

36 Morrow, "Preparation of Coal," 280–1.

37 Johnstone, *Coal Dust*, 12.

38 NSMR, 1867, 48; 1896, 57; 1911, xxi.

39 Pamely, *Colliery Manager's Handbook*, 385. In Cape Breton, in 1863, all
    mines were ventilated naturally with the exception of the large
    Queen Pit at Sydney Mines. NSMR, 1863, 11–24.

40 Galloway, *Annals of Coal Mining*, vol. 2, 269.

41 Lewis, *Coal Mining*, 51; Buxton, *Economic Development*, 131. Buddle's
    system was in place before 1852 at the Albion Mines. Tyro, "Visit to
    the Albion Mines," 177.

42 Gilpin, "Coal Mining in Nova Scotia," 364.

43 Lewis, *Coal Mining*, 51.

44 Gilpin, "Coal Mining in Nova Scotia," 363.

45 BCMR, 1883, 416–18.

46 Morrow, *Springhill Disaster*, 293. No direct correlation can be drawn between the extension of mining underground and the call for trappers. Much depended on the nature of the mine, and the level and type of mining activity at a given time. At Sydney Mines, 192 colliers, 38 drivers, and 15 trappers worked in the mine in 1858; twenty years later, 81 colliers, 11 drivers, and 5 trappers went down the mine in each of two shifts. NSMR, 1858, 376–7; PANS, RG 21, series A, vol. 38, no. 11, Richard Brown Diaries, entries for 6 and 8 June, 1878.

47 NSMR, 1866, 41, cited in MacLeod, "Miners, Mining Men and Mining Reform," 401.

48 NSMR, 1867, 30.

49 Boys were turning fans at Nova Scotia mines into the 1920s. See NA, RG 27, vol. 142, file 611.04:6, Royal Commission on Mining – Sitting at Halifax, 9 August, 1920 Etc. – Minutes of Evidence, Testimony of 13 August, 13.

50 McKay, "Industry, Work and Community," 603.

51 Chrismas, *Coal Dust Grins*, 20.

52 Pamely, *Colliery Manager's Handbook*, 401.

53 CMR, March 1899, 99.

54 Galloway, *Annals of Coal Mining*, vol. 2, 203.

55 CMR, March 1901, 62.

56 An injured trapper boy was reported by the *Maritime Labour Herald*, 3 May 1924. On planning a ventilation system to eliminate doors, see Dick, "Economic Study of Coal Mining," 133–91.

57 Mitchell, *Economic Development*, 75–6. Gunpowder was introduced into Nova Scotian mines by the GMA and was in general use on Vancouver Island by the 1860s. See MacLeod, "Miners, Mining Men and Mining Reform," 314; Gallacher, "Men, Money, Machines," 238.

58 Pit ponies and large tubs were introduced in the United Kingdom during the 1840s. Mitchell, *Economic Development*, 123.

59 Gilpin, "Coal Mining in Nova Scotia," 395.

60 Brown, *Coal Fields*, 113.

61 Burrill, "Class Conflict and Colonialism," 126.

62 Local conditions determined the ratio of drivers to miners. At the Albion Mines, twenty-eight drivers were employed underground with sixty-six colliers in 1836. Gilpin, "Coal Mining in Pictou County," 172. An American visitor observed in 1850 that one boy and one horse "may be sufficient for each two cutters" at the Albion Mines; at Sydney Mines, in contrast, because "a single main road is

made to answer for all the transportation to the pit's bottom ... a much less number of underground horses and drivers is required." See Johnson, *Coal Trade of British America*, 16–17.

63 On the use of chutes in the Crowsnest Pass, see Babaian, *Coal Mining Industry*, 45.

64 Quoted in McKay, "Realm of Uncertainty," 29.

65 Ibid.

66 Springhill Miners' Museum, Springhill, Nova Scotia, Cumberland Railway and Coal Company, Time Books, August 1901.

67 Nicholson, "Past and Present Methods," 468–70.

68 Gilpin, "Coal Mining in Nova Scotia," 357–9.

69 Geological Survey of Canada, *Reports on Progress*, 1866–67, 94.

70 NSMR, 1873, 18–19, indicates the use of back-balances at the Caledonia and Gowrie Mines in Cape Breton.

71 Gilpin, "Coal Mining in Pictou County," 175.

72 Bowen, *Boss Whistle*, 16.

73 Mitchell, "Early Mining of Coal," 551.

74 MacDonald, "Farewell to Coal," 21.

75 LC, *Evidence*, 278.

76 "Horses in the Coal Mines," 38–40; Schwieder, Hraba, and Schwieder, *Buxton*, 69–70.

77 LC, *Evidence*, 437–8.

78 Ibid., 303.

79 Moffat, "Coal Miner's Ears," 413–14. Rats were also valued for their usefulness in warning of impending danger. See Bowen, *Boss Whistle*, 61.

80 See "Horses in the Coal Mines," 42. See also Lawson, *A Man's Life*, 25.

81 McNeil, *Voice of the Pioneer*, 61.

82 "Horses in the Coal Mines," 42–3.

83 McNeil, *Voice of the Pioneer*, 19.

84 NSMR, 1890, 17.

85 TJ, 28 February 1883.

86 Bowen, *Boss Whistle*, 59–60.

87 Nanaimo *Free Press*, 25 January 1901.

88 BCMR, 1887, 288.

89 NSMR, 1867, 33.

90 Boutilier was fined one dollar and costs. See North Sydney *Herald*, 20 March 1895. Societies for the Prevention of Cruelty to Animals were founded before organizations concerned with the prevention of cruelty to children.

91 Bowen, *Boss Whistle*, 60. Mine managers attempted to fine boys they suspected of mistreating horses. At Springhill, if a horse was killed

on account of a driver's negligence, the boy was dismissed. See LC, *Evidence*, 298.

92 Gilpin, "Notes on Nova Scotia Pit Waters," 2.

93 Kingston, "International Colliery," 21.

94 On this point, see Belshaw, "Standard of Living," 45; and Bowen, *Boss Whistle*, 226. Sometimes miners worked with a "buddy": at Springhill, for instance, two miners commonly shared both a bord and the cost of a helper. McKay, "Realm of Uncertainty," 14.

95 See PAA, Royal Commission on the Coal Mining Industry, *Report and Evidence*, 10. The (Duncan) Royal Commission Respecting the Coal Mines of the Province of Nova Scotia heard in 1925 that boys continued to be brought into the mines as helpers for their father. Cited in Penfold, "Have You No Manhood," 24.

96 Glace Bay *Gazette*, 9 March 1933, cited in MacEwan, *Miners and Steelworkers*, 5.

97 As one miner testified in 1920: "Pushing is very hard on the men when they get up to middle life, they find that they have to give up contract work because pushing is attached to it and they are not able to do pushing." See NA, RG 27, vol. 141, file 611.04:6, "Minutes of a Board of Investigation with representatives of Miners and Dominion Coal Company, Glace Bay, Nova Scotia: Proceedings of Conference at Glace Bay, 20 and 21 July 1920," 4.

98 NA, RG 27, vol. 142, file 611.04:6, "Proceedings of the Royal Commission appointed to inquire into Coal Mining Conditions in the Maritime Provinces at Meetings held in Fredericton, N.B., on August 17th and 18th, 1920," 42.

99 NSMR, 1872, 32.

100 NSMR, 1914, 77.

101 Victoria *Daily British Colonist*, 19 September 1867.

102 BCMR, 1895, 723.

103 Miners' work in the bords was accompanied by "pit talk," a "spirited tradition of conversation and debate." Frank, "Coal Masters and Coal Miners," 51.

104 I owe these observations to Del Muise. On production difficulties and weak profitability as spurs to consolidation of ownership in Nova Scotia, see Inwood, "Local Control," 254–82.

105 McLennan, "Screening of Soft Coal," 88; Drummond, *Minerals and Mining*, 226–7.

106 CMJ, 1 November 1911, 710. In 1913 the Dominion Iron and Steel Corporation operated five blast furnaces at Sydney and a large establishment operated at Sydney Mines as well, where Nova Scotia Steel and Coal had coke ovens, a blast furnace, and open hearths. CMJ, 1 September 1914, 593–4.

107 Forty-three mines operated in Nova Scotia that year; thirty-three in British Columbia; and eleven in New Brunswick. *Coal Statistics for Canada, 1927*, 13.

108 Gallacher, "Men, Money, Machines," 4, 146–60; Graham, "Vancouver Island Coal Industry," 456. When the original Wellington site was abandoned in 1900, Dunsmuir opened a new mine at Extension. See Gidney, "From Coal to Forest Products," 38. The Western Fuel Company purchased the Nanaimo mines in 1902. See "Report of the Royal Commission on Industrial Disputes in British Columbia," Canada, *Sessional Papers*, 1903, vol. 37, no. 13, 36a, 35.

109 Inwood, "Local Control," 254–82.

110 Macgillivray, "Henry Melville Whitney," 44–70.

111 The largest collieries remaining outside BESCO were the Intercolonial in Pictou County, the Inverness Railway and Coal Company on Cape Breton Island, and the Maritime Coal, Railway and Power Company in Joggins (Cumberland County). Others included the Port Hood Collieries Ltd. and the Bras d'Or Coal Company Ltd. See Frank, "Rise and Fall," 3–34. BESCO was reorganized, following a series of crises in the 1920s, as the Dominion Steel and Coal Company (DOSCO) in 1928. DOSCO's coal mines were taken over by the Canadian government in 1966.

112 Because coal mining was a labour-intensive industry, salaries and wages accounted for up to 80 percent of the cost of producing coal. CMR, June 1899, 165.

113 Either bords were uneconomically small or the coal left in pillars was wasted, slowly crushed by the weight above. See Millward, "Model of Coalfield Development," 243; and Gallacher, "Men, Money, Machines," 243.

114 McCall, "Some Coal Mining Practices," 490. Mining engineers also looked for seams with a suitable roof, which would bend but not easily break. See Bulman and Redmayne, *Colliery Working and Management*, 163.

115 At the turn of the twentieth century, longwall was in use in the upper seam at Union; "considerable" longwall was used at No. 5 Shaft, Wellington. Both were Dunsmuir mines. *Canadian Mining Manual*, 1899, 594, 627. See also Belshaw, "Mining Technique and Social Division," 49.

116 In the Crowsnest Pass, sharply pitched and irregular seams encouraged the use of bord-and-pillar methods. See Babaian, *Coal Mining Industry*, 39.

117 McCall, "Some Coal Mining Practices," 490–1. Longwall was in use in sections of both the Drummond and Acadia collieries in Pictou County in 1899 and at Joggins in 1900. NSMR, 1899, 7–8; 1900, 9.

118 McCall, "Some Coal Mining Practices," 484.

119 Gray, "Mining Coal under the Sea," 1007; McDougall, "Longwall Operations," 480.

120 McCall, "Some Coal Mining Practices," 470–1.

121 See Bryan, "Coal-Mining," 359–75.

122 Doe, "Practical Application," 162.

123 CMR, March 1891, 85.

124 CMR, August 1891, 196.

125 CMR, June 1891, 160–1.

126 Mitchell, *Economic Development*, 79, 92. The use of electricity is debated, for instance, in CMR, August 1888, 90.

127 Mechanized mining was destructive of lump coal. Only when markets for slack coal emerged with the production of coke for the metallurgical sector – by the middle of the nineteenth century in Great Britain, towards the end of the century in Canada – could coal-cutting machines be widely adopted. See Galloway, *Annals of Coal Mining*, vol. 2, 362. On the adoption of mechanical cutters, see Hudson, "Notes on Coal Cutting Machinery," 156; and Mitchell, *Economic Development*, 81–2.

128 BCMR, 1891, 587; *Canadian Mining Manual*, 1894, 491.

129 Den Otter, *Civilizing the West*, 267; Hardie, "Machine Mining at Lethbridge," 245–8.

130 Alberta Coal Commission, *Report*, 66.

131 CMR, March 1903, 59–60.

132 Dix, "Work Relations," 160–1. Curtis Seltzer estimated that undercutting machines reduced by 75 percent the time required to undermine a coalface by handpick. See Seltzer, *Fire in the Hole*, 12.

133 NA, RG 27, vol. 141, file 611.04:6, "Minutes of a Board of Investigation with representatives of Miners and Dominion Coal Company, Glace Bay, Nova Scotia: Proceedings of Conference at Glace Bay, 20 and 21 July 1920," 43–4.

134 Mitchell, *Economic Development*, 77. Another drawback to the use of steam engines underground is that they weakened the mine roof. See CMR, October 1888, 109.

135 *Historical Review of Coal Mining*, 94–8; Blakemore, "Introduction of Endless Haulage," 151–4.

136 This was in the Queen Pit at Sydney Mines. See NSMR, 1858, 376.

137 Mitchell, *Economic Development*, 78–9. When British Columbia passed restrictive child labour legislation in 1877, legislators' efforts to exclude children from the mines were qualified in one respect. A clause permitted thirteen- to fifteen-year-olds to work in thin seams with special provincial approval, to a maximum of six hours daily. See "The Coal Mines Regulation Act, 1877," 40 Vict., no. 2, s. 2, *Statutes of British Columbia*, 1877.

138 Gilpin, "Coal Mining in Nova Scotia," 363.

139 Brown, *Coal Fields*, 143.

140 CMR, January 1896, 2–3.

141 NSMR, 1891, 5–6.

142 CMR, January 1893, 2; August 1891, 209.

143 Johnston, "Description of Haulage System," 92.

144 BCMR, 1883, 416, 418.

145 Alberta Coal Commission, *Report*, 66.

146 In 1867, 418 horses were employed in Nova Scotian collieries, and
    458 in 1900. See NSMR, 1867, 48; 1900, 71.

147 Johnston, "Description of Haulage System," 92. Submarine mines
    called for very elaborate underground haulage "approximate to that
    of a railway system, with its feeder lines, marshalling sidings, and
    the main line." Gray, *Coal-Fields and Coal Industry*, 43.

148 Mortimer-Lamb, "Coal Industry of Vancouver Island," 14–19, 29–32;
    BCMR, 1892, 550; Planta, "Coal Fields of Vancouver Island," 435; Stra-
    chan, "Coal Mining in British Columbia," 78–9.

149 Even the design of coal tubs was much discussed. See Hyde, "Mine
    Car Design," 226–41.

150 CMR, January 1889, 2; Rotteleur, "Use of Gasoline Locomotives," 506–
    9.

151 McDougall, "Longwall Mining," 428–30.

152 McCall, "Modern Trends," 393–4.

153 McCall, "Some Coal Mining Practices," 479.

154 "The Staff," "Mechanization in the Collieries," 466.

155 "The mines at the [Pacific] coast are not so favourably circumstanced
    as those in the east for the extensive use of coal-cutting machinery
    owing to the irregularity of the pavement and the 'faulty' character of
    the seams, and the tonnage produced in this manner is not large."
    CMR, October 1900, 214. See also Babaian, *Coal Mining Industry*, 39, 42.
    On links between the availability of Asian labourers and the failure to
    mechanize the Vancouver Island mines, see Gallacher, "Men, Money,
    Machines," 224.

156 Dick, *Conservation of Coal*, 172–93.

157 Dominion Bureau of Statistics, *Coal Statistics for Canada, 1927*, 13.

158 Ibid., 45, 81, 89. The mechanization of Nova Scotia's collieries was
    concentrated in Cape Breton. Springhill, for instance, was slow to
    adopt machines. McKay, "Realm of Uncertainty," 17.

159 Dominion Bureau of Statistics, *Coal Statistics for Canada, 1927*, 45, 81, 89.

160 Frank, "Contested Terrain," 105.

161 Canada [Carroll], *Royal Commission on Coal*, 583, 591–4, emphasized
    the extent to which the process of mechanizing Canadian mines was
    incomplete.

162 "Horses in the Coal Mines," 42.

163 Daniel McIntosh, a thirteen-year-old roller-oiler at Sydney Mines, was killed in 1898 when he fell under a trip while trying to get on for a ride. NSMR, 1898, 29. See also PANS, RG 21, vol. 38, no. 14, Richard Brown Diaries, entry for 16 February, 1901; CMR, August, 1891, 201–3. The last prewar agreement between the Western Fuel Company and its employees at Nanaimo specified a number of boys' jobs: door-boys (trappers), drivers, boys on endless ropes, rope riders, winchers. See Canada, Royal Commission on Coal Mining Disputes on Vancouver Island, *Report*, 31–2. As late as 1924, boys' pay scales were even negotiated in Alberta. See Alberta Coal Commission, *Report*, 214.

164 Chrismas, *Coal Dust Grins*, 39.

165 *Labour Gazette*, 1904, 617.

166 NA, RG 27, vol. 142, file 611.04:6, "Proceedings of the Royal Commission appointed to inquire into Coal Mining Conditions in the Maritime Provinces at Meetings held in Fredericton, N.B., on August 17th and 18th, 1920," 68.

167 Managers' dwindling respect for the craft of mining was evident in their use of miners as needed for other kinds of mine work. Miners objected to this practice ("to take men from the face, and put them on shift work") vehemently before the Quirk Commission in 1920. See NA, RG 27, vol. 142, file 611.04:6, "Proceedings of the Royal Commission appointed to inquire into Coal Mining Conditions in the Maritime Provinces at Meetings held in Fredericton, N.B., on August 17th and 18th, 1920," 41.

168 At Springhill, for instance, shot-firers began to be employed from 1884. NSMR, 1890, i–xxiii. Provincial legislation required the certification of all shot-firers by the end of the decade. Logan, *Trade Unions*, 173. By early in the twentieth century, shot-firers were seen as minor officials. See Labour Canada Library, Annual Meeting of the PWA Grand Council, *Minutes*, 1907, 613.

169 Shortly after the First World War, all Dominion Coal mines began to blast exclusively on the night shift as a safety measure. The hole was bored during the day. CMJ, 5 March 1920, 170.

170 *Labour Gazette*, February 1920, 128.

171 On the declining percentage of colliers in the Nova Scotia mining workforce relative to other groups of mine workers, see McKay, "Realm of Uncertainty," 17–18; and CMJ, 8 October 1920, 828.

172 McCall, "Modern Trends," 389.

173 Boys at Springhill complained to the Duncan Royal Commission about the high levels of dust associated with longwall work. See Labour Canada Library, Royal Commission Respecting the Coal Mines of the Province of Nova Scotia, *Minutes of Evidence*, 1925, 3608, 3612.

174 LC, *Evidence*, 452.

175 Testifying before federal officials in 1920, miners gave high priority to a demand for "continuous service of [a] riding rake" in the pits from noon. See NA, RG 27, vol. 141, file 611.04:6, "Minutes of a Board of Investigation with representatives of Miners and Dominion Coal Company, Glace Bay, Nova Scotia: Proceedings of Conference at Glace Bay, 20 and 21 July 1920," 22.

176 Hardie, "Machine Mining at Lethbridge," 248.

177 Bercuson, *Alberta's Coal Industry*, 86.

178 See MacLeod, "Miners, Mining Men and Mining Reform," 536–7. Much research on the impact of longwall on the workforce was undertaken by the Tavistock Institute in postwar Britain. See, for instance, Trist and Bamforth, "Social and Psychological Consequences," 3–38; and Trist, Higgin, Murray, and Pollock, *Organizational Choice*.

179 MacLeod, "Miners, Mining Men and Mining Reform," 543.

180 Not until the 1930s did Nova Scotian miners first wage a major strike against technical innovation, at Glace Bay in 1938, although informal sabotage of mechanical cutters had been reported earlier. See Abbott, "Coal Miners and the Law," 39–40; Earle, "Coalminers and Their 'Red' Union," 135; and MacDonald, "Farewell to Coal," 22. In contrast, worker resistance in the United Kingdom is often cited as contributing to delays in introducing mechanical cutters there. See Taylor, "Labour Productivity," 59–60. Australian resistance to mechanical cutters is discussed in Turner, "Mechanisation of Coal Cutting," 61–7.

181 H.S. Poole, "Mechanical Appliances Past and Present," cited in Macdonald, *Coal and Iron Industries*, 158.

182 LC, *Evidence*, *passim*.

183 Nova Scotia, Commission on Miners' Old Age Pensions, *Report*, 8.

184 By the late nineteenth century, miners' unwillingness to see their sons follow them into the mines distinguished them from other craftsmen. See McKay, "Realm of Uncertainty," 25–6. Hobsbawm, *Age of Empire*, 136, underscored the desire of European miners to see their sons schooled and out of the pits.

Chapter Five

1 Observing the failure to enforce Ontario's compulsory schooling legislation, federal commissioners remarked in 1882: "If education is not enforced the question arises whether the children are not better cared for by spending a portion of their time at work, rather than wasting it on the public streets." See "Report of the Commissioners appointed to

enquire into the working of Mills and Factories of the Dominion, and the labor employed therein," *Sessional Papers*, 1882, vol. 15, 9, no. 42, 3.

2   See Houston and Prentice, *Schooling and Scholars*, 215–23; Davey, "Rhythm of Work," 221–53; Gaffield and Levine, "Dependency and Adolescence," 35–48; and Heron, "High School and the Household Economy," 217–60.

3   Harrigan, "Schooling of Boys and Girls," 805–8. The *Labour Gazette*, March 1919, 317–18, reported that juveniles were out of school prematurely during the war on account of the attractive job market. See also *Labour Gazette*, January 1942, "Employment of Children and School Attendance in Canada," 47–57.

4   Bradbury, *Working Families*, 128; Jean, "Le recul du travail des enfants," 28; Sutherland, "We always had things to do," 105–41.

5   Bullen, "Children of the Industrial Age," 391.

6   Hurl, "Overcoming the Inevitable," 87–121.

7   Tyro, "A Visit to the Albion Mines," 178.

8   Spedon, *Rambles among the Bluenoses*, 192.

9   Gilbert, *Montreal to the Maritime Provinces*, 31.

10   As reported in *TJ*, 15 September 1880.

11   Halifax *Morning Chronicle*, 4 December 1890.

12   Morrow, *Springhill Disaster*, 293–4.

13   *Maritime Mining Review*, 14 August 1907, in NA, Records of the Department of Labour (hereafter RG 27), vol. 3130, file 78.

14   In addition to Morrow, *Springhill Disaster*, see McKnight, "Great Colliery Explosion."

15   Nova Scotia, *Debates*, 1872, 258.

16   Kealey, ed., *Canada Investigates Industrialism*, 22.

17   "Judgments of Full Court in Re: Coal Mines Regulation Amendment Act, 1890," British Columbia, *Sessional Papers*, 1897, 441.

18   Bercuson, *Alberta Coal Industry*, 37.

19   Historians have developed the argument recently that protective legislation reaffirmed both women's secondary status in the labour market and male privilege in the home. Stewart, *Women, Work, and the French State*, vii.

20   "Judgments of Full Court in Re: Coal Mines Regulation Amendment Act, 1890," British Columbia, *Sessional Papers*, 1897, 441.

21   John, *Sweat of Their Brow*.

22   Hazlitt, *British Columbia and Vancouver Island*, 166. Native women were also paid to carry brick and clay to the mines. See Belshaw, "British Coal Miners," 175.

23   See Cameron, *Pictonian Colliers*, 112; and *TJ*, 18 March 1885.

24   Various interpretations of female exclusion from British mines are offered in Humphries, "Protective Legislation"; John, *Sweat of Their*

Brow; Colls, *Pitmen of the Northern Coalfields*, 133–4; Mark-Lawson and Witz, "From 'family labour' to 'family wage'?," 151–74.

25 Quoted in Heesom, "The Coal Mines Act of 1842," 72.

26 John, *Sweat of Their Brow*, 55–7; Colls, *Pitmen of the Northern Coalfields*, 133–4.

27 John, *Sweat of Their Brow*, 21, 24.

28 Mark-Lawson and Witz, "From 'family labour' to 'family wage'?," 162–3.

29 John, *Sweat of Their Brow*, 30.

30 Mark-Lawson and Witz, "From 'family labour' to 'family wage'?" By this process, female labour was confined increasingly to coalfields where antiquated techniques of mining were used. Women were often replaced by boys, for instance, when horses and wheeled tubs were introduced underground in the late eighteenth century. John, *Sweat of Their Brow*, 23.

31 Campbell, *Lanarkshire Miners*, 161–2; John, *Sweat of Their Brow*, 57; Challinor and Ripley, *Miners' Association*; Hartmann, "Capitalism, Patriarchy and Job Segregation."

32 Megaw, "Women Coal-bearers," 87–9.

33 Women were excluded from mine work until well into the twentieth century. During the Second World War, specified surface jobs, including work at picking belts, were made available to them. See Frank, "The Miner's Financier," 139. Owing to the "strenuous opposition" of the UMWA and the "negative" response of mine owners in Alberta and British Columbia, mine jobs were not opened to women in these provinces during the war. See Pierson, *Canadian Women and the Second World War*, 11.

34 Victoria *Daily British Colonist*, 29 March 1877.

35 Links between female wage labour and male idleness were drawn, for instance, by British subcommissioners at the time of the (1840–42) Children's Employment Commission. See John, *Sweat of Their Brow*, 37. During the First World War, high enlistment rates by miners led to severe shortages of skilled workers, "but it has not yet been suggested that women should go underground to work in the mines." See CMJ, 1 April 1916, 156. On the members of the British Columbia legislature in 1877, see Elections British Columbia, *Electoral History of British Columbia*, 22–6.

36 Other legislation to restrict children's employment, including Children's Protection Acts, a range of municipal by-laws, Shops Acts, and Factory Acts, had little or no impact on boys raised in colliery towns and villages.

37 "Public Schools Report, 1875–76," British Columbia, *Sessional Papers*, 1877, 94.

38 See "Annual Report for the Public Schools of Nova Scotia, 1907–08," Nova Scotia, *Journals and Proceedings*, 1908, 81.

39 Hurt, *Elementary Schooling and the Working Classes*, 46.

40 Victoria *Daily British Colonist*, 8 February 1877.

41 LC, *Evidence*, 351.

42 Labour Canada Library, Annual Meeting of the PWA Grand Council, *Minutes*, 1890, 221.

43 Halifax *Herald*, 22 February 1902, cited in McLaren, "Proper Education for All Classes," 141.

44 Labour Canada Library, Annual Meeting of the PWA Grand Council, *Minutes*, 1906, 221.

45 RCTE, 1708.

46 Ibid.

47 NA, RG 27, vol. 141, file 611.04:6, "Proceedings of the Glace Bay Conference, 20–21 July 1920," Baxter to Quirk, 9.

48 While he acknowledged that some protection in law was desirable for both parents and children, it was Drummond's fear that the question of child labour would divert the Labour Commission from the problems faced by adult workers. Drummond recognized that child labour ranked high on the commissioners' agenda. *TJ*, 14 March 1888.

49 Characteristically, for instance, the *Trades Journal* (4 November 1885) chastised parents for their meagre attendance at school examinations.

50 McCreath, "Charles Tupper and the Politics of Education," 203–24; Hamilton, "Society and Schools in Nova Scotia," 86–105; "An Act to Secure Better Attendance at Public Schools," 46 Vict., c. 17, *Statutes of Nova Scotia*, 1883; "An Act to amend and consolidate the Acts relating to Public Instruction," 58 Vict., c. 1, s. 84, *Statutes of Nova Scotia*, 1895; "An Act respecting compulsory attendance at schools in cities and towns," 5 Geo. V, c. 4, *Statutes of Nova Scotia*, 1915.

51 "An Act to amend 'The Education Act,'" 11–12 Geo. V. c. 59, s. 7, *Statutes of Nova Scotia*, 1921; "An Act to amend Chapter 9, *Acts of 1918*, 'The Education Act,'" 13 Geo. V, c. 52, s. 11, *Statutes of Nova Scotia*, 1923. A synopsis of much of this legislation is found in Department of Labour, *Employment of Children*, 98.

52 "Third Annual Report on the Public Schools," British Columbia, *Sessional Papers*, 1875, 22.

53 Department of Labour, *Employment of Children*, 98.

54 Race, "Compulsory Schooling in Alberta," 71.

55 Department of Labour, *Employment of Children*, 99.

56 "An Act respecting Truancy and Compulsory School Attendance," c. 8, *Statutes of the Province of Alberta*, 1910; Department of Labour, *Employment of Children*, 99.

57 Department of Labour, *Employment of Children*, 99.

58 Ibid., 98.

59 See Keeling, *Child Labour in the United Kingdom*, xiv.

60 MacLeod, "Colliers, Colliery Safety, and Workplace Control," 233.

61 "Of the regulation of mines," c. 10, part 1, s. 4, *The Revised Statutes of Nova Scotia*, Fourth Series, 1873.

62 LC, *Evidence*, 351; Labour Canada Library, Annual Meeting of the PWA Grand Council, *Minutes*, October 1890, 221. The 1891 revisions also stipulated that no boy under eighteen years of age would have charge of a hoist, and that no boy under sixteen years of age would normally be employed more than ten hours daily or fifty-four hours weekly. Boys already in the pits were grandfathered. "An Act to amend Chapter 8, *Revised Statutes*, 'Of the regulation of coal mines,'" 54 Vict., c. 9, secs. 3 and 4, *Statutes of Nova Scotia*, 1891.

63 "An Act to consolidate and amend Chapter 19, *Revised Statutes, 1900, 'The Coal Mines Regulation Act,'* and amendments thereto," 8 Ed. VII, c. 8, s. 19 (1), *Statutes of Nova Scotia*, 1908.

64 *Labour Gazette*, 1923, 353. The minimum age for underground employment was raised to seventeen in 1947 ("An Act to Amend Chapter 1 of the Acts of 1927, 'The Coal Mines Regulation Act'," 11 Geo. VI, c. 39, s. 7, *Statutes of Nova Scotia, 1947*) and to eighteen in 1954 ("An Act to Amend Chapter 4 of the Acts of 1951, 'The Coal Mines Regulation Act,'" 3 Eliz. II, c. 56, s. 14, *Statutes of Nova Scotia*, 1954).

65 Nova Scotia, *Debates*, 1872, 258.

66 CMR, May 1891, 115. In fact, the legislation read that no boy under sixteen years of age was to be employed at a mine "unless he be able to read, write, and to count as far as division, and furnish a certificate to that effect from a duly licensed teacher." 54 Vict., c. 9, s. 3, *Statutes of Nova Scotia*, 1891.

67 CMR, November 1890, 162.

68 NA, RG 27, vol. 142, file 611.04:6, "Proceedings of the Royal Commission appointed to inquire into Coal Mining Conditions in the Maritime Provinces at Meetings held in Fredericton, N.B., on August 17th and 18th, 1920," 48.

69 Victoria *Daily British Colonist*, 8, 11 February, 1877.

70 "An Act to Make Regulations with respect to Coal Mines," 40 Vict., no. 15, s. 2, *Statutes of British Columbia*, 1877. The act also excluded women and girls from employment underground, required a minimum age of eighteen for those in charge of hoists used to raise people, and called for a special register of boys, with provisions for fines for offences. In 1911 the minimum age for employment was raised to fifteen (underground) and fourteen (on the surface). "An Act to consolidate and amend the 'Coal-Mines Regulation Act' and Amending Acts," 1 Geo. V, c. 33, s. 3, *Statutes of British Columbia*, 1911.

71 "Judgments of Full Court in Re: Coal Mines Regulation Amendment Act, 1890," British Columbia, *Sessional Papers*, 1897, 441.

72 See "Petition Against Coal-Mining Bill" signed by Vancouver Island coal operators, British Columbia, *Sessional Papers*, 1877, 504; Victoria *Daily British Colonist*, 1 April 1877.

73 BCMR, 1880, 257.

74 See Victoria *Daily British Colonist*, 22, 27 February 1883; "An Act to Amend the Coal Mines Regulation Act, 1877," 46 Vict., c. 2, *Statutes of British Columbia*, 1883.

75 "An Ordinance to amend Chapter 16 of the *Consolidated Ordinances, 1898*, entitled 'An Ordinance to make Regulations with respect to Coal Mines,'" c. 4, s. 1, *Ordinances of the North-West Territories*, 1899.

76 The law, like Nova Scotia's, required the boy to provide a certificate attesting that he had reached the required educational level. The Alberta act exempted mine operators from liability if they employed an underage boy in good faith. In these instances, the parent or guardian was liable for penalty under the act. "An Act to make regulations with respect to coal mines," c. 25, secs. 6, 8, 63, *Statutes of Alberta*, 1906.

77 See PAA, Royal Commission on the Coal Mining Industry, *Report and Evidence*, 277, 129, 383, 398.

78 "An Act respecting Mines," c. 4, s. 6, *Statutes of Alberta*, 1913. By 1930, amendments had been passed whereby boys had to have reached a minimum age of sixteen for mines employment. Department of Labour, *Employment of Children*, Table C.

79 Ibid.

80 "An Act to Amend Chapter 35 of *The Revised Statutes*, 1927, Respecting Mines and Minerals," 23 Geo. V, c. 23, *Acts of the Legislative Assembly of New Brunswick*, 1933. Section 127 stipulated that no woman or girl was to be employed in a mine; section 128, that no boy under sixteen was to be employed underground.

81 NA, RG 27, vol. 3130, file 83, "Correspondence received by Deputy Minister of Labour, William Lyon Mackenzie King, concerning wage earning children, 1902."

82 "We were unable to find any place in which this Act is enforced," royal commissioners observed of the Ontario compulsory education law in 1882. See "Report of the Commissioners appointed to enquire into the working of Mills and Factories of the Dominion, and the labor employed therein," 45 Victoria, *Sessional Papers*, 1882, vol. 15, 9, no. 42, 3.

83 Marshall, *Aux origines sociales de l'État providence*, has written a fine study of the genealogy of mid-twentieth-century legislation focused on children, its impact, and the interaction between its administrators and its "objects."

84 "Report of 1890–91 Provincial Select Committee enquiring into the Wellington Colliery Strike," British Columbia, *Journals* (Victoria, 1891), cccxx; "The Coal Mines Regulation Act," 40 Vict., no. 15, s. 2, *Statutes of British Columbia*, 1877.

85 See BCMR, 1877–1914; and Table 3.1, Chapter 3.

86 Drummond argued at the same time that "[i]t would be a great benefit to the miners if the age limit could be increased. If a boy over 12 even could not go as a driver it would be better for all concerned. It would be better even if men could do boys' work as drivers." Robert Drummond, "The Employment of Boys in Mines," Halifax *Herald*, 22 February 1902, 5, cited in McLaren, "Proper Education for All Classes," 141.

87 *TJ*, 6 December 1882.

88 Bercuson, "Tragedy at Bellevue," 227; *CMJ*, February 1912, 127.

89 LC, *Evidence*, 302.

90 *RCTE*, 1708–10.

91 LC, *Evidence*, 462, 466.

92 "Annual Report on Schools," British Columbia, *Sessional Papers*, 1891, 149, 151.

93 "Seventh Annual Report on the Public Schools (1877–78)," British Columbia, *Sessional Papers*, 1879, 190.

94 "Annual Reports for the Public Schools of Nova Scotia," Nova Scotia, *Journals and Proceedings, passim*.

95 LC, *Evidence*, 294.

96 Robbins, *Dependency of Youth*.

97 *RCTE*, 1712.

98 Sexton, "Industrial Education for Miners," 595.

99 *RCTE*, 1678.

100 *CMJ*, 21 July 1922, 473.

Chapter Six

1 The "family" is defined here as a couple and their co-resident children.

2 Seccombe, "Patriarchy stabilized," 53–76, outlines the emergence of the sexual division of labour. On the question of gender in the coalfields, see Penfold, "Have You No Manhood," 21–44; and Hinde, "Stout Ladies and Amazons," 33–57.

3 Bradbury, *Working Families*, 16.

4 Copp, *Anatomy of Poverty*, 30–42; Piva, *Condition of the Working Class*, 27–60; Bradbury, *Working Families*, chap. 3. By 1928, one historian has argued, "it was possible, for the first time, for the average male manufacturing worker to raise a family on his wages alone." See Palmer, *Working-Class Experience*, 232.

5 Gaffield, "Labouring and Learning," 19.
6 On non-wage survival strategies, see Fingard, "Winter's Tale," 65–94; Bradbury, "Pigs, Cows, Boarders," 9–46; "Fragmented Family," 109–28; Darroch and Ornstein, "Family Coresidence in Canada," 30–55; and Bullen, "Hidden Workers," 163–87.
7 Many of the central themes of this literature are discussed in Bradbury, "Women's History and Working-Class History," 23–44. See also the articles in the "Special Issue on Women and Work," *Labour/Le Travail* 24 (Fall 1989).
8 In the first category, see Bradbury, "Women and Wage Labour," 115–31; Synge, "Transition from School to Work," 249–69; Coulter, "Working Young of Edmonton," 143–59; Jean, "Le recul du travail des enfants," 91–129. In the second category, see Bradbury, "Family Economy and Work in an Industrializing City," 85; Early, "French-Canadian Family Economy," 180–99; and Hurl, "Restricting Child Factory Labour," 118.
9 Even in contemporary Montreal, where a range of opportunities existed for girls to work outside the home, the preferred practice was to send boys out to find waged work and to keep girls at home. See Bradbury, "Gender at Work at Home," 119–40.
10 LC, *Evidence*, 294.
11 NA, Records of the Department of Labour (hereafter RG 27), vol. 142, file 611.04:6, "Proceedings of the Royal Commission appointed to inquire into Coal Mining Conditions in the Maritime Provinces at Meetings held in Fredericton, N.B., on August 17th and 18th, 1920," 87.
12 See RG 27, vol. 141, file 611.04:6, "Minutes of a Board of Investigation with representatives of Miners and Dominion Coal Company, Glace Bay, Nova Scotia: Proceedings of Conference at Glace Bay, 20 and 21 July 1920," 7.
13 Trade unionist J.B. McLachlan protested strongly against that claim. NA, RG 27, vol. 142, file 611.04:6, "Proceedings of the Royal Commission appointed to inquire into Coal Mining Conditions in the Maritime Provinces at Meetings held in Fredericton, N.B., on August 17th and 18th, 1920," 53.
14 Ibid., 114–15. Evans allowed one exception: the sons of a widow. "She is getting a little support from the Parish, and the boys are doing whatever they can and wherever they can." Ibid., 115–16.
15 Recent research on child labour in late-nineteenth-century American industry has argued that working-class parents acted in their own, and not in their children's, interest. See Parsons and Goldin, "Parental Altruism and Self-Interest," 637–57.
16 This discussion will overstate the typical level of adult male earnings in coal communities, because it assumes the adult male breadwinner

to have been a (relatively well paid) miner, rather than a mine
labourer.

17 The comparison is drawn from evidence presented before the federal
labour commission. Miners' annual earnings compared poorly with
those of Toronto carpenters, London iron foundry men, Montreal
moulders, or Saint John brass founders. See Kealey, ed., *Canada Investigates Industrialism*, 77, 126, 248, 317.

18 By one estimate, the Nova Scotia miner's average daily pay was $1.25
in 1875 and $1.75 in 1895 (see "Importance of the Canadian Coal
Industry"). The *Nova Scotian and Weekly Chronicle* (11 December 1903)
estimated that Springhill miners (perhaps the best paid in the province) earned on average $1.95 daily between 1883 and 1900, at mines
that were worked more regularly than other provincial mines.

19 In Ontario, in contrast, only the rare occupation did not offer at least
250 days of work annually in 1889. See Gagan and Gagan, "Working-
Class Standards of Living," 174.

20 NSMR, 1880, K. Desegregated to specific mines, this figure was even
more striking as a reflection of the continued seasonality of mining.
The Gowrie mine, for instance, operated on average between 90 and
120 days annually through the 1880s. See NSMR, 1880–90.

21 In Nova Scotia in 1880, miners' daily average earnings were $1.45;
mine labourers', $.95; and boys, $.65. From their earnings miners
faced deductions that just for rent, doctor, coal, and school amounted
to $2.80 monthly. Macdonald, *Coal and Iron Industries*, 45. A correspondent from Cow Bay (Cape Breton) indicated that family income
was generally not above $300 annually. *TJ*, 18 January 1888. On
Ontario wage earnings, see Gagan and Gagan, "Working-Class Standards of Living," 176.

22 At the Reserve Mines in Cape Breton, for instance, if a tub contained
too much slack, the miner was fined one-fifth of the tub's value.
"Fines [were] pretty frequent." Macdonald, *Coal and Iron Industries*,
57.

23 Western Canadian nominal wage rates were considerably higher than
in Nova Scotia. At Nanaimo, for instance, mine workers earned from
$1.75 to $5.00 daily over the period 1875 to 1900 (this figure takes
into account the small number of skilled workers employed at mines,
such as carpenters and blacksmiths). Miners earned from $2.50 to
$5.00 daily. See BCMR, 1875–1900.

24 Accidents were recorded in provincial mines reports in British
Columbia, Alberta, Saskatchewan, and Nova Scotia.

25 New Glasgow *Eastern Chronicle*, 27 March 1873. In Sydney Mines, in
1908, the disabled were generally supported "by their families." See
Nova Scotia, Commission on Miners' Old Age Pensions, *Report*, 64.

26 Bowen, "Friendly Societies," 67.

27 NSMR, 1873, 37. The *Trades Journal* refers to a benefit fund at Bridge-port (14 November 1883) and to the publication of the third annual report of the Albion Mines Relief Fund (23 January 1884).

28 Angus L. Macdonald Library, St Francis Xavier University, Minutes of Pioneer Lodge No. 1, PWA, 28 March, 18 April 1883; (Stellarton) *Journal*, 1 February 1891.

29 Macdonald, *Coal and Iron Industries*, 47, 145.

30 Robert Drummond remarked that frequently a large sum of money was collected, and complained that it was occasionally misspent. He recommended that a Board of Charity be established to oversee these funds, pending the establishment of a compulsory insurance program. See *TJ*, 3 June 1885. On the persistence of informal pit collections into the twentieth century, see Nova Scotia, Commission on Miners' Old Age Pensions, *Report*, 61, 118.

31 Seager, "Miners' Struggles," 167.

32 Nova Scotia, Commission on Miners' Old Age Pensions, *Report*, 132.

33 Sydney *Post*, 30 April 1925, quoted in Frank, "Cape Breton Coal Miners," 79.

34 Mathers, *Evidence*, 3703.

35 "An Act to Incorporate the Sydney Mines Industrial and Provident Society," 31 Vict., c. 44, *Statutes of Nova Scotia*, 1868. A similar society was incorporated at Cow Bay in 1869. "An Act to Incorporate the Cow Bay Industrial and Provident Society," 32 Vict., c. 66, *Statutes of Nova Scotia*, 1869.

36 Mathers, *Evidence*, 3693. See also the testimony of Mrs Bailey, a miner's widow on Vancouver Island, in "Minutes of Evidence of the Royal Commission on Industrial Disputes in the Province of British Columbia," Canada, *Sessional Papers*, 1904, vol. 38, no. 13, 36a, 67.

37 Mathers, *Evidence*, 3684.

38 Ibid., 3686.

39 Nova Scotia, Commission on Miners' Old Age Pensions, *Report*, 64.

40 NSMR, 1890, 23.

41 *CMR*, June 1905, 149.

42 Halifax *Herald*, 24 November 1906.

43 Mortimer-Lamb, "Coal Industry of Vancouver Island," 19. It was a further complaint against the Chinese on Vancouver Island that they took surface jobs from old men. See "Report of the Royal Commission on Chinese and Japanese Immigration," *Sessional Papers*, 1902, vol. 36, no. 13, 54, "Chapter IX – Coal Mining Industry," 84.

44 Mathers, *Evidence*, 3707.

45 See Muise, "Industrial Context of Inequality," 3–31.

46 Seager and Perry, "Mining the Connections," 73.

47 Migration out of the region has been a feature of Maritime life since the mid-nineteenth century. See Thornton, "Problem of Out-Migration," 3–34.

48 *TJ*, 14, 21 October 1885, cited in Hornsby, *Nineteenth-Century Cape Breton*, 189.

49 Cameron, *Pictonian Colliers*, 109.

50 See NA, RG 27, vol. 141, file 611.04:6, "Minutes of a Board of Investigation with representatives of Miners and Dominion Coal Company, Glace Bay, Nova Scotia: Proceedings of Conference at Glace Bay, 20 and 21 July 1920," 38.

51 Cameron, *Pictonian Colliers*, 111.

52 This account of women's domestic labour draws on McKay, "Realm of Uncertainty," 24 (from which the quotation is drawn); Frank, "The Miner's Financier"; Schwieder, Hraba, and Schwieder, *Buxton*, 114; Jones, "Serfdom and Slavery," 92–5; and Corbin, *Life, Work, and Rebellion*, 92.

53 Haines, "Fertility, Nuptiality, and Occupation," 245–80; Haines, "Fertility, Marriage, and Occupation," 28–55.

54 The miner was considerably older, at 27.5 years of age. Belshaw, "Cradle to Grave," 57; Ward, *Courtship, Love, and Marriage*, 53.

55 Macnab, *British Columbia for Settlers*, 200.

56 Belshaw, "British Immigrants in British Columbia," 27.

57 Nova Scotia, Royal Commission into Hours of Work, *Report*, 114.

58 NA, RG 27, vol. 141, file 611.04:6, Quirk Commission, *Report*, 1920, 4.

59 Mathers, *Evidence*, 3897.

60 Seager, "Minto, New Brunswick," 97.

61 Forsey, *Economic and Social Aspects*, 92.

62 LC, *Evidence*, 288, 273.

63 Quoted in Penfold, "Have You No Manhood," 30. In another view of women's role as purchasers, W. Henderson, a mine operator at Drumheller, remarked in 1919 that "[t]he women of Calgary and other cities have had to pay pretty high this last winter for their coal – pretty high." See Mathers, *Evidence*, 698.

64 Wylie, *Coal Culture*, 133. The rapid growth of the industrial Cape Breton mines after the formation of Dominion Coal in 1893 swelled in-migration (and the incidence of boarding). In the absence of boarding houses, young migrants lived with families. See Muise, "Making of an Industrial Community," 83.

65 Seager and Perry, "Mining the Connections," 75.

66 See Bullen, "Hidden Workers," 166.

67 *TJ*, 6 March 1889.

68 Glace Bay *Standard*, 5 June 1911.

69 See Bradbury, "Pigs, Cows, Boarders," 9–46. Nanaimo homes were surrounded by cows, horses, and piggeries in 1859. See Victoria *Daily British Colonist*, 8 June 1859, cited in Belshaw, "British Coal Miners," 234. On hunting and fishing on Vancouver Island, see Belshaw, "Standard of Living," 58; and Seager, "Miners' Struggles," 168. On Nova Scotian miners gardening and hunting, see *TJ*, 9 November 1882.

70 Boarders were relatively rare in Sydney Mines until the turn of the twentieth century. The manuscript census records 13 in 1871, 29 in 1881, 10 in 1891, but 130 in 1901, a jump that reflects the rapid growth of the community (boarders have been defined as non-related household co-residents). See Sydney Mines, Mss Census, 1871–1901.

71 Gilbert, *Montreal to the Maritime Provinces*, 34–5.

72 See NSMR, 1876, 29; 1878, 17.

73 Macdonald, *Coal and Iron Industries*, 215.

74 Belshaw, "Standard of Living," 52–3; Seager, "Miners' Struggles," 168; Macnab, *British Columbia for Settlers*, 203.

75 Corbin, *Life, Work, and Rebellion*, 123. See Labour Canada Library, Royal Commission Respecting the Coal Mines of the Province of Nova Scotia, *Minutes of Evidence*, 1925, 2743. This allegation made its way into the final report of the commission. "We were struck with the general absence of any attempt on the part of the tenants to make any use of the land that is at their disposal." See Nova Scotia, Royal Commission Respecting the Coal Mines, *Report*, 42.

76 Seager, "Miners' Struggles," 168.

77 Zelizer, *Pricing the Priceless Child*, 60.

78 Baskerville and Sager, *Unwilling Idlers*, 121–5.

79 See also Bradbury, *Working Families*, 131–3.

80 *North Sydney Herald*, 11 February 1891, quoted in Hornsby, *Nineteenth-Century Cape Breton*, 180.

81 LC, *Evidence*, 365, 359.

82 If a father brought his son into a Pennsylvania mine as a helper, he was provided with 50 percent more coal cars. See Corbin, *Life, Work, and Rebellion*, 16. See also Schwieder, Hraba, and Schwieder, *Buxton*, 65, on the "increased turn." Chinese haulage workers in Vancouver Island mines were alleged in 1879 to have favoured Caucasian miners who employed a Chinese helper by bringing them more boxes. See Bowen, *Three Dollar Dreams*, 177. See also McKay, "Industry, Work and Community," 725, on the "square turn."

83 *TJ*, 14 March 1888.

84 McKay, "Realm of Uncertainty," 26.

85 McTagarth lived in Springhill; Terrance in Pictou County. LC, *Evidence*, 301–2. See also Bowen, *Boss Whistle*, 58. In the nineteenth

century, British boys generally received simply some pocket money if they were employed by an older relative. See Benson, *British Coalminers*, 68.

86 On boys boarding, see Nova Scotia, Commission on Miners' Old Age Pensions, *Report*, 123–4. See also Table 6.2 on boys' wages.

87 BCMR, 1880, 257.

88 Nanaimo *Free Press*, 4, 8, 9 October 1900, 1 February 1901.

89 Belshaw, "Standard of Living," 57.

90 For a recent defence of the manuscript census as a historical record, see Baskerville and Sager, *Unwilling Idlers*, especially Appendix A.

91 Population figures are for the Sydney Mines census subdivision and are drawn from the manuscript census. See Sydney Mines, Mss Census, 1871–1901. Employment figures are drawn from NSMR, 1871, 36; 1901, xiv.

92 A computer-readable database has been assembled which incorporates information recorded on Schedule One of the Canadian manuscript census. All individuals resident in the Sydney Mines census subdivision have been included in this database for the years 1871, 1891, and 1901. The census has its drawbacks: most notably, it reveals only what people chose to declare in response to questions that census officials chose to ask. It is also unhelpful with respect to casual or subcontracted (often women's) labour. Angela John, for instance, has pointed to the non-inclusion of women in the earliest British censuses if they were working in the pit for their miner-husband (John, *Sweat of Their Brow*, 24). On neither of these counts, however, should major problems emerge regarding the reporting of boys' labour. Enumerators were local residents, acquainted with the community. Boys' wage labour was common enough in Sydney Mines not to be considered blameworthy at this time. In determining whether boys were to be recorded as employed, the enumerators' instructions were clear: regular labour for wages (the conditions under which most pit boys laboured) was to be reported; they made provision also for those circumstances where a miner might bring his son into the mine as his helper – "when sons follow the professions or occupations of their fathers, and are associated with them, the same description is to be inserted [for the boy as for the father]." See "Manual Containing 'The Census Act,'" 1871, 134.

93 See Hurt, *Elementary Schooling*, 34–5; and Gillis, *Youth and History*, 61.

94 Chrismas, *Coal Dust Grins*, 18.

95 See NSMR, 1891, xxiii–xxvi; Morrow, *Springhill Explosion*, 84.

96 See the comments of Ontario factory inspectors in Chapter 2.

97 LC, *Evidence*, 380.

98 Ibid., 460.

99 Ibid., 304.

100 Ibid., 301.

101 McKay, "Realm of Uncertainty," 26. A fictitious pit boy in a short story by C.W. Lunn claimed: "I hated school and was more anxious to work in the mine than I was to learn me lessons ... I choose the goin' to work [over further school attendance], 'cause 'twas just what I wanted." See Lunn, "From Trapper Boy to General Manager," 225.

102 MacDonald, "Farewell to Coal," 21.

103 Quoted in Bowen, *Boss Whistle*, 58.

104 Quoted in Chrismas, *Coal Dust Grins*, 248.

105 Sexton, "Industrial Education for Miners," 594. George Orwell, describing English mining towns in the 1930s, claimed that "there is not one working-class boy in a thousand who does not pine for the day when he will leave school." See *The Road to Wigan Pier*, 148. See also Lawson, *A Man's Life*, 69.

106 See Oren, "Welfare of women in labouring families," 226–44; and Humphries, "Protective Legislation," 20.

107 K. Durland, *Among the Fife Miners*, paraphrased in Harrison, "Class and Gender," 124.

108 Lawson, *A Man's Life*, 74.

109 Quoted in McKay, "Realm of Uncertainty," 26.

110 McKay, "Industry, Work and Community," 598.

111 Labour Canada Library, Annual Meeting of the PWA Grand Council, *Minutes*, 1890, 221; McKay, "Realm of Uncertainty," 25; McKnight, "Great Colliery Explosion," 8; Morrow, *Springhill Disaster*, 83.

112 McNeil, *Voice of the Pioneer*, 19.

113 Extant time sheets for January 1858 indicate that the collieries at Sydney Mines employed only twenty trappers; ten years later, manager R.H. Brown noted that ten trappers were used over two shifts (more than ten boys may have been employed, of course, for this work). See Beaton Institute, MG 1, E59 f(48), Workmen's Time Books, Sydney Mines, January 1858; and PANS, RG 21, Series A, vol. 38, no. 11, Richard Brown diaries, entries for 6, 8 June 1878; and LC, *Evidence*, 269–70.

114 *TJ*, 22 June 1887.

115 Amherst *Daily News*, 26 July 1899.

116 Bowsfield, ed., *Fort Victoria Letters*, lxxiii, 111.

117 Johnstone, *Coal Dust in My Blood*, 27.

118 Katz and Davey, "Youth and Early Industrialization," S116. The scope of individual choice was tempered by the powerful working-class commitment to "repaying one's childhood." See Parr, *Labouring Children*, 23.

119 Cited in Labour Canada Library, Drummond, *Reflections and Recollections*, 184–5.
120 See Barnsby, "Standard of Living," 220–39. According to Barnsby's calculations (based on a family of four), a bare level of comfort involved twice the expenditure of subsistence. For other approaches to the standard of living issue, see Gagan and Gagan, "Working-Class Standards of Living," 171–93.
121 Ian McKay has argued that the additional income earned by boys was necessary to "independence and home ownership." See McKay, "Realm of Uncertainty," 25.
122 At the Dominion Coal Company, employer of nearly half of Nova Scotian mine workers, collieries operated on average nearly three hundred days annually by the first decade of the twentieth century. Dominion Coal was based on Cape Breton, where mines had been far more subject to seasonal slowdowns than mainland Nova Scotian mines in the nineteenth century. See NSMR, 1901, xiv; 1906, xiv; 1911, xxi.
123 Macdonald, *Coal and Iron Industries*, 70.
124 It was non-universal, like earlier funds. Orphan children were to receive benefits to fourteen; before reorganization, it had generally been thirteen. CMJ, 15 July 1910, 441; 1 August 1910, 472; 1 September 1910, 534–5; *Labour Gazette*, February, 1911, 880–1.
125 The Nova Scotia Workmen's Compensation Board was established effective 1 January 1917. It provided benefits for injured workers and for survivors. It was established in time to provide benefits to families bereaved by the explosion at New Waterford on 25 July 1917, which killed sixty-five. See Nova Scotia, Workmen's Compensation Board, *Report*, 6. British Columbia passed legislation respecting workmen's compensation in 1902; and a more comprehensive act in 1916. See "An Act respecting compensation to workmen from accidental injuries suffered in the course of their employment," 2 Ed. VII, c. 74, *Statutes of British Columbia*, 1902; "An Act to provide for compensation to workmen for injuries sustained and industrial diseases contracted in the course of their employment," 6 Geo. V, c. 77, *Statutes of British Columbia*, 1916. On the Alberta Workmen's Compensation Board, established in 1918, see Alberta Coal Commission, *Report*, 286–309.
126 Nova Scotia introduced Mother's Allowances in 1930. See Strong-Boag, "Wages for Housework," 25, 29.
127 It aimed in part to address the failure of miners' sons to take up the occupation: "[A]ny legislation which would make the occupation more attractive to our own people would be desirable." See Nova Scotia, Commission on Miners' Old Age Pensions, *Report*, 8. Over a

decade later, when the federal (Mathers) Royal Commission on Industrial Relations toured provincial coalfields, miners made repeated reference to the pensions inquiry, expressing their disappointment that the province had failed to act. Mathers, *Evidence*, 3690–1, 3894. Nova Scotia did not begin to issue cheques under the federal old-age pension program until 1934. See Bryden, *Old Age Pensions*, 86.

128 Its significance should not be overstated: there were only 247 recipients in 1945. There were over 700 others over the age of sixty-five still employed by the company (of whom 115 had applied for the pension, waiting for death to open room on the pension list). See Canada [Carroll], *Royal Commission on Coal*, 300–1.

Chapter Seven

1 Victoria *Daily British Colonist*, 27 January 1861.
2 Scott, *Springhill*; Norcross, *Nanaimo Retrospective*; Den Otter, *Civilizing the West*, 161–96; 238–65.
3 Brown, *Coal Fields*, 53–4.
4 Bercuson, *Alberta's Coal Industry*, 182–204.
5 *Census of Canada*, vol. 1, 1881, 1891, 1901.
6 Den Otter, *Civilizing the West*, 239.
7 Belshaw, "Cradle to Grave," 46; Seager and Perry, "Mining the Connections," 64–5; Norcross, *Nanaimo Retrospective*.
8 Belshaw, "British Collier in British Columbia," 11–36; Cameron, *Pictonian Collier*, 103.
9 Muise, "Making of an Industrial Community," 83.
10 Wylie, *Coal Culture*, 136.
11 Seager and Perry, "Mining the Connections," 68–9.
12 Babaian, *Coal Mining Industry*, 43.
13 Seager, "Socialists and Workers," 56.
14 Belshaw, "Cradle to Grave," 49–50.
15 Bowen, *Three Dollar Dreams*, 144.
16 Seager and Perry, "Mining the Connections," 70.
17 See Bercuson, *Alberta's Coal Industry*.
18 Ibid., 84.
19 Seager and Perry, "Mining the Connections," 71.
20 Belshaw, "British Coal Miners," 274–5, 285.
21 Muise, "Making of an Industrial Community," 77, 82–3.
22 *Census of Canada*, vol. 1, 1901.
23 NA, Records of Statistics Canada, RG 31, Manuscript Census, Sydney Mines, 1871–1901.
24 Muise, "Making of an Industrial Community," 83.

25 McNeil, *Voice of the Pioneer*, 61.

26 See Angus L. Macdonald Library, St Francis Xavier University, United Mine Workers of America, Local 4514, *Minutes*, 8 January 1927.

27 Macdonald, *Coal and Iron Industries*, 57.

28 LC, *Evidence*, 459.

29 Macdonald, *Coal and Iron Industries*, 72.

30 *CMJ*, 11 June 1908, as quoted in Frank, "Company Town, Labour Town," 178.

31 Cameron, *Pictonian Colliers*, 103–4. The Hudson's Bay Company provided a teacher at Nanaimo as early as 1853. Norcross, *Nanaimo Retrospective*, 40–6.

32 *CMR*, June 1902, 166.

33 See Bercuson, *Alberta's Coal Industry.*

34 Forbes, *Vancouver Island*, 57.

35 Belshaw, "Standard of Living," 53.

36 Wylie, *Coal Culture*, 172; Cameron, *Pictonian Colliers*, 24–5; Howe, *Western and Eastern Rambles*, 159.

37 Wylie, *Coal Culture*, 182.

38 McKay, "Wisdom, Wile or War," 18–19.

39 Hornsby, *Nineteenth-Century Cape Breton*, 103–5, 178; LC, *Evidence*, 412.

40 LC, *Evidence*, 412; *CMJ*, 1 July 1914, 442.

41 These events were also commonly followed by legal action against striking miners. McKay, "Crisis of Dependent Development," 37–9.

42 Mouat, "Politics of Coal," 8.

43 Macdonald, *Coal and Iron Industries*, 219.

44 Brown, *Coal Fields*, 53.

45 Belshaw, "Standard of Living," 50–1.

46 See Bercuson, *Alberta's Coal Industry*, 127, 133.

47 Hornsby, *Nineteenth-Century Cape Breton*, 171.

48 *TJ*, 16 March 1881, cited in McKay, "Wisdom, Wile or War," 20.

49 Macdonald, *Coal and Iron Industries*, 219–22.

50 Frank, "Company Town, Labour Town," 181.

51 Cameron, *Pictonian Colliers*, 103.

52 Canada [Carroll], *Royal Commission on Coal*, 599. Similar concern over company towns in Cape Breton had been expressed earlier. See Nova Scotia, Royal Commission Respecting the Coal Mines, *Report*, 10.

53 PANS, RG 21, series A, vol. 38, no. 10, Richard Brown diary, entry for 7 February 1874.

54 PANS, RG 21, series A, vol. 32, Letter Books, Henry Swift to J.R. Cowans, 24 November 1890.

55 In 1903 nearly all Nova Scotia's colliery managers were former workmen. Even at the massive Dominion Coal Company, in 1910 virtually all officials "were ex-miners trained in the mining schools." See

MacLeod, "Colliers, Colliery Safety and Workplace Control," 251.
Mine-owner Robert Dunsmuir first entered the mines as a boy of
sixteen. See Gallacher, "Robert Dunsmuir," 290–4.

56 *TJ*, 20 April 1881.
57 Companies would levy a charge for instance just for the cost of delivering the coal. Macdonald, *Coal and Iron Industries*, 59.
58 Forbes, *Vancouver Island*, 57.
59 Cameron, *Pictonian Colliers*, 104.
60 *TJ*, 9 January 1889.
61 Macdonald, "Industrial Relations Department," 326; Scott, *Springhill*,
51.
62 McKay, "Wisdom, Wile or War," 31.
63 *TJ*, 28 January 1885, 27 March 1889.
64 McKay, "Wisdom, Wile or War," 31.
65 Cameron, *Pictonian Colliers*, 122.
66 Macdonald, *Coal and Iron Industries*, 223–5. Others, such as the
Pioneer Co-operative at Springhill, only lasted a few years. See *TJ*,
21 June 1882, 4 May 1887. On reasons for the failure of cooperative
stores in mining communities, see MacPherson, *Each for All*, 23.
67 MacPherson, "Patterns in the Maritime Cooperative Movement," 68–70.
68 Bowen, *Boss Whistle*, 197–8; Babaian, *Coal Mining Industry*, 77–8.
69 *TJ*, 8 January 1882.
70 McKay, "Wisdom, Wile or War," 43.
71 Ibid., 45.
72 Frank, "Company Town, Labour Town," 181–6.
73 Wylie, *Coal Culture*, 121.
74 Frank and Reilly, "The Emergence of the Socialist Movement," 99.
75 Seager, "Miners' Struggles," 176.
76 Ibid., 176–7.
77 Seager, "Socialists and Workers," 37–42; Schwantes, *Radical Heritage*,
73–4, 100–1.
78 On the development of miners' unions, see Chapter 3.
79 See Chapter 5.
80 Halifax *Herald*, 26 September 1910.
81 Halifax *Herald*, 31 July 1909.
82 Nanaimo *Free Press*, 28 November 1912, cited in Wargo, "The Great
Coal Strike," 94.
83 *CMJ*, 1 November 1913, 690.
84 *Maritime Labour Herald*, 15 April 1922, cited in Penfold, "Have You No
Manhood," 27.
85 Cited in McKay, "Realm of Uncertainty," 52.
86 PANS, RG 21, series A, vol. 38, no. 13, Richard Brown diary, entry for
24 February 1894.

87 *TJ*, 29 May 1889.

88 Chrismas, *Alberta Miners*, 29.

89 As one woman wrote to the PWA's official newspaper in 1882, "I am precluded by sex from joining your society." *TJ*, 11 October 1882.

90 Labour Canada Library, Annual Meeting of the PWA Grand Council, *Minutes*, 1907, 611.

91 Quoted in Aurand, *From the Molly Maguires*, 37.

92 Cited in McKay, "Realm of Uncertainty," 52.

93 Morrow, *Springhill Disaster*, 83–4.

94 Ibid., 84–6; Scott, *Springhill*, 72.

95 PANS, MG 2, Box 675, folder 1, F1/15295, A.M. MacLeod to E.H. Armstrong, 26 January 1924.

96 Penfold, "Have You No Manhood," 21.

97 Ibid., 27.

98 Sydney *Post*, 4 April 1925, cited in Penfold, "Have You No Manhood," 29.

99 "Minutes of Evidence, Royal Commission on Industrial Disputes in the Province of British Columbia," Canada, *Sessional Papers*, 1904, vol. 38, no. 13, 36A, 4.

100 Halifax *Herald*, 31 March 1909.

101 See Penfold, "Have You No Manhood," 30–2; and Frank, "Miner's Financier," 137–43.

102 Wylie, *Coal Culture*, 133–4. Lynne Marks observed that church groups offered the only organized associational life in small towns for married women in contemporary Ontario. See Marks, *Revivals and Roller Rinks*, 137.

103 Corbin, *Life, Work, and Rebellion*, 92–3.

104 Hinde, "Stout Ladies and Amazons," 44. A One Big Union women's auxiliary was formed in Minto in 1926. Seager, "Minto, New Brunswick," 110–11.

105 Penfold, "Have You No Manhood," 38–42.

106 See *TJ*, 11 May 1883, 21 November 1888, 2 January 1889; and CMR, December 1894, 237, for references to intoxicated boys.

107 See also *TJ*, 5 October 1887.

108 McKay, "Wisdom, Wile or War," 21.

109 Victoria *Daily British Colonist*, 17 March, 5 May 1877.

110 Nanaimo *Free Press*, 25 November 1912.

111 Hinde, "Stout Ladies and Amazons," 33–4.

112 Penfold, "Have You No Manhood," 33–4.

113 See, for instance, LC, *Evidence*; "Minutes of Evidence, Royal Commission on Industrial Disputes in the Province of British Columbia," Canada, *Sessional Papers*, 1904, vol. 38, no. 13, 36A; PAA, Royal Commission on the Coal Industry, *Report and Evidence*; Commission on

Miners' Old Age Pensions, *Report*; Mathers, *Evidence*; and Labour Canada Library, Royal Commission Respecting the Coal Mines of the Province of Nova Scotia, *Minutes of Evidence*, 1925.

114 Penfold, "Have You No Manhood," 36; Hinde, "Stout Ladies and Amazons," 33–4.

115 Seager, "Minto, New Brunswick," 119.

116 McKay, "Realm of Uncertainty," 24.

117 Lunn, "Trapper Boy to General Manager," 226; Bowen, *Boss Whistle*, 17.

118 Bercuson, *Alberta's Coal Industry*, 84.

119 See Bailey, *Leisure and Class in Victorian England*. The *Trades Journal* conveyed an assessment of the relative cultural balance of Nova Scotian coal communities in 1889: "Considering the occupation of the miner the wonder is not that a third of them drink, but that two-thirds of them are admitted to be sober men." *TJ*, 26 June 1889. On the threats to traditional popular culture from industrialization and its associated ethic, see Thompson, *Customs in Common*. On cultural divisions in contemporary small-town Ontario, see Marks, *Revivals and Roller Rinks*.

120 *TJ*, 13 April 1881. The view of the miner as a degraded brute was captured in popular novels such as *Germinal* by Emile Zola and Hugh MacLennan's *Each Man's Son*.

121 On the traditional weekly "idle spell" of urban craftsmen, often called "Blue" or "Saint" Monday, see Kealey, *Toronto Workers Respond*, 54, 68; and Palmer, *Culture in Conflict*, 21.

122 *TJ*, 18 July 1883. Drummond failed to acknowledge that companies operated nineteenth-century mines irregularly.

123 PANS, RG 21, series A, vol. 38, no. 10, Richard Brown diary, entries for 21 March, 6 January, 17 March, 3 April, 1 May 1874.

124 Drummond, *Minerals and Mining*, 276–7.

125 *TJ*, 1 August 1888.

126 Cameron, *Pictonian Collier*, 215; McKay, "Realm of Uncertainty," 47.

127 PANS, RG 21, series A, vol. 38, no. 10, Richard Brown diary, entry for 4 May 1874.

128 PANS, RG 21, series A, vol. 38, no. 12, Richard Brown diary, entry for 2 April 1881.

129 *TJ*, 13 April 1887.

130 Macdonald, *Coal and Iron Industries*, 73.

131 Frank, "Cape Breton Coal Miners," 232; McKay, "Realm of Uncertainty," 55–6.

132 See *CMR*, December 1894, 236; *CMJ*, 15 June 1913, 381.

133 *CMR*, September 1903, 198.

134 *TJ*, 8 November 1882.

135 A circus, which the boys apparently found disappointing, closed the mine at River Hebert for a day. See *TJ*, 13 August 1884. A baseball game once shut the Joggins mine. See Halifax *Herald*, 7 June 1906.

136 *TJ*, 25 April 1883.

137 *TJ*, 17 May 1882

138 *TJ*, 14 January 1885.

139 *TJ*, 14 September 1887.

140 *TJ*, 11 October 1882.

141 *CMJ*, 15 April 1914, 254.

142 See Labour Canada Library, [Duncan] Royal Commission Respecting the Coal Mines of the Province of Nova Scotia, *Minutes of Evidence*, 1925, 2648–9, 2953.

143 *TJ*, 23 December 1885.

144 *TJ*, 5 October 1887. The Canada Temperance [Scott] Act had been declared in force in Pictou County in 1882. See *TJ*, 27 September 1882.

145 *TJ*, 7 March 1883.

146 Quoted in Den Otter, *Civilizing the West*, 164.

147 Quoted in Seager and Perry, "Mining the Connections," 66.

148 *TJ*, 21 January 1885.

149 See Harvey, "Love, Honour and Obey," 128–40.

150 *TJ*, 25 April 1883.

151 *TJ*, 24 October 1883.

152 *TJ*, 12 August 1885.

153 On prostitution in the Alberta mining camps, see Den Otter, *Civilizing the West*, 174, 242–8; and Bercuson, *Alberta's Coal Industry*, 190–1.

154 See Samson, "Dependency and Rural Industry," 129.

155 See Angus L. Macdonald Library, St Francis Xavier University, *Minutebooks*, Pioneer Lodge, PWA, 14 August 1884.

156 Belshaw, "Standard of Living," 61–2.

157 *TJ*, 12 August 1885. Other reports of dog-fighting are found in the issues of 30 September 1885 and 11 January 1888; and in the Sydney *Daily Post*, 31 July 1909.

158 See *TJ*, 9 January 1889, and the *Nanaimo Free Press*, 6 February 1901.

159 McLaren, "Proper Education for All Classes," 33, 44–6.

160 Ibid., 54–5.

161 Axelrod, *Promise of Schooling*, 57–9.

162 McLaren, "Proper Education for All Classes," 19.

163 *TJ*, 9 May 1888. See LC, *Evidence*, 437, 447.

164 LC, *Evidence*, 454.

165 *TJ*, 1 April 1885.

166 Lawson, *A Man's Life*, 74.

167 Halifax *Morning Chronicle*, 4 December 1890.

168 On this point, see Marks, *Revivals and Roller Rinks*, 81–5.

169 *TJ*, 8 November 1882 (bowling alley), 19 December 1888 (on the shooting gallery as a "drop-in" for boys).

170 See *TJ*, 3 June 1885. On nineteenth-century courting, see Ward, *Courtship, Love, and Marriage*, esp. chaps 4 and 5.

171 *TJ*, 18 July, 31 October 1883; 2 January 1889.

172 *TJ*, 11 May 1883.

173 *TJ*, 21 November 1888.

174 *TJ*, 2 January 1889.

175 *CMR*, December 1894, 237.

176 LC, *Evidence*, 437.

177 *TJ*, 24 August 1887.

178 See Palmer, "Discordant Music," 5–62; and Thompson, "Rough Music," 285–312. Philippe Ariès remarked on how activities at one time common to all age groups eventually came to be confined to the young. See *Centuries of Childhood*, 62–99.

179 *TJ*, 10 September 1884.

180 *TJ*, 15 May 1889.

181 *TJ*, 2 November 1887.

182 New Glasgow *Eastern Chronicle*, 30 June 1870; *TJ*, 28 October 1885.

183 *TJ*, 6 June 1888.

184 *TJ*, 22 May 1889.

185 Nanaimo *Free Press*, 24 March 1900.

186 *TJ*, 24 April 1889.

187 Marks, *Revivals and Roller Rinks*, 15, 230–2 (Tables 3–5).

188 *TJ*, 2 November 1887, 7 March 1888.

189 Scott, *Springhill*, 50.

190 Labour Canada Library, Annual Meeting of the PWA Grand Council, *Minutes*, 1894, 281.

191 Labour Canada Library, Drummond, *Recollections and Reflections*, 198.

192 He first made the suggestion in *TJ*, 21 July 1880, when he observed that pay-day at Stellarton had been switched to Thursdays with considerable success, "there being much less dissipation than has followed Saturday pay-days."

193 Marks, *Revivals and Roller Rinks*, 109.

194 Bowen, "Friendly Societies in Nanaimo," 67–92.

195 *TJ*, 15 November 1882.

196 *TJ*, 7 January 1885.

197 Cameron, *Pictonian Collier*, 328.

198 Norcross, *Nanaimo Retrospective*, 49.

199 *TJ*, 13 December 1882, 11 November 1885; Angus L. Macdonald Library, St Francis Xavier University, *Minutebooks*, Pioneer Lodge, PWA, 26 November 1885.

200 *TJ*, 20 June 1883.

201 *TJ*, 7 January 1885.

202 *TJ*, 14 October 1885. The lodge made another effort to establish a library in 1889. See *TJ*, 30 October 1889.

203 LC, *Evidence*, 272.

204 *CMJ*, 15 January 1914, 42–3.

205 *TJ*, 18 November 1885, 20 April 1887.

206 Cameron, *Pictonian Colliers*, 102.

207 Scott, *Springhill*, 65–9; *TJ*, 1 June 1887.

208 *Maritime Mining Review*, 21 December 1906, in NA, Records of the Department of Labour, RG 27, vol. 3130, file 78.

209 Belshaw, "Standard of Living," 61.

210 *TJ*, 24 May 1882.

211 *TJ*, 10 July 1889.

212 Glace Bay *Standard*, 5, 10 June 1911.

213 *TJ*, 29 September 1880.

214 *TJ*, 15 May 1889; Belshaw, "Standard of Living," 62.

215 For baseball, see *TJ*, 22 July 1885, 24 April 1889. For a report on the reorganization of the Pictou County Cricket Club, see *TJ*, 20 May 1885. On baseball in the Maritimes, see Howell, *Northern Sandlots*.

216 Sydney Mines *Star*, 18 October 1905.

217 Frank, "Cape Breton Coal Miners," 128.

218 See Halifax *Christian Messenger*, 6 August 1873, 250. On the juvenile templars, see *TJ*, 2 November 1887.

219 Scott, *Springhill*, 79. A temperance lecturer was at the Albion Mines in 1866. See New Glasgow *Eastern Chronicle*, 6 September 1866.

220 *TJ*, 7 March 1888.

221 *TJ*, 23 November 1887.

222 Scott, *Springhill*, 108.

223 "The Boys brigade, which embraces among its membership about fifty boys, nearly all of whom are employed in the pits, has been organized through the efforts of Rev. David Wright in connection with the Presbyterian Sunday school [at Stellarton]. The brigade is doing splendid work. An effort is now being put forth to have the boys supplied with uniforms and other equipments. They are drilled regularly." See Stellarton *Journal and Pictou News*, 28 October 1891. See also Morrow, *Springhill Disaster*, 139.

224 The Nanaimo *Free Press*, 10 October 1900, reported a football match between the high school and the Boys' Brigade teams.

225 Glace Bay *Standard*, 25 May 1911.

226 Scott, *Springhill*, 110.

227 Bowen, "Friendly Societies in Nanaimo," 87.

228 Lunn, "From Trapper Boy to General Manager," 233.

229 Lovejoy, "Child Labor in the Coal Mines," 297.

230 *The Bulletin* (Dartmouth), 15 December 1886, cited in McKay, "Realm of Uncertainty," 27; and Sexton, "Industrial Education for Miners," 594.

231 A Nova Scotian "new model boy" is presented in McKay, "From Trapper Boy to General Manager," 211–40.

Chapter Eight

1 The expression is from McKay, "Industry, work and community," 605.

2 Frank, "Contested Terrain," 104–5.

3 On rats in the pit, see McNeil, *Voice of the Pioneer*, 18.

4 Ibid., 18.

5 Bowen, *Boss Whistle*, 16.

6 McKay, "Realm of Uncertainty," 28.

7 MacDonald, "Farewell to Coal," 21.

8 (Stellarton) *Journal and Pictou News*, 21 October 1889.

9 Halifax *Morning Chronicle*, 4 December 1890. For other pranks played on novice mine workers, see Bowen, *Boss Whistle*, 59.

10 On the experience of one English boy, see Lawson, *A Man's Life*, 70.

11 (Stellarton) *Journal*, 21 January 1891.

12 An elderly British miner recalled starting as a trapper in 1906: "It was a job to keep awake – especially if you were left in the dark all by yourself." See Storm-Clark, "The Miners," 56. On trapper boys falling asleep, see also McKay, "Realm of Uncertainty," 28–9.

13 See Lawson, *A Man's Life*, 73.

14 LC, *Evidence*, 301–2, 288, 269–70.

15 These included James Baird, who started work at the age of eleven as a driver, and Henry Swift, who entered the mines at twelve. CMR, April 1894, 64; Morrow, *Springhill Disaster*, 121–2, CMR, March 1891, 75. John Casey, manager of Dominion Coal's Caledonia Colliery, had also started as a trapper boy. See his obituary, CMJ, 23 January 1920, 55. D.H. MacLean, future resident superintendent at the Acadia Mines, started to work in the mines at the age of twelve in 1892; John C. Nicholson, future BESCO general superintendent, started at the same age in 1893; Charles Mackenzie, also a future Acadia manager, first entered the mines at the age of fourteen in 1921. See Cameron, *Pictonian Colliers*, 66–8.

16 Belshaw, "Standard of Living," 45.

17 See PAA, Royal Commission on the Coal Mining Industry, *Report and Evidence*, 10.

18 See Williamson, *Class, Culture and Community*, 29.

19 Cameron, *Pictonian Colliers*, 109.

20 On job trading, see McKay, "Industry, work and community," 603.

21 LC, *Evidence*, 281, 437, 301; RCTE, 1708.

22 Halifax *Herald*, 20 March 1906.

23 Beaton Institute, MG 1, E 59, f(33), Workmen's Time Book (Sydney Mines), August 1839, and f(48), Workmen's Time Book (Sydney Mines), January 1858.

24 One boy, Eddie Hudson, just hired, only worked the last $2\frac{1}{4}$ days of the pay period. These variations in days worked persisted. In a time sheet for August 1901, twelve drivers were identified. They worked from a minimum of 2 to a maximum of 15 days that month, most working 10 to 12 days. Among seven trappers, the range was from 4 to 14 days. In September 1908 twenty-eight drivers worked anywhere between 8 and $29\frac{1}{2}$ days; nine trappers worked from $12\frac{1}{2}$ to $27\frac{6}{10}$ days. Springhill Miners' Museum, Springhill, Nova Scotia, Cumberland Railway and Coal Company, Time Books, February 1891, August 1901, September 1908.

25 McKay, "Realm of Uncertainty," 47.

26 Miners' unions sought by various means to exclude the unskilled from mine work. See Chapter 3.

27 Cited in Frank, "Contested Terrain," 106.

28 Typical dangers included "pot-holes," lens-shaped large stones; "lypes," fractures in the seam that allowed huge masses of coal to roll forward onto the miner; and fossilized tree stumps known as "chaldron bottoms." See MacLeod, "Colliers, Colliery Safety and Workplace Control," 230.

29 The balance of fatalities had a variety of other causes. McKay, "Realm of Uncertainty," 43–5.

30 McNeil, *Voice of the Pioneer*, 60.

31 Drummond, *Minerals and Mining*, 341; (Halifax) *Christian Messenger*, 21 May 1873.

32 BCMR, 1887, 290; 1888, 324.

33 34. Alberta, *Mines Report*, 179–87, in *Annual Report of the Department of Public Works*, 1914.

34 NSMR, 1917.

35 LC, *Evidence*, 482. The *Trades Journal* (21 March 1888) was less categorical about the boys' irresponsibility: "Two boys named McMillan and McCormick were burned slightly with gas last Monday week [at Bridgeport]. They opened a small door going into a sump when a small quantity of gas ignited. Gas was never found in the place before."

36 *TJ*, 24 April 1889.

37 *TJ*, 26 June 1889.

38 BCMR, 1911, K280.

39 NSMR, 1891, 12.

40 NSMR, 1866, 40–1.

41 BCMR, 1891, 559.

42 NSMR, 1868, 34.

43 NSMR, 1882, 12.

44 NSMR, 1884, 34.

45 Lovejoy, "Child Labor in the Coal Mines," 297. Lovejoy, at the time assistant-secretary of the National Child Labor Committee, drew his statistics from the anthracite coalfields of Pennsylvania, defining boys to be under sixteen years. Boys under sixteen comprised one-ninth of the South Wales mines workforce in the 1850s, yet accounted for one-fifth of accidents. Benson, *British Coalminers*, 37.

46 CMJ, 16 February 1923, 127.

47 These calculations are based on statistics for deaths in the mines, on the assumption that they were far more likely to be recorded than non-fatal accidents. This also allows for a clear measure of an accident's severity. Unlike the mainland reports on accidents, in Cape Breton from 1889 the victim's age was recorded. Statistics from the Inverness and other small coalfields were not examined; thus, after 1904, when Cape Breton was divided into three mining districts, reference was made only to the northern and southern districts (industrial Cape Breton). NSMR, 1890, 23; 1898, 28; 1894, 29; 1898, 29.

48 See Lazonick, "Production Relations," 491–516.

49 See Daunton, "Down the Pit," 591.

50 Labour Canada Library, Annual Meeting of the PWA Grand Council, *Minutes*, 1906, 532.

51 An elderly miner requested permission "to get up in the first Rake with the Boys ... on account of his age and no House Keeper." Dalhousie University Archives, Halifax, Joggins *Minutebooks*, Holdfast Lodge, PWA, 22 November 1905.

52 (Halifax) *Christian Messenger*, 21 May 1873.

53 Labour Canada Library, Annual Meeting of the PWA Grand Council, *Minutes*, 1906, 532.

54 Thus the legislated eight-hour day, not necessarily well received by miners who worked on piece rates, was uniformly welcomed by mine labourers who received a fixed daily rate of pay. See Forsey, *Economic and Social Aspects*, 51, citing the *Labour Gazette*, March 1919, 307–8. The eight-hour day for underground work was legislated in British Columbia in 1903 and in Alberta in 1908. See Seager, "Socialists and Workers," 54. In Nova Scotia, an accord in February 1919 between the UMWA and the Dominion Coal Company included a clause establishing the eight-hour day. See Frank, "Cape Breton Coal Miners," 308.

55 TJ, 11 August 1880.

56 *TJ*, 15 February 1888.

57 *TJ*, 13 June 1888.

58 Dalhousie University Archives, Halifax, Joggins *Minutebooks*, Holdfast Lodge, PWA, 30 May 1906.

59 (Stellarton) *Journal*, 4 February 1891.

60 *TJ*, 11 August 1880.

61 (Stellarton) *Journal*, 21 January 1891.

62 See Labour Canada Library, "Constitution, Rules, By-Laws and Rules of Order of the Provincial Workmen's Association of Nova Scotia and New Brunswick," Article 12. Pioneer delegates to the annual meeting of the PWA were instructed to vote against "admitting boys under age." See Angus L. Macdonald Library, St Francis Xavier University, Springhill *Minutebooks*, Pioneer Lodge, entry for 8 April 1886.

63 *TJ*, 17 October 1883.

64 *TJ*, 27 February 1885.

65 Halifax *Morning Chronicle*, 6 September 1890. On this legislation, see McCallum, "Mines Arbitration Act," 303–25.

66 (Stellarton) *Journal*, 21 January 1891.

67 The boys' lodge at the Reserve Mines was first noted in the *Trades Journal* in 1883. The issue of 26 October 1887 referred to "Stedfast" lodge, [re?]organized that year at the Reserve Mines. The following year the *Trades Journal* (8 February 1888) noted that some Stedfast lodge members, like those of its mother lodge, were poor attenders. Unity, the "mother" lodge at the Reserve Mines, recommended the organization of boys at other mines at the annual meeting of the PWA Grand Council in 1899. See Labour Canada Library, Annual Meeting of the PWA Grand Council, *Minutes*, 1899, 359. Forsey, *Trade Unions in Canada*, 348, noted that Stedfast lodge re-emerged at the Reserve Mines in 1901. In 1907 Stedfast was dissolved and its members were brought into the adult PWA lodge, Unity. See the *Labour Gazette*, 1907, 889. The *Labour Gazette*, 1904, 675, noted a boys' lodge (called Bayview) at the Caledonia mines. The issue of February 1905, 878, noted two boys' lodges on Cape Breton shortly after the turn of the twentieth century: Standard, at Dominion No. 3, and Redpath, at New Aberdeen. In 1907 King Edward lodge (Junior) amalgamated with the senior lodge at Dominion No. 1. See *Labour Gazette*, 1907, 889. King George lodge (Sydney Mines) was organized in 1908. See Labour Canada Library, Annual Meeting of the PWA Grand Council, *Minutes*, 1908, 676.

68 *TJ*, 11 October 1882.

69 Although the colliery manager undertook "to advance the Boys['] wages as they advanced in work," in this case he simply put Downie back driving. Dalhousie University Archives, Halifax, Joggins *Minutebooks*, Holdfast Lodge, PWA, 23, 30 November, 21 December 1904.

70 *Ibid.*, 18 January, 25 July 1905; 22 August 1906.

71 Amherst *Semi-Weekly News*, 19 March 1895.

72 *Maritime Mining Record*, 16 May 1900.

73 UMWA inclusiveness was designed at least in part to subject mine labourers (and not just miners) to union discipline. See Amsden and Brier, "Coal Miners on Strike," 583–616.

74 The "Boys' Committee" at Springhill is mentioned on 21 January 1922. On 8 September 1923 and 6 February 1926, for instance, the cases of discharged boys are addressed. See Angus L. Macdonald Library, St Francis Xavier University, Springhill *Minutebooks*, Local 4514, UMWA.

75 NA, Records of the Department of Labour (hereafter RG 27), vol. 142, file 611.04:6.

76 On the conciliation procedure spelled out in the Montreal Agreement, see Frank, "Cape Breton Coal Miners," 234–6. Eugene Forsey credited the UMWA with putting a stop to "irresponsible" boys' strikes. See Forsey, *Economic and Social Aspects*, 51.

77 Nardinelli, "Corporal Punishment and Children's Wages," 294.

78 LC, *Evidence*, 294, 418.

79 *TJ*, 17 April 1889.

80 See the testimony of twelve-year-old Robert McTagarth. LC, *Evidence*, 302.

81 "[M]anagers would occasionally swing their cane at boys, and bluster and threaten them in an appropriate manner." See McKay, "Realm of Uncertainty," 29–30.

82 LC, *Evidence*, 301–2, 367.

83 New Glasgow *Eastern Chronicle*, 3 April 1873, cited in MacLeod, "Miners, Mining Men and Mining Reform," 435.

84 *TJ*, 17 August 1887.

85 PANS, RG 21, Series A, vol. 35, Letter Books of Henry Swift, entry for 14 May 1890, as quoted in McKay, "Realm of Uncertainty," 31.

86 Halifax *Herald*, 5 December 1906.

87 Sydney *Post*, 7 April 1924.

88 LC, *Evidence*, 269–70, 302.

89 Quoted in McKay, "Realm of Uncertainty," 33.

90 Simpson described his trappers as aged from twelve to fourteen; and his drivers as fourteen to sixteen years old. See LC, *Evidence*, 381.

91 Ferguson also observed that drivers who worked in pairs (two to a horse) only earned seventy-five cents daily. LC, *Evidence*, 437.

92 Labour Canada Library, Royal Commission Respecting the Coal Mines of the Province of Nova Scotia, *Minutes of Evidence*, 1925, 2554. In the United Kingdom at the turn of the twentieth century, eighteen was seen as the age to graduate to collier. See Storm-Clark, "The Miners," 68.

93 PANS, RG 21, Series A, vol. 35, Letter Books of Henry Swift, entries for 14 November, 29 November, and 2 December, as quoted in McKay, "Realm of Uncertainty," 32.

94 *TJ*, 20 July 1887.

95 There is a fictional account of another boys' delegation in Lunn, "From Trapper Boy to General Manager," 231–3.

96 Labour Canada Library, Royal Commission Respecting the Coal Mines of the Province of Nova Scotia, *Minutes of Evidence*, 1925, 2555.

97 NA, RG 27, vol. 332, no. 2, John Moffat to H.H. Ward, 26 April 1924.

98 Johnston, "Description of Haulage System," 92.

99 Amsden and Brier, "Coal Miners on Strike," 601.

100 Samuel, "Mineral Workers," 89.

101 Hickey, *Workers in Imperial Germany*, 181, 199–202.

102 Ibid., 199.

103 Douglass, "The Durham Pitman," 252.

104 "Horses in the Coal Mines," 40.

105 Halifax *Herald*, 5 December 1906.

106 *TJ*, 2 June 1880.

107 *TJ*, 1 July 1885.

108 *TJ*, 22 June 1887.

109 Amherst *Semi-Weekly News*, 19 March 1895; Amherst *Daily News*, 4 November 1895.

110 Amherst *Daily News*, 7 May 1900.

111 *Maritime Mining Record*, 16 May 1900.

112 NA, RG 27, vol. 323, file nos. 361, 364.

113 *Labour Gazette*, March 1904, 937, 939; Halifax *Herald*, 30 January, 2 February 1904.

114 *Maritime Mining Record*, 10 February 1904.

115 NA, RG 27, vol. 327, no. 4.

116 *TJ*, 27 June 1883.

117 North Sydney *Herald*, 20 March 1895.

118 *Labour Gazette*, August 1906, 174.

119 *Maritime Mining Record*, 6 November 1901.

120 Halifax *Herald*, 24 March 1904, *Maritime Mining Record*, 23 March 1904; NA, RG 27, vol. 143, file 611.04:10.

121 *Labour Gazette*, October 1907, 468; NA, RG 27, vol. 327, no. 171.

122 *Labour Gazette*, July 1909, 124; NA, RG 27, vol. 296, no. 3150 (23).

123 *Labour Gazette*, August 1921, 993; NA, RG 27, vol. 327, no. 171; NA, RG 27, vol. 143, file 611.04:10.

124 Sydney *Record*, 9 July 1921.

125 Macdonald, *Coal and Iron Industries*, 60.

126 Halifax *Herald*, 10 March 1909; NA, RG 27, vol. 296, no. 3118.

127 *TJ*, 17 August 1887; Halifax *Morning Chronicle*, 2 December 1890; Amherst *Evening Press*, 2, 3 December 1890.

128 *Maritime Mining Record*, 18 June 1902.

129 Halifax *Herald*, 10, 11, 14 July 1905. The quotation is from the issue of July 14.

130 *Labour Gazette*, August 1905, 204–5; NA, RG 27, vol. 143, file 611.04:10. The quotation is from Halifax *Herald*, 17 July 1905.

131 Halifax *Herald*, 21, 29, 30 November; 4, 15 December 1906; *Labour Gazette*, December 1906, 688; January 1907, 790.

132 *Maritime Mining Record*, 12 December 1906, in NA, RG 27, vol. 3130, file 78.

133 Amherst *Daily News*, 14 December 1906.

134 PANS, RG 21, Series A, vol. 38, no. 14, Richard Brown diaries, entries for 26, 27 February, 4 March 1901.

135 *TJ*, 8 June 1887.

136 NA, RG 27, vol. 143, file 611.04:10.

137 Amherst *Daily News*, 29 March 1901. The quotation is from the *Labour Gazette*, May 1901, 460.

138 Halifax *Herald*, 11 September 1920.

139 NA, RG 27, vol. 143, file 611.04:10. NA, RG 27, vol. 321, no. 185, reports that the new tubs weighed 2,600 pounds and replaced tubs of 2,300 pounds.

140 LC, *Evidence*, 472.

141 *TJ*, 11 August 1880.

142 *TJ*, 20 July 1887, 10 August 1887.

143 Amherst *Daily News*, 24 July 1899; *Industrial Advocate*, August 1899, 12.

144 Amherst *Daily News*, 29 March 1901; *Maritime Mining Record*, 17 April 1901.

145 "An Act relating to the Combination of Workmen," 27 Vict., c. 11, *Statutes of Nova Scotia*, 1864.

146 "Of the regulation of mines," c. 10, s. 26, *The Revised Statutes of Nova Scotia, Fourth Series*, 1873. See, for instance, Albion Mines, "Special Rules."

147 *TJ*, 16 June 1880.

148 Halifax *Herald*, 14 July 1905.

149 The shortcomings of common law in regulating relations between the employer and employees is discussed in Craven, "Law of Master and Servant," 175–211. For the maturing legal context and the turning of employers to the courts, see Tucker and Fudge, "Forging Responsible Unions," 81–120.

150 *Labour Gazette*, July 1906, 96; September 1906, 322.

151 Frank, "Class Conflict in the Coal Industry," 173–4. Boys were the "first to rebel" in 1876, at the time of a large strike of all workers at Sydney Mines. McKay, "Crisis of dependent development," 37.

152 Amherst *Daily News*, 24 July 1899.

153 *TJ*, 27 April 1881.

154 (Stellarton) *Journal*, 21 January 1891.

155 *TJ*, 20 July 1887.

156 Halifax *Herald*, 24 March 1904.

157 NA, RG 27, vol. 296, file 3150(23); vol. 143, file 611.04:10.

158 See McKay, "Realm of Uncertainty," 31.

Chapter Nine

1 *CMJ*, 1 January 1918, 4; 20 August 1919, 616.

2 Even by 1913 provincial coal was becoming significantly more costly to extract than American bituminous. See Inwood, "Local control," 265–6.

3 *CMR*, May 1902, 135; *CMJ*, 25 February 1921, 145. See also the discussion of the displacement of coal by petroleum in BCMR, 1911, K217.

4 Graham, "Problems of the Vancouver Island Coal Industry," 474.

5 *CMJ*, 15 June 1912, 390.

6 Den Otter, "Railways and Alberta's Coal Problem," 84–98.

7 A prewar depression had hit the metallurgical sector extremely hard, but output surged in response to the demands of the war effort. After the war, Nova Scotian collieries lost their major market with the "practical cessation" of pig-iron and ingot steel manufacturing in Cape Breton. See *CMJ*, 21 January 1921, 45.

8 Forsey, *Economic and Social Aspects of the Nova Scotia Coal Industry,* 112; "Is Coal Losing Ground as a Fuel?," 14.

9 McCall, "Modern Trends in Mechanized Mining," 395.

10 Gray, "Development of the Coal Industry in Canada," 218.

11 The balance of energy consumption was accounted for by water, petroleum fuels, and natural gas. Canada [Carroll], *Royal Commission on Coal*, 655.

12 BCMR, 1911, K222; Dominion Bureau of Statistics, *Coal Statistics for Canada, 1927*, 87. Mainland coal was undercutting Vancouver Island coal, even on the island itself, by 1925. Many marginal mines closed altogether shortly after the war. *Western Canadian Coal Review* 8, no. 2 (February 1925): 26.

13 Villiers, "Problems of the Coal Industry," 567–72.

14 Dominion Bureau of Statistics, *Coal Statistics for Canada, 1939*, 30.

15 NSMR, 1911, xxi; Dominion Bureau of Statistics, *Coal Statistics for Canada, 1927*, 44.

16 Dominion Bureau of Statistics, *Coal Statistics for Canada, 1939*, 45.

17 Ibid., 30; Dominion Bureau of Statistics, *Coal Statistics for Canada, 1927*, 78. In Saskatchewan, employment increased from 515 in 1927 to 726 in 1939. In New Brunswick, employment more than doubled over this period, from 558 to 1,326. Dominion Bureau of Statistics, *Coal Statistics for Canada, 1927*, 66, 51; *Coal Statistics for Canada, 1939*, 30, 51.

18 Angus L. Macdonald Library, St Francis Xavier University, Springhill *Minutebooks*, Local 4514, UMWA, entries for 4 January 1922, 20 January 1923. The presence of a handful of boys in British Columbian mines is recorded until the Second World War. See BCMR, 1939.

19 Discontinuities between juvenile and adult labour markets contributed to the development of a substantial pool of unskilled and unemployable young adults in most occupations. See Department of Labour, *Employment of Children*, 7; Bullen, "Children of the Industrial Age," 144. When the campaign against child labour revived in Great Britain at the turn of the century, it focused on its wastefulness: wage work performed by boys imparted no training, no skills. Both the minority and majority reports of the 1909 British Royal Commission on the Poor Laws identified "boy labour" as a serious source of adult unemployment. See also Bray, *Boy Labour and Apprenticeship*; Dunlop, *English Apprenticeship and Child Labour*; Freeman, *Boy Life and Labour*; Dale, "Child Labour under Capitalism"; and Tawney, "Economics of Boy Labour," 517–37.

20 Sutherland, "We always had things to do," 139.

21 Raymond, *Nursery World of Dr. Blatz*, 40.

22 Glace Bay *Gazette*, 9 March 1933, cited in MacEwan, *Mines and Steelworkers*, 5.

23 Johnstone, *Coal Dust in My Blood*, 16.

24 "The strain and anxiety shown by working and wandering youngsters and their precocity and sharpness in pursuit of a living worried Christian child-savers more than their physical deprivations. It was this very acuity and independence that made their childhoods seem unnatural." Parr, *Labouring Children*, 37.

25 Quoted in Bullen, "Children of the Industrial Age," 150.

26 See Ontario, "Reports of Factory Inspectors for 1892," *Sessional Papers*, 18; ibid., 1898, 17; ibid., 1896, 22.

27 *Critic*, 4 December 1891, quoted in MacLeod, "Miners, Mining Men and Mining Reform," 353–4. "What shocked middle-class commentators on factory life in mid-Victorian England as much as the alleged immorality was the independence of the young." See Musgrove, *Youth and the Social Order*, 67.

28 Mackintosh, "Social Significance of Child Labour," 9.

Bibliography

PRIMARY SOURCES

Manuscript Sources

The Beaton Institute, University College of Cape Breton
MG 1, E 59, f(33), Workmen's Time Book (Sydney Mines), August 1839 and f(48), Workmen's Time Book (Sydney Mines), January 1858
New Aberdeen Minutebooks, Keystone Lodge, Provincial Workman's Association; Victory Local, United Mine Workers of America, 1907–9

Dalhousie University Archives
Joggins Minutebooks, Holdfast Lodge, Provincial Workman's Association, 1894–98, 1904–6

Labour Canada Library
Amalgamated Mine Workers of Nova Scotia, "Minutes of Second Annual Convention, Sydney, 18–23 November 1918"
"Constitution, Rules, By-Laws and Rules of Order of the Provincial Workmen's Association of Nova Scotia and New Brunswick, 1916"
John Moffatt, "Valedictory Report," 1917
PWA, Annual Meeting of Grand Council, *Minutes*, 1879–1917
Robert Drummond, *Recollections and Reflections of a Former Trades Union Leader* (unpublished manuscript, circa 1926)
Royal Commission on the Coal Mining Industry of Nova Scotia, [A.R. Duncan], *Minutes of Evidence*, 1925
Trades and Labour Congress of Canada, *Annual Proceedings*, 1883–1920

Angus L. Macdonald Library, St Francis Xavier University
Springhill Minutebooks: Pioneer Lodge, Provincial Workman's Association, 1882–86; Local 4514, United Mine Workers of America, 1923–27

National Archives of Canada

MG 20, Records of the Hudson's Bay Company

MG 28, I 10, Records of the Canadian Council for Social Development

MG 28, I 25, Records of the National Council of Women of Canada

MG 28, I 129, Records of the Montreal Society for the Protection of Women and Children

RG 27, Records of the Department of Labour

RG 33, series 95, [Mathers] Royal Commission on Industrial Relations, *Minutes of Evidence*, 1919

RG 81, Records of the Dominion Coal Board

RG 84, Records of the Canadian Parks Service

Public Archives of Nova Scotia

RG 7, Records of the Provincial Secretary

RG 21, Records of Mines and Mining in Nova Scotia, Series A
  Richard Brown Papers
  Letter Books of Henry Swift, 20 July 1890–20 February 1891

Springhill Miners' Museum

Cumberland Railway and Coal Company, Time Books, February 1891, August 1901, September 1908

Provincial Archives of Alberta

Department of Mines and Minerals, Mines Division, 1888–1967, acc. 72.90

Energy Resources Conservation Board, Mining Division, 1898–1976, acc. 77.237

Report and Evidence of the Royal Commission on the Coal Mining Industry in the Province of Alberta, 1907, Arthur L. Sifton (chairman), acc. 76.396

Newspapers

Christian Messenger (Halifax), 1873

Colonial Patriot (Pictou), 1827–29

Daily British Colonist (Victoria), 1860–1900

Eastern Chronicle (New Glasgow), 1866–73

Eastern Labour News (Moncton), 1909–13

Free Press (Nanaimo), 1899–1901

Herald (Halifax), 1879–1920

Maritime Labour Herald (Glace Bay), 1921–26

Morning Chronicle (Halifax), 1876–1890

Nova Scotian and Weekly Chronicle, 1903

Standard (Glace Bay), 1909–11

Trades Journal (*Journal, Journal and Pictou News*) (Springhill/Stellarton), 1880–1891

Industry Periodicals

British Columbia Mining Record, 1895–1908
Canadian Mining Journal, 1907–23
Canadian Mining and Metallurgical Bulletin, 1917–50
Canadian Mining Manual, 1890–1903
Canadian Mining Review, 1884–1906
Journal of the Canadian Mining Institute, 1898–1911
Journal of the Federated Canadian Mining Institute, 1896–97
Journal of the Mining Society of Nova Scotia, 1892–1915
Transactions of the Canadian Institute of Mining and Metallurgy and of the Mining
    Society of Nova Scotia, 1921–40
Transactions of the Canadian Mining Institute, 1912–20
Transactions of the Canadian Society of Civil Engineers, 1887–1917
Western Canadian Coal Review, 1918–26

Published Sources

Abbott, Kirby. "The Coal Miners and the Law in Nova Scotia: From the 1864
    Combination of Workmen Act to the 1947 Trade Union Act." In *Workers
    and the State in Twentieth Century Nova Scotia*, edited by Michael Earle, 24–
    46. Fredericton: Acadiensis Press 1989
Abella, Irving, and David Millar. *The Canadian Worker in the Twentieth Century*.
    Toronto: University of Toronto Press 1978
Acheson, T.W. "The National Policy and the Industrialization of the Mari-
    times, 1880–1910." *Acadiensis* 1, no. 2 (Spring 1972): 3–28
Alberta. *Annual Report of the Mines Branch of the Department of Public Works
    of the Province of Alberta*. Edmonton: Government Printer 1918–24
Alberta. Department of Public Works. *Annual Reports: The Mines Branch*.
    Edmonton: Government Printer 1905–17
Alberta. [H.M.E. Evans]. *Report of Alberta Coal Commission, 1925*. Edmonton:
    W.D. McLean, Acting King's Printer 1926
Alberta. Royal Commission on the Coal Industry in the Province of Alberta.
    Report. Edmonton: Government Printer 1907
Alberta. *Statutes of the Province of Alberta*. Edmonton: Government Printer
    1906–15
Albion Mines. "Special Rules for the Conduct and Guidance of the Persons
    Acting in the Management and of All Persons Employed in or about the
    Albion Mines." Halifax: n.p. 1880
Allen, Richard. *The Social Passion: Religion and Social Reform in Canada, 1914–
    28*. Toronto: University of Toronto Press 1973
Ambrose, Linda. *For Home and Country: The Centennial History of the Women's
    Institutes in Ontario*. Erin, Ont.: Boston Mills Press 1996

Amsden, John, and Stephen Brier. "Coal Miners on Strike: The Transformation of Strike Demands and the Formation of a National Union." *Journal
of Interdisciplinary History* 7, no. 4 (Spring 1977): 583–616

Ariès, Philippe. *Centuries of Childhood: A Social History of Family Life.* New
York: Knopf 1962

Arnup, Katherine. *Education for Motherhood: Advice for Mothers in Twentieth
Century Canada.* Toronto: University of Toronto Press 1994

Ashton, T.S. "The Coalminers of the Eighteenth Century." *Economic History* I
(1928): 307–34

Audet, Pierre H. "Apprenticeship in Early Nineteenth Century Montreal,
1790–1812." MA thesis, Concordia University 1975

Aurand, Harold W. *From the Molly Maguires to the United Mine Workers: The
Ecology of an Industrial Union, 1869–1897.* Philadelphia: Temple University
Press 1971

Axelrod, Paul. *The Promise of Schooling: Education in Canada, 1800–1914.* Toronto: University of Toronto Press 1997

Babaian, Sharon. *The Coal Mining Industry in the Crow's Nest Pass.* Edmonton:
Alberta Culture 1985

Backhouse, Constance. "Shifting Patterns in Nineteenth Century Canadian
Custody Law." In *Essays in the History of Canadian Law.* Vol. 1, edited by
David H. Flaherty, 218–48. Toronto: University of Toronto Press for the
Osgoode Society 1981

Baedeker, Karl. *Dominion of Canada with Newfoundland and an Excursion to
Alaska.* Leipsic: K. Baedeker 1894

Baehre, Rainer. "Paupers and Poor Relief in Upper Canada." In Canadian
Historical Association, *Historical Papers/Communications historiques,* 1981:
57–80

Bagnell, Kenneth. *The Little Immigrants: The Orphans Who Came to Canada.*
Toronto: Macmillan 1980

Bailey, Loring Woart. "Report on the Mines and Minerals of New Brunswick." Fredericton: G.E. Fenety 1864

Bailey, Martha J. "Servant Girls and Upper Canada's *Seduction Act:* 1837–
1946." In *Dimensions of Childhood: Essays on the History of Children and Youth
in Canada,* edited by Russell Smandych, Gordon Dodds, and Alvin Esau,
159–82. Winnipeg: Legal Research Institute of the University of Manitoba
1991

Bailey, P.C. *Leisure and Class in Victorian England: Rational Recreation and the
Contest for Control, 1830–1885.* London: Routledge and Kegan Paul 1978

Baird, James. "Joggins Mine, Cumberland County, N.S." *Canadian Mining
Review,* June 1893: 59–60

Baker, G. Blaine. "The Juvenile Advocate Society, 1821–1826: Self-Proclaimed
Schoolroom for Upper Canada's Governing Class." In Canadian Historical
Association, *Historical Papers/Communications historiques,* 1985: 74–101

Baker, William M. "The Miners and the Mediator: The 1906 Lethbridge Strike and Mackenzie King." *Labour/Le Travail* 11 (Spring 1983): 89–117
– "The Miners and the Mounties: The Royal North West Mounted Police and the 1906 Lethbridge Strike." *Labour/Le Travail* 27 (Spring 1991): 55–96
Bancroft, Hubert Howe. *History of British Columbia 1792–1887*. San Francisco: History Co. 1890
Barman, Jean. "'Knowledge is Essential for Universal Progress but Fatal to Class Privilege': Working People and the Schools in Vancouver during the 1920s." *Labour/Le Travail* 22 (Fall 1988): 9–66
Barnsby, George J. "The Standard of Living in the Black Country during the Nineteenth Century." *Economic History Review*, ser. 2, 24, no. 2 (1971): 220–39
Bartlett, James Herbert. *The Manufacture, Consumption and Production of Iron, Steel and Coal in Canada*. Montreal: Dawson Brothers 1885
Baskerville, Peter, and Eric W. Sager. *Unwilling Idlers: The Urban Unemployed and Their Families in Late Victorian Canada*. Toronto: University of Toronto Press 1998
Behiels, Michael. "L'Association catholique de la jeunesse canadienne-française and the Quest for a Moral Regeneration, 1903–1914." *Journal of Canadian Studies/Revue d'études canadiennes* 13, no. 2 (Summer 1978): 27–41
Belshaw, John Douglas. "British Coal Miners on Vancouver Island, 1848–1900: A Social History." PhD dissertation, University of London 1987
– "The British Collier in British Columbia: Another Archetype Reconsidered." *Labour/Le Travail* 34 (Fall 1994): 11–36
– "Mining Technique and Social Division on Vancouver Island, 1848–1900." *British Journal of Canadian Studies* 1, no. 1 (June 1986): 45–65
– "The Standard of Living of British Miners on Vancouver Island, 1848–1900." *BC Studies*, no. 84 (Winter 1989–90): 37–64
Bennett, Paul W. "Taming the 'Bad Boys' of the 'Dangerous Class': Child Rescue and Restraint at the Victoria Industrial School, 1887–1935." *Histoire sociale/Social History* 21, no. 41 (May 1988): 71–96
– "Turning 'Bad Boys' into 'Good Citizens': The Reforming Impulse of Toronto's Industrial Schools Movement, 1883 to the 1920's." *Ontario History* 78, no. 3 (September 1986): 209–32
Benson, John. *British Coalminers in the Nineteenth Century: A Social History*. Dublin: Gill 1980
Bercuson, David, ed. *Alberta's Coal Industry*. Calgary: Historical Society of Alberta 1978
– "Tragedy at Bellevue: Anatomy of a Mine Disaster." *Labour/Le Travailleur* 3 (1978): 221–31
Biglow, R.S. "Progress in Mechanical Loading." *The Canadian Mining and Metallurgical Bulletin* (July 1931): 822–35
Bitterman, Rusty. "Farm Households and Wage Labour in the Northeastern Maritimes in the Early 19th Century." *Labour/Le Travail* 31 (Spring 1993): 13–45

Bjarnason, Emil. "Collective Bargaining in the Coal Mining Industry of Canada, 1825–1938." MA thesis, Queen's University 1965

Blakemore, William. "The Frank Disaster." *Canadian Mining Review*, 1903: 121–2

– "The Introduction of Endless Haulage into Cape Breton." *Canadian Mining Review*, 1894: 151–4

Bliss, Michael. "'Pure Books on Avoided Subjects': Pre Freudian Sexual Ideas in Canada." In Canadian Historical Association, *Historical Papers/Communications historiques*, 1970: 89–108

Bouchard, Gérard. *Quelques Arpents d'Amérique: Population, économie, famille au Saguenay, 1838–1971*. Montréal: Boréal 1996

Bourinot, J.G. "Cape Breton and Its Memorials of the French Regime." *Proceedings and Transactions of the Royal Society of Canada* 9, section 2 (1891): 173–343

Bowen, Lynn. *Boss Whistle: The Coal Miners of Vancouver Island Remember*. Lantzville, B.C.: Oolichan Books 1982

– "Friendly Societies in Nanaimo: The British Tradition of Self-Help in a Canadian Coal-Mining Community." *BC Studies*, no. 118 (Summer 1998): 67–92

– *Three Dollar Dreams*. Lantzville, B.C.: Oolichan Books 1987

Bowsfield, Hartwell, ed. *Fort Victoria Letters, 1846–1851*. Winnipeg: Hudson's Bay Record Society 1979

Bradbury, Bettina. "The Family Economy and Work in an Industrial City: Montreal in the 1870s." In Canadian Historical Association, *Historical Papers/Communications historiques*, 1979: 71–96

– "The Fragmented Family: Family Strategies in the Face of Death, Illness and Poverty, Montreal, 1860–1885." In *Childhood and Family in Canadian History*, edited by Joy Parr, 109–28. Toronto: McClelland and Stewart 1982

– "Gender at Work at Home: Family Decisions, the Labour Market and Girls' Contributions to the Family Economy." In *Canadian and Australian Labour History: Towards a Comparative Perspective*, edited by Gregory S. Kealey and Greg Patmore, 119–40. Sydney: Australian-Canadian Studies 1990

– "Pigs, Cows, Boarders: Non-Wage Forms of Survival among Montreal Families, 1861–91." *Labour/Le Travail* 14 (Fall 1984): 9–46

– "Women and Wage Labour in a Period of Transition: Montreal, 1861–1881." *Histoire sociale/Social History* 17, no. 33 (May 1984): 115–31

– "Women's History and Working-Class History." *Labour/Le Travail* 19 (Spring 1987): 23–44

– *Working Families: Age, Gender, and Daily Survival in Industrializing Montreal*. Toronto: McClelland and Stewart 1993

Bray, Reginald A. *Boy Labour and Apprenticeship*. London: Constable and Company 1911

Bremner, Robert H., ed. *Children and Youth in America: A Documentary History*. 3 vols. Cambridge, Mass.: Harvard University Press 1970–74

Briggs, Asa. *The Age of Improvement, 1783–1867*. London: Longman 1959

British Columbia. *Annual Report of the Minister of Mines. Sessional Papers*, 1875–1940

British Columbia. *Journals*, 1891, "Report of the 1890–1 Provincial Select Committee enquiring into the Wellington Colliery Strike."

British Columbia. "Judgments of Full Court in Re: Coal Mines Regulation Amendment Act, 1890." *Sessional Papers*, 1897

British Columbia. *Statutes*, 1877–1916

Brophy, John. *A Miner's Life: An Autobiography*. Madison: University of Wisconsin Press 1964

Brown, Richard. *The Coal Fields and Coal Trade of the Island of Cape Breton*. Stellarton: Maritime Mining Record Office 1899 [1872]

Brown, Richard H. "Submarine Coal Mining." *Transactions of the Mining Society of Nova Scotia* 9 (1904–5): 43–53

Brown, Robert. *On the Geographical Distribution and Physical Characteristics of the Coal-fields of the North Pacific Coast*. Edinburgh: n.p. 1869

Bryan, Andrew. "Coal-Mining." In *A History of Technology*. Vol. 6, pt 1, edited by Trevor I. Williams, 359–75. Oxford: Clarendon Press 1978

Bryden, Kenneth. *Old Age Pensions and Policy-Making in Canada*. Montreal and Kingston: McGill-Queen's University Press 1974

Buckham, A.F. "The Nanaimo Coal Field." *Transactions of the Canadian Institute of Mining and Metallurgy*, 1947: 460–72

Buckingham, James Silk. *Canada, Nova Scotia, New Brunswick and the other British Provinces in North America, with a Plan of National Colonization*. London and Paris: Fisher, Son, and Co. 1843

Buckley, Suzann. "Ladies or Midwives? Efforts to Reduce Infant and Maternal Mortality." In *A Not Unreasonable Claim: Women and Reform in Canada, 1880's–1920's*, edited by Linda Kealey, 131–49. Toronto: Women's Educational Press 1979

Bullen, John. "Children of the Industrial Age: Children, Work and Welfare in Late Nineteenth-Century Ontario." PhD dissertation, University of Ottawa 1989

– "Hidden Workers: Child Labour and the Family Economy in Late Nineteenth Century Urban Ontario." *Labour/Le Travail* 18 (Fall 1986): 163–87

– "J.J. Kelso and the 'New' Child-Savers: The Genesis of the Children's Aid Movement in Ontario." *Ontario History* 82, no. 2 (June 1990): 107–28

Bulman, H.F., and R.A.S. Redmayne. *Colliery Working and Management, Comprising the Duties of a Colliery Manager, the Superintendence and Arrangement of Labour and Wages and the Different Systems of Working Coal Seams*. London: Crosby, Lockwood and Son 1896

Burgess, Joanne. "Le travail des enfants au Québec, 18e–19e siècles: problèmes de définition et de mesure." *Bulletin du RCHTQ*, 22, no. 2 (automne 1996): 27–34

Burrill, William. "Class Conflict and Colonialism: The Coal Miners of Vancouver Island during the Hudson's Bay Company Era, 1848–1862." MA thesis: University of Victoria 1987

Buxton, Neil K. *The Economic Development of the British Coal Industry: From Industrial Revolution to the Present Day.* London: Batsford Academic 1978

Cameron, James M. *The Pictonian Colliers.* Halifax: Nova Scotia Museum 1974

Campbell, Alan. *The Lanarkshire Miners: A Social History of Their Trade Unions, 1775–1874.* Edinburgh: John Donald 1979

– "Skill, Independence, and Trade Unionism in the Coalfields of Nineteenth-Century Britain, with Particular Reference to Scotland." In Canadian Historical Association, *Historical Papers/Communications historiques,* 1981: 155–74

Campbell, Alan, and Fred Reid. "The Independent Collier in Scotland." In *Independent Collier: The Coal Miner as Archetypal Proletarian Reconsidered,* edited by Royden Harrison, 54–74. Hassocks, Sussex: Harvester 1978

Canada. Department of the Interior. *Annual Report.* Ottawa: Queen's/King's Printer 1874–1905

Canada. Department of Labour. *The Employment of Children and Young Persons in Canada.* Ottawa, 1930

Canada. Department of Labour. *The Labour Gazette,* 1901–25

Canada. Department of Labour [F.A. Acland]. *Report of the Deputy Minister of Labour on Industrial Conditions in the Coal Fields of Nova Scotia* Ottawa, 1909

Canada. Department of Labour [R.C. Clute]. Royal Commission on Mining Conditions in British Columbia. Vol. 1, *Report of Commissioner;* vol. 2, *Evidence.* Ottawa, 1900

Canada. Geological Survey of Canada. *Reports on Progress,* 1866–72

Canada. House of Commons. *Debates,* 1944

Canada. *Journals of the House of Commons.* "Select Committee on Chinese Labour and Immigration," vol. 13, app. 4, 1879

Canada. *Report of the Royal Commission on Coal Mining Disputes on Vancouver Island.* Ottawa, 1913

Canada. *Report of Royal Commission Regarding Coal Mining Operations in the Provinces of Nova Scotia and New Brunswick.* Ottawa, 1920

Canada. [W.F. Carroll]. *Report of the Royal Commission on Coal, 1946.* Ottawa: Edmond Cloutier 1947

Canada. Royal Commission on the Relations between Capital and Labour. *Nova Scotia Evidence.* Ottawa, 1889

Canada. Royal Commission on the Relations between Capital and Labour. *Ontario Evidence.* Ottawa, 1889

Canada. Royal Commission on the Relations between Capital and Labour. *Report.* Ottawa, 1889

Canada. *Sessional Papers,* 1871, vol. 4, no. 64, 19, "Manual Containing 'The Census Act' and Instructions to officers employed in the taking of the First Census of Canada, 1871."

Canada. *Sessional Papers*, 1882, vol. 15, no. 9, 42, *Report of the Commissioners appointed to enquire into the working of Mills and Factories of the Dominion, and the labor employed therein.*

Canada. *Sessional Papers*, 1885, vol. 18, no. 11, 54a, *Report of the Royal Commission on Chinese Immigration.*

Canada. *Sessional Papers*, 1902, vol. 36, no. 13, 54, *Report of the Royal Commission on Chinese and Japanese Immigration.*

Canada. *Sessional Papers*, 1903, vol. 37, no. 13, 36a, *Report of the Royal Commission on Industrial Disputes in British Columbia.*

Canada. *Sessional Papers*, 1904, vol. 38, no. 13, 36a, *Minutes of Evidence of the Royal Commission on Industrial Disputes in British Columbia.*

Canada. *Sessional Papers*, 1913, vol. 47, no. 28, 191d, *Report of the Royal Commission on Technical Education.*

Casey, John. "Accidents in Coal Mines and their Causes." *Transactions of the Mining Society of Nova Scotia* 19 (1914–15): 80–96

Census of Canada, 1881, vol. 1. Ottawa: MacLean, Roger and Co. 1882

Census of Canada, 1891, vol. 1. Ottawa: S.E. Dawson, Queen's Printer 1893

Census of Canada, 1901, vol. 1. Ottawa: S.E. Dawson, King's Printer 1902

Challinor, Raymond. *The Lancashire and Cheshire Miners*. Newcastle upon Tyne: Graham 1972

Challinor, Raymond, and Brian Ripley. *The Miners' Association: A Trade Union in the Age of the Chartists*. London: Lawrence 1968

Chan, Anthony. *Gold Mountain: The Chinese in the New World*. Vancouver: New Star Books 1983

Charles, Enid. *The Changing Size of the Family in Canada*. Ottawa: Dominion Bureau of Statistics 1948

Chiasson, Paulette M. "Travellers in Nova Scotia, 1770–1860." MA thesis, Queen's University 1981

Childs, Michael J. *Labour's Apprentices: Working-Class Lads in Late Victorian and Edwardian England*. Montreal and Kingston: McGill-Queen's University Press 1992

Chisholm, Jessie. "Organizing on the Waterfront: The St. John's Longshoremen's Protective Union (LSPU), 1890–1914." *Labour/Le Travail* 26 (Fall 1990): 37–59

Chrismas, Lawrence. *Alberta Miners: A Tribute*. Calgary: Cambria Publishing 1993

– *Coal Dust Grins: Portraits of Canadian Coal Miners*. Calgary: Cambria Publishing 1998

Christie, Nancy, and Michael Gauvreau. *A Full-Orbed Christianity: The Protestant Churches and Social Welfare in Canada, 1900–1940*. Montreal and Kingston: McGill-Queen's University Press 1996

Clapham, J.H. *An Economic History of Modern Britain*. Vol. 3, *Free Trade and Steel, 1850–1886*. Cambridge: Cambridge University Press 1932

Clapp, C.H. "The Geology of the Nanaimo Coal District." *Transactions of the Canadian Institute of Mining and Metallurgy,* 1912: 334–53

Clark, C.S. *Of Toronto the Good. A Social Study. The Queen City of Canada as it is.* Montreal: Toronto Publishing 1898

Cliché, Marie-Aimée. "Les filles-mères devant les tribunaux de Québec, 1850–1969." *Recherches sociographiques* 32, no. 1 (1991): 9–42

Cohen, Marjorie Griffin. *Women's Work, Markets, and Economic Development in Nineteenth-Century Ontario.* Toronto: University of Toronto Press 1988

Coll, Charles J. "Remarks on Some Recent Explosives in Coal Mines." *Transactions of the Mining Society of Nova Scotia* 13 (1908–9): 51–67

Le collectif Clio. *L'histoire des femmes au Québec depuis quatre siècles.* Rev. ed. Montréal: Le Jour 1992

Colls, Robert. *The Pitmen of the Northern Coalfield: Work, Culture and Protest, 1790–1850.* Manchester: Manchester University Press 1987

Comacchio, Cynthia R. "Beneath the 'Sentimental Veil': Families and Family History in Canada." *Labour/Le Travail* 33 (Spring 1994): 279–302

– *"Nations Are Built of Babies": Saving Ontario's Mothers and Children, 1900–1940.* Montreal and Kingston: McGill-Queen's University Press 1993

Cook, Ramsay. *The Regenerators: Social Criticism in Late Victorian English Canada.* Toronto: University of Toronto Press 1985

Cook, Sharon Anne. "Educating for Temperance: The Woman's Christian Temperance Union and Ontario Children, 1880–1916." *Historical Studies in Education/Revue d'histoire de l'éducation* 5, no. 2 (Fall 1993): 251–77

– *"Through Sunshine and Shadow": The Woman's Christian Temperance Union, Evangelicalism, and Reform in Ontario, 1874–1930.* Montreal and Kingston: McGill-Queen's University Press 1995

Copp, Terry. *The Anatomy of Poverty: The Condition of the Working Class in Montreal, 1897–1929.* Toronto: McClelland and Stewart 1974

Corbin, David Alan. *Life, Work, and Rebellion in the Coal Fields: The Southern West Virginia Miners, 1880–1922.* Urbana: University of Illinois Press 1981

Corless, C.V. "The Coal Creek Colliery of the Crow's Nest Pass Coal Co." *Canadian Mining Review,* 1901: 60–7

Coulter, Rebecca. "'Not to Punish but to Reform': Juvenile Delinquency and the Children's Protection Act in Alberta, 1909–1929." In *Studies in Childhood History: A Canadian Perspective,* edited by Patricia T. Rooke and R.L. Schnell, 167–84. Calgary: Detselig Enterprises 1982

– "The Working Young of Edmonton, 1921–1931." In *Childhood and Family in Canadian History,* edited by Joy Parr, 143–59. Toronto: McClelland and Stewart 1982

Cousins, W.J. "A History of the Crow's Nest Pass." MA thesis: University of Alberta 1952

Cowles, J.P. "The Juvenile Employment System of Ontario." Ottawa: Canadian Council on Child Welfare 1923

Craven, Paul. "The Law of Master and Servant in Mid-Nineteenth Century Ontario." In *Essays in the History of Canadian Law.* Vol. 1, edited by David H. Flaherty, 175–211. Toronto: University of Toronto Press for the Osgoode Society 1981

Crawley, Ron. "Off to Sydney: Newfoundlanders Emigrate to Industrial Cape Breton, 1890–1914." *Acadiensis* 17, no. 2 (Spring 1987): 27–51

Crevier, Claudette. "État et travail des enfants au Québec (1880–1900)." Mémoire de maîtrise, Université du Québec à Montréal 1992

Crosby, T.H. "Storage Battery Locomotives for Mine Service." *Transactions of the Canadian Institute of Mining,* 1922: 260–5

Crowley, Terry. "Madonnas before Magdalenes: Adelaide Hoodless and the Making of the Canadian Gibson Girl." *Canadian Historical Review* 67, no. 4 (December 1986): 520–47

Cunningham, Hugh. "The Employment and Unemployment of Children in England c. 1680–1851." *Past and Present,* no. 126 (February 1990): 115–50

Curtis, Bruce. *Building the Educational State: Canada West, 1836–1871.* London, Ont.: Falmer Press; Althouse Press 1988

– "The Playground in Nineteenth-Century Ontario: Theory and Practice." *Material History Bulletin/Bulletin d'histoire de la culture matérielle* 22 (Fall/ Automne 1985): 21–9

– *True Government by Choice Men? Inspection, Education, and State Formation in Canada West.* Toronto: University of Toronto Press 1992

Dale, Mrs Hylton. "Child Labour under Capitalism." London: Fabian Society 1908

Darroch, Gordon, and Michael Ornstein. "Family Coresidence in Canada in 1871: Family Life-Cycles, Occupations and Networks of Mutual Aid." In Canadian Historical Association, *Historical Papers/Communications historiques,* 1983: 30–55

Daunton, M.J. "'Down the Pit': Work in the Great Northern and South Wales Coalfields, 1870–1914." *Economic History Review,* ser. 2, 34, no. 4 (November 1981): 578–97

– "Miners' Houses: South Wales and the Great Northern Coalfield, 1880– 1914." *International Review of Social History* 25, pt 2 (1980): 143–75

Davey, Ian. "The Rhythm of Work and the Rhythm of School." In *Egerton Ryerson and His Times,* edited by Neil McDonald and Alf Chaiton, 221–53. Toronto: Macmillan 1978

Davin, Anna. "Working or Helping? London Working-Class Children in the Domestic Economy." In *Households and the World Economy,* edited by Joan Smith, Immanuel Maurice Wallerstein, and Hans-Dieter Evers, 215–32. Beverly Hills: Sage 1984

Dawes, Albert. "The New Coal Raising and Screening Arrangements at Jubilee Colliery, Sydney Mines, Nova Scotia." *Transactions of the Canadian Institute of Mining and Metallurgy,* 1921: 299–308

Den Otter, A.A. *Civilizing the West: The Galts and the Development of Western Canada*. Edmonton: University of Alberta Press 1982
- "Railways and Alberta's Coal Problem, 1880–1960." In *Western Canada: Past and Present*, edited by A.W. Rasporich, 84–98. Calgary: McClelland and Stewart West 1975
- "Sir Alexander Galt, the Canadian Government and Alberta's Coal." In Canadian Historical Association, *Historical Papers/Communications historiques*, 1973: 21–42
- "A Social History of the Alberta Coal Branch." MA thesis, University of Alberta 1967
Dick, W.J. "Coal Problems of Alberta." *Transactions of the Canadian Institute of Mining and Metallurgy*, 1936: 573–84
- *The Conservation of Coal in Canada with Notes on the Principal Coal Mines*. Ottawa: Commission of Conservation 1914
- "An Economic Study of Coal Mining in Alberta and South Eastern British Columbia." *Transactions of the Canadian Institute of Mining and Metallurgy*, 1923: 133–91
Dickson, James. "Submarine Coal Mining at Nanaimo, Vancouver Island, British Columbia." *Transactions of the Canadian Institute of Mining and Metallurgy*, 1935: 465–77
Dirks, Patricia. "'Getting a Grip on Harry': Canada's Methodists Respond to the 'Big Boy' Problem, 1900–1925." *Canadian Methodist Historical Society Papers*, 1989: 67–82
Dix, Keith. *Work Relations in the Coal Industry: The Hand-Loading Era, 1880–1930*. Morgantown, W.Va.: Institute for Labor Studies, West Virginia University 1977
- "Work Relations in the Coal Industry: The Handloading Era, 1880–1930." In *Case Studies in the Labor Process*, edited by Andrew Zimbalist, 156–69. New York: Monthly Review Press 1979
Dobson, George H. *A Pamphlet Compiled and Issued under the Auspices of the Boards of Trade of Pictou and Cape Breton on the Coal Industry of the Dominion, its Relation to the Iron, Shipping and Carrying Trade of Canada*. Ottawa: Maclean, Roger and Company 1879
Dodd, Dianne. "Advice to Parents: The Blue Books, Helen MacMurchy, MD, and the Federal Department of Health, 1920–34." *Canadian Bulletin of Medical History/Bulletin canadien d'histoire de la medicine* 8, no. 2 (1991): 203–30
Doe, J.S. "The Practical Application of Electricity to Coal Mines." *Canadian Mining Review*, 1891: 162
Dominion Bureau of Statistics. *Coal Statistics for Canada for the Calendar Year 1927*. Ottawa: F.A. Acland, King's Printer 1928
Dominion Bureau of Statistics. *Coal Statistics for Canada for the Calendar Year 1939*. Ottawa: Edmond Cloutier, King's Printer 1941
Douglass, Dave. "The Durham Pitman." In *Miners, Quarrymen and Saltworkers*, edited by Raphael Samuel, 205–95. London: Routledge and Kegan Paul 1977

Dowling, D.B. "Notes on the Progress of Development Work in Coal Areas of Alberta and Saskatchewan." *Transactions of the Canadian Mining Institute*, 1912: 354–63

Doyle, Andrew. "Reply of Mr. Doyle to Miss Rye's Report on the Emigration of Pauper Children." In *British Parliamentary Papers: Papers Relating to Canada 1875–77*. Vol. 28, edited by P. Ford, 489–504. Shannon: Irish University Press 1970

– "Report to the Right Honourable the President of the Local Government Board, by Andrew Doyle, Esquire, Local Government Inspector, as to the Emigration of Pauper Children to Canada." In *British Parliamentary Papers: Papers Relating to Canada 1875–77*. Vol. 28, edited by P. Ford, 259–300. Shannon: Irish University Press, 1970

Drummond, Robert. "The Beginnings of Trade Unionism in Nova Scotia." In New Glasgow *Evening News*, 7 July 1924, 5.

– *Minerals and Mining, Nova Scotia*. Stellarton: Mining Record Office 1918

Duckham, Baron Frederick. *History of the Scottish Coal Industry.* Vol. 1, *A Social and Industrial History, 1700–1815*. Newton Abbot: David and Charles 1970

Dumont, Micheline. "Des garderies au 19e siècle: les salles d'asile des sœurs Grises à Montréal." *Revue d'histoire de l'amérique française* 34, no. 1 (juin 1980): 27–55

Dunlop, O. Jocelyn. *English Apprenticeship and Child Labour: A History.* London: Unwin 1912

Earle, Michael. "The Coalminers and Their 'Red' Union: The Amalgamated Mine Workers of Nova Scotia, 1932–1936." *Labour/Le Travail* 22 (Fall 1988): 99–137

–, ed. *Workers and the State in Twentieth Century Nova Scotia*. Fredericton: Acadiensis Press 1989

Earle, Michael, and H. Gamberg. "The United Mine Workers and the Coming of the CCF to Cape Breton." *Acadiensis* 19, no. 1 (Fall 1989): 3–26

Early, Frances H. "The French-Canadian Family Economy and Standard of Living in Lowell, Massachusetts, 1870." *Journal of Family History* 7, no. 2 (Summer 1982): 180–99

Eid, Nadia F. *Le clergé et le pouvoir politique au Québec: une analyse de l'idéologie ultramontaine au milieu du XIXe siècle*. Montréal: Hurtubise HMH 1978

Elections British Columbia. *An Electoral History of British Columbia, 1871–1986*. Victoria: Elections British Columbia 1988

Engels, Friedrich. *The Condition of the Working Class in England*. Stanford: Stanford University Press 1968 [1845]

Fauteux, Joseph-Noël. *Essai sur l'industrie au Canada sous le Régime français*. Québec: Proulx 1927

Fergusson, C.B. *W.S. Fielding: The Mantle of Howe*. Windsor: Lancelot 1970

Fielding, W.S. "The Coal Mines of Nova Scotia: The Government's Scheme for Extending the Coal Trade." Halifax: Nova Scotia Printing Co. 1893

Fingard, Judith. *The Dark Side of Life in Victorian Halifax*. Porter's Lake, N.S.: Pottersfield Press 1989

- "The Winter's Tale: The Seasonal Contours of Pre-Industrial Poverty in British North America, 1815–1860." In Canadian Historical Association, *Historical Papers/Communications historiques,* 1974: 65–94
Forbes, Charles. *Vancouver Island, Its Resources and Capabilities as a Colony.* Victoria, B.C.: Colonial Government 1862
Forsey, Eugene. *Economic and Social Aspects of the Nova Scotia Coal Industry.* Toronto: Macmillan 1926
- "A Note on the Dominion Factory Bills of the Eighteen-Eighties." *Canadian Journal of Economic and Political Science* 13 (1947): 580–3
- *Trade Unions in Canada 1812–1902.* Toronto: University of Toronto Press 1982
Frank, David. "The Cape Breton Coal Industry and the Rise and Fall of the British Empire Steel Corporation." *Acadiensis* 7, no. 1 (Autumn 1977): 3–34
- "The Cape Breton Coal Miners, 1917–1926." PhD dissertation, Dalhousie University 1979
- "Class Conflict in the Coal Industry: Cape Breton 1922." In *Essays in Canadian Working Class History,* edited by G.S. Kealey and Peter Warrian, 161–84. Toronto: McClelland and Stewart 1976
- "Coal Masters and Coal Miners: The 1922 Strike and the Roots of Class Conflict in the Cape Breton Coal Industry." MA thesis, Dalhousie University 1974
- "Company Town/Labour Town: Local Government in the Cape Breton Coal Towns, 1917–1926." *Histoire sociale/Social History* 14, no. 27 (May 1981): 177–96
- "Contested Terrain: Workers' Control in the Cape Breton Coal Mines in the 1920s." In *On the Job: Confronting the Labour Process in Canada,* edited by Craig Heron and Robert Storey, 102–23. Montreal and Kingston: McGill-Queen's University Press 1986
- "The Miner's Financier: Women in the Cape Breton Coal Towns, 1917." *Atlantis* 8, no. 2 (Spring 1983): 137–43
- "Richard Smith." *Dictionary of Canadian Biography, 1861–1870* Vol. 9, 730–2. Toronto: University of Toronto Press 1976
- "Tradition and Culture in the Cape Breton Mining Community in the Early Twentieth Century." In *Cape Breton at 200: Historical Essays in Honour of the Island's Bicentennial, 1775–1985,* edited by Kenneth Donovan, 203–18. Sydney: University College of Cape Breton Press 1985
- "The Trials of James B. McLachlan." In Canadian Historical Association, *Historical Papers/Communications historiques,* 1983: 208–25
Frank, David, and John Manley. "The Sad March to the Right: J.B. McLachlan's Resignation from the Communist Party of Canada, 1936." *Labour/Le Travail* 30 (Fall 1992): 115–31
Frank, David, and Nolan Reilly. "The Emergence of the Socialist Movement in the Maritimes, 1899–1916." *Labour/Le Travailleur* 4 (1979): 85–113
Freeman, Arnold James. *Boy Life and Labour: The Manufacture of Inefficiency.* London: P.S. King and Son 1914

Gaffield, Chad. "Boom and Bust: The Demography and Economy of the Lower Ottawa Valley in the Nineteenth Century." In Canadian Historical Association, *Historical Papers/Communications historiques*, 1982: 172–95

– "Canadian Families in Cultural Context: Hypotheses from the Mid-Nineteenth Century." In Canadian Historical Association, *Historical Papers/Communications historiques*, 1979: 48–70

– "Children, Schooling and Family Reproduction in Nineteenth-Century Ontario." *Canadian Historical Review* 72, no. 2 (June 1991): 157–91

– "Labouring and Learning in Nineteenth-Century Canada: Children in the Changing Process of Family Reproduction." In *Dimensions of Childhood: Essays on the History of Children and Youth in Canada*, edited by Russell Smandych, Gordon Dodds, and Alvin Esau, 13–27. Winnipeg: Legal Research Institute of the University of Manitoba 1991

– *Language, Schooling, and Cultural Conflict: The Origins of the French-Language Controversy in Ontario*. Montreal and Kingston: McGill-Queen's University Press 1987

– "Schooling, the Economy and Rural Society in Nineteenth-Century Ontario." In *Childhood and Family in Canadian History*, edited by Joy Parr, 69–92. Toronto: McClelland and Stewart 1982

Gaffield, Chad, and David Levine. "Dependency and Adolescence on the Canadian Frontier: Orillia, Ontario in the Mid-19th Century." *History of Education Quarterly* 18, no. 1 (Spring 1978): 35–48

Gagan, David, and Rosemary Gagan, "Working-Class Standards of Living in Late-Victorian Urban Ontario: A Review of the Miscellaneous Evidence on the Quality of Material Life." In *Journal of the Canadian Historical Association*, 1990: 171–93

Gagan, Rosemary R. *A Sensitive Independence: Canadian Methodist Women Missionaries in Canada and the Orient, 1881–1925*. Montreal and Kingston: McGill-Queen's University Press 1992

Gagnon, Louise. *L'apparition des modes enfantines au Québec*. Québec: Institut québécois de recherche sur la culture 1992

Gallacher, Daniel T. "John Muir." *Dictionary of Canadian Biography, 1881–1890*. Vol. 11, 626–7. Toronto: University of Toronto Press 1982

– "Men, Money, Machines: Studies Concerning Colliery Operations and Factors of Production in British Columbia's Coal Industry to 1891." PhD dissertation, University of British Columbia 1979

– "Robert Dunsmuir." *Dictionary of Canadian Biography, 1881–1890*. Vol. 11, 290–4. Toronto: University of Toronto Press 1982

Galloway, Robert. *Annals of Coal Mining and the Coal Trade*. 2 vols. Newton Abbot: David and Charles Reprints 1971

Gerriets, Marilyn. "The Impact of the General Mining Association on the Nova Scotia Coal Industry, 1826–1850." *Acadiensis* 21, no. 1 (Autumn 1991): 54–84

Gesner, Abraham. *The Industrial Resources of Nova Scotia*. Halifax: A. and W. MacKinlay 1849

Gidney, Norman. "From Coal to Forest Products: The Changing Resource Base of Nanaimo, B.C." *Urban History Review* 1 (June 1978): 18–47

Gidney, R.D, and W.P.J. Millar. *Inventing Secondary Education: The Rise of the High School in Nineteenth-Century Ontario.* Montreal and Kingston: McGill-Queen's University Press 1990

Gilbert, Alexander Glen. *From Montreal to the Maritime Provinces and Back.* Montreal: Montreal Print and Pub. Co. 1867

Gill, Pauline. *Les enfants de Duplessis.* Montréal: Libre expression 1991

Gillis, Hugh B. "The Use of Mechanical Loading Machines in Mines." *Transactions of the Canadian Mining Institute,* 1921: 309–16

Gillis, John R. *Youth and History: Tradition and Change in European Age Relations, 1770–Present.* New York: Academic 1981

Gilpin, Edwin. "Coal Mining in Nova Scotia." *Transactions of the Canadian Society of Civil Engineers* 2 (1888): 350–400

– "Coal Mining in Pictou County." *Transactions of the Royal Society of Canada* 4 (1896): 167–79

– "Notes on Nova Scotia Pit Waters." Halifax: n.p. [1877]

– "Presidential Address." Nova Scotian Institute of Science, *Proceedings for 1896–7,* 1897: lxxix–lxxxv

– "Underground certificates in Nova Scotian coal-mines: a paper read before the Institution of Mining Engineers, annual general meeting at Birmingham, September 13th, 1898." London and Newcastle-upon-Tyne: Andrew Reid and Company, Ltd 1899

Gleason, Mona. "Psychology and the Construction of the 'Normal' Family in Postwar Canada, 1945–60." *Canadian Historical Review* 78, no. 3 (September 1997): 442–77

Gooderich, Carter. *The Miner's Freedom: A Study of the Working Life in a Changing Industry.* Boston: Marshall Jones Company 1925

Gouett, Paul M. "The Halifax Orphan House 1752–1787." *Nova Scotia Historical Quarterly* 6, no. 3 (September 1976): 281–91

Gough, Barry M. "Fort Rupert, Its Coal and Its Spar Trade." In *The Company on the Coast,* edited by E. Blanche Norcross, 29–41. Nanaimo: Nanaimo Historical Society 1983

Graff, Harvey J. "Remaking Growing Up: Nineteenth-Century America." *Histoire sociale/Social History* 24, no. 47 (May 1991): 35–59

Graham, Charles. "The Problems of the Vancouver Island Coal Industry." *Transactions of the Canadian Institute of Mining and Metallurgy,* 1924: 456–77

Grant, John Webster. *A Profusion of Spires: Religion in Nineteenth-Century Ontario.* Toronto: University of Toronto Press 1988

Grant, W. Colquhoun. *Description of Vancouver Island by its First Colonist.* London: n.p. 1857

Gray, Francis W. *The Coal Fields and Coal Industry of Eastern Canada: A General Survey and Description.* Ottawa: Department of Mines 1917

- "The Development of the Coal Industry in Canada from 1920 to 1935." *Transactions of the Canadian Institute of Mining and Metallurgy,* March 1936, 217–34
- "Fifty Years of the Dominion Coal Company." *Dalhousie Review* 22 (1942–43): 461–19
- "Mining Coal under the Sea in Nova Scotia." *Transactions of the Canadian Institute of Mining and Metallurgy,* 1927: 986–1176
Green, Raoul. "The Frank Disaster." *Canadian Mining Review,* 1903: 103–110
- "Methods of Mining in Crowsnest Pass District, Alberta." *Transactions of the Canadian Mining Institute,* 1917: 400–8
Greer, Allan. "The Sunday Schools of Upper Canada." *Ontario History* 67 (September 1975): 169–84
Griffiths, N.E.S. *The Splendid Vision: Centennial History of the National Council of Women of Canada, 1893–1993.* Ottawa: Carleton University Press 1993
Grove, Allan and Ross Lambertson. "Pawns of the Powerful: The Politics of Litigation in the Union Colliery Case." BC *Studies* 103 (Autumn 1994): 3–31
Guildford, Janet. "Coping with De-industrialization: The Nova Scotia Department of Technical Education, 1907–1930." *Acadiensis* 16, no. 2 (Spring 1987): 69–84
Haines, Michael R. "Fertility, Marriage, and Occupation in the Pennsylvania Anthracite Region, 1850–1880." *Journal of Family History* 2 (1977): 28–55
- "Fertility, Nuptiality, and Occupation: A Study of Coal Mining Populations and Regions in England and Wales in the Mid-Nineteenth Century." *Journal of Multidisciplinary History* 8, no. 2 (Autumn 1977): 245–80
Hair, Paul Edward Hedley. "A Social History of British Coalminers, 1800–1845." PhD dissertation, University of London 1955
Haliburton, T.C. *A Historical and Statistical Account of Nova Scotia.* Halifax: J. Howe 1829
Hamel, Thérèse. "L'Obligation scolaire au Québec: enjeu pour le mouvement syndical et agricole." *Labour/Le Travail* 17 (Spring 1986): 83–102
- "Obligation scolaire et travail des enfants au Québec, 1900–1950." *Revue d'histoire de l'amérique française* 38, no. 1 (été 1984): 39–58
Hamilton, Sally Anne. "A Historical Geography of the Coal Mining Industry of the City of Edmonton." MA thesis, University of Alberta 1971
Hamilton, William B. "Society and Schools in Nova Scotia." In *Canadian Education: A History,* edited by J. Donald Wilson, Robert M. Stamp, and Louis Philippe Audet, 86–105. Scarborough: Prentice-Hall 1970
Hammond, J.L., and Barbara Hammond. *The Bleak Age.* London: Penguin Books 1947
- *The Town Labourer, 1760–1832.* New York: Augustus M. Kelley 1967
Hardie, W.D.L. "Machine Mining at Lethbridge, N.W.T." *Canadian Mining Review,* 1899: 245–8

Hardy, Jean-Pierre, and David-Thiéry Ruddel. *Les apprentis artisans à Québec.* Montréal: Presses de l'Université du Québec 1977

Harper, Marjory. "Cossar's Colonists: Juvenile Migration to New Brunswick in the 1920s." *Acadiensis* 28, no. 1 (Autumn 1998): 47–65

Harrigan, Patrick. "The Schooling of Boys and Girls in Canada." *Journal of Social History* 23, no. 4 (Summer 1990): 803–16

Harrison, Brian. "Class and Gender in Modern British Labour History." *Past and Present*, no. 124 (August 1989): 121–58

Harrison, Phyllis, ed. *The Home Children: Their Personal Stories.* Winnipeg: Watson and Dwyer 1979

Harrison, Royden, ed. *Independent Collier: The Coal Miner as Archetypal Proletarian Reconsidered.* Hassocks, Sussex: Harvester 1978

Hartmann, Heidi. "Capitalism, Patriarchy and Job Segregation by Sex." In *Capitalist Patriarchy and the Case for Socialist Feminism*, edited by Zillah R. Eisenstein, 206–47. New York: Monthly Review Press 1979

Harvey, Katherine. "To Love, Honour and Obey: Wife-Battering in Working-Class Montreal, 1869–79." *Urban History Review* 19, no. 2 (October 1990): 128–40

Hatch, Alison J., and Curt T. Griffiths. "Child Saving Postponed: The Impact of the Juvenile Delinquents Act on the Processing of Youth Offenders in Vancouver." In *Dimensions of Childhood: Essays on the History of Children and Youth in Canada*, edited by Russell Smandych, Gordon Dodds, and Alvin Esau, 233–66. Winnipeg: Legal Research Institute of the University of Manitoba 1991

Hazlitt, William C. *British Columbia and Vancouver Island.* London: G. Routledge 1858

Heeley, William G. "Methods of Haulage in Coal Mines." *Transactions of the Canadian Institute of Mining*, 1925: 371–86

Heesom, Alan. "The Coal Mines Act of 1842, Social Reform, and Social Control." *Historical Journal* 24, no. 1 (1981): 69–88

Hendrick, Harry. *Images of Youth: Age, Class, and the Male Youth Problem, 1880–1920.* Oxford: Clarendon Press 1990

Herd, W. "Notes on Working Two Coal Seams Lying Near One Another." *Transactions of the Mining Society of Nova Scotia* 19 (1914–15): 97–102

Heron, Craig. *The Canadian Labour Movement: A Short History.* 2nd ed. Toronto: James Lorimer 1996

– "The High School and the Household Economy in Working-Class Hamilton, 1890–1940." *Historical Studies in Education/Revue d'histoire de l'éducation* 7, no. 2 (Fall 1995): 217–60

Heywood, Colin. *Childhood in Nineteenth-Century France: Work, Health and Education among the "classes populaires."* Cambridge: Cambridge University Press 1988

– "The Market for Child Labour in Nineteenth Century France." *History* 66, no. 216 (February 1981): 34–49

Hickey, S.H.F. *Workers in Imperial Germany: The Miners of the Ruhr.* Oxford: Clarendon 1985

Hind, Henry Youle. "Report on Sydney Colliery, Cape Breton." Halifax: n.p. 1871

- "Report on the Point Aconi Coal Property, Sydney Coal Field, Cape Breton." Halifax: n.p. 1870

- "Report on the Victoria Coal Mines at Low Point, Sydney, Cape Breton." Halifax: n.p. 1867

- "A Sketch of the Mineral Resources of Part of Cumberland Co., Nova Scotia." Halifax: C. Annand 1872

Hinde, John R. "'Stout Ladies and Amazons': Women in the British Columbia Coal Mining Community of Ladysmith, 1912–1914." BC *Studies,* no. 114 (Summer 1997): 33–57

Historical Review of Coal Mining. London: Fleetway Press for the Mining Association of Great Britain [1924]

Hobsbawm, E.J. *The Age of Empire, 1875–1914.* New York: Pantheon Books 1987

Holden, James. "The Relation of the Size of the Car and Gauge of the Track to the Economic Working of a Coal Seam." *Transactions of the Canadian Mining Institute,* 1916: 242–6

Hopkins, Eric. "The Victorians and Child Labour." *The Historian,* no. 48 (Winter 1995): 10–14

Hopkins, J. Castell. "Youthful Canada, and the Boys' Brigade." *The Canadian Magazine* 4, no. 6 (April 1895): 551–6

Hornsby, Stephen J. *Nineteenth-Century Cape Breton: A Historical Geography.* Montreal and Kingston: McGill-Queen's University Press 1992

"Horses in the Coal Mines." *Cape Breton's Magazine,* no. 32 (1983): 36–43

Houston, Susan E. "Late Victorian Juvenile Reform: A Contribution to the Study of Educational History." In *Monographs in Education.* Vol. 5, *Approaches to Educational History,* edited by David C. Jones, Nancy M. Sheehan, Robert M. Stamp, and Neil G. McDonald, 7–23. Winnipeg: University of Manitoba 1981

- "The Role of the Criminal Law in Redefining 'Youth' in Mid-Nineteenth-Century Upper Canada." *History of Education Review* 23, no. 3, and *Historical Studies in Education/Revue d'Histoire de l'Éducation* 6, no. 3 (1994): 39–55

- "The 'Waifs and Strays' of a Late Victorian City: Juvenile Delinquents in Toronto." In *Childhood and Family in Canadian History,* edited by Joy Parr, 129–42. Toronto: McClelland and Stewart 1982

Houston, Susan E., and Alison Prentice. *Schooling and Scholars in Nineteenth-Century Ontario.* Toronto: University of Toronto Press 1988

Hovey, H.C. "Coal Dust as an Element of Danger in Mining; Shown by the Explosion in the Albion Mines, Nov. 12, 1880." In *Proceedings of the American Association for the Advancement of Science* 30 (Cincinnati Meeting, August 1881).

Howe, Joseph. *Western and Eastern Rambles,* edited by M.G. Parks. Toronto: University of Toronto Press 1973

Howell, Colin D. *Northern Sandlots: A Social History of Maritime Baseball.* Toronto: University of Toronto Press 1995

Howell, David, and Peter Lindsey. "Social Gospel and the Young Boy Problem, 1895–1925." *Canadian Journal of the History of Sport/Revue canadienne de l'histoire des sports* 17, no. 1 (May 1986): 75–87

Hudson, Joseph G.S. "Investigation of the Coal Mine Disaster at Bellevue Mine near Frank, Alberta." Canada. *Sessional Papers,* 1911, 26a.

– "Notes on Coal Cutting Machinery at the Collieries of the Dominion Coal Company." *Canadian Mining Review,* 1894: 156

Hughes, Herbert W. *A Text-Book of Coal-Mining for the Use of Colliery Managers and Others.* 4th ed. London: Charles Griffin and Company 1901

Humphries, Jane. "Protective Legislation, the Capitalist State, and Working Class Men: The Case of the 1842 Mines Regulation Act." *Feminist Review* 7 (Spring 1981): 1–33

Humphries, Stephen. *Hooligans or Rebels? An Oral History of Working-Class Childhood and Youth, 1889–1939.* Oxford: Basil Blackwell 1981

Hurl, Lorna F. "Restricting Child Factory Labour in Late Nineteenth Century Ontario." *Labour/Le Travail* 21 (Spring 1988): 87–121

Hurt, J.S. *Elementary Schooling and the Working Classes, 1860–1918.* London: Routledge and Kegan Paul 1979

Hyde, Marcus L. "Mine Car Design." *Transactions of the Canadian Institute of Mining and Metallurgy,* 1916: 226–41

"Importance of the Canadian Coal Industry." N.p., 1897

Intercolonial Coal Mining Co. "Reports on the Property of the Intercolonial Coal Mining Company Situated in Pictou, Nova Scotia." Halifax: J. Lovell 1866

Inwood, Kris E. "Local control, resources, and the Nova Scotia Steel and Coal Company." In Canadian Historical Association, *Historical Papers/Communications historiques,* 1986: 254–82

"Is Coal Losing Ground as a Fuel?" *Western Canadian Coal Review* 6, no. 12 (December 1923): 14.

Jaffray, William. "A Day at the Waterloo Poor House and What I Learned There." Lecture at Berlin Town Hall on 20 June 1870, reprinted in *Waterloo Historical Society Annual* 57 (1969): 72–8

Jean, Dominique. "Le recul du travail des enfants au Québec entre 1940 et 1960: une explication des conflits des familles pauvres et l'État providence." *Labour/Le Travail* 24 (Fall 1989): 91–129

John, Angela. *By the Sweat of Their Brow: Women Workers at Victorian Coal Mines.* London: Croom Helm 1980

Johnson, Moses. "Notes on Operating Conditions of the Lethbridge Collieries." *Transactions of the Canadian Mining Institute,* 1919: 296–300

Johnson, Walter R. *The Coal Trade of British America (with researches on the characters and practical values of American and Foreign Coals).* Washington: Taylor and Maury 1850

Johnston, John. "Description of Haulage System Installed to take the Place of Horses at No. 3 and No. 4 Collieries." *Journal of the Mining Society of Nova Scotia* 15 (1910–11): 89–92

– "Submarine Coal Mining." *Transactions of the Mining Society of Nova Scotia* 13 (1908–9): 47–50

Johnstone, Bill. *Coal Dust in My Blood: The Autobiography of a Coal Miner.* Victoria: British Columbia Provincial Museum 1980

Jones, Andrew, and Leonard Rutman. *In the Children's Aid: J.J. Kelso and Child Welfare in Ontario.* Toronto: University of Toronto Press 1981

Jones, David C. "'We can't live on air all the time': Country Life and the Prairie Child." In *Studies in Childhood History: A Canadian Perspective,* edited by Patricia T. Rooke and R.L. Schnell, 185–202. Calgary: Detselig Enterprises 1982

Jones, Dot. "Serfdom and Slavery: Women's Work in Wales." In *Class, Community and the Labour Movement: Wales and Canada, 1850–1930,* edited by Deian R. Hopkin and Gregory S. Kealey, 86–100. N.p.: Society for Welsh Labour History and the Canadian Committee on Labour History 1989

Joyal, Renée. "L'acte concernant les écoles d'industrie (1869): Une mesure de prophylaxie sociale dans un Québec en voie d'urbanisation." *Revue d'histoire de l'amérique française* 50, no. 2 (autumne 1996): 227–40

– "L'évolution des modes de contrôle de l'autorité parentale et son impact sur les relations entre parents et enfants dans la société québécoise." *International Journal of Canadian Studies/Revue internationale d'études canadiennes,* Winter 1993: 73–83

Joyal, Renée, et Carole Chatillon. "La Loi québécoise de protection de l'enfance de 1944: génèse et avortement d'une réforme." *Histoire sociale/ Social History* 27, no. 53 (May 1994): 33–63

Karas, F.P. "Labour and Coal in the Crow's Nest Pass, 1925–1935." MA thesis, University of Calgary 1972

Katz, Michael B., and Ian E. Davey. "Youth and Early Industrialization in a Canadian City." In *Turning Points, Historical and Sociological Essays on the Family,* edited by John Demos and S.S. Bocock, S81–S119. Chicago: University of Chicago Press 1978

Kealey, Gregory, ed. *Canada Investigates Industrialism: The Royal Commission on the Relations of Labor and Capital, 1889.* Toronto: University of Toronto Press 1973

–, ed. *Class, Gender and Region: Essays in Canadian Historical Sociology.* St John's: Committee on Canadian Labour History 1988

– "Labour and Working-Class History in Canada: Prospects in the 1980s." *Labour/Le Travail* 7 (Spring 1981): 67–94

– *Toronto Workers Respond to Industrial Capitalism, 1867–1892.* Toronto: University of Toronto Press 1980

Kealey, Gregory S., and Peter Warrian, eds. *Essays in Canadian Working Class History.* Toronto: McClelland and Stewart 1976

MacFie, Matthew. *Vancouver Island and British Columbia*. London: Longman, Green, Longman, Roberts, and Green 1865

Macgillivray, Don. "Cape Breton in the 1920's: A Community Besieged." In *Essays in Cape Breton History*, edited by B.D. Tennyson, 49–67. Windsor, N.S.: Lancelot 1973

– "Henry Melville Whitney Comes to Cape Breton: The Saga of a Guilded Age Entrepreneur." *Acadiensis* 9, no. 1 (Autumn 1979): 44–70

– "Industrial Unrest in Cape Breton, 1919–1925." MA thesis, University of New Brunswick 1971

– "Military Aid to the Civil Power: The Cape Breton Experience in the 1920's." *Acadiensis* 3, no. 1 (Autumn 1973): 45–64

Macgillivray, Don, and Brian Tennyson, eds. *Cape Breton Historical Essays*. Sydney: College of Cape Breton Press 1980

McIntosh, Robert. "The Boys in the Nova Scotian Coal Mines, 1873–1923." *Acadiensis* 16, no. 2 (Spring 1987): 35–50

McKavanagh, T.J. "Electricity in the Mines." *Transactions of the Mining Society of Nova Scotia* 13 (1908–9): 75–82

McKay, Ian. "'By Wisdom, Wile or War': The Provincial Workmen's Association and the Struggle for Working-Class Independence in Nova Scotia, 1879–97." *Labour/Le Travail* 18 (Fall 1986): 13–62

– "The Crisis of Dependent Development: Class Conflict in the Nova Scotian Coalfields, 1872–1876." In *Class, Gender, and Region: Essays in Canadian Historical Sociology*, edited by Gregory S. Kealey, 9–48. St John's: Committee on Canadian Labour History 1988

– "Industry, Work and Community in the Cumberland Coalfields, 1848–1927." PhD dissertation, Dalhousie University 1983

– "The Realm of Uncertainty: The Experience of Work in the Cumberland Coal Mines, 1873–1927." *Acadiensis* 16, no. 1 (Autumn 1986): 3–57

– "Strikes in the Maritimes, 1901–1914." *Acadiensis* 13, no. 1 (Autumn 1983): 3–46

McKendrick, Neil. "Home Demand and Economic Growth: A New View of the Role of Women and Children in the Industrial Revolution." In *Historical Perspectives: Studies in English Thought and Society in Honour of J.H. Plumb*, edited by Neil McKendrick, 152–210. London: Europa 1974

Mackintosh, Margaret. "The Social Significance of Child Labour in Agriculture and Industry." Ottawa: Canadian Council on Child Welfare 1924

McKnight, H.A. "The Great Colliery Explosion at Springhill, Nova Scotia, February 21, 1891." Springhill: H.A. McKnight 1891

McLaren, Angus. *Our Own Master Race: Eugenics in Canada, 1885–1945*. Toronto: McClelland and Stewart 1990

McLaren, Katherine I. "'The Proper Education for All Classes': Compulsory Schooling and Reform in Nova Scotia, 1890–1930." MEd thesis, Dalhousie University 1984

McLennan, J.S. "The Screening of Soft Coal." *Transactions of the Canadian Society of Civil Engineers* 4 (1890): 82–96

MacLeod, David. "'A Live Vaccine': The YMCA and Male Adolescence in the United States and Canada 1870–1920." *Histoire sociale/Social History* 11, no. 21 (May 1978): 5–25

MacLeod, Donald. "Colliers, Colliery Safety and Workplace Control: The Nova Scotian Experience, 1873–1910." In Canadian Historical Association, *Historical Papers/Communications historiques*, 1983: 226–53

– "Miners, Mining Men and Mining Reform: Changing the Technology of Nova Scotian Gold Mines and Collieries." PhD dissertation: University of Toronto 1981

– "Practicality Ascendant: The Origins and Establishment of Technical Education in Nova Scotia." *Acadiensis* 15, no. 2 (Spring 1986): 53–92

McLeod, J.A. "Haulage by Electric Storage-Battery Locomotives." *Transactions of the Canadian Mining Institute*, 1920: 196–201

Macmillan, Charles J. "Trade Unionism in District 18, 1900–1925: A Case Study." MA thesis, University of Alberta 1969

Macnab, Frances. *British Columbia for Settlers: Its Mines, Trade and Agriculture.* London: Chapman and Hall 1898

MacNeil, A.S., and Joseph Kalbheen. "Advances in Mechanization in Collieries of the Sydney Coal Field." *Canadian Mining and Metallurgical Bulletin*, June 1932: 289–302

McNeil, Bill. *Voice of the Pioneer.* Toronto: Macmillan 1978

MacPherson, Ian. *Each for All: A History of the Co-operative Movement in English Canada, 1900–1945.* Toronto: Macmillan of Canada in Association with the Institute of Canadian Studies, Carleton University 1979

– "Patterns in the Maritime Cooperative Movement, 1900–1945." *Acadiensis* 5, no. 1 (Autumn 1975): 67–83

Makahonuk, Glen. "Labour Relations in the Saskatchewan Coal Mines during the 1930s." MA thesis, University of Saskatchewan 1976

– "Trade Unions in the Saskatchewan Coal Industry, 1907–1945." *Saskatchewan History* 31, no. 2 (Spring 1978): 51–68

Mark-Lawson, Jane, and Anne Witz. "From 'family labour' to 'family wage'? The case of women's labour in nineteenth-century coalmining." *Social History* 12, no. 2 (May 1988): 151–74

Marks, Lynne. *Revivals and Roller Rinks: Religion, Leisure, and Identity in Late-Nineteenth-Century Small-Town Ontario.* Toronto: University of Toronto Press 1996

Marr, Lucille M. "Church Teen Clubs, Feminized Organization? Tuxis Boys, Trail Rangers, and Canadian Girls in Training, 1919–1939." *Historical Studies in Education/Revue d'histoire de l'éducation* 3 (1991): 249–67

– "Sunday School Teaching: A Women's Enterprise. A Case Study from the Canadian Methodist, Presbyterian and United Church Tradition,

1919–1939." *Histoire sociale/Social History* 26, no. 52 (November 1993): 329–44

Marshall, David B. *Secularizing the Faith: Canadian Protestant Clergy and the Crisis of Belief, 1850–1940.* Toronto: University of Toronto Press 1992

Marshall, Dominique. "The Cold War, Canada, and the United Nations Declaration of the Rights of the Child." In *Canada and the Early Cold War, 1943–1957,* edited by Greg Donaghy, 183–212. Ottawa: Department of Foreign Affairs and International Trade 1998

– "The Language of Children's Rights, the Formation of the Welfare State, and the Democratic Experience of Poor Families in Quebec, 1940–1955." *Canadian Historical Review* 78, no. 3 (September 1997): 409–41

– *Aux origines sociales de l'État providence: Familles québécoises, obligations scolaires et allocations familiales, 1940–1955.* Montréal: Les Presses de l'université de Montréal 1998

– "Reconstruction Politics, the Canadian Welfare State and the Ambiguity of Children's Rights, 1940–1950." In *Uncertain Horizons: Canadians and Their World in 1945,* edited by Greg Donaghy, 261–83. Ottawa: Canadian Committee for the History of the Second World War 1996

Martell, J.S. "Early Coal Mining in Nova Scotia." In *Essays in Cape Breton History,* edited by Donald Macgillivray and Brian Tennyson, 41–53. Sydney: College of Cape Breton Press 1980

Martin, R. Montgomery. *History of Nova Scotia, Cape Breton, the Sable Islands, New Brunswick, Prince Edward Island, the Bermudas, Newfoundland, etc.* London: Whittaker 1837

Marx, Karl. *Capital: A Critique of Political Economy.* Vol. 1. Moscow: Progress Publishers 1954

Mayne, Richard Charles. *Four Years in British Columbia and Vancouver Island.* London: John Murray 1862

Megaw, B.R.S. "Women Coal-Bearers in a Midlothian Mine." *Scottish Studies* 10, pt 1 (1965): 87–9

Michel, Joël. "Politique syndicale et conjoncture économique: La limitation de la production de charbon chez les mineurs européens au XIX siècle." *Le mouvement social,* no. 119 (avril–juin 1982): 63–90

Mifflin, P.S. "A History of Trade Unionism in the Coal Mines of Nova Scotia." MA thesis, Catholic University of America 1951

Mill, John Stuart. *On Liberty: The Subjection of Women.* Ware, Hertfordshire: Wordsworth Editions 1996

Millward, Hugh. "The Development, Decline and Revival of Mining on the Sydney Coalfield." *Canadian Geographer* 28 (1984): 180–5

– "Mine Locations and the Sequence of Coal Exploitation on the Sydney Coalfield, 1720–1980." In *Cape Breton at 200: Historical Essays in Honour of the Island's Bicentennial 1785–1985,* edited by Kenneth Donovan, 183–202. Sydney: University of Cape Breton Press 1985

- "A Model of Coalfield Development." *Canadian Geographer* 29 (1985): 234–48

Mimeault, Mario. "Le capital industriel des pêches dans la baie de Gaspé de 1760 à 1866." *Acadiensis* 25, no. 1 (Autumn 1995): 33–53

Mitchell, Brian R. *The Economic Development of the British Coal Industry, 1800–1914*. Cambridge: Cambridge University Press 1984

Mitchell, J.C. "Early Mining of Coal in Glace Bay District, Cape Breton." *Canadian Mining Journal*, 1912: 547–51

Mitchinson, Wendy. "Early Women's Organizations and Social Reform: Prelude to the Welfare State." In *The 'Benevolent' State: The Growth of Welfare in Ontario*, edited by Alan Moscovitch and Jim Albert, 77–92. Toronto: Garamond Press 1987

- "The WCTU: 'For God, Home and Native Land': A Study in Nineteenth Century Feminism." In *A Not Unreasonable Claim: Women and Reform in Canada, 1880's–1920's*, edited by Linda Kealey, 151–67. Toronto: Women's Educational Press 1979

- "The YWCA and Reform in the Nineteenth Century." *Histoire sociale/Social History* 12, no. 24 (November 1979): 368–84

Moffatt, Ben Lawrence. "A Community of Working Men: The Residential Environment of Early Nanaimo, British Columbia, 1875–1891." MA thesis, University of British Columbia 1982

Moffatt, John. "A Coal Miner's Ears." *Canadian Mining Journal*, 1922: 413–4

Moogk, Peter N. "Apprenticeship Indentures: A Key to Artisan Life in New France." In Canadian Historical Association, *Historical Papers/Communications historiques*, 1971: 65–83

- "Apprenticeship of Edward Davis, an Abandoned Child, by the Town Wardens of Waterloo to Christian Schwartzentruber, A Farmer of Wilmot Township, 1 June 1839." *Waterloo Historical Society* [annual] 57 (1969): 80–1

- "'Les petits sauvages': Children of Eighteenth Century New France." In *Children and Family in Canadian History*, edited by Joy Parr, 17–43. Toronto: McClelland and Stewart 1982

Moorsom, W.S. *Letters from Nova Scotia: Comprising Sketches of a Young Country*. London: H. Colburn and R. Bentley 1830

Morrow, J.B. "The Preparation of Coal." *Transactions of the Canadian Institute of Mining and Metallurgy*, 1932: 412–30

Morrow, R.A.H. *The Story of the Springhill Disaster*. Saint John: R.A.H. Morrow 1891

Mortimer-Lamb, H. "The Coal Industry of Vancouver Island." *British Columbia Mining Record* 4, no. 2 (February 1898): 14–9, and no. 3 (March 1898): 29–32

Morton, Desmond. "Aid to the Civil Power: Use of the Canadian Militia in Support of Social Order, 1867–1914." *Canadian Historical Review* 51, no. 4 (December 1970): 407–25

- "The Cadet Movement in the Moment of Canadian Militarism, 1909–1914." *Journal of Canadian Studies/Revue des études canadiennes* 13, no. 2 (Summer 1978): 56–68

Morton, Desmond, with Terry Copp. *Working People: An Illustrated History of the Canadian Labour Movement.* Rev. ed. Ottawa: Deneau Publishers 1984

Morton, James. *In the Sea of Sterile Mountains: The Chinese in British Columbia.* Vancouver: J.J. Douglas 1973

Mouat, Jeremy. "The Politics of Coal: A Study of the Wellington Miners' Strike of 1890–91." *BC Studies* 77 (Spring 1988): 3–29

Moyles, R.G. "A Boy's Own View of Canada." *Canadian Children's Literature/ Littérature canadienne pour la jeunesse,* no. 34 (1984): 41–56

Muise, D.A. "The 1860s: Forging the Bonds of Union." In *The Atlantic Provinces in Confederation,* edited by E.R. Forbes and D.A. Muise, 13–47. Toronto: University of Toronto Press 1993

- "The GMA and the Nova Scotia Coal Industry." *Bulletin of Canadian Studies* 6, no. 2/7, no. 1 (Autumn 1983): 70–87

- "The Great Transformation: Changing the Urban Face of Nova Scotia, 1871–1921." *Nova Scotia Historical Review,* December 1991, 1–42

- "The Industrial Context of Inequality: Female Participation in Nova Scotia's Paid Labour Force, 1871–1921." *Acadiensis* 20, no. 2 (Spring 1991): 3–31

- "The Making of an Industrial Community: Cape Breton Coal Towns 1867–1900." In *Cape Breton Historical Essays,* edited by Don Macgillivray and Brian Tennyson, 76–94. Sydney: College of Cape Breton Press 1980

Muise, Delphin A., and Robert G. McIntosh. *Coal Mining in Canada: A Historical and Comparative Overview.* Ottawa: National Museum of Science and Technology 1996

Munro, John A. "British Columbia and the 'Chinese Evil': Canada's First Anti-Asiatic Immigration Law." *Journal of Canadian Studies* 6, no. 4 (November 1971): 42–51

Murphy, John. "Longwall Mining Operations in Jubilee Lower Seam, Sydney Mines, Nova Scotia." *Transactions of the Canadian Mining Institute,* 1921: 281–3

Murray, D.R. "The Cold Hand of Charity: The Court of Quarter Sessions and Poor Relief in the Niagara District, 1828–1841." In *Canadian Perspectives on Law and Society: Issues in Legal History,* edited by W.W. Pue and B. Wright, 179–206. Ottawa: Carleton University Press 1988

Musgrove, Frank. *Youth and the Social Order.* London: Routledge and Kegan Paul 1964

Myers, Sharon. "Revenge and Revolt: The Boys' Industrial Home of East Saint John in the Inter-War Period." In *Children's Voices in Atlantic Literature and Culture: Essays on Childhood,* edited by Hilary Thompson, 104–13. Guelph, Ont.: Canadian Children's Press 1995

Nardinelli, Clark. "Corporal Punishment and Children's Wages in Nine-teenth-Century Britain." *Explorations in Economic History* 19, no. 3 (July 1982): 283–95

Nasaw, David. *Children of the City: At Work and at Play.* New York: Oxford University Press 1985

National Council of Women of Canada. *Appendix to Women Workers of Canada Being the Reports and Discussions on the Laws for the Protection of Women and Children, and on Pernicious Literature at the Third Annual Meeting of the National Council of Women of Canada.* Montreal: n.p. 1896

– *Report of Sub-Committee on Laws for the Protection of Women and Children.* Toronto: n.p. May 1896

Neary, Peter. "The Bradley Report on Logging Operations in Newfoundland, 1934: A Suppressed Document." *Labour/Le Travail* 16 (Fall 1985): 193–232

Nef, J.U. *The Rise of the British Coal Industry (1550–1700).* London: Routledge 1932

Neff, Charlotte. "The Ontario Industrial Schools Act of 1874." *Canadian Journal of Family Law/Revue canadienne de droit familial* 12, no. 1 (1994): 171–208

New Brunswick. *Journals of the House of Assembly.* Fredericton: n.p. 1880–1930

Newsome, Eric. *The Coal Coast, 1835–1900: The History of Coal Mining in B.C.* Victoria: Orca Book Publishers 1989

Nicholson, J.C. "Past and Present Methods of Working No. 2 Mine, Spring-hill, Nova Scotia." *Canadian Mining Journal,* 1922: 468–70

Nicholson, Neil A. "Practical and Economical Mining." *Transactions of the Mining Society of Nova Scotia* 15 (1910–11): 83–7

Norcross, E. Blanche, ed. *The Company on the Coast.* Nanaimo: Nanaimo His-torical Society 1983

– *Nanaimo Retrospective: The First Century.* Nanaimo: Nanaimo Historical Society 1979

Norris, John. "The Vancouver Island Coal Mines, 1912–1914: A Study of an Organizational Strike." *BC Studies* 45 (1990): 56–72

North-West Territories. *The General Ordinances of the North-West Territories in Force September 1, 1905,* edited by Reginald Rimmer. Regina: John A. Reid, Government Printer 1907

– *Ordinances of the North-West Territories, 1899.* Regina: John A. Reid, Govern-ment Printer 1904

Nova Scotia. House of Assembly. *Debates and Proceedings for 1872.*

Nova Scotia. *Journals and Proceedings of the House of Assembly, 1859–1931. Mines Reports, 1858–1930*

Nova Scotia. *Journals and Proceedings of the House of Assembly of Nova Scotia, 1908.* "Report of Commission on Old Age Pensions and Miners' Relief Societies."

Nova Scotia. *Report of the Workmen's Compensation Board, 1917.* Halifax, King's Printer 1918

Nova Scotia. Royal Commission into Hours of Work. *Report*. Halifax 1910

Nova Scotia. Royal Commission Respecting the Coal Mines of the Province of Nova Scotia [Andrew Rae Duncan]. *Report*. Halifax: Minister of Public Works and Mines, King's Printer 1926

Nova Scotia. *Statutes*. Halifax, 1868–1954

O'Brian, George. "Ancient and Modern Methods of Testing for Gas in Coal Mines." *Bulletin of the Canadian Mining Institute*, 1924: 205–12

Odell, C.M. "Men and Methods of the Early Days of Mining in Cape Breton." *Transactions of the Canadian Institute of Mining*, 1922: 503–30

Ontario. "Report of the Commissioners Appointed to Enquire into the Prison and Reformatory System of Ontario." *Sessional Papers*, 1891, vol. 23, pt 4, no. 18

Ontario. *Report of Committee on Child Labor*. Toronto: K. Cameron 1907

Ontario. "Reports of Factory Inspectors." *Sessional Papers*, 1892–1907

Oren, L. "The Welfare of Women in Labouring Families: England, 1860–1950." In *Clio's Consciousness Raised: New Perspectives on the History of Women*, edited by M. Hartman and L.W. Banner, 226–44. New York: Octagon Books 1974

Ormsby, Margaret. *British Columbia: A History*. Toronto: Macmillan 1958

Orr, Allan Donald. "The Western Federation of Miners and the Royal Commission on Industrial Disputes in 1903 with Special Reference to the Vancouver Island Coal Miners' Strike." MA thesis: University of British Columbia 1968

Orwell, George. *The Road to Wigan Pier*. New York: Harcourt 1958

Paine, J.S. "The Men and the Mines on Vancouver Island." *British Columbia Magazine* 9, no. 9 (September 1913): 526–33

Palmer, Bryan. *A Culture in Conflict: Skilled Workers and Industrial Capitalism in Hamilton, Ontario, 1860–1914*. Montreal: McGill-Queen's University Press 1979

– "Discordant Music: Charivaris and Whitecapping in Nineteenth-Century North America." *Labour/Le Travailleur* 3 (1978): 5–62

– *Working-Class Experience: Rethinking the History of Canadian Labour*. 2nd ed. Toronto: McClelland and Stewart 1992

Pamely, Caleb. *The Colliery Manager's Handbook: A Comprehensive Treatise on the Laying Out and Working of Collieries*. London: Crosby Lockwood and Son 1893

Parenteau, Bill. "Bonded Labour: Canadian Woods Workers in the Maine Pulpwood Industry, 1940–55." *Forest and Conservation History* 37, no. 3 (July 1993): 108–19

Parr, Joy. *Labouring Children: British Immigrant Apprentices to Canada, 1869–1924*. London: Croom Helm 1980

– "'Transplanting from Dens of Iniquity': Theology and Child Emigration." In *A Not Unreasonable Claim: Women and Reform in Canada, 1880's–1920's*, edited by Linda Kealey, 169–83. Toronto: Women's Educational Press 1979

Parsons, Donald O., and Claudia Goldin. "Parental Altruism and Self-Interest: Child Labor among Late Nineteenth-Century American Families." *Economic Inquiry* 27, no. 4 (October 1989): 637–59

Patterson, Rev. Dr George. "The Early History of Mining in Pictou County." *Canadian Mining Review*, 1892: 116

– *A History of the County of Pictou, Nova Scotia.* Montreal: Dawson Bros. 1877

Pedersen, Diana. "'Keeping Our Good Girls Good': The YMCA and the 'Girl Problem,' 1870–1930." *Canadian Women's Studies* 7, no. 4 (Winter 1986): 20–4

Pemberton, J.D. *Facts and Figures relating to Vancouver Island and British Columbia, Showing What to Expect and How to Get There.* London: Longman, Green, Longman and Roberts 1860

Penfold, Steven. "'Have You No Manhood in You?': Gender and Class in the Cape Breton Coal Towns, 1920–1926." *Acadiensis* 23, no. 2 (Spring 1994): 21–44

Petherick, Thomas. "Report on the Property of the Acadia Coal Company, Nova Scotia." New York: n.p. 1865

Phillips, Paul A. *No Power Greater: A Century of Labour in British Columbia.* Vancouver: Boag Foundation 1967

Pierson, Ruth Roach. *Canadian Women and the Second World War.* Ottawa: Canadian Historical Association 1983

Pigot, David. *The Mining Society of Nova Scotia, 1887–1987.* Glace Bay: Mining Society of Nova Scotia 1987

Pinchbeck, Ivy, and Margaret Hewitt. *Children in English Society.* Vol. 1, *From Tudor Times to the Eighteenth Century.* Toronto: University of Toronto Press 1969

– *Children in English Society.* Vol. 2, *From the Eighteenth Century to the Children's Act 1948.* Toronto: University of Toronto Press 1973

Piva, Michael J. *The Condition of the Working Class in Toronto – 1900–1921.* Ottawa: University of Ottawa Press 1979

Planta, S.P. "The Coal Fields of Vancouver Island, B.C." *Canadian Mining Manual*, 1893: 279–97

Pollock, Linda A. *Forgotten Children: Parent-Child Relations from 1500 to 1900.* Cambridge: Cambridge University Press 1983

Poole, H.S. "Notes on the Legislation Affecting the Working and Regulation of Mines in Nova Scotia." *Journal of the Mining Society of Nova Scotia* 1, pt 4 (1892–93): 26–35

– "Pumping with Compressed Air." *Canadian Mining Journal*, 1896: 56–7

Porter, Marilyn. "'She was Skipper of the Shore-Crew': Notes on the History of the Sexual Division of Labour in Newfoundland." *Labour/Le Travail* 15 (Spring 1985): 105–23

Porter, Marion R., J. Porter, and Bernard R. Blishen. *Does Money Matter? Prospects for Higher Education in Ontario.* Ottawa: Carleton University Press 1979

Prang, Margaret. "'The Girl God Would Have Me Be': The Canadian Girls in Training, 1915–1939." *Canadian Historical Review* 66, no. 2 (June 1985): 154–84

Prentice, Alison. *The School Promoters: Education and Social Class in Mid-Nineteenth Century Upper Canada.* Toronto: McClelland and Stewart 1977

Province of Canada. Legislative Assembly. *Journals.* Vol. 8 (1849), app. no. 3, B.B.B.B.B., *First Report of the Commissioners appointed to inquire into and report upon the conduct, economy, discipline and management of the Provincial Penitentiary,* 16 March 1849; *Second Report of the Commissioners of the Penitentiary Inquiry,* 16 April 1849.

Purvey, Diane. "Alexandra Orphanage and Families in Crisis in Vancouver, 1892–1938." In *Dimensions of Childhood: Essays on the History of Children and Youth in Canada,* edited by Russell Smandych, Gordon Dodds, and Alvin Esau, 107–33. Winnipeg: Legal Research Institute of the University of Manitoba 1991

Race, Cecil L. *Compulsory Schooling in Alberta (1888–1942).* MEd thesis, University of Alberta 1978

Radforth, Ian. *Bush Workers and Bosses: Logging in Northern Ontario, 1900–1980.* Toronto: University of Toronto Press 1987

Ralston, H. Keith. "Miners and Managers: The Organization of Coal Production on Vancouver Island by the Hudson's Bay Company, 1848–1862." In *The Company on the Coast,* edited by E. Blanche Norcross, 42–55. Nanaimo: Nanaimo Historical Society 1983

Ralston, H. Keith, and Gregory S. Kealey. "Samuel H. Myers." *Dictionary of Canadian Biography, 1881–1890.* Vol. 11, 637–9. Toronto: University of Toronto Press 1982

Raymond, Jocelyn Motyer. *The Nursery World of Dr. Blatz.* Toronto: University of Toronto Press 1991

Reid, Donald. "Industrial Paternalism: Discourse and Practice in Nineteenth-Century French Mining and Metallurgy." *Comparative Studies in Society and History* 27, no. 4 (October 1985): 579–607

– *The Miners of Decazeville: A Genealogy of Deindustrialization.* Cambridge, Mass.: Harvard University Press 1985

Reilly, Sharon. "The Provincial Workmen's Association of Nova Scotia, 1879–1898." MA thesis: Dalhousie University 1979

Robb, Charles. "Mineral Resources of British North America." Montreal: n.p. 1863

Robbins, J.E. *Dependency of Youth.* Ottawa: King's Printer 1937

Robinson, Marina. "The Child, the Family and Society in Ontario, 1850–1900, According to Four Educational Journals." MA thesis, Lakehead University 1978

Roland, Charles G. "Darby Bergin." In *Dictionary of Canadian Biography, 1891–1900.* Vol. 12, 94–7. Toronto: University of Toronto Press 1990

Rooke, Patricia T., and R.L. Schnell. "Childhood and Charity in Nineteenth Century British North America." *Histoire sociale/Social History* 15, no. 29 (May 1982): 157–79

‒ *Discarding the Asylum: From Child Rescue to the Welfare State in English Canada (1800‒1950)*. New York: University Press of America 1983
‒ "Guttersnipes and Charity Children: Nineteenth Century Child Rescue in the Atlantic Provinces." In *Studies in Childhood History: A Canadian Perspective*, edited by Patricia T. Rooke and R.L. Schnell, 82‒104. Calgary: Detselig Enterprises 1982
‒ "Imperial Philanthrophy and Colonial Response: British Juvenile Emigration to Canada, 1896‒1930." *Historian* 46, no. 1 (November 1983): 56‒77
‒ *Studies in Childhood History: A Canadian Perspective*. Calgary: Detselig Enterprises 1982
Rose, Lionel. *The Erosion of Childhood: Child Oppression in Britain, 1860‒1918*. London and New York: Routledge 1991
Ross, David P., Katherine Scott, and Mark A. Kelly. "Overview: Children in Canada in the 1990s." In *Growing Up in Canada: National Longitudinal Survey of Children and Youth*. Ottawa: Statistics Canada 1996
Rotteleur, A. "The Use of Gasoline Locomotives in Coal Mines." *Transactions of the Canadian Mining Institute*, 1913: 506‒9
Rouillard, Jacques. *Les travailleurs du coton au Québec, 1900‒1915*. Montréal: Les presses de l'université du Québec 1974
Roy, Patricia. *A White Man's Province: British Columbia Politicians and Chinese and Japanese Immigrants, 1858‒1914*. Vancouver: University of British Columbia Press 1989
Rutherford, J.G. "Pictou County." *Journal of the Mining Society of Nova Scotia* 1, pt 4 (1892‒93): 47‒53
Rutherford, John. "The Coal-fields of Nova Scotia." Newcastle: n.p. 1871
‒ "The Early History and Progress of Coal Mining in Nova Scotia." *Canadian Mining Review*, 1891: 201‒3
Rutman, Leonard. "Importation of British Waifs into Canada 1868 to 1916." *Child Welfare* 52, no. 2 (March 1973): 158‒66
‒ "J.J. Kelso and the Development of Social Welfare." In *The 'Benevolent' State: The Growth of Welfare in Canada*, edited by Allan Moscovitch and Jim Allen, 68‒76. Toronto: Garamond Press 1987
Ryder, Bruce. "Racism and the Constitution: The Constitutional Fate of British Columbia Anti-Asian Immigration Legislation, 1844‒1909." *Osgoode Hall Law Journal* 29, no. 3 (Fall 1991): 619‒76
Samson, Daniel. "Dependency and Rural Industry: Inverness, Nova Scotia, 1899‒1910." In *Contested Countryside: Rural Workers and Modern Society in Atlantic Canada, 1800‒1950*, edited by Daniel Samson, 105‒49. Fredericton: Acadiensis Press 1994
‒ "The Making of a Cape Breton Coal Town: Dependent Development in Inverness, Nova Scotia, 1899‒1915." MA thesis, University of New Brunswick 1988
Samuel, Raphael. "Mineral Workers." In *Miners, Quarrymen and Saltworkers*, edited by Raphael Samuel, 1‒97. London: Routledge and Kegan Paul 1977

Saskatchewan. *Annual Report of the Department of Public Works of the Province of Saskatchewan*. Regina: J.W. Reid, Government Printer 1906–15

Saskatchewan. *Revised Statutes of Saskatchewan, 1920*. Regina: J.W. Reid, King's Printer 1921

Schlereth, Thomas J. "The Material Culture of Childhood. Problems and Potential in Historical Explanation." *Material History Bulletin/Bulletin d'histoire de la culture matérielle* 21 (1985): 1–15

Schnell, R.L "Childhood as Ideology: A Reinterpretation of the Common School." *British Journal of Educational Studies* 27 (February 1979): 7–28

– "A Children's Bureau for Canada: The Origins of the Canadian Council on Child Welfare, 1913–1921." In *The 'Benevolent' State: The Growth of Welfare in Canada*, edited by Allan Moscovitch and Jim Allen, 95–110. Toronto: Garamond Press 1987

Schwantes, Carlos A. *Radical Heritage: Labor, Socialism, and Reform in Washington and British Columbia, 1885–1917*. Seattle and London: University of Washington Press 1979

Schwieder, Dorothy, Joseph Hraba, and Elmer Schwieder. *Buxton: Work and Racial Equality in a Coal Mining Community*. Ames, Iowa: Iowa State University Press 1987

Scott, Bertha Isabel. *Springhill, a Hilltop in Cumberland*. Springhill: n.p. 1926

Scott, Jean Thomson. "The Conditions of Female Labour in Ontario." Toronto: Warwick 1892

Seager, Allen. "A History of the Mine Workers' Union of Canada, 1925–1936." MA thesis, McGill University 1977

– "Miners' Struggles in Western Canada, 1890–1930." In *Class, Community and the Labour Movement: Wales and Canada, 1850–1930*, edited by Deian R. Hopkin and Gregory S. Kealey, 160–98. N.p.: Society for Welsh Labour History and the Canadian Committee on Labour History 1989

– "Minto, New Brunswick: A Study in Class Relations between the Wars." *Labour/Le Travailleur* 5 (Spring 1980): 81–132

– "Socialists and Workers: The Western Canadian Coal Miners, 1900–1921." *Labour/Le Travail* 16 (Fall 1985): 23–59

Seager, Allen, and Adele Perry. "Mining the Connections: Class, Ethnicity, and Gender in Nanaimo, British Columbia, 1891." *Histoire sociale/Social History* 30, no. 59 (May 1997): 55–76

Seale, R.G. "Some Geographical Aspects of the Coal Industry in Alberta." MA thesis, University of Alberta 1966

Seccombe, Wally. "Patriarchy stabilized: the construction of the male breadwinner wage norm in nineteenth-century Britain." *Social History* 11, no. 1 (January 1986): 53–76

Seguin, Normand. *La conquête du sol au XIXe siècle*. Québec: Editions du Boréal express 1977

Seltzer, Curtis. *Fire in the Hole: Miners and Managers in the American Coal Industry.* Lexington: University Press of Kentucky 1985

Semple, Neil. "'The Nurture and Admonition of the Lord': Nineteenth Century Canadian Methodism's Response to Childhood." *Histoire sociale/Social History* 14, no. 27 (May 1981): 157–75

Sexton, Frederick H. "Industrial Education for Miners." *Transactions of the Canadian Mining Institute*, 1912: 582–97

– "The Relation of Technical Education to Industrial Progress." *Transactions of the Mining Society of Nova Scotia* 11 (1906–7): 1–26

Shanks, J. "Notes on the Use of Storage-Battery Locomotives and Storage-Batteries Underground." *Transactions of the Canadian Institute of Mining and Metallurgy*, 1924: 533–45

Sharp, Alexander. "Some Notes on the Longwall Method of Mining Coal." *Transactions of the Canadian Institute of Mining and Metallurgy*, 1913: 417–33

Shiman, Lilian Lewis. "The Band of Hope Movement: Respectable Recreation for Working Class Children." *Victorian Studies* 18 (1973): 49–74

Sider, Gerald M. *Culture and Class in Anthropology and History: A Newfoundland Illustration.* Cambridge: Cambridge University Press 1986

Siegel, Linda S. "Child Health and Development in English Canada, 1790–1850." In *Health, Disease, and Medicine: Essays in Canadian History,* edited by Charles Roland, 360–80. Toronto: Hannah Institute for the History of Medicine 1984

Silverman, P.G. "Aid of the Civil Power: The Nanaimo Coal Miners' Strike, 1912–1914." *Canadian Defence Quarterly* 4, no. 1 (Summer 1974): 46–52

Silverman, Peter. "Military Aid to the Civil Power in British Columbia: The Labor Strikes in Wellington and Steveston, 1890 and 1900." *Pacific Northwest Quarterly* 61, no. 3 (1970): 156–64

Sloan, William. "The Crowsnest Pass during the Depression: A Socio-economic history of Southeastern British Columbia, 1918–1939." MA thesis, University of Victoria 1968

Smelser, Neil J. *Social Change in the Industrial Revolution: An Application of Theory to the British Cotton Industry.* Chicago: University of Chicago Press 1959

Smith, Michael J. "Female Reformers in Victorian Nova Scotia: Architects of a New Womanhood." MA thesis, St Mary's University 1986

Spedon, Andrew Leamont. *Rambles Among the Bluenoses: or Reminiscences of a Tour Through New Brunswick and Nova Scotia During the Summer of 1862.* Montreal: J. Lovell 1863

Splane, Richard B. *Social Welfare in Ontario, 1791–1893: A Study of Public Welfare Administration.* Toronto: University of Toronto Press 1965

The Staff. "Mechanization in the Collieries of the Dominion Steel and Coal Corporation." *Canadian Mining and Metallurgical Bulletin* 42 (1949): 463–501

Stamp, Robert M. "Canadian High Schools in the 1920's and 1930's: The Social Challenge to the Academic Tradition." In Canadian Historical Association, *Historical Papers/Communications historiques*, 1978: 76–93

– *The Schools of Ontario, 1876–1976*. Toronto: University of Toronto Press for the Ontario Historical Studies series 1982

Stansell, Christine. *City of Women: Sex and Class in New York 1789–1860*. Urbana and Chicago: University of Illinois Press 1987

Stewart, Mary Lynn. *Women, Work, and the French State: Labour Protection and Social Patriarchy, 1879–1919*. Montreal and Kingston: McGill-Queen's University Press 1989

Stone, Laurence. *The Family, Sex and Marriage in England, 1500–1800*. Harmondsworth: Penguin Books 1979

Storm-Clark, Christopher. "The Miners, 1870–1970: A Test Case for Oral History." *Victorian Studies* 15, no. 1 (1971): 49–71

Strachan, Robert. "Coal Mining in British Columbia." *Transactions of the Canadian Institute of Mining and Metallurgy*, 1923: 70–132

Strong-Boag, Veronica. *The Parliament of Women: The National Council of Women of Canada, 1893–1929*. Ottawa: National Museums of Canada 1976

– "'Wages for Housework': Mother's Allowances and the Beginnings of Social Security in Canada." *Journal of Canadian Studies/Revue d'études canadiennes* 14, no. 1 (Spring 1979): 24–34

Sutherland, Neil. *Childhood in English Canadian Society: Framing the Twentieth Century Consensus*. Toronto: University of Toronto Press 1976

– *"Growing Up": Childhood in English Canada from the Great War to the Age of Television*. Toronto: University of Toronto Press 1997

– "'I can't recall when I didn't help': The Working Lives of Pioneering Children in Twentieth-Century British Columbia." *Histoire sociale/Social History* 24, no. 48 (November 1991): 263–88

– "'We always had things to do': The Paid and Unpaid Work of Anglophone Children between the 1920s and the 1960s." *Labour/Le Travail* 25 (Spring 1990): 105–41

Sutherland, Neil, Jean Barman, and Linda L. Hale, comps. *History of Canadian Childhood and Youth: A Bibliography*. Westport, Conn.: Greenwood Press 1992

Synge, Jane. "The Transition from School to Work: Growing Up Working Class in Twentieth Century Hamilton, Ontario." In *Childhood and Adolescence in Canada*, edited by K. Ishwaren, 249–69. Toronto: McGraw-Hill Ryerson 1979

Tawney, R.H. "The Economics of Boy Labour." *Economic Journal* 19 (December 1909): 517–37

Taylor, Arthur J. "Labour Productivity and Technical Innovation in the British Coal Industry, 1850–1914." *Economic History Review*, ser. 2, 14, no. 1 (1961): 48–70

Tennyson, Brian D. "Economic Nationalism and Confederation: A Case Study in Cape Breton." *Acadiensis* 2, no. 1 (Autumn 1972): 39–53

– *Essays in Cape Breton History.* Windsor, N.S.: Lancelot Press 1973

Thompson, E.P. *Customs in Common: Studies in Traditional Popular Culture.* New York: New Press 1991

– *The Making of the English Working Class.* Harmondsworth: Penguin Books 1968

– "'Rough Music': Le charivari anglais." *Annales. Economies. Sociétés. Civilisations* 27 (1972): 285–312

Thompson, John Herd, with Allen Seager. *Canada, 1922–1939: Decades of Discord.* Toronto: McClelland and Stewart 1985

Thornton, P.A. "The Problem of Out-Migration from Atlantic Canada, 1871–1921." *Acadiensis* 15, no. 1 (Autumn 1985): 3–34

Trépanier, Jean. "The Origins of the Juvenile Delinquents Act of 1908: Controlling Delinquency through Seeking Its Causes and through Youth Protection." In *Dimensions of Childhood: Essays on the History of Children and Youth in Canada*, edited by Russell Smandych, Gordon Dodds, and Alvin Esau, 205–32. Winnipeg: Legal Research Institute of the University of Manitoba 1991

Trevelyan, George Macaulay. *British History in the Nineteenth Century (1782–1901).* London: Longmans 1933

Trist, E., and K. Bamforth. "Some Social and Psychological Consequences of Longwall Method of Coal Getting." *Human Relations* 4, no. 1 (February 1951): 3–38

Trist, E.L., G.W. Higgin, H. Murray, and A.B. Pollock. *Organizational Choice: Capabilities of Groups at the Coal Face under Changing Technologies: The Loss, Re-Discovery and Transformation of a Work Tradition.* London: Tavistock Publications 1963

Trottner, Walter I. *Crusade for the Children: A History of the National Child Labor Committee and Child Labor Reform in America.* Chicago: Quadrangle Books 1970

Tucker, Eric. *Administering Danger in the Workplace: The Law and Politics of Occupational Health and Safety Regulation in Ontario, 1850–1914.* Toronto: University of Toronto Press 1990

Tucker, Eric, and Judy Fudge. "Forging Responsible Unions: Metal Workers and the Rise of the Labour Injunction in Canada." *Labour/Le Travail* 37 (Spring 1996): 81–120

Turmel, André. "Folie, épidémie et institution: contrôle et régulation sociale de l'enfance." *Recherches sociographiques* 34, 1 (1993): 111–27

Turner, J.W. "The Mechanisation of Coal Cutting in Pelaw Main Colliery, 1902–5." *Labour History* (Australia), no. 18 (May 1970): 61–7

Turner, Wesley B. "Miss Rye's Children and the Ontario Press, 1875." *Ontario History* 68, no. 3 (September 1976): 169–200

Tyro. "A Visit to the Albion Mines." *The Provincial or Halifax Monthly Magazine* 1, no. 5 (May 1852): 175–81

United Kingdom. Parliamentary Papers. Factory Inquiry Commission, *Report of the Central Board of His Majesty's Commissioners appointed to collect Information in the Manufacturing Districts as to the employment of Children in Factories. First Report, June 1833. Second Report, July 1833.*

United Kingdom. Parliamentary Papers. *Report of Commission of Inquiry into the Employment of Children and Young Persons in Mines and Collieries. First Report, 1842, Second Report, 1843.*

United Kingdom. Parliamentary Papers. *Report of Select Committee on Factory Children's Labour* (Sadler's Report), 1831–2.

Ursel, Jane. *Private Lives, Public Policy: 100 Years of State Intervention in the Family.* Toronto: Women's Press 1992

Valverde, Mariana. *The Age of Light, Soap, and Water: Moral Reform in English Canada, 1885–1925.* Toronto: McClelland and Stewart 1991

Veinott, Rebecca. "Child Custody and Divorce: A Nova Scotia Study, 1866–1910." In *Essays in the History of Canadian Law.* Vol. 3, *Nova Scotia*, edited by Philip Girard and Jim Phillips, 273–302. Toronto: University of Toronto Press for the Osgoode Society 1990

Vernon, C.W. "Child Labour in the Country." In Fourth Annual Canadian Conference on Child Welfare, *Proceedings and Papers, Winnipeg, 1923*, 115–21. Ottawa: Acland 1924

Villiers, Charles W. "Problems of the Coal Industry in British Columbia." *Transactions of the Canadian Institute of Mining and Metallurgy* 39 (1936): 567–72

Wagner, Gillian. *Children of the Empire.* London: Weidenfeld and Nicolson 1982

Ward, W. Peter. *Courtship, Love, and Marriage in Nineteenth-Century English Canada.* Montreal and Kingston: McGill-Queen's University Press 1990

Wargo, Alan John. "The Great Coal Strike: The Vancouver Island Coal Miners' Strike, 1912–1914." BA essay, University of British Columbia 1962

Warsh, Cheryl Krasnick, ed. *Drink in Canada: Historical Essays.* Montreal: McGill-Queen's University Press 1993

Watkin, Edward. *Canada and the States: Recollections, 1851–1886.* London: Ward 1887

Webber, Jeremy. "Labour and the Law." In *Labouring Lives: Work and Workers in Nineteenth-Century Ontario*, edited by Paul Craven, 105–21. Toronto: University of Toronto Press 1995

Weissbach, Lee Shai. *Child Labor Reform in Nineteenth-Century France: Assuring the Future Harvest.* Baton Rouge: Louisiana State University Press 1989

Whalen, James M. "The Nineteenth Century Almshouse System in Saint John County." *Histoire sociale/Social History* 7 (April 1971): 5–27

– "Social Welfare in New Brunswick, 1784–1900." *Acadiensis* 2, no. 1 (Autumn 1972): 54–64

Wickberg, Edgar. *From China to Canada: A History of the Chinese Communities in Canada*. Toronto: McClelland and Stewart 1982

Williamson, Bill. *Class, Culture and Community: A Biographical Study of Social Change in Mining*. London and Boston: Routledge and Kegan Paul 1982

Wright, C.H. "Electrical Transmission for Mining and Other Purposes in the Maritime Provinces." *Transactions of the Mining Society of Nova Scotia* 18 (1912–13): 44–9

Wylie, William N.T. *Coal Culture: The History and Commemoration of Coal Mining in Nova Scotia*. Ottawa: Historic Sites and Monuments Board of Canada 1997

Wynne, Robert Edward. *Reaction to the Chinese in the Pacific Northwest and British Columbia, 1850 to 1910*. New York: Arno Press 1978

Zelizer, Vivana. *Pricing the Priceless Child: The Changing Social Value of Children*. New York: Basic Books 1985

Zimbalist, Andrew, ed. *Case Studies in the Labor Process*. New York: Monthly Review Press 1979

Zola, Emile. *Germinal*. Paris: Garnier-Flammarion 1968 [1885]

Zucchi, John E. *The Little Slaves of the Harp: Italian Child Street Musicians in Nineteenth-Century Paris, London, and New York*. Montreal and Kingston: McGill-Queen's University Press 1992

Index